MEDIEVAL ITALY, MEDIEVAL AND EARLY MODERN WOMEN

Medieval Italy, Medieval and Early Modern Women

ESSAYS IN HONOUR OF CHRISTINE MEEK

Conor Kostick

EDITOR

FOUR COURTS PRESS

Typeset in 10.5 pt on 12.5 pt Ehrhardt for
FOUR COURTS PRESS LTD
7 Malpas Street, Dublin 8, Ireland
www.fourcourtspress.ie
and in North America
FOUR COURTS PRESS
c/o ISBS, 920 NE 58th Avenue, Suite 300, Portland, OR 97213.

A catalogue record for this title is available
from the British Library.

ISBN 978-1-84682-222-3

Printed in England
by Antony Rowe Ltd, Chippenham, Wilts.

Contents

Abbreviations

AAAG	*Annals of the Association of American Geographers*
AAL	Archivio Arcivescovile di Lucca
ACL	Archivio Capitolare di Lucca
A. Conn.	*Annala Connacht: the annals of Connacht 1224–1544*, ed. A.M. Freeman (Dublin, 1844, rpt. 1970)
AFM	*Annala rioghachta Eireann: Annals of the kingdom of Ireland from the earliest period to the year 1616 by the Four Masters*, ed. J. O Donovan, 7 (Dublin, 1854)
AI	*The Annals of Inisfallen (MS Rawlinson B 503)*, ed. Seán Mac Airt (Dublin, 1951)
ALC	*The Annals of Loch Cé: a Chronicle of Irish Affairs 1014–1590*, ed. W.M. Hennessy (London, 1871)
AM	*Archeologia medievale*
ASDL	Archivio Storico Diocesano di Lucca, formerly AAL.
ASI	*Archivio Storico Italiano*
ASL	Archivio di Stato di Lucca
ASF	Archivio di Stato di Firenze
AU	*Annála Uladh: Annals of Ulster 431–1541*, ed., W.M. Hennessy and Bartholomew MacCarthy, 4 (Dublin, 1877–1901)
BBKL	Biographisch-Bibliographisches Kirchlexikon. Nordhausen, 1996 ff. [digitized]
BEFAR	Bibliothèque des Écoles Français d'Athènes et de Rome
CCCM	*Corpus Christanorum continuatio mediaevalis*
CPL	*Calendar of entries in the papal registers relating to Great Britain and Ireland: Papal Letters*, ed. W.H. Bliss, et al. (London and Dublin, 1893–)
DBI	*Dizionario biografico degli Italiani*
Dipl.	*Diplomatico*
EHR	*English Historical Review*
MEFRM	*Mélanges de l'École française de Rome: Moyen Age-Temps modernes*
MGH SS	*Monumenta Germaniae Historica Scriptores, Scriptores* in Folio, 32 (1826–1934)
MVGN	*Mitteilungen des Vereins für Geschichte der Stadt Nürnberg*
PL	J.P. Migne (ed.), *Patrologiae cursus completus. Series Latina* (1844–66)
RHC Oc.	*Recueil des historiens des croisades, Historiens occidentaux* 1–5 (Académie des inscriptions et belles-lettres: Paris 1841–95)
RIN	*Rivista italiana di numismatica e scienze affini*
RIS	*Rerum Italicarum Scriptores*, 2nd series (Città di Castello and Bologna, 1906–40)
TRE	*Theologische Realenzyklopädie*
ZCP	*Zeitschrift für Celtische Philologie*

ACKNOWLEDGMENT

The editor gratefully acknowledges the support of the Trinity Foundation and the Grace Lawless Lee fund in providing grants towards the production of this book.

Christine Meek's publications

MONOGRAPHS

The Italian Renaissance (Dublin, 1974).

Lucca, 1369–1400: politics and society in an early Renaissance city-state (Oxford, 1978).

Lucca under Pisan rule, 1342–1369 (Cambridge, MA, 1980).

Donne italiane, donne inglesi a confronto tra due e quattrocento (Perugia, 1997).

EDITED VOLUMES

Co-editor with M.K. Simms, *'The fragility of her sex'? Irish women in their European context* (Dublin, 1996).

Editor, *Women in Renaissance and Early Modern Europe: Studies on women in Medieval and Early Modern Europe* 2 (Dublin, 2000).

Co-editor with Catherine Lawless, *Pawns or Players? Studies on women in Medieval and Early Modern Europe* 3 (Dublin, 2003).

Co-editor with Catherine Lawless, *Victims or Viragos? Studies on women in Medieval and early Modern Europe* 4 (Dublin, 2005).

Co-editor with Brenda Bolton, *Aspects of power and authority in the Middle Ages* (Turnhout, 2007).

ARTICLES

'The trade and industry of Lucca in the fourteenth century' in T.W. Moody (ed.), *Historical Studies* VI (London, 1968), pp 39–58.

'Il debito pubblico nella storia finanziaria di Lucca nel XIV° secolo', *Actum Luce* III (1974), pp 7–46.

'Le finanze e l'amministrazione finanziaria di Lucca al tempo di Castruccio' in *Castruccio Castracani e il suo tempo* (Convegno Internazionale, Lucca 5–10 ottobre 1981) Istituto Storico Lucchese (1984–5), pp 157–72.

'Finanze comunali e finanze locali nel quattordicesimo secolo: l'esempio di Montecarlo' in *Castelli e borghi nella Toscana tardo medievale* (Atti di

Convegno di Studi, Montecarlo, 28–9 maggio 1983) (Lucca, 1988), pp 139–53.

'Il tempo di Giovanni Sercambi', in *Giovanni Sercambi e il suo tempo* (Lucca, 1991), pp 1–30.

'Public policy and private profit: tax farming in fourteenth-century Lucca', in T.W. Blomquist & M.F. Mazzaoui (eds), *The other Tuscany* (Kalamazoo, MI, 1994), pp 41–82.

'Dante's life in Dante's time', in J.C. Barnes & C.O. Cuilleanáin (eds), *Dante and the Middle Ages* (Dublin, 1995) pp 11–31.

'Beyond the frontier: Irishmen and Irish goods in Lucca in the later Middle Ages', in R. Frame, T.B. Barry & M.K. Simms (eds), *Colony and frontier in medieval Ireland: essays presented to J.F. Lydon* (London, 1995), pp 229–41.

'Women, the church and the law: matrimonial litigation in Lucca under bishop Nicolao Guinigi (1394–1435)', in M. O'Dowd & S. Wichert (eds), *Chattel, servant or citizen: women's status in church, state and society* (Belfast, 1995), pp 82–90.

'La donna, la famiglia e la legge nell'epoca di Ilaria del Carretto' in *Ilaria del Carretto e il suo monumento: la donna nell'arte, la cultura e la società del '400* a cura di Stéphane Toussaint (Lucca, 1995), pp 137–63.

'Women, dowries and the family in late medieval Italian cities' in C.E. Meek and M.K. Simms (eds), *'The fragility of her sex'? Irish women in their European context* (Dublin, 1996), pp 136–52.

'Men, women and magic: some cases from late medieval Lucca', in Christine Meek (ed.), *Women in Renaissance and Early Modern Europe* (Dublin, 2000), pp 43–66.

'Liti matrimoniali nel tribunale eccelsiastico lucchese sotto il vescovo Nicolao Guinigi (1394–1435)', *Quaderni Lucchesi di Studi sul Medioevo e sul Rinascimento* Anno 1, 1 (2000), pp 182–93.

'Women between the law and social reality in early Renaissance Lucca' in L. Panizza (ed.), *Women in Italian Renaissance culture and society* (Oxford, 2000), pp 182–93.

'"Simone ha aderito alla fede di Maometto". La "fornicazione spirituale" come causa di separazione (Lucca, 1424)', in *Coniugi nemici. La separazione in Italia dal XII al XVIII secolo* a cura di Silvana Seidel Menchi e Diego Quaglioni (Annali dell'Istituto Storico Italo-Germanico di Trento, Quaderni 53, Bologna, Il Mulino, 2000), pp 121–39.

'Un unione incerta: la vicenda di Neria, figlia dell'organista, e di Baldassino, merciaio pistoiese (Lucca 1396–7)' in *Matrimoni in dubbio. Unioni contrverse e nozze clandestine in Italia dal XIV al XVIII secolo*, a cura di Silvana Seidel Menchi e Diego Quaglioni (Il Mulino, Bologna, 2002), pp 107–21 plus Latin document on CDRom.

'Carlo IV come figura europea', in *Medioevo europeo: Giovanni e Carlo di Lussemburgo in Toscana (1331–1369), Atti del Convegno Internazionale di Studi, Montecarlo, 14 luglio 2002, Quaderni Lucchesi di Studi sul Medioevo e sul Rinascimento*, III (2002), pp 19–34.

'Paolo Guinigi, parenti e amici', Atti del Convegno 'Paolo Guinigi e il suo Tempo' (Lucca, 24–25 maggio 2001), *Quaderni Lucchesi di Studi Sul Medioevo e Sul Rinascimento* IV, 1/2, gennaio–dicembre (2003).

'Il matrimonio e le nozze: sposarsi a Lucca nel tardo Medio Evo' in Silvana Seidel Menchi & Diego Quaglioni (eds), *I tribunali del matrimonio (secoli XV–XVIII). I processi matrimoniali degli archivi ecclesiastici italiani* (Bologna, 2006), pp 359–73.

'Divorce and separation in the Middle Ages' in Margaret Schaus (ed.), *Women and gender in medieval Europe. An Encyclopaedia* (London, 2006), pp 214–16.

'The gonfaloniere appeals to local patriotism' in Katherine L. Janson, Joanna Drell & Frances Andrews (eds), *Medieval Italy: a documentary history* (Philadelphia, PA, 2009), pp 74–6.

'In Memoriam Thomas W. Blomquist (1931–2007)', *Perspectives on History, Newsmagazine of the American Historical Association* (January 2009), co-authored with Duane Osheim.

'Obituary: Louis Ferdinand Green (1929–2008)', *Renaissance Studies* 23 (2009), pp 758–762, co-authored with F. William Kent.

'"Whatever's best administered is best": Paolo Guinigi, *signore* of Lucca, 1400–1430' in John E. Law & Bernadette Paton (eds), *Communes and despots in late medieval and Renaissance Italy* (Farnham, 2010).

ENTRIES

On Uguccione della Faggiuola, Francesco della Faggiuola, Napoleone della Gherardesca, Bonifazio della Gherardesca, Enrico del Carretto e Nicoletto Diversi in *Dizionario Biografico degli Italiani* (1988–9).

On Lucca in *Garland Encyclopaedia of Medieval Italy*, ed. C. Kleinhenz (London, 2004), pp 658–64.

Introduction: Christine Meek – an appreciation

CONOR KOSTICK

Christine Meek's research career centres on the medieval archives at Lucca. In 1961 when Christine first began to work in Italian archives the influx of 'Anglo-sassoni' had hardly begun, even in Florence much less Lucca: Italy was only just emerging from post-war austerity. In Lucca archive opening hours were very limited, three desks placed one under each of the windows in the reading room were more than sufficient to cater for any likely number of readers, and restaurants and cafes all closed by eight in the evening. But by the 1970s a resurgence was well under way. More local Italian scholars and 'tesi di laurea' students began to appear in the archives, opening hours were extended, new societies were founded and new journals began to be published.

The staff of the Lucchese archives under three successive Directors, Domenico Corsi, Vito Tirelli and Giorgio Tori, and the Istituto Storico Lucchese under its President, Antonio Romiti, were always very welcoming to non-Italians and happy to include them in conferences and in other initiatives. Christine was flattered to be elected a Corresponding Fellow of both the newly-founded Istituto Storico Lucchese and the old-established Accademia Lucchese in 1981. Non-Italian scholars who first met in the Lucchese archives – Tom Blomquist, Louis Green, Duane Osheim, Michael Bratchel, Chris Wickham, Andreas Meyer – became life-long friends, and although several years might pass between periods when visits to the archives coincided, these scholars kept in touch by correspondence and from the 1980s onwards through meetings at international conferences.

In recent years more international graduate students have begun to appear in Lucca from North America, Britain, France, Germany and even Japan and it is sometimes difficult to find a seat, especially in the Archivio Diocesano, while Lucca itself has become a major tourist centre. It is all a far cry from 1961 and Christine was glad to have benefited from and contributed to the increased appreciation of the riches of the Lucchese archives.

Thirteenth- and fourteenth-century Lucca was overshadowed by its larger neighbours – Florence in the fourteenth century probably averaged annual revenues five times those of Lucca – and the city came under the domination various external powers from 1328, being subject to Pisa from 1342 until 1369. As a consequence, until Christine's seminal monographs *Lucca, 1369–1400: politics and society in an early Renaissance city-state* (Oxford, 1978) and *Lucca under Pisan rule, 1342–1369* (Cambridge, MA, 1980), modern historians had rather neglected the material available to them from the archives of the smaller city, despite the fact that it compared favourably with that from Florence. Yet the study of Lucca proves to be extremely valuable, not just in its own terms as an important medieval capital city but as a means of comparison. With the benefit of Christine's work it becomes much clearer, for example, how representative or otherwise were the much more closely scrutinized economic and political developments in Florence.

It is all too easy for the modern historian to sift material in the light of paradigms established by earlier scholarship, but Christine's interpretation of the material in the Lucchese archives is firmly independent of such preceding influences. In particular, she found that while elsewhere in Tuscany the conflict between city and countryside was bitter and had a significant impact on political developments, for Lucca the relations between city and countryside were fairly harmonious and tax burdens were relatively equally distributed between town and country. Again, unlike Florence, Siena and Pisa, Lucca had a form of direct election to political office, rather than any kind of lottery. As a result the dominant families of the city had no great difficulty monopolizing the highest offices.

Lucca experienced factional conflict between the Guinigi and the Rapondi and their allies the Forteguerra leading to a period of despotic rule by the Guinigi from 1400. Unlike the norms established for such conflicts in other cities, Christine Meek did not find in the archives any evidence that such events were in any way a reflection of different social interests. In the Lucchese case, the wealthier merchants and bankers were deeply influential on both sides and the struggle for power was therefore a struggle within the elite rather than – as was the case for Florence – between the highest order and those social layers below them.

Christine's peers quickly appreciated that these findings were important for providing comparisons and contrasts with the patterns established for the history of Florence and Siena. As Duane Osheim explains in much greater depth below, Christine's findings have 'offered a subtle critique and amendment to general studies of late medieval Italian cities'. Aspects of these discoveries were first published in two articles that appeared before her monographs: 'The trade and industry of Lucca in the fourteenth century' in T.W. Moody (ed.), *Historical Studies* VI (London, 1968), pp 39–58 and 'Il debito pubblico nella storia finanziaria di Lucca nel XIV° secolo', *Actum Luce* III (1974), pp 7–46 and in several articles subsequent to the monographs, notably 'Le finanze e l'amministrazione finanziaria di Lucca al tempo di Castruccio' in *Castruccio Castracani e il suo tempo* (Convegno Internazionale, Lucca 5–10 ottobre 1981) (Istituto Storico Lucchese, 1984–5), pp 157–72; 'Finanze comunali e finanze locali nel quattordicesimo secolo: l'esempio di Montecarlo' in *Castelli e borghi nella Toscana tardo medievale* (Atti di Convegno di Studi,

Montecarlo, 28–9 maggio 1983) (Lucca, 1988), pp 139–53 and 'Public policy and private profit: tax farming in fourteenth-century Lucca', in T.W. Blomquist & M.F. Mazzaoui (eds), *The other Tuscany* (Kalamazoo, MI, 1994), pp 41–82.

The other field in which the legacy of Christine Meek's work will be of lasting impact is in uncovering the history of medieval women as active agents in the societies in which they lived. Both by her own direct investigations and also by her energies in bringing together other scholars working in this area, Christine has brought into being a considerable body of published work that significantly clarifies and enhances our understanding of the roles and status of women in a variety of medieval contexts. Her own research is best represented by a number of articles that utilized the material in the archives at Lucca to investigate the status of women and their roles in the medieval city. Christine used the relatively rich body of case studies available in the archives to not only provide fascinating glimpses into women's lives in medieval Lucca, but also to broaden our general understanding of women's status in late medieval Italian cities. The full and impressive range of these studies is listed in the bibliography of her works.

Perhaps a more important contribution to the uncovering of the lives and activities of medieval women than her individual essays were the series of conferences that Christine organized and the series of volumes that were published as a result: *Studies on Medieval and Early Modern Women*. Together with M.K. Simms, Christine edited *'The fragility of her sex'? Irish women in their European context* (1996); as sole editor she oversaw the appearance of *Women in Renaissance and early modern Europe* (2000); with Catherine Lawless as her co-editor she produced *Pawns or Players? Studies on women in medieval and early modern Europe 3* (2003) and also *Victims or Viragos? Studies on women in medieval and early modern Europe 4* (2005), all published by Four Courts Press, Dublin.

These conferences provided an important focus for medievalists and early modernists in Ireland and internationally who were working in the field. The first of the meetings was organized in 1993 in Trinity College as the annual conference of the Women's History Association of Ireland, with Christine an executive member of the association at the time. All too often the interest generated by the themes of a successful history conference can quickly dissipate. To keep up the momentum of a stimulating dialogue between historians requires a commitment by a person with the respect of their peers and strong organizational skills. Ireland's community of historians interested in the roles of medieval and early modern women were fortunate in having just such a person in Christine Meek. By seeing the conference contributions into print and then by organizing a succession of follow-up conferences, Christine helped the emergence of a strong culture of research in Ireland in the area of women's history. Among those who regularly attended the conferences (which increasingly attracted scholars from overseas) a distinct sense of identity and purpose arose, cemented by the series of publications.

In addition to her intellectual achievements, Christine Meek also, quietly and unassumingly but with great ability, played a pathbreaking role for the involvement of women at the highest levels of administration in Trinity College. She became Junior Proctor for the college, 1988–9; Senior Proctor, 1989–91 and 1997–9 and was the College Registrar 1999–2001. As such she was a member of the Council of the University and the Board of the College, and of committees such as, College Officers' Committee, Academic Affairs Committee, Deans' Committee, Staff Appointments' Committee and Finance Committee. Christine was Chairman of the Academic Appeals' Committee and of the Coordinating Committees for the B.Ed., B.Ed. (Home Economics), B.Th., M.Phil. in Peace Studies, M.Phil. in Ecumenics.

Outside of Trinity College, Christine became a member of the Management Committee of the Women's History Project, a government-funded research project, employing a Director and five other people. It has produced a very valuable Directory of Sources for Irish Women's History (now available via the National Archives website at http://www.nation-alarchives.ie/wh/), and several volumes of edited letters. She is also a member of the Processi Matrimoniali research project at the University of Trent and Istituto Storico Italo-Germanico di Trento. This runs regular multi-lingual (mainly Italian and German) research seminars twice a year and has so far published one volume of articles and edited documents.

The essays published here reflect both strands of Christine Meek's research interests. The first half of the collection begins with a passionate call for a revival of an economic approach to our understanding of medieval Italy by George Dameron. Having made the case that the trend in recent historiography has been to turn away from economic approaches, Dameron convincingly connects this trend to the much broader Western philosophical movements of the 1980s and in particular to the rise of post-structuralism and post-modern theory and makes the case that this has come at the price of neglecting not only a powerful methodology but also the vast and under-utilized quantity of sources that still remain to be incorporated into our understanding of Italian history. One of the seminal works of the 'economic' tradition highlighted by Dameron is Duane Osheim's: *An Italian lordship: the bishopric of Lucca in the late Middle Ages* and fewer historians are better placed appreciate Christine's contribution to the history of Lucca and Italy more generally than Duane Osheim, who does so for this volume.

Amongst other observations, Osheim notes that Christine Meek's work on Lucca amended the prevailing view of late medieval Italian cities. Once the

Lucchese case is properly understood, then the pattern of exploitation, colonization and integration by which regional states came into being around the major cities no longer can be held to be universal. Lucca followed a different path. In the same spirit of nuanced and concrete investigation of a relatively neglected town comes William Day's examination of the evolution of Empoli in the lower Arno Valley *c.*1100–1300.

Situated between the much more powerful cities of Florence and Pisa, Empoli functioned as frontier location at the western edge of the Florentine *contado* from *c.*1254. Its central position gave the town a political importance and it became the principal site at which the parliaments of the Tuscan League were regularly convened. Day persuasively makes the case that the importance of securing safe passage through the territory of Empoli shaped the policy of the rulers of Florence towards the market town. The rapid development of Empoli itself as a major supplier of foodstuffs to the capital, Day attributes above all to the actions of the Guidi counts and the fact that Empoli failed to go on to achieve greater independence to a number of factors, the most important being the decline of that family.

Edward Coleman's contribution takes another important medieval Italian city, Cremona, as the setting for a case study in the development of elite factional politics very much in the spirit of Christine Meek's work on Lucca. In this example, Coleman analyses the roots of the rise to power of Boso da Dovara to the point where in 1266 he could become 'perpetual podestà and lord of the community'. These roots were deep and it was the adept utilizations of ecclesiastical and communal offices, as well as the accretion of both extensive landholdings, vassals, clients and allies by the da Dovara family from the eleventh century that paved the way for one of their number to eventually achieve a position of complete political dominance.

Christine Meek's discovery of a 1424 marriage dispute in Lucca, which reveals an extraordinary relationship between two apostate Christians, provides the launching pad for Brenda Bolton's exploration of a hitherto neglected aspect of Pope Innocent III's pontificate: his concern for Christian prisoners, particularly those in Iberia, North Africa and the Near East who were at risk of adopting the Muslim faith in return for their freedom. Amongst the material that she analyses are consolatory letters from the papacy, whose contents echo the themes addressed later in this volume by Stephen Hanaphy and Katharine Simms. Innocent was, however, subordinating his literary skills to what he saw as a most urgent practical task and Brenda Bolton highlights how the pope attempted to give a strong lead to the secular rulers of all Christendom, that they assist the thousands of Christian slaves in Muslim hands.

Another lawsuit, this time from the Lucchese archives for 1237 is published for the first time in this volume, thanks to the research of Andreas

Meyer. His selection of this document is particularly apt, combining as it does material that allows for a rich prosopographical discussion of the participants with gender-related themes that are central to the case. Andreas Meyer's familiarity with the Lucchese archive material means that we are presented here with not only a useful edition of an important source, but we also get a fascinating glimpse into the social and personal relations between people who were members of the elite social circles of their day.

Another document to be edited and published for the first time in this Festschrift comes from the Fondo Diplomatico of the Archivio di Stato di Lucca courtesy of Ignazio Del Punta, who has chosen the document for the information it provides with regard to the relationship between the merchant-banks of Lucca and the Commune. This set of accounts from the thirteenth century illustrates the methods by which Lucchese companies were working in financial activities in north-western Europe from the 1280s, and in particular that the fairs of Champagne were used as a favourable site for the repayment of loans contracted by the Commune. Given this testimony, there can be no doubting the sophistication of the fiscal systems of Lucca by the later thirteenth century.

There is an enormous historiographical tradition associated with the discussions around the emergence of national identity in Europe. Jennifer Petrie has found a way to provide some illumination on the question with regard to the concept of the Italian nation, which is to examine how Petrarch understood the content of the idea of 'Italy'. By convincingly demonstrating that Petrarch – and therefore by implication other literate figures of the fourteenth century – had a clear understanding that Italy was nation, Jennifer Petrie provides us with an important landmark in the evolution of national concepts at the same time as helping us better understand Petrarch's works.

The English Mercenary, John Hawkwood, is a fascinating figure and the subject of William Caferro's discussion. The city of Florence was Hawkwood's last employer and did the mercenary proud at his funeral 20 March 1394, making the event a huge public spectacle and at a stroke doing much to establish a myth about the prowess and importance of Hawkwood. For as Caferro convincingly shows, the propaganda around the life of the mercenary was out of all proportion to his actual services to the city. By drawing attention to this discrepancy and in offering an explanation for it, Caferro ably reveals to us that a tradition was evolving in which rival Italian cities competed to sacralize their respective heroes. Hawkwood died at a convenient time for the Florentines to outdo the enormous public display at the Sienese funeral in honour of one of their own captains, Giovanni d'Azzo degli Ubaldini.

The value of utilizing the relatively rich economic material that is available for medieval Tuscany to better understand the workings of that society is demonstrated here by Duane Osheim, whose detailed examination of tax-books for the fourteenth and early fifteenth centuries allows for a reconstruction of the patterns of land ownership. In particular, Osheim is able to show that what would have once been a large body of independent farmers in the thirteenth century had significantly declined, succumbing to the pressures of war, plague and from being drawn into an unfavourable system of loans and short-term leases by patrician speculators who come to dominate the agricultural land in the years after 1500.

Synchronizing with Osheim, but this time using legal documents for the same period, M.E. Bratchel illuminates in just as intimate a manner the decline in population of the inhabitants of the Lucchese plain in the early fifteenth century. The criminal proceedings of that era are replete with vivid cases that demonstrate that the main difficulties facing all social classes in the region were raiding parties of Florentines, banditry, and pestilence. Moreover, the incidental details of the more colourful cases allow Bratchel to provide wonderfully precise snapshots of the activities and settlement patterns of the residents in the countryside around Lucca. These in turn provide the material for Bratchel to make important generalizations about the economic changes in the region and once again Lucca provides an important point of comparison with Florence and Siena precisely because of the different pattern of its evolution.

If the essays on medieval Italian history in this volume do justice to Christine Meek's interest in the subject then the same can certainly be said for the impressive collection of studies related to the lives and activities of women in the medieval and early modern periods. I.S. Robinson's painstaking piecing together of the fragments of evidence relating to a reform-minded visionary, Herluca (*c.*1060–1127/8), and her circle of associates is like a flash of lightning in the darkness, one that reveals quite an unexpected sight. For here was a woman of very modest origins – probably a domestic servant – commanding the respect of aristocratic champions of reform who gathered under her mentorship at Epfach on the River Lech. Not only does Herluca's life, when reconstructed, tell us a great deal about gender and social mobility *c.*1100, it also reveals the existence of a distinct type of community whose existence has barely been noted: that of pious refugees from the battle between papal reformers and their imperial opponents. This group adhered to the reform papacy at a time of adversity, their resolve stiffened by their belief in the blessed nature and visionary powers of Herluca. Their attempt to build a reform-minded community at Epfach was destroyed when 'wicked peasants' expelled Herluca, who spent her final years at Bernreid, celebrated as a saintly figure whose life supported the purest form of Gregorian ideal.

No woman of the medieval era has attracted more attention than Eleanor of Aquitaine and we are in the fortunate position of being able to present two original studies related to Eleanor for this Festschrift. The first, that by myself, discusses the role of the French queen on the Second Crusade in the context of a more general comparison of the part played by women in the crusading movement of 1096–9 and that of 1147–8. In the intervening two generations, I argue, it seems to be the case that the opportunity for large numbers of women to join the crusade declined. While crowds of women from the lower social orders were less prominent on the Second Crusade than the First, for one woman, Eleanor, the expedition provided a momentary opportunity for her to assert her own goals against those of her husband, Louis VII. At Antioch in the spring of 1148, Eleanor broke from the French king's desire to march south to Jerusalem, preferring to campaign with her uncle, Prince Raymond of Antioch, in the local vicinity. This incident has been rather downplayed by modern historians, even those who search the career of Eleanor for examples of autonomous political decision-making by aristocratic women, perhaps because of the allegations of incest that sprang up almost immediately. But the moment does provide an important case study of the exceptional circumstances that allowed for a married noble-woman of such seniority to be able to oppose her husband.

In composing three letters that purported to express the thoughts of Eleanor of Aquitaine, Peter of Blois provided perhaps the most vivid examples of a distinct characteristic of his writing style, that of drawing upon the literary tradition of *locus consolationis* or 'topic of consolation'. By focusing on the strength of this mode of writing in Peter's work, in our second study related to Eleanor, Stephen Hanaphy helps us understand the works of one of the finest writers of the twelfth century. Hanaphy's insights represent an important addition to even the most recent and thorough monographs on the subject of Peter's writings. Eleanor's letters demonstrate in practice the theoretical approaches to the language of consolation outlined in *Libellus de arte dictandi*, a handbook in all probability written by Peter of Blois. This new understanding of the phrasing and themes of the letters is important for anyone wanting to treat them as historical sources for the career of Queen Eleanor, as it makes clear the rhetorical passages. But this study is perhaps even more valuable in highlighting the importance of the topic of consolation in the evolution of European literary practice.

The theme of consolation in literature is continued by Katharine Simms in her analysis of the works of Irish bardic poets composed for bereaved ladies. A comparison of the work of poets across the decades and centuries allows for some confidence to be given to Katharine Simms' observation that the growing practice of poets addressing their works to noblewomen from the fifteenth century onwards indicates an increased social and economic status for the female members of the Irish and Anglo-Irish noble families in the early modern period. And again, a cluster of seventeenth-century poems allows Simms to connect the favourable material circumstances of wives or sisters of exiled Gaelic chiefs – who obtained pensions from the Spanish – with their ability to act as patrons in Gaelic Ireland. The poems that were composed in their honour, therefore, are not just valuable for their internal evidence of the poet's assumptions with regard to the feelings of the patroness, but they also provide a measure of the upward evolution of the social status of noblewomen in Gaelic Ireland.

That the life and works of St Jerome (*c*.362–420) proved important for the devotion both individual women and movements of women in the medieval era is demonstrated by Catherine Lawless. In particular, Lawless' examination of the paintings of the Clarissan order, and the letters relating to the female branch of the Gesuati and the followers of St Birgitta of Sweden, allow her to anaylse with precision the aspects of the life and works of St Jerome that appealed to these women. One part of this appeal lay in the fact that unlike other early Christian saints, Jerome's reputation was based on penitence, prayer, fasting and teaching rather than martyrdom. These were qualities that could be emulated by communities of Christian women in the thirteenth and fourteenth centuries. St Jerome's paternal relationship to a number of pious female contemporaries also provided a useful authority for the establishment of a form of governance by male mendicant houses over female ones acceptable to both.

Turning from the religious to the secular lives of medieval women, Gillian Kenny examines the evidence for the participation of women in warfare in Ireland. This material is fascinating in its own right, but the similarities and differences of this experience between Gaelic Ireland and the Anglo-Irish regions allows for an original method of comparison and Kenny is able to reach a conclusion of great importance to Irish medievalists as well as those interested in the limits of action for medieval noblewomen: that Gaelic married women were able to take more prominent parts in the prosecution of conflict through a variety of roles that were quite unavailable to their Anglo-Irish contemporaries due to their greater independence within the legal framework of the contemporary institution of marriage.

Nothing could be more appropriate to this volume than a study of a woman of great learning and skilful political acumen and in Helga Robinson-Hammerstein's examination of the career of Caritas Pirckheimer, abbess of the Nuremberg Convent of the Poor Clares from 1503 to her death in 1532, we have a perfect example. Caritas was under enormous pressure from her brother Willibald to become a conduit for humanist 'secularist' learning. It was a path that – for the sake of good communal order – Caritas wished to resist, but not so openly as to turn away from her love of learning. And in the ebb and flow of the exchanges between brother and sister two major themes dovetail with discussions earlier in this collection. Among the books presented to the convent by leading humanist intellectuals, the most treasured by Caritas was by St Jerome, thus extending our insights into female adherence to the cult of the saint – provided by Catherine Lawless – into the early modern period. Similarly, the letters exchanged between Caritas and her brother give us more insight into the theme of consolation literature, a topic that interested them both.

The collection of essays close with a discussion of one of the more fascinating female figures of the early modern period: Lucrezia Borgia. Maria Grazia Nico Ottaviani places the experience of Lucrezia as a governor of Spoleto and Foligno in Umbria (1499) alongside that of Caterino Cibo Varano who inherited the governorship of Camerino as regent for her daughter on the death of her husband in 1527. The comparison is fruitful and interesting. As a political appointee of her father, Pope Alexander VI, Lucrezia had much less freedom for her own initiatives than did Caterino as a widow of a former governor and appreciating this is valuable reminder of the centuries long difficulties faced by medieval and early modern women who managed to come to positions of authority.

Far more of Christine's colleagues than are published here sent their good wishes and expressions of appreciation of her work and friendship. And, I hope it will be recognized by all, that those who did have the time and material on hand to make a contribution to the Festschrift have helped bring into being a splendid volume of essays that stands as a worthy tribute to Christine on her retirement from teaching.

Becoming invisible: the role of economic history in medieval studies and in the historiography on medieval Italy

GEORGE DAMERON

Since the 1970s economic history has been receding from medieval studies, especially in North America.[1] It could be in danger of becoming invisible. This is true not only for medieval historiography in general but also for the field of Italian medieval history in particular. A generation ago, in 1977, when research into the history of women and gender in European history was still in its early stages, Renate Bridenthal and Claudia Koontz edited a collection of chronologically arranged essays that helped revolutionize European historiography: *Becoming visible: women in European history*.[2] A classic in the field of women's history, it included essays that were among the earliest syntheses of current research regarding European women. Today, women's history, and increasingly, gender studies, remain some of the most influential and important areas of historical study, regardless of period or region. The four volumes of essays on medieval and early modern women edited by Christine Meek are significant additions to this literature.[3] In the more than thirty years since Bridenthal and Koontz's collection appeared, women's history and gender studies have indeed made themselves very visible in European historiography, including economic history.[4]

In the same year that *Becoming Visible* appeared, 1977, Duane Osheim published his first book: *An Italian lordship: the bishopric of Lucca in the late Middle Ages*.[5] This monograph, which developed out of his dissertation, was

1 An earlier draft of this essay was presented as 'Becoming visible: the study of economic history and the medieval Italian church' at the 36th International Congress on Medieval Studies (5 May 2001) in Kalamazoo, Michigan. I am most grateful to David Peterson for his helpful suggestions and comments on this paper.   2 Renate Bridenthal and Claudia Koontz (eds), *Becoming visible: women in European history* (Boston, 1977), now in its 3rd edition (1998), ed. Renate Bridenthal, S.M. Stuard, & M.E. Wiesner.   3 Christine Meek & Katharine Simms (eds), *'The fragility of her sex'?: medieval Irishwomen in their European context* (Dublin, 1996); Meek (ed.), *Women in Renaissance and early modern Europe* (Dublin, 2000); Meek & Catherine Lawless (eds), *Studies on medieval and early modern women: pawns or players?* (Dublin, 2003); Meek & Lawless (eds), *Victims or viragos?* (Dublin, 2005).   4 This essay does not argue that women's history and gender studies are responsible for the lack of attention to economic history. Indeed, for some examples in economic history, see David Herlihy, *Opera Muliebria: women and work in medieval Europe* (New York, 1990); Martha Howell, *Women, production, and patriarchy in late medieval cities* (Chicago, 1986); and Lisa Bitel, chapter 5, *Women in early medieval Europe, 400–1100* (Cambridge 2002). 5 Duane Osheim, *An Italian lordship: the bishopric of Lucca in the late Middle Ages*

a detailed economic analysis of the development of the temporal possessions of the Lucchese bishopric and its role in the history of the commune. Its focus reflected a historiographical trend that was current and common in medieval Italian studies at that time: the study of the economy. Indeed, in Anglophone scholarship on the medieval Italian economy, the 1960s and 1970s were rich and creative decades. Philip Jones had published his two seminal studies on medieval Italian agrarian history in 1966 and 1968. Roberto Lopez's *The commercial revolution of the Middle Ages*, which offered a comprehensive explanation of the economic take-off of the High Middle Ages by one of the foremost economic historians of medieval Italy, appeared in 1971. With regards to the history of the medieval Italian Commune, understanding the economy was deemed essential at the time. David Herlihy's *Medieval and Renaissance Pistoia: the social history of an Italian town: 1200–1430* had appeared in 1967, and Frederic Lane's *Venice: a maritime republic* came out in 1973. Just three years before, William Bowsky had examined in a comprehensive fashion the finances of the regime of the Nine in *The finance of the commune of Siena: 1287–1355*. Christine Meek's *Lucca, 1369– 1400: politics and society in an Early Modern Renaissance city-state*, appeared eight years later, in 1978. Although primarily political in focus, this book was comprehensive in scope, examining industry, loans, and taxation from a comparative perspective. Osheim's 1977 history of the Lucchese bishopric was therefore in the mainstream of medieval historiography regarding the economy. Yet, it was also innovative in that it was among the earliest studies in medieval Italian historiography to focus extensively on church property.[6]

A generation after both Osheim's monograph and *Becoming visible* appeared, the field of medieval studies continues to flourish. It has certainly been enriched by new research in gender studies, law and conflict resolution, liturgy and spirituality, hagiography, cultural studies, politics, the social history of elites, and heresy.[7] Politics and the narrative are back, but economic

(Berkeley, 1977). **6** Philip Jones, 'Medieval agrarian society at its prime: Italy', in M.M. Postan and H.J. Habakuk (eds), *Cambridge economic history*, 2nd ed. (Cambridge, 1966), pp 340–431; 'From manor to mezzadria: a Tuscan case-study in the medieval origins of modern agrarian society', in N. Rubinstein (ed.), *Florentine studies: politics and society in Renaissance Florence* (London, 1968), pp 193–241; Roberto Lopez, *The commercial revolution of the Middle Ages, 950–1350* (Englewood Cliffs, NJ, 1971); David Herlihy, *Medieval and Renaissance Pistoia: the social history of an Italian town, 1200–1430* (New Haven, 1967); Frederic C. Lane, *Venice: a maritime republic* (Baltimore, 1973); William Bowsky, *The finance of the commune of Siena, 1287–1355* (Oxford, 1970); Christine Meek, *Lucca, 1369– 1400: politics and society in an early Renaissance city-state* (Oxford, 1978). Since 1977, Osheim has continued to publish on medieval Italy. See Sharon Dale, Alison Lewin, and Duane Osheim (eds), *Chronicling history: chroniclers and historians in medieval and Renaissance Italy* (University Park, PA, 2008); *A Tuscan monastery and its social world: San Michele of Guamo (1156–1348)* (Rome, 1989). **7** See Paul Freedman & G.M. Spiegel, 'Medievalisms old and new: the rediscovery of alterity in North American medieval studies', *American Historical Review* 103:3 (June 1998), 677–704, especially 693ff.

history has been in danger of disappearing. This essay, which takes as its premise the assumption that medieval Italian historiography is broadly emblematic of medieval studies in general, will explore the problem in more detail. It will consist of four sections. First, it will describe the situation and offer evidence. Second, it will explore possible explanations for this neglect. Third, it will suggest why historians need to make the economy visible again. Finally, it will lay out reasons for hope for the future.

A couple of points, however, are worth mentioning at the outset. For purposes of discussion, this essay limits itself to the Middle Ages, defined here as the period that spans the centuries between AD 600 and 1400. The so-called High Middle Ages, AD 1000–1400, is the principal focus. The Early Modern Period and Renaissance (*c.*1400–*c.*1700) lies outside its scope and deserves its own study.[8] Second, the essay concentrates primarily on the Anglophone historiographical tradition, particularly North American. Italian historiography on medieval Italy is relevant to this discussion, but it also rightfully deserves its own separate essay. Third, by arguing that economic history is currently not getting the attention it deserves, the essay does not suggest that historians should return to economic history at the expense of other fields. Indeed, newer trends in modern historiography since the mid-1970s – transnational history, gender studies, cultural studies, and so on – should ideally enrich the field of economic history, and conversely, more economic analyses should be brought into these fields as well. Finally, this is not meant to be a full review of the historiography on the medieval economy. Its primary aim is to argue for a return of economic analysis into the mainstream. The scholarship cited here are examples to demonstrate broad points, not to offer a comprehensive bibliography.

Until the late 1970s there had been a significant and continuous stream of scholarship on the medieval Italian economy for at least three generations. The origins of this tradition reach deep into the late nineteenth century. Marxism and socialist theory, with their emphasis on the primacy of class, economic structure, and social relations, informed and influenced the work of many late nineteenth- and early twentieth-century historians of medieval Italy. Among them was Romolo Caggese, whose work, on one of many other issues, emphasized conflict between city (exploiting) and countryside

---

8 Studies of the Italian economy after 1400 are therefore excluded from this analysis. This includes most of the work of S.K. Cohn, Jr, including *Creating the Florentine state: peasants and rebellion, 1348–1434* (Cambridge, 1999) and *The Black Death transformed: disease and culture in early Renaissance Europe* (London, 2002). Richard Goldthwaite's *The economy of Renaissance Florence* (Baltimore, 2009), except for the Introduction, is also beyond the scope of this essay, as is J.C. Brown's *In the shadow of Florence: provincial society in Renaissance Pescia* (Oxford, 1982). For the historiography on the Renaissance Italian church, see David Peterson, 'Out on the margins: religion and the Church in Renaissance Italy', *Renaissance Quarterly* 53:3 (Autumn 2000), 835–79.

(exploited). Johann Plesner's still-influential *L'Émigration de la campagne à la ville libre de Florence au XIIIe siècle* in 1934 argued that economic oppression by lords in the countryside could not account for urban immigration in the thirteenth century. Cinzio Violante followed his classical study of Milan in 1953 (*La società milanese nell'eta precomunale*) with numerous studies of churches and communes that highlighted economic developments. Enrico Fiumi's classic studies on the Florentine economy and Philip Jones' influential analyses of ecclesiastical property appeared in the 1950s. Like Plesner's study, which relied on the case study method, Elio Conti's highly important *La formazione della struttura agraria moderna nel contado fiorentino* (1965) concentrated on the economic and social development of specific communities, particularly Passignano in the Val di Pesa (south of Florence). David Herlihy's innovative work on Pistoia and the rural commune of Santa Maria Impruneta integrated economic history into the story of medieval communes and their ecclesiastical institutions. Marvin Becker's two-volume *Florence in Transition* (1967) made the economy central to his argument that communal governance had declined by the 1340s from a 'gentle' to a stern *paideia*. Pierre Toubert's path breaking focus on the development of *castelli* in medieval Latium (1973) made rural economic history and *incastellamento* (castle-building) central to any understanding of the medieval Italian (not just Roman) countryside. In addition, Christine Meek, Thomas Blomquist, and William Bowsky all zeroed in on the history of finance and taxation to illuminate the history of various communes in Tuscany, specifically Florence, Lucca, Pistoia, and Siena.[9] In 1974 Giovanni Cherubini collected several of his most influential essays on the economic and social history of central and northern Italy into a single volume, *Signori, Contadini, and Borghesi*, and two years later Charles de La Roncière published his detailed economic analysis of fourteenth-century Florence and its region.[10] When Duane Osheim's work on the

9 Romolo Caggese, *Classi e comuni rurali nel medio evo* (Florence, 1908); Johan Plesner, *L'Émigration de la campagne à la ville libre de Florence au XIIIe siècle*, trans. F. Gleizal (Copenhagen, 1934); Cinzio Violante, 'I vescovi dell'Italia centro-settentrionale e lo sviluppo dell'economia monetaria,' in *Vescovi e diocesi* (Padua, 1964), pp 193–217; Enrico Fiumi, 'Sui rapporti economici tra città e contado nell'età comunale', *Archivio Storico Italiano* 114 (1956), 18–68; Philip Jones, 'Le finanze della Badia Cistercense di Settimo nel XIV secolo', *Rivista di storia della chiesa in Italia* 10 (1956), 90–122; Elio Conti, *La formazione della struttura agraria moderna nel contado fiorentino* (Florence, 1965); Herlihy, *Medieval and Renaissance Pistoia*; 'Santa Maria Impruneta: a rural commune in the late Middle Ages', in *Florentine Studies*, pp 242–76; David Herlihy, 'Direct and indirect taxation in Tuscan urban finance, c.1200–1400', in *Finances et comptabilité urbaines du 13e siècle au 16e siècle* (Brussels, 1964), pp 385–405; Marvin Becker, *Florence in transition*, 2 (Baltimore, 1967); Pierre Toubert, *Les structures du Latium médiévale* (Rome, 1973); Meek, *Lucca, 1369–1400*; Thomas Blomquist, *Merchant families, banking, and money in medieval Lucca* (Aldershot, 2005); W.M. Bowsky, *The finance of the commune of Siena* (Oxford, 1970). 10 Giovanni Cherubini, *Signori, Contadini, Borghesi* (Florence, 1974); Charles-M de La Roncière, *Florence, centre économique régional au XIVe siècle*, 5 (Aix-en-Provence,

bishopric of Lucca appeared in 1977, therefore, the study of the Italian medieval economy had been a valued part of medieval (and medieval Italian) historiography for several generations. The twenty-five year period between 1955 and 1980 therefore constituted an era of great productivity in the historiography on the medieval Italian economy.

In the past three decades, however, the profile of economic history in the historiography on medieval Italy has receded. Indeed, economic history – whether it concerns the Commune, rural history, or ecclesiastical institutions in both city and countryside – seems to be largely (though not totally) neglected, especially among English-speaking (particularly North American) historians. This is surprising, since Italian archives are burgeoning with documents and manuscripts relating to economic history. This is not to say however that economic history has become invisible. There are exceptions. Significant work has indeed been published since 1980 by non-Europeans and Europeans in fields associated with trade and the Mediterranean (Abulafia, McCormick), the economic impact of military (Caferro), banks (Tognetti and Mueller), industry (Franceschini and Hoshino), the economic history of individual communes and regions (Steven A. Epstein, Wickham, Marshall, S.R. Epstein, Goldthwaite), women and work (Herlihy), hospitals (S.R. Epstein), fiscality and state formation (Cohn), and the economic development of ecclesiastical institutions (Dameron, Osheim).[11] However, within the broader context of the historiography on medieval Italy, in both Europe and North America, since 1980 the economy of medieval Italy has increasingly remained in the background. This is in contrast to the situation among Italian historians, who have for the most part maintained an uninterrupted and vibrant tradition of economic and social history for generations. The emphasis here may be on social history and lordship, but the disposition of property is also crucial to their concerns. In Tuscan historiography alone, local studies continue

---

1976). 11 David Abulafia, *The two Italies: economic relations between Norman Kingdom of Sicily and the northern communes* (Cambridge, 1977); William Caferro, *Mercenary companies and the decline of Siena* (Baltimore, 1998); Sergio Tognetti, *Il banco Cambini* (Florence, 1999); Reinhold Mueller, *The Venetian money market* (Baltimore, 1997); Franco Franceschi, *Oltre il 'tumulto': i lavoratori fiorentini dell'Arte della Lana fra Tre e Quattrocento* (Florence, 1993); David Herlihy, *Opera Muliebria*, which pays particular attention to Italy; Stephan R. Epstein, *An island for itself: economic development and social change in late medieval Sicily* (Cambridge, 1992); C.J. Wickham, *The mountains and the city: the Tuscan Appennines in the early Middle Ages* (Oxford, 1988); Richard Marshall, *The local merchants of Prato: small entrepreneurs in the late medieval economy* (Baltimore, 1999); Stephan R. Epstein, *Alle origini della fattoria toscana: l'Ospedale della Scala di Siena e le sue terre (metà '200–metà '400)* (Florence, 1986); Richard Goldthwaite, *The economy of Renaissance Florence* (Baltimore, 2009), Introduction; Michael McCormick, *Origins of the medieval economy: communications and commerce, AD 300–AD 900* (Cambridge, 2001); Samuel Kline Cohn, Jr, *Creating the Florentine state*; George Dameron, *Episcopal power and Florentine society, 1000–1320* (Cambridge, MA, 1991); *Florence and its church in the age of Dante* (Philadelphia, 2005); Duane Osheim, *A Tuscan monastery*.

to appear to address major issues in economic and social history, based on meticulous archival research.[12]

As economic history loses visibility in medieval Italian historiography (less so in the United Kingdom, more so in North America), it has ceded its place to other fields, particularly cultural and political history. Even though study of the economy has ebbed, the quality of recent historical literature on medieval Italy has continued to advance. Indeed, medieval Italian historiography is flourishing. The field of cultural history has been particularly rich, especially in the areas of religion, the visual arts, gender studies, education, and legal history. Politics and governance of the Commune, private life, and Franciscan studies have especially been productive fields of inquiry.[13] Southern Italy has also been the subject of several new and innovative studies by historians who have delved into the rich archives of the region to examine new as well as traditional historical problems. Churches in southern Italy are continuing to get the attention they deserve, and the social and political history of the South is increasingly the focus of innovative research.[14]

---

12 For some examples in Tuscan historiography, see Paolo Pirillo, *Famiglia e mobilità sociale nella Toscana medievale: i franzese Della Foresta da Figline Valdarno (secolo XII–XV)* (Florence, 1992); E. Faini, 'Firenze nei secoli X–XII. Economia, società, istituzioni' (PhD dissertation in Storia Medievale, Università degli Studi di Firenze, XVII ciclo (2005)); Maria Elena Cortese, *Signori, castelli, città: l'aristocrazia del territorio fiorentino tra X e XII secolo* (Florence, 2007).   13 For examples, see Carol Lansing, *Passion and order: restraint of grief in the medieval Italian communes* (Ithaca, NY, 2008); Sharon Dale, Alison Lewin, and Duane Osheim (eds), *Chronicling history*; Judith Steinhoff, *Sienese painting after the Black Death* (Cambridge, 2007); Robert Black, *Education and society in Florentine Tuscany* (Leiden, 2007); Rosalind Brooke, *The image of Saint Francis* (Cambridge, 2006); John Najemy, *A history of Florence, 1200–1575* (Malden, MA, 2006); Augustine Thompson, *Cities of god: the religion of the Italian communes, 1125–1325* (University Park, PA, 2005); William Cook (ed.), *The art of the Franciscan Order in Italy* (Leiden, 2005); Louise Bourdua, *The Franciscans and art patronage in late medieval Italy* (Cambridge, 2004); Samantha Kelly, *The new Solomon: Robert of Naples (1309–1343) and fourteenth century kingship* (Leiden, 2003); Chris Wickham, *Courts and conflict in twelfth-century Tuscany*; William Connell and Andrea Zorzi (eds), *Florentine Tuscany* (Cambridge, 2000); Jean-Claude Maire Vigueur (ed.), *I podestà dell'Italia comunale* (Rome, 2000); Frances Andrews, *The early Humiliati* (Cambridge, 1999); M. Michèle Mulchahey, *'First the bow is bent in study' – Dominican education before 1350* (Toronto, 1998); Benjamin Kohl, *Padua under the Carrara, 1318–1405* (Baltimore, 1998); Mary Stroll, *The medieval Abbey of Farfa* (Leiden, 1997); Philip Jones, *The Italian city-state* (Oxford, 1997); Steven A. Epstein, *Genoa and the Genoese, 958–1578* (Chapel Hill, NC, 1996); Daniel Bornstein, *The Bianchi of 1399: popular devotion in late medieval Italy* (Ithaca, NY, 1993); Grado G. Merlo, *Tra eremo e città: studi su Francesco d'Assisi e sul francescanesimo medievale* (Assisi, 1991); André Vauchez, *Ordini mendicanti e società italiana: XIII–XV secolo*, trans. Michele Sampaolo (Milan, 1990); Merlo, *Eretici e eresie medievale* (Bologna, 1989); Daniel Waley, *The Italian city-republics*, 3rd ed. (London, 1988).   14 Graham Loud, *The Latin church in Norman Italy* (Cambridge, 2007); Valerie Ramseyer, *Transformation of a religious landscape: medieval Southern Italy, 850–1150* (Ithaca, NY, 2006); Joanna Drell, *Kingship and conquest: family strategies in the principality of Salerno during the Norman period, 1077–1194* (Ithaca, NY, 2002); Graham Loud, *Conquerors and churchmen in Norman Italy* (Brookfield, VT, 1999);

Furthermore, the historiography of medieval Italian religion continues to advance, enriched by new research regarding cults of saints, confraternities, ecclesiastical patronage, institutional development, heresy, the development of piety, women's spirituality, and gender. New understanding about the history of women and gender is prompting us to rethink and re-conceptualize religious history and political power in new ways. Institutional history of the church continues to thrive, as is evident from the studies by William Bowsky on the chapter of San Lorenzo in Florence, Maureen Miller's on the episcopal palace, Valerie Ramseyer's on southern Italy (particularly Salerno), and Robert Brentano's examination of the diocese of Rieti.[15] Paralleling and enriching Anglophone and French ecclesiastical historiography is a thriving tradition of local church history in Italy. Since the late 1970s a new generation of Italian scholars have turned their attention to the Italian church. They include Antonio Rigon, Anna Benvenuti, Roberto Bizzocchi, Daniela Rando, Paolo Golinelli, and Mauro Ronzani.[16] Their work has underscored the relevance of the spiritual and ecclesiastical traditions to the political, cultural, and institutional development of the Italian Commune.

Barbara Kreutz, *Before the Normans: southern Italy in the ninth and tenth centuries* (Philadelphia, 1991). 15 See previous note and also Susan Boynton, *Shaping a monastic identity: liturgy and history at the Imperial Abbey of Farfa, 1000–1125* (Ithaca, NY, 2006); Thomas Luongo, *The saintly politics of Catherine of Siena* (Ithaca, NY, 2006); Marica Tacconi, *Cathedral and civic ritual in late medieval and Renaissance Florence: the service books of Santa Maria del Fiore* (Cambridge, 2005); Dameron, *Florence and its church in the age of Dante* (Philadelphia, 2005); Susan Twyman, *Papal ceremonial in the twelfth century* (London, 2002); Maureen Miller, *The bishop's palace: architecture and authority in medieval Italy* (Ithaca, NY, 2000); William Bowsky, *La chiesa di San Lorenzo nel medioevo* (Florence, 1999); Carol Lansing, *Power and purity: Cathar heresy in medieval Italy* (Oxford 1998); Daniel Bornstein, *Women and religion in medieval and Renaissance Italy* (Chicago, 1996); Robert Brentano, *A new world in a small place: church and religion in the Diocese of Rieti, 1188–1378* (Berkely, 1994); Charles de La Roncière, *Réligion paysanne et réligion urbaine en Toscane (c.1250–c.1450)* (Aldershot, 1994); John Henderson, *Piety and charity in late medieval Florence* (Oxford, 1994); Giorgio Chittolini, 'Civic religion and the countryside in late medieval Italy', in *City and countryside in late medieval and Renaissance Italy*, ed. Chris Wickham and Trevor Dean (London, 1990); Anna Benvenuti Papi, *In Castro poenitentiae: santità e societa femminile nell'Italia medievale*, Italia Sacra 45 (Rome, 1990); D. Osheim, *A Tuscan monastery*; G. Dameron, *Episcopal power and Florentine society*. 16 See Mauro Ronzani, *La chiesa di San Martino* (Pisa, 2007); *Un idea trecentesca di cimitero: la costruzione e l'uso del Camposanto nella Pisa del secolo XIV* (Pisa, 2005); Daniela Rando, *Una Chiesa di frontiera: le istituzioni ecclesiastiche veneziane nei secoli VI–XII* (Bologna, 1994); Paolo Golinelli, *Città e culto dei santi nel medioevo italiano* (Bologna, 1996); M. Ronzani, 'La 'plebs' in città. La problematica della pieve urbana in Italia centro-settentrionale fra il IX e XIV secolo', in C. Fonseca and C. Violante (eds), *Chiesa e città* (Galatina, 1990), pp 23–43; Anna Benvenuti, *In Castro poenitentiae*; Antonio Rigon, *Clero e città: 'fratalea cappellanorum', parroci, cura d'anime in Padova dal XII al XV secolo* (Padua, 1988); Ronzani, 'L'Organizzazione della cura d'anime nella città di Pisa (secoli XII–XIII)', in Cinzio Violante and C. Fonseca (eds), *Istituzioni ecclesiastiche della Toscana medioevale* (Galatina, 1980), pp 35–85; Robert Brentano, 'Italian ecclesiastical history: the Sambin Revolution', *Medievalia et Humanistica*, n.s., no. 14 (Totowa, NJ, 1986), 189–97; Giorgio Chittolini and

Nevertheless, economic concerns in general – not to mention in the field of ecclesiastical history – remain largely peripheral to medieval Italian historiography, especially among North American scholars. They have been barely visible, mirroring general trends in medieval studies itself. Indeed, they parallel developments in the historical profession as a whole. A survey of the articles published between 1999 and 2009 in the volumes of *Speculum: A Journal of Medieval Studies*, the most prestigious journal of medieval studies in North America, reveals that a very small percentage of these essays concerned economic history, either directly or indirectly. Of the estimated 160 articles published in that decade (about four per quarter), only seven seemed to concern economic topics.[17] What has been happening in medieval studies is simply the part of a much larger trend in the profession as a whole, particularly among American historians. A glance at the programs for the annual conferences of the American Historical Association for 2008 and 2009, for example, reveal that relative to other fields represented at those meetings, economic history played a small role. In 2008, there were 48 sessions on comparative history, 19 on cultural history, and 18 on historiography. Economic history was represented by eight. The same trend was evident a year later. At the 2009 meeting in New York City, comparative history had 32 sessions, cultural 24, and historiography (a major increase) 33. Only six sessions in 2009 concerned economic topics.[18]

In her 2009 Presidential Address, 'The Task of the Historian,' Gabrielle Spiegel surveyed recent developments in historiography that may help us understand the reasons for this situation. Observing that the legacy of the 'linguistic turn' of the post-World War II period regarding modern historiography 'has run its course,' she argues that much of poststructural theory still 'might be worth saving.' Noting that we are currently living in a period of 'rapid change,' 'not least in the realm of technology and the spread of global capital,' she offers a short list of concerns for historians to consider for

Giovanni Miccoli (eds), *Storia d'Italia. Annali 9. La chiesa e il potere politico dal Medioevo all'età contemporanea* (Turin, 1986).   17 James Masschaele, 'The public space of the marketplace in medieval England', *Speculum* 77:2 (April 2002), 383–421; M.M. Bullard, S.R. Epstein, Benjamin G. Kohl, & Susan Mosher Stuard, 'Where history and theory interact: Frederic C. Lane on the emergence of Capitalism', *Speculum* 79:1 (January 2004), 88–119; Paul Freedman, 'Spices and late-medieval European ideas of scarcity and value', *Speculum* 80:4 (October 2005), 1209–27; Florin Curta, 'Merovingian and Carolingian gift giving', *Speculum* 81:3 (July 2006), 671–99; Stephen Perkinson, 'Courtly splendor, urban markets: some recent exhibition catalogues', *Speculum* 81:4 (October 2006), 1150–7; Michael McCormick, P.E. Dutton, and P.A. Mayewski, 'Volcanoes and the climate forcing of Carolingian Europe, AD 750–950', *Speculum* 82:4 (October 2007), 865–95; Leor Halevi, 'Christian impurity versus economic necessity: a fifteenth century fatwa on European paper', *Speculum* 83:4 (October 2008), 917–45.   18 *The American Historical Association Program of the 123rd Annual Meeting (New York City, NY), January 2–5, 2009*, Sharon Tune (ed.), p. 137; *The American Historical Association Program of the 122nd Annual Meeting (Washington, DC), January 3–6, 2008*, ed. Sharon Tune, p. 211.

the future. They include 'diaspora, migration, immigration, and the rapidly developing field of transnational history.' Study of the economy, though implied, is absent from that list. Although she notes that the impact of 'the spread of global capitalism and its impact on all forms of social formation' will continue to be an important influence on the work of historians, she does not include economic history or economic concerns in her choice of current and future topics for historical research. Those subjects, 'as in the case of poststructuralism,' are 'concerned with the problematics of displacement and absent or fractured memory.'[19] The expansion of global capitalism may well have a decisive impact on the future work of historians, but we are here still in the realm of culture, not economics.

The neglect of economic history is therefore simply one manifestation of a much larger trend: the virtual disappearance of economic history in current historical discourse. Why? There are several reasons worth mentioning here. First, since the 1960s and 1970s, the period which marked the so-called 'linguistic turn' and the emergence of postmodern (or post-structural) theory, modern historical research has increasingly focused on culture and cultural studies. This has come largely at the expense of economic history. Though never completely dismissive of economic structures, postmodern theory identified language as the primary vehicle for social understanding and meaning, elevating the study of culture and marginalizing topics such as the economy.[20] As the literary critic Terry Eagleton has suggested, the appeal of post-structuralism stemmed from the fact that for many disillusioned intellectuals after 1968, it offered a way to subvert the status quo in the abstract (in the realms of language, cultural interpretation, and ideology) when actual state and economic structures seemed impervious to change. Similarly, for Gabrielle M. Spiegel, post-structuralism appealed specifically to those historians who had suffered a 'loss of confidence and optimism in post-Enlightenment progress'.[21] If language itself is indeterminate and unstable in meaning, so are the ideas, beliefs, and texts that it articulated. The impact of the 'linguistic turn' was certainly less pronounced in historiography than in literary theory, a field where the theoretical work of Jacques Derrida on deconstruction was most

---

19 Gabrielle M. Spiegel, 'Presidential address: the task of the historian', *American Historical Review* 114:1 (February 2009), 1–15. The quotations are from pages 3, 11, and 13, respectively. For another excellent (but thematically different) analysis of the influence of postmodernism or the cultural turn on the work of historians, see Caroline W. Bynum, 'Perspectives, connections, and objects: what is happening in history now?', *Daedalus* 38:1 (Winter 2009), 71–86. Although she notes that current interest in material objects is 'a flight from postmodern textuality' (p. 79), she too has nothing to say about the role of economic history in past or future historiography. I am grateful to Mac McCorkle for having brought Bynum's essay to my attention.   20 G.M. Spiegel, 'Presidential address: the task of the historian', pp 1–11; Freedman and Spiegel, 'Medievalisms old and new', pp 693–704.   21 Terry Eagleton, *Literary theory: an introduction* (Minneapolis, 1983), p. 142; Spiegel, 'Presidential address: the task of the historian', p. 8.

influential. More important to historians was the influence of the symbolic anthropology of the late cultural anthropologist, Clifford Geertz. Here the focus for the scholar was on 'systems of meaning rather than behaviour'. The 'linguistic turn' did indeed exert a significant influence on historians, particularly with regards to the identification of the types of historical problems to be investigated and the ways by which primary sources were to be interpreted as 'texts' rather than as primary sources.

Also central to historical practice has been the legacy of the work of Michel Foucault, a legacy that highlighted the study of culture and focused on exposing the underlying ideological and linguistic structures of the dominant elites. His interest in the connections between knowledge and power, and, in particular, in the social groups that included 'the marginal and excluded,' has been highly influential.[22] In the last quarter of the twentieth century, therefore, the analysis of material life and economic structures receded as subjects of investigation. What mattered most in postmodern theory was the study of the perceptions and repressive ideologies that helped socially construct the dominant institutions and cultural traditions of the modern world. One of the disadvantages of this approach, as the modern historian, Chris Bayly, has pointed out in a 2006 forum on transnational history in the *American Historical Review*, is that it tends to assume that the economy emerges from culture. 'There is a related danger of positing culture as an entity prior to economy in some way: this simply reverses the old catchphrase of Marxist materialism.' He added: 'Economy transforms culture as much as vice versa.'[23]

A second related factor that has contributed to the marginalization of economic history has been the nature of the historical profession itself. In the last quarter of the twentieth century and the beginning of the twenty-first, as the emphasis on cultural studies has loomed larger and larger as a focus of study, there seem to be fewer and fewer opportunities for economic and social historians to secure tenure-track positions and to advance within the profession. With fewer opportunities come fewer rewards. An unscientific survey of job openings in the field of medieval history in the past few years, for example, reveals little if any demand for economic and social historians. Third, a final factor contributing to the paucity of practicing economic historians in the

---

22 Freedman and Spiegel, 'Medievalisms old and new', pp 694–7 ('the marginal and excluded', quoted from p. 697); Peter Novick, *That noble dream: the 'objectivity question' and the American historical profession* (Cambridge, 1988), pp 551–5 ('systems of meaning rather than behavior', quoted from p. 553). See also the influential essay by N.Z. Davis, 'Some tasks and themes in the study of popular religion', in Charles Trinkaus and Heiko Oberman (eds), *The pursuit of holiness in late medieval and Renaissance religion* (Leiden, 1974), pp 307–36.   23 Chris Bayly, '*AHR* conversation: on transnational history', *American Historical Review* 111:5 (December 2006), p. 1452; Spiegel and Freedman, 'Medievalisms old and new', pp 697–9; Mark T. Gilderhus, *History and historians: a historiographical introduction* (5th ed., Upper Saddle River, NJ, 2003), pp 132–40.

field of medieval history is demographic. There are certainly exceptions, but there seem to be fewer economic and social historians of the Middle Ages currently training graduate students than there were four decades ago. Many of the most productive Anglophone economic and social historians who were working in Italian medieval economic history and published some of their most innovative work in the 1960s, 1970s, and 1980s have either passed away or retired.[24] A final (and fourth) factor is historiographical. The study of politics and the Commune remains the dominant focus of historical research on Italy in the Middle Ages. As a result, many current historians of medieval Italy tend to pay attention to the economy only in so far as it illuminates their understanding of the development of the Commune. Economic history becomes a means to an end rather than an end in itself. With fewer and fewer senior historians and graduate students exploring problems in economic history, and with fewer professional opportunities for jobs and advancement, economic concerns have become secondary to other issues. And where anti-clerical and anti-ecclesiastical traditions may still be strong, as in Italy, there are few incentives among many Italian scholars to examine the economic history of ecclesiastical institutions.

Why should neglect of the economy be considered a problem? Why is it worthwhile to make economic history visible again? Several reasons come to mind. First, there is simply the need to know for the sake of knowing. There is still much for historians to learn about the medieval Italian economy, especially for the period after 1000. Italian archives contain some of the most extensive and comprehensive collections of primary sources relating to economic history, and they remain unexplored. Second, understanding the evolution of the medieval Italian economy can significantly enhance and enrich our understanding of other aspects of the history of the peninsula, including the development of the Commune, the Church, gender relations, the social history of elites, patronage of the arts, the law, and politics. For example, a greater understanding of the economic history of ecclesiastical institutions can help us clarify the relationship between the city and countryside, the history of rural communes, the balance of economic and political forces within the Commune, and the emergence of the territorial state at the end of the Middle Ages. Ecclesiastical institutions were among the wealthiest landlords in city and countryside and among the most powerful economic players in any commune. At this point, we still need to have more basic information about them: the location of their properties, the impact of taxation on various ecclesiastical constituencies, the evolution of rents, the relationship of urban to rural holdings, the names of those engaged in significant economic transactions, the

---

24 Among those who have passed on are Marvin Becker, Elio Conti, David Herlihy, Philip Jones, Frederic Lane, Harry Miskiman, and Roberto Lopez. Within the past few years, the profession has also lost S.R. Epstein and Thomas Blomquist.

history of prices, the economics of church building, and the economic impact of war on urban and ecclesiastical finance. The list could continue. Until such issues are more fully explored, there will always be gaps in what we know about the history of the Commune, about patronage, gift-giving, the development of the territorial state, power structures, and the balance of social and political forces in medieval Italian cities.[25] Third, and certainly not the least, the study of the medieval economy itself nurtures a high level of intellectual rigor and analytical understanding that is both quantitative and qualitatve. For undergraduates and practicing historians alike, the study of the economy enhances and develops critical thinking skills. As Susan Mosher Stuard described Frederic Lane's approach to the teaching of history, 'Careful study makes us conscious of the sources, and an evidence-based discipline supplies correctives for various kinds of misunderstandings. Developing a critical habit of mind inoculates us against uncritical acceptance.'[26]

Regarding the future of economic history, there are indeed reasons for optimism, especially since the turn of the millenium. There does seem to be a growing consensus today among many historians that the legacies of the 'linguistic turn' and 'cultural studies' have indeed run its course. This may offer an opening for economic history to return, and more and more historians are calling precisely for that to happen. The current popularity of transnational history is a good case in point. As Sven Beckert, a historian of nineteenth-century America, wrote in the recent American Historical Association-sponsored forum on transnational history in 2006, 'I am cautiously optimistic that questions of economic change, state formation, and political economy might again become more central to historical inquiries as part of an embrace of transnational history.' He also called for more research on the global economy (his own work, as he observed, implies a 'distancing from cultural history'). The growing importance of global history has indeed drawn attention to the decisive importance of economic developments, and medievalists have contributed significantly to this growing field. Furthermore, volumes 5 and 6 of the *New Cambridge Medieval History* (1999–2000) highlight social and economic developments and include several chapters in each volume on urban life, rural society, and commerce.[27] New areas of study are also stimulating renewed interest in the economy. Within the last decade the study of seas and oceans has emerged as a significant field of historical

25 See Dameron, *Florence and its church in the age of Dante*, p. 10.   **26** Melissa Meriam Bullard et al., 'Where history and theory interact', p. 89.   **27** Sven Beckert, '*AHR* conversation: on transnational history', pp 1453–4. For two contributions by medievalists to pre-modern global history, see J.L. Abu-Lughod, *Before European hegemony: the world system AD 1250–1350* (Oxford, 1989) and Alfred Andrea and James Overfield (eds), *The human record: sources for global history*, 2 (3rd ed., Boston, 1998). Vol. 5 (*c.*1198–*c.*1300) of *The New Cambridge Economic History* was edited by David Abulafia (Cambridge, 1999); Vol. 6 (*c.*1300–*c.*1415) by Michael Jones (Cambridge, 2000).

research. In a recent essay, 'The Mediterranean and "the New Thalassology"', a medieval and an ancient historian, Peregrine Horden and Nicholas Purcell, respectively, identified 'regimes of risk', the 'logic of production', 'internal connectivity', and 'topographical fragmentation' as crucial constitutive elements of their four-fold model of Mediterranean history. David Abulafia, historian of the medieval Mediterranean, continues to publish extensively in this field, as he has for decades. Trade in the Mediterranean world and on the Iberian peninsula has also for more than a decade been a principal focus of attention for another medievalist, Olivia Remie Constable.[28]

In the 2004 essay on Frederic Lane, the late S.R. Epstein lamented that 'economic history is no longer much practiced by medievalists'.[29] That may still unfortunately be true in the early twenty-first century, but developments in the medieval historiography of Italy in the past decade offer us reasons for hope. Abulafia's continued focus on the Mediterranean and Chris Wickham's work on early medieval Italy reminds us that medieval economic history in general has never totally gone away in British historiography, even if the field has become less and less visible in North America.[30] And even in North America, trends are promising. Michael McCormick's massive study, *Origins of the European economy: communications and commerce, AD 300–900*, published in 2001, is a good case in point. William Caferro's work on military history is also helping us return the economy to the study of the Commune. There are still a few American historians of medieval Italy teaching in American colleges and universities who are training graduate students, suggesting that the field will persist well into the twenty-first century. Economic history is also increasingly becoming more prominent in the field of medieval studies as a whole. The publication in 2009 of a new synthesis on the economic and social history of Europe by Steven A. Epstein, himself a historian of the medieval Italian economy, is a significant, promising development. It follows by seven years three other syntheses: Peter Spufford's study of the merchant, Diana Wood's survey of medieval economic thought, and Angeliki Laiou's overview of the Byzantine economy.[31]

28 Peregrine Horden and Nicholas Purcell, 'The Mediterranean and "the New Thalassology"', in '*AHR* forum: oceans of history', *American Historical Association* 113:3 (June 2006), 722–40; David Abulafia, 'Mediterraneans', in William Harris (ed.), *Rethinking the Mediterranean* (Oxford, 2005), pp 64–93; David Abulafia (ed.), *The Mediterranean in history* (Los Angeles, 2003); *Italy, Sicily, and the Mediterranean* (London, 1987); *The two Italies: economic relations between the Norman Kingdom of Sicily and the northern communes* (Cambridge, 1977); O.R. Constable, *Trade and traders in Muslim Spain* (Cambridge, 1996); *Housing the stranger in the Mediterranean world* (Cambridge, 2003). 29 S.R. Epstein, in M. Bullard et al., 'Where history and theory interact', p. 97. 30 Christopher Dyer, Peter Coss & Chris Wickham (eds), *Rodney Hilton's Middle Ages: an exploration of historical themes* (Oxford, 2007). 31 Chris Wickham, *Framing the early Middle Ages* (Oxford, 2005) and 'Rural economy and society', in Cristina La Rocca (ed.), *Italy in the early Middle Ages (Short Oxford History of Italy)* (Oxford, 2002), pp 118–143; Abulafia, *Mediterranean*

If economic history is indeed to return to visibility in the twenty-first century, it will depend on those students currently enrolled in the high schools, universities, and graduate schools who are now learning about the Middle Ages for the first time or who are presently beginning their careers as young scholars. It will be they who will take the field well into this century, examining the material life of the medieval dead with new questions and new insights. Hopefully, their passion for the economic history of the Middle Ages will be enriched but not constrained by the historiographical traditions of the past generation. In this respect, the work of Christine Meek can play a pivotal role in the historiography of the coming decades. It will serve as a useful and inspiring model for future historians of the pre-modern European economy.

---

encounters, economic, religious, political, 1100–1550 (Aldershot, 2000); S.A. Epstein, *The economic and social history of later medieval Europe, 1000–1500* (Cambridge, 2009); Peter Spufford, *Power and profit: the merchant in medieval Europe* (New York, 2002); Diana Wood, *Medieval economic thought* (Cambridge, 2002); Angeliki Laiou, *The economic history of Byzantium* (Washington, D.C., 2002). See also, 'Trade and navigation', 'Material life', and, 'Rural Italy', in David Abulafia (ed.), *Italy in the central Middle Ages (Short Oxford History of Italy)* (Oxford, 2004), pp 127–82.

Christine Meek and the history of Lucca

DUANE OSHEIM

A recent review of historical works on Lucca virtually conceded the period before 1500 to the '*anglosassoni*'. Although many at the university where Christine Meek taught might prefer to be designated anglophone rather than Anglo-Saxon, the observation is largely correct. Scholars from the British Isles, North America, South Africa, and Australia have contributed important studies to Lucca's economic, political and religious history.[1] Beginning in the late 1950s Robert S. Lopez's[2] call to investigate the rich notarial archives of Lucca was answered first by the late Thomas Blomquist, perhaps Christine Meek's closest friend among the North Americans. He completed a series of studies of the merchants of bankers of thirteenth-century Lucca that remain fundamental to the economic history of medieval Italy. It was shortly after he arrived in Lucca that Christine Meek and Louis Green began work that called attention to Lucca's equally important political history. They were among the first of these modern English-speaking explorers of Lucca's unusual history.

Among the first, because in some respects we can look at Christine Meek's work as a clarification of Thomas Hobbes' *Leviathon*: perhaps the first of these *anglosassoni*. Hobbes was highly critical of notions of civic humanism that had arrived in England from Italy and particularly Tuscany. He noted Lucca's engraving of *Libertas* on its city walls. It was typical, he thought. Communes praise this liberty as an individual civic right. But, he observed, a Lucchese has no more *libertas* than a resident of Constantinople. He would have rejected Lucchese complaints of lost liberty and bitter subjection to the Pisan yoke. In one sense, true liberty only belongs to the sovereign and not to individuals. The implication was clearly that Italians and Hobbes' contemporaries

---

1 In addition to Christine Meek, see F.M. Edler, 'The silk trade of Lucca during the thirteenth and fourteenth centuries' (PhD, University of Chicago, 1930); T.W. Blomquist, *Merchant families, banking and money in medieval Lucca* (Farnham, Surrey, 2005); Louis Green, *Lucca under many masters: a fourteenth-century Italian commune in crisis (1328–1342)* (Florence, 1995); *Castruccio Castracani: a study on the origins and character of a fourteenth-century Italian despotism* (Oxford, 1986); D.J. Osheim, *A Tuscan monastery and its social world, San Michele of Guamo (1156–1348)* (Rome, 1989); *idem, An Italian lordship: the bishopric of Lucca in the late Middle Ages* (Berkeley, 1977); Chris Wickham, *Community and clientele in twelfth-century Tuscany: the origins of the rural commune in the Plain of Lucca* (Oxford, 1998); *idem, Courts and conflict in twelfth-century Tuscany* (Oxford, 2003). 2 Roberto S. Lopez, 'The unexplored wealth of the notarial archives of Pisa and Lucca' in Charles-Edmond Perrin (ed.), *Mélanges d'histoire de moyen-âge dédiés à la mémoire de Louis Halphen* (Paris, 1951), pp 417–32.

39

misunderstood their situation. And, he would add, we have continued to misunderstand the true nature of liberty (Hobbes' point is about the nature of personal liberty, which he defines as the absence of external restraint. His is thus a critique of what Italians thought of as civic humanism).[3]

It is one of the great virtues of Christine Meek's studies that they make clear the extent to which Lucchese certainly, and Italians generally, grappled with the nature of liberty. Lucca's own chronicler, Giovanni Sercambi, whose work Christine both relies on and corrects, put the problem of liberty at the center of his own work. He thanked eternal Providence, he said, that 'Lucca was removed from tyrannical servitude and put in a state of liberty …'[4] Machiavelli had his own doubts about whether a republic, once it had lost the virtues fostered by independent government, could ever truly regain its liberty.[5] The Lucchese discussions of their liberty, as recounted by Meek, make clear the extent to which they understood that at root, their liberty depended on the commune. Giovanni Sercambi's open letter to the Guinigi which is included as the end of Bongi's edition of Sercambi's chronicle[6] makes clear that *libertas* and the 'salvation of Lucca' depend on the leadership of the Guinigi family. The debate over *Libertas* and its changing definition is at the heart of her narrative of Lucca. As Meek shows, the locus of Lucca's liberty shifts dramatically by 1400 from the popular government to the Guinigi family.

Christine Meek's first book, *Lucca, 1369–1400*, appeared in the wake of polemics about Florentine *Libertas*, as defined in a series of studies by Hans Baron.[7] Baron argued that a modern sense of republican freedom arose in Florence in opposition to a traditional sense of authority represented by despots and monarchs. Baron's work raised the critical question of just how communes understood themselves and the nature of their communities. Many of Baron's critics argued that his emphasis on ideology obscured the role of faction based on family or social standing. These were the issues that Meek's work addressed. In *Lucca*, Meek narrates the careful process by which the Lucchese debated the nature of their government, a commune of the old style or a government by the popolo. In Lucca the critical issue was how to maintain independence.

3 Hobbes' observation is in *Leviathan*, Bk 2, ch. 21: 'Of the liberty of subjects'. On Hobbes' comment, see Quentin Skinner, *Hobbes and republican liberty* (Cambridge, 2008), pp 157–62.   4 Giovanni Sercambi, *Le chroniche di Giovanni Sercambi, Lucchese*, ed. Salvatore Bongi, Fonti per la Storia d'Italia, 3 (Lucca, 1892), 1, 141–42.   5 Machiavelli discusses the problem in *Discourses on the first ten Books of Livy*, Bk 1, ch. 17.   6 G. Sercambi, *Le chroniche di Giovanni Sercambi*, 3, 399–407.   7 Hans Baron, *The crisis of the early Italian Renaissance* (Princeton, 1966); and *idem, In search of Florentine civic humanism: essays on the transition from medieval to modern thought* (Princeton, 1988). On Baron's work see J.M. Najemy, 'In search of Florentine civic humanism; review article', *Renaissance Quarterly* 45 (1992), 340–50; and James Hankins (ed.), *Renaissance civic humanism: reappraisals and reflections* (Cambridge, 2000).

Meek carefully outlines the political, diplomatic and even fiscal issues at play. And finally she describes the political factions that concentrate around the Forteguerra and the eventually triumphant Guinigi parties. The first decades after Liberty were, in fact, a period of relative internal peace. And she argues that when factional parties do emerge, there is little evidence that these parties were based on, or benefited from, social divisions within the city. Since the thirteenth century Lucca had been a city dominated by merchants and bankers. Guinigi power, she argues, derived from the family's wealth and was evident even before 1369. And the opposing party concentrated around the Foretguerra and the Rapondi families was really a response to the extent to which the Guinigi could dominate the mercantile oligarchy at Lucca. The two factions appear remarkably similar. There was, Christine concludes, 'no real distinction between the Guinigi and the Forteguerra parties as far as their social or economic composition is concerned …'[8]

The resulting picture of Lucchese government at the end of the fourteenth century is an interesting counter example to the Florentine norm. The difference is striking. In Meek's Lucca social differences are clearly present, but their economic and political importance fades. In his recent summation of a lifetime's work on Florentine politics and political thought, John Najemy has reiterated the ways in which the basic struggle in Florence was and remained between a class of elites and the more modest.[9] Florence grew more rapidly in the late thirteenth century than did Lucca. Its class of workers, artisans, and newly rich merchants was larger and more vocal than Lucca's. They placed continuous pressure on Florence's rulers. The names can change, but the various crises of the magnates, the new citizens, the Ciompi, and the *grandi*, can be reduced in Najemy's view, to the various attempts to control the elite, or strategies of the elite themselves to maintain influence. The clientage typical of Gene Brucker's sort of face-to-face community or Melissa Bullard's political *botteghe* does not disappear,[10] but Najemy argues that at base political struggles in Florence were and remained socio-economic.

Faction in Lucca and the eventual triumph of the Guinigi is strikingly different. While Lucchese historical sources lack the depth and variety of Florentine materials, they do allow Meek to flesh out the changed political dialogue. Giovanni Sercambi concluded that it was the devil: 'The greater the evil, the greater his pleasure because the penalties [of sin] continue to grow …'[11] Sercambi's chronicle does not describe fear of new citizens, prepotent magnates or restive underclasses. It was jealousy and strife within the ruling

8 C. Meek, *Lucca*, p. 224.   9 J.M. Najemy, *A history of Florence, 1200–1575* (Malden, MA, 2006).   10 The classic statement of Brucker's view remains his elegant introduction in G.A. Brucker, *Renaissance Florence* (Berkeley, 1983); see also M.M. Bullard, *Lorenzo il Magnifico, image and anxiety, politics and finance* (Florence, 1994), especially the essay 'Heroes and their workshops', pp 109–30.   11 G. Sercambi, *Le chroniche di Giovanni Sercambi*, 2, 406.

oligarchy caused by the Evil One: who he blames regularly. While Meek does not blame the Devil, she too describes factional struggles, effectively among peers. They do have allies among the various classes and they certainly are aware of social differences, but socio-economic differences do not seem to translate into predictable political alliances. The marked social tensions of Florence seem more muted in Lucca. More than one historian of Florence has remarked on the ways Lucca does not seem to measure up. If one simply looks at political groupings, the reasons are difficult to see; if however, you follow Meek's other major works on Lucca, there are suggestions as to why Lucca was different. And these differences are fundamental to Lucchese *Libertas*.

Lucca's fiscal records offer a good introduction into the differences between Lucca and much of the rest of Tuscany. Christine Meek discounts Giovanni Sercambi's claim that *Libertas* cost Lucca 300,000 florins, but it was nonetheless expensive. The Lucchese owed 100,000 florins to the emperor, and 40,000 florins annually to the imperial vicar. And more expenses as well. To pay for its Liberty, the government borrowed 50,000 florins from Urban V, 29,000 from the Florentines and numerous other amounts from foreign as well as internal sources. Her description of how the Lucchese handled this ongoing fiscal problem again underlines some of the differences between Lucca and its neighbors. Like most other communes, the Lucchese preferred loans to direct taxes. The government used *prestanze*, voluntary loans paid by the merchant oligarchs, to pay off its outstanding debts. Again, a number of these loans were by the Guinigi themselves. Other members of the oligarchy were also involved. What is interesting is that repayment of most of these prestanze was tied to specific revenues. The government seemed to feel that repayment of debts was the price of liberty: 'as is fitting in a free city', one councilor maintained. Meek describes how as the financial needs deepened, the commune created a pyramid or a kiting scheme such that virtually all current revenues were tied up in repayment of outstanding loans. Eventually, the government was forced to restrict repayment to interest only. And finally as the crisis deepened, the government created a public debt fund, the so-called Massa (*Dovana Salis et Massa Creditorum*). As in other funded debt schemes, outstanding debts were folded in along with new forced loans.[12]

One can understand Lucchese actions as the typical story of an elite feathering its own nest. But as Meek makes clear, it is at this point that Lucca's Massa begins to differ from the various Florentine *Monti*. That the Lucchese guaranteed repayment of loans made them a reasonable financial instrument for oligarchs, especially when interest rates could be ten or twelve per cent a rate higher than that paid in most other communes. But the Lucchese never turned them into the same sort of vehicle for speculation they became in

12 C. Meek, *Lucca*, pp 48–76, esp. 64.

Florence. In Florence there was a lively discount market,[13] in Lucca trade in *Massa* claims was restricted to the government. As Meek concludes, 'the *Massa* never became as important in the public life of Lucca as the *Monte* was in Florence'.[14] Lucchese oligarchs clearly protected their own interests but they never seemed to have exploited government finance as systematically as did the Florentines. The limits the Lucchese put on themselves, may well have to do with their view of their place in Tuscan politics.

Even before writing her big book on Lucca, Meek published a shorter work on *Lucca under Pisan rule*.[15] It investigated part of the period that Louis Green later characterized as *Lucca under many masters*.[16] After the death of Castruccio Castracane in 1328, Lucca endured over 40 years as a sort of political prize of the emperor, the Scaligieri, and finally the Pisans. Since the fourteenth century Lucchese have complained about the harsh rule they endured under the Pisans. Meek is not so sure. And her explanation fits well with the political and fiscal issues we have already discussed. The Pisans certainly maintained control of the levers of government. Yet certain critical functions like law and taxation remained in the hands of the Lucchese. And even though they complained regularly, Meek concludes that Pisan rule was, in many respects, mild. The sums, she observes, that Lucca had to pay to Pisa 'seem to have been carefully calculated with regard to the expenditure they were to cover'.[17] The reason seems to be that the Pisans recognized that Lucca was strategically important and that it would be a difficult subject to control. And Pisan exactions did not impoverish their subject city. The Lucchese were able to raise an immense sum to buy their freedom in 1369. Thus, while Lucca did lose territories (about which it would continue to complain), '[Pisan] rule', she concludes, 'does not seem to have been tyrannical'.[18]

Meek observes a similar sort of restraint when she studies Lucca's economic and fiscal policies in the years after it regained its *Libertas*. Lucca in the fourteenth century was past its brightest years. Its cloth industry, especially its silk industry, was probably at its height at the end of the thirteenth century. Its rich contado was reduced in size by Florentine and Pisan depredations, and the remaining areas were ravaged by war and plague. Its remaining strength lay in its merchants, though even they were more modest than their Florentine competitors. After 1369, the government worked to recover artisans the area had lost, to regain its influence in the silk market and to rebuild its small woolen manufacture. But it remained a struggle and its econ-

13 On the institutional structure of communal finance see W.M. Bowsky, *The finance of the commune of Siena, 1287–1355* (Oxford, 1970); on the politics of finance and public debt in Florence, Anthony Molho, *Florentine public finances in the early Renaissance, 1400–1433* (Cambridge, MA, 1971). 14 C. Meek, *Lucca*, p. 46. 15 Christine Meek, *The commune of Lucca under Pisan rule, 1342–1369* (Cambridge, MA, 1980). 16 Louis Green, *Lucca under many masters: a fourteenth-century Italian commune in crisis (1328–1342)* (Florence, 1995). 17 C. Meek, *The commune of Lucca*, p. 63. 18 Ibid., p. 127.

omy was never a match for its neighbors. It had to and it did recognize limits.[19]

And these limits may have played a role in the restrained exploitation of its contado. Meek shows that the Lucchese never taxed their countryside as aggressively as the Florentines did. They were quicker to renegotiate the liabilities of broken communes (those so reduced in population they could no longer meet their obligations). And when they taxed land, they seem to have taxed landlords as well as tenants: a policy quite at variance with the Florentine or Pistoian experience.[20] Lucca then, offers an interesting counter narrative to Tuscan history as viewed from Florence.

Since Meek's first publications on politics and society in Lucca, her work has offered a subtle critique and amendment to general studies of late medieval Italian cities. Building on the work of Anglophone historians as well as a tradition of Italian writing, Giorgio Chittolini has argued since the 1970s that one could see the formation of regional states that naturally came to replace the medieval city-republics.[21] In Tuscany that seemed to mean exploitation, colonization and integration. But the Lucchese model seems different. Both as a subject of Pisa and later in the period of its *Libertas*, as Meek describes it, Lucca followed a different path. The point seems to be that since the end of Castruccio's short-lived dominance, Lucca found itself on the edge of Italian economic and political life. Meek noted that the Lucchese recognized their limited economic power. There were attempts to repopulate the countryside, to insure the continued presence of artisans, all recognizing Lucca's weakened economic position. This theme of relative weakness is taken up by M.E. Bratchel in *Medieval Lucca*, where he notes Lucca's difficulties continued through the fourteenth and much of the fifteenth centuries. Bratchel argues that the sort of institutional and economic integration described for Florence and its subject territories is largely absent at Lucca.[22]

Elites could not exploit the very peasants and artisans they hoped to keep attached to the commune.[23] The Lucchese tried to revive their silk industry, to create a woolen industry, but in the end their successes were not dramatic.[24] The city's own resources remained modest. Lucca's primary wealth remained its international merchants and bankers. The marginal role of its

---

19 C. Meek, *Lucca*, pp 31–47. 20 Ibid., pp 77–112, esp. pp 108–9; exploitation of the countryside was an important thesis of David Herlihy, see e.g., 'Santa Maria Impruneta: a rural commune in the late Middle Ages,' in Nicolai Rubinstein (ed.), *Renaissance Florence* (London, 1968), pp 242–76. It is also for S.K. Cohn, *Creating the Florentine state: peasants and rebellion, 1348–1434* (Cambridge, 1999). 21 Giorgio Chittolini, *La formazione dello stato regionale e le istituzioni del contado, secoli XIV e XV* (Turin, 1979). 22 M.E. Bratchel, *Medieval Lucca* (Oxford, 2008) esp. pp 170–203. 23 D.J. Osheim, 'Countrymen and the law in late medieval Tuscany', *Speculum* 64 (1989), 317–38; and M.E. Bratchel, *Medieval Lucca*, pp 196, 266. 24 C. Meek, *Lucca*, pp 31–41.

economy is also reflected in the modest support it could claim from its contado. Meek's work shows that the contado was taxed, but the government was always aware that *contadini* could emigrate, that the tenuous loyalty of countrymen could easily be lost. The Lucchese could not confidently exploit their countryside as the Florentines did. It may be as well, although Meek is too careful to make such an argument, that the relative restrain of social groupings as opposed to elite factions, may be because all Lucchese recognized the dangers the commune faced. In all these respects, the Lucchese state had to operate with a strong sense of its status relative to its very aggressive neighbors. Giovanni Sercambi summed up the dangers Lucca faced with a piece of Italian doggeral that I have translated into English doggeral:

The frog and the mouse prepared to fight,
'til they were devoured by a passing kite![25]

Christine Meek would have said this much more carefully than either Sercambi or this reviewer. But this is the importance of her contribution. While aware of the general direction of the historiography on the late medieval city-state, she has made clear how Lucca's experience differed. Lucca did maintain her *Libertas* until 1799, but as her work has shown, *Libertas* as understood by Lucca was neither that of Florence nor of Hobbes.

---

25 G. Sercambi, *Le chroniche di Giovanni Sercambi*, 1, 85.

Quasi-*città irredenta*: Empoli (*c.*1100–1325)

WILLIAM R. DAY, JR

In a seminal article in reference to towns on the Po plain in Lombardy, Giorgio Chittolini put forward his conception of the quasi-*città*.[1] This was a place that had many of the salient characteristics of a city, typically including an effectively independent government and a subject territory, but it still was not quite a city or *civitas* in the way that Italian historians have traditionally understood the term because it did not have metropolitan status. It lacked, in other words, the fundamental institution of the bishop. In late-medieval Tuscany, cities such as Colle Val d'Elsa, Prato, San Gimignano, and San Miniato al Tedesco had all possessed at one time or another the essential pre-requisites of a quasi-*città*.[2] Situated near diocesan frontiers, they had managed to break free of their metropolitan churches, urban communal governments and sometimes 'feudal' overlords, and to carve out their own subject territories and to exercise independent rule. In some places, for example Prato on the diocesan frontier between Florence and Pistoia, the early harbingers of this process can be distinguished already in the later eleventh century, but most Italian historians conventionally regard the phenomenon as a later one, stretching over the long period from the later twelfth through the fifteenth century.

There are of course problems in defining the concept of city or *civitas* strictly in terms of metropolitan status, partly because the boundaries within which bishops exercised ecclesiastical jurisdiction did not always coincide with the extent of the corresponding municipal government's civil jurisdiction. The two disconnected segments of the diocese of Fiesole, for example, both lay entirely within the jurisdictional boundaries of the Florentine *comitatus* or *contado*, which obviously also included the diocese of Florence.[3] Another prob-

---

1 G. Chittolini, '"Quasi-città": borghi e terre in area lombarda nel tardo medioevo', *Società e storia* 13:47 (1990), 3–26.   2 F. Salvestrini, 'Gli statuti delle "quasi città" toscane (secoli XIII–XV)' in *Signori, regimi signorili e statuti nel tardo medioevo (Atti del VII Convegno del Comitato nazionale per gli studi delle fonti e le edizioni normative, Ferrara, 5–7 ottobre 2000)*, ed. Rolando Dondarini, G.M. Varanini & Maria Venticelli (Bologna, 2003), pp 217–42.   3 The diocese of Fiesole is divided into two parts, the 'island' of Fiesole, an area of about ten square kilometres around Fiesole itself, though for the most part north and east of the town, and completely surrounded by the diocese of Florence, and the larger and more distant part of the diocese to the south and southeast along the frontiers of the dioceses of Siena and Arezzo. The precise contours of diocesan boundaries in Tuscany, both medieval and modern, are delineated on the maps that accompany P. Guidi (ed.), *Rationes Decimarum Italiae: Tuscia*, 1: *La decima degli anni 1274–1280* (Vatican City 1932; *Studi e testi* 58); M. Giusti & P. Guidi (eds), *Rationes Decimarum Italiae: Tuscia*, 2: *la decima degli anni 1295–1304* (Vatican City, 1942; *Studi e testi* 98). From the middle of the ninth cen-

lem in conflating the concept of *civitas* with the seat of an episcopal see during the period under consideration here is simply that geography and history had conspired to diminish the importance of many metropolitan cities over the course of the preceding centuries. Chiusi in the Val di Chiana south of Arezzo is a good case in point. Although an important administrative centre on the via Cassia during the Lombard period, the *impaludamento* of the Val di Chiana had gradually turned Chiusi into a provincial backwater, fought over by its larger and more powerful neighbours and almost always under the sway of one of them but no longer of any real importance.[4]

There are also problems in seeing quasi-*città* exclusively as places of non-metropolitan status that were ultimately successful in disentangling themselves from the previously existing jurisdictional and territorial framework and establishing an independent structure of governance. This is not only because many metropolitan cities, for example Cortona and Massa Marittima and perhaps even Volterra, looked a lot more like quasi-*città* than *civitates*. It is also because this view does not take account of those places that were clearly beginning to assume some of the essential characteristics of the quasi-*città*, most notably around 1200, but whose trajectory of development towards jurisdictional and territorial independence was somehow arrested. The simple point here is that the sort of retrospective clarity afforded historians by the passage of centuries and the ultimate unravelling of events sometimes throws a brilliant light on events that was not at all apparent to the people who were wrapped up in them.

This paper focuses on these kinds of places, which I call quasi-*città irredente*, with particular reference to the *contado fiorentino*. This ancillary subject

tury, the bishops of Fiesole were effectively subordinate to those of Florence, and in the early eleventh century, a Florentine administrator was even managing the properties of the bishops of Fiesole. See R. Davidsohn, *Storia di Firenze*, trans. Giovanna Battista Klein, 8 (Florence 1977–9), I, 129, 196–7; R. Davidsohn (ed.), *Forschungen zur Geschichte von Florenz*, 4 (Berlin, 1896–1908), I, 27–8, 33. 4 The decline of Chiusi is best approached through M. Marrocchi, 'La disgregazione di un'identità storica: il territorio di Chiusi tra l'Alto medioevo e il Duecento' (Tesi di dottorato di ricerca in Storia medievale, Università degli Studi di Firenze, 2001). On the *impaludamento* of the Val di Chiana, see D. Alexander, 'The reclamation of the Val-di-Chiana (Tuscany)', *AAAG* 74:4 (1984), pp 527–50; M. Marrocchi, 'L'impadulamento della Val di Chiana in epoca medievale' in *Incolti, fiumi, paludi: utilizzazione delle risorse naturali nella Toscana medievale e moderna*, ed. Alberto Malvolti & Giuliano Pinto; Biblioteca storica toscana 42 (Florence, 2003), pp 73–93. Curiously, though, Chiusi did manage to exert full independence for 18 years around the middle of the fourteenth century and even managed to produce its own multi-denominational coinage. On the rare silver *grosso* of Chiusi, struck 1337–55, see W.R. Day, Jr & L. Travaini, 'L'Agontano di Chiusi' in *L'Agontano: una moneta d'argento per l'Italia medievale (Convegno in ricordo di Angelo Finetti, Trevi [Perugia], 11–12 ottobre 2001)*, ed. Lucia Travaini (Perugia, 2003), pp 141–52. In addition, a unique and evidently genuine billon or base silver *denaro* of Chiusi weighing 0.41g, modelled after the popular *denari* of Ancona and Ravenna, and probably also struck during Chiusi's brief period of independence has since turned up on the antiquities market in Italy. The specimen was put up for auction by the Milanese coin dealer Raffaele Negrini, auction 21 (26 May 2005), lot 659.

is a not an entirely new one. In connection with the designs of the bishops of Fiesole to transfer the seat of their diocesan see from Fiesole to Figline Valdarno in the twelfth century, Chris Wickham likened the urban aspirations of the Figlinesi to movements in the direction of independence then occurring in places like Prato and the altogether new foundation of the Alberti counts at Semifonte above the Elsa Valley near Certaldo.[5] These are not the only such places. The development of Empoli, Montevarchi, Poggibonsi, and perhaps a few other towns in the Florentine *contado* also need to be considered in the context of discussions concerning the quasi-*città*. The late Riccardo Francovich and his students have indeed put forward a powerful argument on the basis of the comparatively rich documentary and archaeological record for seeing Poggibonsi as a quasi-*città*,[6] and Paolo Pirillo, without exactly describing it as such, has effectively made a similar case for the less well-documented town of Montevarchi.[7] Towards the end of the twelfth century and through the first half of the thirteenth century at least, these places probably looked not very different from some of the ultimately successful Tuscan quasi-*città*, but they never eventually managed to pull themselves entirely free of the capital.

The quintessential quasi-*città irredenta fiorentina* was Poggibonsi, which appears to be the only town in the Florentine *contado* documented as having negotiated treaties on its own behalf in the thirteenth century,[8] but Poggibonsi is well covered in the recent literature. For this collection in honour of the distinguished career of Christine Meek, I will discuss the one place among these quasi-*città irredente fiorentine* that has received the least attention in the literature in recent years and was closest in proximity to Lucca and its *contado* on which much of Professor Meek's attention has focused, namely Empoli in the lower Arno Valley. The starting point for

5 C. Wickham, 'Ecclesiastical dispute and lay community: Figline Valdarno in the twelfth century', *MEFRM* 108:1 (1996), 7–93, here 11.   6 R. Francovich, C. Tronti, and M. Valenti, 'Il caso di Poggio Bonizio (Poggibonsi, Siena): da castello di fondazione signorile a "quasi città"' in *Le terre nuove: atti del seminario internazionale organizzato dai Comuni di Firenze e San Giovanni Valdarno (Firenze–San Giovanni Valdarno, 28–30 gennaio 1999)*, ed. David Friedman & Paolo Pirillo (Florence, 2004; *Biblioteca storica toscana* 44), pp 201–56.   7 P. Pirillo, 'Montevarchi: nascita, sviluppo e rifondazione di un centro del Valdarno' in *Lontano dalle città: il Valdarno di Sopra nei secoli XII–XIII*, ed. Giuliano Pinto and Paolo Pirillo (Rome, 2005), pp 343–77; P. Pirillo, *Creare comunità: Firenze e i centri di nuova fondazione della Toscana medievale* (Rome 2007), pp 127–59.   8 That is, if one excludes Empoli's qualified submission to Florentine authority in 1182. For this, see below. For some of the treaties negotiated by Poggibonsi in the thirteenth century, see F. Schneider (ed.), *Regestum senense: regesten der Urkunden von Siena*, vol. 1: *Bis zum Frieden von Poggibonsi, 713–30 juni 1235* (Rome 1911; *Regesta chartarum Italiae* 8), pp 265–6 doc. 595 (10–12 July 1221), p. 315 doc. 710 (21–26 November 1226); G. Cecchini (ed.), *Il Caleffo Vecchio del comune di Siena*, 5 (Siena, 1932–1991), I, 239–50 doc. 170 (10–12 July1221), pp 336–45 doc. 234 (21–26 November 1226). See also L. Fumi (ed.), *Codice diplomatico della città d'Orvieto: documenti e regesti dal secolo XI al XV* (Florence, 1884; *Documenti di storia italiana* 8), pp 203–5 (11 June 1254), 323 (1280).

what follows is around 1325, when the capital city of Florence was at or very near maximum demographic and economic expansion and Empoli is relatively well documented. The paper then looks back to the twelfth and early thirteenth centuries, but it pays particular attention to the second half of the thirteenth century when the written evidence, which is so exiguous beforehand, first begins to take on bulk.

Empoli is situated on the left bank of the Arno nearly 30 kilometres west of Florence and some 35 kilometres east of Pisa, on what was in the later thirteenth and early fourteenth centuries the main road between the two cities,[9] very near the western frontier of the Florentine diocese. Before the middle of the thirteenth century, the diocesan boundary in the lower Arno Valley still coincided more or less with the theoretical western extent of Florentine authority,[10] though territorial expansion over the course of the later thirteenth and fourteenth centuries extended the reach of the Florentine *distretto* to take in parts of neighbouring dioceses. In the parlance of the central-place theorist, at any rate, Empoli functioned as both an interstitial centre, situated at the interstice between the dominant centres of Florence and Pisa, and, because of its frontier location within the Florentine *contado*, as a 'gateway', with all that these categorizations entail.[11]

9 R. Caggese (ed.), *Statuti della Repubblica fiorentina*, 1: *Statuto del Capitano del popolo degli anni 1322–25* (Florence 1999; *Documenti di storia italiana*, ser. 2, 6), pp 158–63 (bk iv.8): *strata per quam itur Pisas que summitur a porta seu Burgo Sancti Frediani*. This was one of the ten Florentine 'master' roads described as radiating out from the city in the statutes of 1322, and it must have been one of the seven master roads attested in the deliberations of the Florentine communal consuls in September 1285. See A. Gherardi (ed.), *Le consulte della repubblica fiorentina dall'anno MCCLXXX al MCCXCVIII*, 2 vols (Florence, 1896–1898), I, 294. The radial system of master roads that converged on Florence functioned not only to facilitate regional and supra-regional communications but also to reinforce the centrality of the city within the *contado*. On this latter point, see A. Zorzi, 'L'organizzazione del territorio in area fiorentina tra XIII e XIV secolo' in Giorgio Chittolini & Dietmar Willoweit (eds), *L'organizzazione del territorio in Italia e Germania: secoli XIII–XIV (Atti della XXXV° settimana di studio del Istituto storico italo-germanico)*, (Bologna, 1994), pp 279–349 esp. 305. For more on the Florentine road network in the lower Arno Valley, see W.R. Day, Jr, 'The early development of the Florentine economy, *c.*1100–1275' (Doctoral dissertation, London School of Economics and Political Science, 2000), pp 391–5. **10** Ferdinando Ughelli found evidence to suggest that Empoli was once under the civil and ecclesiastical jurisdiction of Pisa, but later historians have found the document to be spurious. See F. Ughelli (ed.), *Italia Sacra sive de Episcopis Italiae et insularum adiacentium*, 2nd ed., 10 vols (Venice, 1717–22), coll. XX; G. Lami (ed.), *Sanctae Ecclesiae Florentinae Monumenta*, 4 (Florence, 1758), IV, 104, 108; E. Repetti, *Dizionario geografico-fisico-storico della Toscana*, 5 (Florence, 1833–45), II, 56–7; G. Lastraiolo, 'Empoli tra feudo e comune (revisione di giudizi e motivi dominanti dei primi secoli di storia empolese)', *Bullettino storico empolese* 4 (1960), 83–154 esp. 97–103; E. Antonini and P. Tinagli, 'Il territorio empolese nel XII secolo (proposte e quesiti)', *Bullettino storico empolese* 6, anno 16, 1 (1972), 17–78 esp. 21–4. **11** These categorizations of Empoli deserve more attention than space and the scope of this essay permit. Suffice it to say that the starting points for research on the genesis, function, and development of

The modern town of Empoli is stretched out along a bend in the Arno, roughly midway between the confluence of the Arno with the river Elsa to the west and with the *torrente* Pesa to the east. It is actually an amalgam of three adjacent settlements: Empoli *vecchio* in the west, Empoli *nuovo* in the east, and the *Cittadella* between them. Tradition holds that the place-name Empoli is classical in origin and derives from *Emporium Arni*,[12] but the form *Emporium Arni* occurs for the first time only during the Renaissance and therefore might have been more an invention of humanist writers.[13] The actual origins of the place-name Empoli remain obscure.

The statutes of the *capitani* of Florence of 1323–5 show that Empoli was by then the administrative centre of one of the rural *leghe*, or leagues, in the Florentine *contado*. The *lega empolese* consisted of Empoli itself, the important towns of Monterappoli and Borgo Santa Fiora (the latter now known as Bastia but called Torre Benni in the twelfth century), plus the subsidiary league of Pontorme and Sammontano.[14] Documents of various sorts, from papal bulls of

interstitial market centres are W. Christaller, *Central places in southern Germany*, C.W. Baskin trans. (Englewood Cliffs, NJ, 1966) and G.W. Skinner, 'Marketing and social structure in rural China', *Journal of Asian Studies* 24 (1964–5), 3–43, 195–228, 363–99; G.W. Skinner, 'Mobility strategies in late Imperial China: a regional system analysis' in C.A. Smith (ed.), *Regional analysis regional economic systems* (New York, 1976), pp 328–30. Christaller focused on the optimal location for retail suppliers on the bases of the range and threshold for various levels of goods and services, while Skinner set aside the problem of origins and concentrated on the evolution of interstitial centres as a result of population pressure. Their views are summarized in C.A. Smith, 'Regional economic systems: linking geographical models and socioeconomic problems' in Smith (ed.), *Regional analysis*, pp 12–15, 47–50, respectively.   12 For a claim that Empoli was the *portus ad Arnum* of antiquity, see A. Solari, *Topografia storica dell'Etruria*, 4 (Pisa, 1914–18), III, 98; app. 72 no. 41. Emanuale Repetti was more equivocal, allowing the possibility on the basis of its favourable geographic circumstances but also noting that Empoli enters the written record only in the 780s. See Repetti, *Dizionario geografico*, II, pp 55, 57, 66. The archaeological record nevertheless suggests that the site had been settled in antiquity. For the numismatic evidence from coin finds during archaeological excavations in Empoli, see A. Degasperi, 'I ritrovamenti numismatici dallo scavo ad Empoli: prime riflessioni sulla circolazione monetale empolese tra l'età romana e rinascimentale', *RIN* 105 (2004), 173–203 esp. 174–8. 13 Lastraiolo, 'Empoli', 92 n. 3. On other possible etymological roots of the term, see S. Pieri, *Toponomastica della valle dell'Arno* (Rome, 1919), p. 374.   14 Caggese (ed.), *Statuto del Capitano*, 254 bk v.80. The bronze seal matrix of the *lega*, preserved in the Museo nazionale del Bargello in Florence, has the inscription +SIGILLV LIGhE · ✠ · ✠ ✠ DE · EMPOLI ✠ (retrograde) with grained borders around a stylized image of the church of Empoli with a mound surmounted by a vine on the left and a loggia and tower on the right against a background punctuated by small stars. See D.M. Manni, *Osservazioni storiche sopra i sigilli antichi de' secoli bassi* (Florence, 1739–86), X, 87–97; Repetti, *Dizionario geografico*, II, 64, and IV, 542; A. Muzzi, B. Tomasello, & A. Tori (eds), *Sigilli nel Museo nazionale del Bargello*, 3 vols (Firenze, 1988–90), pp 24–6 no. 46. The compilers of the Bargello catalogue dated the seal to 1250 when the Florentines reorganized the administration of the *contado* around the 96 baptismal churches (*pivieri*) in the *contado*, but a somewhat later date, after the Florentines had completed their acquisition of the interests of the Guidi counts in and around Empoli in 1273, is perhaps more likely. On the

the eleventh, twelfth, and thirteenth centuries to the so-called *Libro di Montaperti* of 1260,[15] make it possible to delineate the contours of Empoli's territory, which broadly coincide with the extent of the interests of the powerful Guidi counts in Empoli as described in documents of 1254, 1255, and 1273.[16] In the later thirteenth and early fourteenth centuries, local government in Empoli was sometimes administered by a Florentine *podestà* evidently sent at the request of the Empolesi themselves, as in 1294, but it was sometimes also under a more autonomous consular regime, as it was even as late as 1326.[17]

By that time, the fortified circuit of walls that enclosed Empoli had at least four main gates.[18] The Guidi counts originally constructed Empoli's fortifica-

reorganization of the administration of the Florentine *contado* around 1250, see G. Villani, *Nuova cronica*, ed. Giuseppe Porta (Parma, 1991), I, 329 (vii.39).   **15** Papal bulls identifying the thirty churches in and around Empoli dependent on the *pieve* of Sant'Andrea are attested for Nicholas II in 1059 (11 December), Celestine III in 1192 (27 May), and Alexander IV in 1258 (3 July). For register summaries of the bulls of Nicholas and Celestine, see P. Jaffé & W. Wattenbach (eds), *Regesta Pontificum Romanorum ab condita Ecclesia ad annum post Christum natum MCXCVIII*, 2, 2nd ed. (Leipzig, 1881–8), I, 561 doc. 4417, and II, 591 doc. 16885 (10378); P.F. Kehr (ed.), *Italia Pontificia sive Repertorium Privilegiorum et Litterarum a Romanis Pontificibus ante annum MCLXXXXVIII*, 3: *Etruria* (Berlin, 1908), pp 56–7 docc. 2–3. For somewhat more complete descriptions of the bulls of Celestine III and Alexander IV with lists of the churches mentioned, see Lami (ed.), *Monumenta*, IV, 109–14. See also Repetti, *Dizionario geografico*, II, 58. The dependent churches were: (1) San Donnino between Empoli *nuovo* and Empoli *vecchio* (annexed to the chapter of Empoli in 1473); (2) San Lorenzo a Empoli *vecchio*; (3) Santa Lucia in *Cittadella* (between Empoli and Ripa); (4) Santa Maria in *Castello* (now under the name of Ripa); (5) San Donato a Empoli *vecchio* (annexed to Santa Maria a Ripa); (6) San Mamente a Empoli *vecchio* (annexed to San Michele a Empoli *vecchio* in 1442); (7) San Michele a Empoli *vecchio* (aggregated with Santa Maria a Ripa in 1787); (8) Santo Stefano a Cassiana (long destroyed); (9) San Cristofano a Strada (united with Cortenuova); (10) San Jacopo d'Avane (11) San Pietro sull'Arno (now called *a Riottoli*); (12) San Martino a Vitiana (united with Santa Cristina a Pagnanacanina in 1783); (13) Santa Cristina a Pagnanacanina; (14) San Leonardo a Cerbaiola; (15) Santi Simone e Guida a Corniola; (16) Sant'Ippolito e Cassiano a Valle oltr'Arno (annexed to Santa Maria a Petroio in 1459); (17) San Giusto a Petroio (chapel joined to the *pieve* of Empoli in 1754); (18) San Ruffino in Padule (long destroyed, near the cloister of the church of San Giovanni Battista de' Cappuccini); (19) San Jacopo a Bagnolo (annexed to San Donato in Val di Botte); (20) San Frediano in Val di Botte (near Cotone, long united to San Donato in Val di Botte); (21) San Donato in Val di Botte; (22) Santa Maria a Fibbiana; (23) San Michele a Lignano (annexed to San Donato in Val di Botte); (24) Santa Maria a Cortenuova; (25) San Martino a Pontorme; (26) San Michele nel Castello di Pontorme; (27) San Ponziano a Pratignone (chapel of the same parish as the *pieve* of Empoli); (28) Santa Maria a Pagnanamini (otherwise called *a Spicchio*); (29) San Bartolomeo a Sovigliana oltr'Arno; (30) Santa Maria a Petroio oltr'Arno. Most of these communities are unambiguously listed in the relevant section in C. Paoli (ed.), *Il Libro di Montaperti (anno MCCLX)*, *Documenti di storia italiana* 9 (Florence, 1889), pp 104–5. For a detailed assessment of Empoli's territorial makeup in the sixteenth century, see W. Simeoni & L. Guerrini, *Il territorio empolese nella seconda metà del XVI secolo*, *Documenti inediti di cultura toscana*, n.s. 1 (Florence, 1987), pp 177–330.   **16** See below, pp 54, 58–9.   **17** Gherardi (ed.), *Consulte*, II, 347; Davidsohn, *Storia*, V, 363; F. Berti, 'Vita empolese del XIII secolo nelle imbreviature di ser Lasta', *Bullettino storico empolese* 7, 21:1–2 (1977), 34 n. 73.   **18** See again Davidsohn,

tions around 1120 as a bulwark against the twin nemeses of the rival Alberti counts and the still embryonic urban commune of Florence.[19] At that time, the Alberti presented a greater threat than Florence and main object of the enterprise must have been to siphon off clients and revenue from them.[20] In the early fourteenth century, however, the most significant threat to Empoli and its immediate environs was that posed by Castruccio Castracane, lord of Lucca.[21] The walls of Empoli outlasted the Lucchese ruler, who died in 1328, but not by much, as tracts of the enclosure succumbed in 1333 to the same flooding that inundated Florence and many other places in the Arno valley.[22]

At the time of the Florentine tax survey (*catasto*) of 1427–30, despite a sharp decline in population during the decades around 1400, Empoli lay at the western edge of the most densely populated part of the Florentine *contado*.[23] In 1356, just eight years after the Black Death of 1348, Florentine tax records (*estimi*) show that Empoli itself (Empoli *vecchio*, that is, the *piviere* of Sant'Andrea) had 323 hearths and that the ten other *popoli* subordinate to Empoli in close proximity to the old town had an additional 255.[24] On the

Storia, V, 363. **19** The *incastellamento* of Empoli deserves more attention than space here permits. Suffice it to say that Count Guido IV (d. 1101/3) had wisely established close ties with both the Church Reform movement, through his support of the Vallombrosan order, and the Great Countess Matilda di Canossa, the powerful marquise of Tuscany (d. 1115), with his heir Guido V Guerra even appearing as Matilda's adopted son in a document of 1099. In 1113, Count Alberto's son Goffredo was nominated to succeed Ranieri as bishop of Florence, possibly through agency of Matilda, as Dameron argued, presumably in the interest of maintaining a balance of power in the region between the Guidi and the Alberti. Count Ugo, the last male heir of the Cadolingi counts, died in the same year. His ecclesiastical properties and rights reverted to the Church, but his large secular patrimony, which included properties in the lower Arno and Elsa Valleys near Empoli, passed into the possession of his widow Cecilia. By February 1120, Cecilia had married another of Count Alberto's sons, Tancredi Nontigiova, effectively bringing much of her inheritance, including the important *castelli* of Vernio in the Bisenzio Valley and Mangona in the western Mugello, under Alberti control. This, in brief, is the broader context against which the Guidi counts' *incastellamento* of Empoli must be considered. See R. Davidsohn, *Storia di Firenze*, trans. Giovanna Battista Klein, 8 (Florence, 1956–68); G.W. Dameron, *Episcopal power and Florentine society, 1000–1320* (Cambridge, MA, 1991). **20** Pirillo, *Creare comunità*, pp 93, 168. **21** In March 1326, Castruccio gained control of Greti, attacked Vinci and Cerreto, crossed the Arno and occupied the town of Petroio just outside Empoli, inflicting heavy damage on it but abandoning it towards the end of June because of concerns about the arrival of the duke of Athens and King Robert of Anjou. See Villani, *Nuova cronica*, II, 511–12 (x.345). Six years earlier, Castruccio had advanced through Cappiano and Montefalcone, burning the area around Fucecchio, Vinci, and Cerreto, and reaching as far as Empoli before turning back to besiege and eventually capture Santa Maria a Monte. See Villani, *Nuova cronica*, II, 308–10 (bk x.106). **22** Villani, *Nuova cronica*, III, 9 (xii.1). On 18 March 1336, the Florentine government granted the Empolesi licence to rebuild their walls. See E. Repetti, *Dizionario geografico-fisico-storico della Toscana: supplemento* (Florence, 1846), p. 88. **23** D. Herlihy & C. Klapisch-Zuber, *Les Toscans et leurs familles: une étude du catast florentin de 1427* (Paris, 1978), p. 223; D. Herlihy & C. Klapisch-Zuber, *Tuscans and their families: a study of the Florentine Catasto of 1427* (New Haven, CT, 1985), p. 47. **24** E. Fiumi, 'La demografia fiorentina nelle

basis of four persons per hearth,[25] this works out to about 1300 inhabitants in the old town and a further 1020 in Empoli *nuovo*, the *Cittadella*, and the surrounding suburbs for a total population of about 2310. If Empoli and its constituent *communities* had lost only a quarter of their inhabitants to the Plague, the total population before 1348 would have been over 3000.

The political importance of Empoli in the later thirteenth and early fourteenth centuries is suggested first by the fact that it was the site at which an important treaty between Pistoia on the one hand and Florence, Lucca, and Prato on the other was redacted and ratified in 1254.[26] Documents of the period sometimes also refer to Empoli specifically as a *civitas*.[27] The town subsequently became the principal site at which the parliaments of the Tuscan League were regularly convened. Empoli as well as the other sites sometimes used for these assemblies, namely Castelfiorentino and more rarely Fucecchio,[28] were chosen precisely because of their political importance and because of their centrality in northern Tuscany between the cities of Florence, Lucca, Pisa, Pistoia, and Siena as well as the fact that all three were accessible by river transport.[29]

The first such assembly in Empoli was apparently the famous one that Count Giordano d'Anglano, *vicario* of King Manfred in Tuscany, called together after the defeat of the Florentines at Montaperti in September 1260 to discuss plans to raze Florence to the ground. Initially, the object of the deliberations was not so much to consider whether to destroy the city but how to go about it, as most of the Ghibelline delegates in attendance presumably favoured the plan. The one voice of dissent came from a Florentine Ghibelline named Manente degli Uberti, better known as Farinata, who vowed to defend his city 'with sword in hand' against the very men alongside of whom he had fought to defeat a Florentine army only a short time earlier. His intervention ruptured the seeming unanimity of the assembly and ultimately resulted in the abandonment of the plan.[30]

pagine di Giovanni Villani', *ASI* 108 (1950), 93, 151. Fiumi also used the 1356 figure for 1350, since the incomplete *estimi* for that year do not include data for Empoli. The earliest records are for 1343, which survive in a fifteenth-century copy. They suggest that Empoli then had only 300 hearths, despite the demographic contraction that the Black Death of 1348 must have brought about. The incongruence between the data for 1343 and 1350/6 is widespread. Fiumi accounted for the discrepancy by supposing that the records for 1343, though comprehensive in terms of their territorial extent, were perhaps not so complete in terms of the number of hearths. See Fiumi, 'Demografia fiorentina', pp 94–7. **25** Fiumi, 'Demografia fiorentina', p. 106; Herlihy & Klapisch-Zuber, *Les Toscans*, pp 211, 472–9; Herlihy & Klapisch-Zuber, *Tuscans*, pp 63, 73, 90, 91, 282–90. **26** P. Santini (ed.), *Documenti dell'antica costituzione del comune di Firenze, Appendice, Documenti di storia italiana* 15 (Florence, 1952), pp 38–47 doc. 15 (1 and 3 February 1254). **27** In October 1254, for example, a contract for the conveyance of immovable property in a place called Camagio describes the vendor of the property as an inhabitant of the *civitas* of Empoli. See ASF, *Dipl.* Santo Stefano di Empoli, 18 ottobre 1254. **28** Davidsohn, *Storia*, II, 721. **29** The evidence for the river-port at Empoli is given below, n. 63. **30** Villani, *Nuova cron-*

By the beginning of the second quarter of the fourteenth century, Empoli had been more or less unambiguously under Florentine jurisdiction for some seventy years, effectively since 1254–5 when the heads of three of the four main branches of the Guidi counts sold their shares of properties and rights in the town to Florence; the remaining branch, under Count Guido Salvatico, alienated the last share of the Guidi counts' properties and rights in Empoli to the Florentine communal government in 1273.[31] The men of Empoli had already submitted to Florence in 1182, guaranteeing all Florentine citizens safe passage through the *fortia* of Empoli and promising to consign to the commune an annual payment of fifty *lire* in whatever coinage happened to be circulating in Florence when payment was due as well as an offering of wax on the day of the feast of San Giovanni, but Florentine control over Empoli remained subordinated to that of the Guidi counts in as much as the treaty of submission obliged the men of Empoli to defend Florence against all enemies except the Guidi.[32]

In practical terms, the 1182 treaty of submission was probably sufficient to satisfy the Florentines, despite the fact that it stopped short of making Count Guido VII a Florentine subject. Even the rolling back of all Florentine territorial and jurisdictional gains in the *contado* by Emperor Frederick I Barbarossa (1152–90, emp. from 1155) in 1185 and the more modest delimitation of Florentine jurisdiction by Frederick's son King Henry VI in 1187 evidently failed to undermine the treaty.[33] More important for Florence than the

---

ica, I, 384–7 (vii.81); Davidsohn, *Storia*, II, 702–3. For Dante's encounter with Farinata in the *Inferno*, see D. Alighieri, *The Divine Comedy: Inferno*, 1: *Italian text and translation*, trans. C.S. Singleton, *Bollingen Series* 80 (Princeton, 1975), pp 98–106 (canto x); for Farinata's reference to the council of Empoli, see p. 104 (x.91–3).   **31** The conveyances are discussed below.   **32** P. Santini (ed.), *Documenti dell'antica costituzione del comune di Firenze, Documenti di storia italiana* 10 (Florence, 1895), pp 17–18 doc. 12 (3 February 1282). On the significance of candle or wax offerings in communal Italy, see A. Thompson, *Cities of god: the religion of the Italian communes, 1125–1325* (University Park, IL, 2005), pp 160–6.   **33** In 1185, Frederick responded to complaints about the encroachments of the Florentine communal government on seigniorial interests in the *contado* by confirming the properties and rights of the rural nobility, monasteries, and bishops, and by divesting Florence of all jurisdiction in the *contado* up to the walls of the city itself. Because the record of Frederick's pronouncement survives only in chronicle accounts, it is impossible to know whether it actually entailed the complete suppression of Florentine jurisdiction in the *contado*. See Villani, *Nuova cronica*, I, 240–241 (bk vi.12). The Florentine chronicler Giovanni Villani dated Frederick's arrival in Florence to 31 July 1184, but he was mistaken about the year. The emperor was north of the Alps in 1184 but was in Tuscany during the summer of 1185, even issuing a charter from Florence on 1 August. See *MGH Dipl.* X, pt 4, 173–4 doc. 912. Frederick's charter of 2 August 1185 to the Camaldolese convent of San Pietro di Luco di Mugello north of Florence taking the nunnery and its possessions under imperial protection very well might have been an immediate result of the protest. See ASF *Dipl.* Monache di Luco, 1185 agosto 2; *MGH Dipl.* X, 175–6 doc. 913. Several months later, perhaps also stemming from the protests, Frederick took the aristocratic Ranieri, Ubertini, and Guidi households under imperial protection and declared them free from any jurisdiction other than that of the emperor.

subjugation of the Guidi must have been the facility of safe passage through the territory of Empoli. Such a facility very well might have even antedated the 1182 treaty, perhaps going back to about 1175 or even as far back as 1158, when relations between Florence and the Guidi, which had been fairly hostile until then, first appear to have taken on an increasingly cooperative aspect and were certainly less bellicose.³⁴ It is also notable that trade between Florence

See ASF *Dipl.* Riformagioni, Atti pubblici, 1185 dicembre 8; *MGH Dipl.* X, 191–2 doc. 924. On the itinerary of Frederick in Italy from September 1184 to June 1186, see F. Opll, *Das Itinerar Kaiser Friedrich Barbarossas (1152–1190)*, *Forschungen zur Kaiser- und Papstgeschichte des Mittelalters, Beihefte zu J.F. Böhmer, Regesta Imperii* 1 (Vienna, 1978), pp 82–90; C. Brühl, *Fodrum, gistum, servitium regis: Studien zu den wirtschaftlichen Grundlagen des Königtums im Frankenreich und in den fränkischen Nachfolgestaaten Deutschland, Frankreich und Italien vom 6. bis zur Mitte des 14. Jahrhunderts*, Kölner historische Abhandlungen 14:2 (Cologne, 1968), I, 580. For earlier chronicle accounts of Frederick's proclamation, see the pseudo-Brunetto Latini in O. Hartwig (ed.), *Quellen und Forschungen zur Ältesten Geschichte der Stadt Florenz*, 2 (Marburg Halle, 1875–1880), II, 221; A. Schiaffini (ed.), *Testi fiorentini del dugento e dei primi del trecento, con introduzione, annotazioni linguistiche e glossario* (Florence, 1926), p. 108. See also the *Gesta Florentinorum (Codex Neapolitanus)* in Hartwig (ed.), *Quellen und Forschungen*, p. 273. Finally, see P. Pieri, *Cronica di Paolino Pieri Fiorentino delle cose d'Italia dall'anno 1080 fino all'anno 1305*, Antonio Filippo Adami ed. (Rome, 1755), p. 9. In 1187, Frederick's son Henry VI partially restored Florentine jurisdiction in the *contado* in exchange for an annual payment of silk, limiting it in most directions to a radius of ten *miliaria* from the city, probably no more than about 16.5 km, but to only three *miliaria* from the city in the direction of Settimo and Campi to the west in the Arno Valley and to only one *miliarium* in the direction of Fiesole. Empoli and most other important towns in the *contado* thus lay beyond the reach of Florentine jurisdiction and Henry's charter exempted the nobility from Florentine jurisdiction even within the area of Florentine control. See ASF *Dipl.* Riformagioni, atti pubblici, 1187 giugno 24; J. Ficker (ed.), *Forschungen zur reichs- und rechtsgeschichte Italiens*, 4 (Innsbruck 1868–74), IV, 213–14 doc. 170. Henry's 'restoration' of Florentine jurisdiction limited it to an area that extended at most only to just beyond Cerbaia, San Casciano in Val di Pesa, and Strada in Chianti in south, but it fell just short of Rignano sull'Arno, and it only barely embraced Pontassieve in the east. North of Florence, urban jurisdiction extended only to just beyond Vaglia, but Fiesole and much of the Sieve Valley evidently lay beyond its bounds. In the west, it was limited to the area east of the river Greve on the left bank of the Arno and it extended only as far as Peretola and Quarto on the right bank. **34** The relative calm was briefly broken only in 1174 by a Florentine assault on Poggibonsi, where the Guidi had considerable interests, but the more cordial relations are attested in two treaties of 1158 and about 1175. The treaty of 1158 settled a conflict between Florence and Lucca on the one hand and Pisa and its allies on the other, including the Guidi counts, while the one of 1175 was evidently expressly between Florence and the Guidi. The other parties involved in the 1158 settlement, in addition to Florence and Lucca on one side and Pisa and the Guidi counts on the other, were Pistoia, Siena, and the Alberti counts, all allies of Pisa. The record of the agreement survives in an undated 'minuta' and in the summary account of the Pisan chronicler Bernardo Maragone, who very well might have used the 'minuta' as his source. For the 'minuta', see N. Caturegli (ed.), *Regesto della Chiesa di Pisa, Regesta Chartarum Italiae* 14 (Rome, 1938), p. 312 doc. 456; N. Rauty (ed.), *Documenti per la storia dei conti Guidi in Toscana: le origine e i primi secoli, 887–1164*, Deputazione di storia patria per la Toscana, Documenti di storia italiana, ser. 2:10 (Florence, 2003), p. 291 doc. 220. For Maragone's account, see *MGH SS* XIX,

and Pisa, which would have had to pass through territory under the control of Empoli, is clearly attested in the documentary record only from after 1158, first in a commercial treaty between the two cities in 1171 and then in the depositions of witnesses in a court case of 1209 concerning tolls on the Arno at the *passagium* of Ricavo over the previous 40 years.[35] The commercial and industrial development of Empoli, which is well attested in the thirteenth-century alienations of Guidi property and rights there, must have been undertaken largely to exploit the town's position on the main trade route between Florence and Pisa and the commercial opportunities that this presented. Count Guido VII was less concerned about the qualified submission of the Empolesi in 1182 than he was about keeping the lines of trade open. Already by March 1180, moreover, he had established direct ties with Florence by having his earlier marriage to Agnese of Montferrat[36] dissolved and then by marrying 'la buona Gualdrada',[37] the purportedly beautiful and well-spoken only child of a prominent Florentine citizen, Bellincione Berti de' Ravignani, himself of rural aristocratic lineage.[38] Gualdrada's dowry included important property near the Porta San Piero in Florence and the marriage very well might have even afforded Guido a grant of Florentine citizenship.[39]

244; B. Maragone, *Rerum Italicarum Scriptores: Raccolta degli storici italiana* 6, pt 2: *Gli annales pisani di Bernardo Maragone*, Michele Lupo Gentile ed. (Bologna, 1936), pp 17–18. The treaty of about 1175 is known only through the depositions of several witnesses in a court case of 1203 concerning the disposition of the convent of Rosano in the Arno Valley about 15 kilometres above Florence. For the relevant depositions, see L. Passerini, 'Un monaco del secolo XIII', *ASI* ser. 3:23 (1876), 385, 389, 391, 396–7, 399. The depositions might have been in reference to Guido's renunciation of his properties and rights in Poggibonsi in 1177. See K.F. Stumpf-Brentano (ed.), *Die Reichskanzler vornehmlich des X., XI. und XII. Jahrhunderts*, 3 (Innsbruck, 1865–81), III, 526 (22 August 1177).   35 For the 1171 commercial treaty between Florence and Pisa, see F. Dal Borgo (ed.), *Raccolta di scelti diplomi pisani* (Pisa, 1765), pp 307–8; Santini (ed.), *Documenti*, pp 5–6 doc. 4. See also the chronicle account of the treaty in Maragone, *Annales pisani*, p. 53. For the court case of 1209, see Davidsohn (ed.), *Forschungen*, III, 1 doc. 1; Caturegli (ed.), *Regesto della Chiesa di Pisa*, pp 83–5 doc. 47.   36 Agnese belonged to another of the more powerful aristocratic families in Italy at the time. She was the daughter of Marquis Guglielmo IV *il Vecchio* of Montferrat (d. 1183) and sister of Guglielmo's son and eventual successor Bonifacio I (d. 1207).   37 Quoted from Alighieri, *The divine comedy: Inferno*, p. 164 (xvi. 37).   38 Villani, *Nuova cronica*, I, 161 (v.1). Villani described Gualdrada as the daughter of Bellincione Berti de' Ravignani, perhaps using as his source an early anonymous commentator on Dante. See A. Torri (ed.), *L'ottimo commento della Commedia*, I: *Inferno* (Pisa, 1827), p. 299. On Count Guido's divorce of Agnese and marriage to Gualdrada, see also L. Eckenstein, 'The Guidi and their relations with Florence [pt 2]', *EHR* 14:55 (1899), 444–5; Davidsohn, *Storia*, I, 814–18.   39 The author of the late thirteenth-century pseudo-Brunetto Latini chronicle named one Tegrimo of the Guidi counts as a Florentine consul in 1192, also stating that the Guidi and many other rural nobles had taken up residence in the city at the same time. See Schiaffini (ed.), *Testi fiorentini*, pp 110–11. It is unclear exactly who this Tegrimo was, since Guido VII is not known to have had any male siblings and his son Tegrimo appears in the sources only from 1220, was married only in 1225, and died by 1250. See Santini (ed.), *Documenti*, p. xl. This would

The Guidi counts were exceedingly important for the history of Empoli. They had been the dominant figures there from before December 1119, when the Countess Imilia, wife of Count Guido V (d. 1124),[40] promised with her husband's consent to uphold his earlier pledge to the *pievano* of Sant'Andrea d'Empoli to grant to anyone who would come to live within the *piviere* a parcel of land on which they could build their own house. She further reiterated her husband's promise to construct a new *castello*, to defend it against any enemy, to rebuild it immediately should it ever be destroyed, and to prevent the construction of any church or monastery within the *piviere* without the approval of the curate or his successors. She also invested the *pievano* with the movable and immovable properties of fourteen other churches in the environs of Empoli for the benefit of the *pieve*.[41] The document indeed suggests that the Guidi were, in effect, re-founding Empoli as a 'new town' (*terra nuova*), and the development of Empoli should therefore be seen in this context.[42]

Before the middle of the thirteenth century, the documentary evidence for Empoli and particularly for the extent of Guidi interests in and around the town and throughout the lower Arno Valley in the *contado fiorentino* is extremely exiguous. The fact that Count Guido V owned the movable and immovable properties of at least fourteen churches in the area already before 1119 is nevertheless instructive. Otherwise, neither the three imperial charters issued to Count Guido VII by Frederick I in 1164,[43] to Guido's five sons

have made him far too young to serve as a consul in 1192, but if the chronicle reference were to Guido VII, it would indicate that he had indeed obtained citizenship. **40** Imilia's husband Guido Guerra is last attested alive in 1124 and had died by October of that year. See Rauty (ed.), *Documenti per la storia dei conti Guidi*, pp 232–4 docc. 167–8. For the numbering of the Guidi counts, I am following the scheme laid out by Rauty instead of that used by Repetti and Davidsohn. **41** The churches named in the document were described simply as (1) San Lorenzo; (2) Santa Maria; (3) San Donato; (4) San Mamme; (5) San Michele; (6) Santo Stefano; (7) Santi Cristoforo e Jacopo; (8) San Pietro; (9) San Martino a Vitiana; (10) San Bartolomeo; (11) Santa Maria a Pagnana; (12) San Rufino; (13) Santo Giusto; and (14) Santi Simone e Giuda. See Rauty (ed.), *Documenti per la storia dei conti Guidi*, pp 226–8 docc. 162–3; Davidsohn, *Storia*, I, 575. Cf. also the list given above of the 30 churches dependent on the *pieve* of Sant'Andrea of Empoli as delineated in papal bulls of the eleventh, twelfth, and thirteenth centuries (n. 15). **42** On the refoundation of Empoli, see Pirillo, *Creare comunità*, pp 56, 93, 149–50, 168. On Florentine new towns more generally, see C. Higounet, 'Les "terre nuove" florentines du XIVe siècle' in *Studi in onore di Amintore Fanfani*, 6 (Milan, 1962), III, 1–17; D. Friedman, 'Le terre nuove fiorentine', *AM* 1 (1974); D. Friedman, *Florentine new towns: urban design in the late Middle Ages* (New York, 1988); M.E. Cortese, '*Castra* e terre nuove: strategie signorili e cittadine per la fondazione di nuovi insediamenti in Toscana (metà XII–fine XIII sec.)' in David Friedman & Paolo Pirillo (eds), *Le terre nuove: atti del seminario internazionale organizzato dai Comuni di Firenze e San Giovanni Valdarno (Firenze–San Giovanni Valdarno, 28–30 gennaio 1999)*, *Biblioteca storica toscana* 44 (Florence, 2004). See also the other papers collected in David Friedman & Paolo Pirillo (eds), *Le terre nuove*. **43** *MGH Dipl.* X, pt 2, 369–71 doc. 462; Rauty (ed.), *Documenti per la storia dei conti Guidi*, pp 298–301 doc. 226.

– Guido, Tegrimo, Ruggero, Marcovaldo, and Aghinolfo – by Frederick II (1217–50, emp. from 1220) in 1220,[44] and to Counts Guido Novello and Simone by Frederick II in 1247,[45] nor the documents relating to the division of Guidi properties and rights in 1230[46] provide anything but the barest of notions about the true extent of the Guidi holdings in and around Empoli.

It is only in the lengthy instruments by which the heads of three of the four main branches of the Guidi counts conveyed their properties and rights in and around Empoli to the Florentine communal government in 1254 and 1255 for the combined sum of 27,700 *lire* that any real sense of the sheer scale of these holdings becomes apparent.[47] They show that the Guidi possessions in and around Empoli were indeed extensive. The heads of these three branches each controlled a quarter interest in the *pieve* of Sant'Andrea itself, in the market at Empoli and in 10 commercial shops bordering on the marketplace, in 18 mills in the lower Arno Valley in and around Empoli,[48] in the hospital of San Giovanni in Cerbaiola, and in the *castello* of Empoli and the *palazzo vecchio*, the latter of which being the building that later became known as the Palazzo Ghibellino where the famous parliament of 1260 took place. In addition, the heads of each branch owned other properties outright, including not only agricultural lands on which they collected rents but also churches. Elsewhere in the lower Arno Valley around Empoli, at Cerreto, Collegonzi, Colle di Pietra (now Colle Alberti), Greti, Monterappoli, Musignano, Petroio, San Donato, Sovigliana, and Vinci, among other places, the situation was very much the same as it was in Empoli, with the heads of each branch controlling a quarter

---

44 J.L.A. Huillard-Bréholles (ed.), *Historia Diplomata Friderici Secundi: sive constitutiones, privilegia, mandata, instrumenta quae supersunt istius Imperatoris et filiorum ejus*, 6 (Paris, 1852–60), II, pt 1, 58–64 esp. 61.   **45** Huillard-Bréholles (ed.), *Historia Diplomata*, VI, pt 1, 518–24 esp. 522.   **46** ASF *Dipl.* Riformagioni, Atti pubblici, 17 marzo 1229 (*st. fior.*), 19 marzo 1229 (2 pezzi, *st. fior.*), 21 marzo 1229 (*st. fior.*), 17 aprile 1230. The documents are published in P. Santini, 'Nuovi documenti dall'antica costituzione del comune di Firenze', *ASI* ser. 5, 19 (1897), pp 300–25 docc. 9–13 (17 March–17 April 1230).   **47** For the conveyances, see Santini (ed.), *Documenti, Appendice*, pp 65–72 doc. 20 (12 August 1254), pp 78–86 doc. 22 (10 September–10 November 1254), pp 130–41 doc. 43 (6 May–28 July 1255). The three branches involved in the alienations of 1254–5 were: (1) Guido and Ruggero, the sons of Count Marcovaldo; (2) Guido di Romena, the son of Count Aghinolfo; and (3) Guido Novello, the son of Count Guido VIII. The remaining branch, led by Count Guido Salvatico of Dovadola, finally released his hold on the fourth share of properties and rights in and around Empoli as well as his share of properties in and around Monetmurlo and Montevarchi in 1273 explicitly to satisfy his debts. See Ildefonso di San Luigi (ed.), *Delizie degli eruditi toscani*, 24 (Firenze, 1770–89), VIII, 129–35. Unfortunately, the published version of the 1273 document is less detailed than the instruments of 1254–5 and therefore does not permit a more complete picture of the full extent of Guidi possessions in and around Empoli before the alienations.   **48** There were 4 mills in Empoli and 2 each in Cerreto (Campo Streda), Cintoia, Colle di Pietra (Colle Alberti, Confienti or Gonfienti), Pagnana, Petroio, Ripa, and Sovigliana included in the sale. There were also others that did not belong to the Guidi, such as one at Riottoli on the left bank of the Arno near Avane. See Berti, 'Vita empolese', pp 29–30 n. 60.

share in the *pieve* and/or in other important local churches and hospitals, and in any *castelli* and/or *palazzi*, and then owning other properties individually. In each place, the heads of each branch collected an annual tax, the imperial *fodro*, of two *staia* of wheat and two *staia* of spelt typically from several dozen households as well as various other dues in services, money, and kind. In all of these places, the branch heads also shared jurisdictional and seigniorial rights, including the rights to revenues from tolls 'per terram et per aquam'.

The main beneficiaries of the dismemberment of Guidi holdings in and around Empoli were evidently the Adimari, creditors of the Guidi who acquired from Florence many of the fertile agricultural properties that had belonged to the counts around Empoli and Vinci and on the lower slopes of Monte Albano.[49] Entries in the *Libro degli estimi* (*Liber extimationum*) of 1269, an inventory of the damages that Ghibellines inflicted on Guelf property in Florence and its *contado* during Guido Novello's rule of 1260–6, perhaps reflect some of the recent acquisitions of the Adimari in and around Empoli. Buonaccorso Bellincione [degli Adimari], who is named specifically as one of the Guidi creditors in a document of 1240, is recorded to have sustained the loss of two *palazzi* with four houses in the *castello* of Empoli valued at 620 *lire* and a house in Vinci valued at 40 *lire*, plus six houses and a *palazzo* in a place called Toricchie, probably somewhere in the environs of nearby Fucecchio, valued at 400 *lire*.[50] One Ruggero Rossi [di Bellincione], presumably related to Buonaccorso Bellincione, lost a tower with four small houses in Empoli valued at 400 *lire* plus a large house 'cum curia' with three other houses in the *popolo* of Santa Maria di Empoli vecchio, two in the *popolo* of San Jacopo d'Avane, and one each in the *popolo* of Sant'Angelo di Empoli vecchio and in the *castello* of Empoli valued collectively at 400 *lire*.[51] In addition, the sons of Filigno [degli Adimari] lost a house at Petriolo Cerreti in Colle di Pietra valued at 60 *lire*.[52]

49 In his chronicle, Simone della Tosa wrote that the Florentine commune purchased Greti from the Guidi counts and then resold it in 1250 to certain men of Florence, mentioning only the Adimari among those acquiring the Guidi properties. See D.M. Manni (ed.), *Cronichette antiche di vari scrittori del buon secolo della lingua toscana* (Florence, 1733), p. 135. Because no large-scale alienations of Guidi property in the lower Arno Valley are known for 1250, Davidsohn supposed, almost certainly correctly, that the chronicler erred in his dating and that the account was in reference to the conveyances of 1254 and 1255. See Davidsohn, *Storia*, II, 599–600. The resale of Guidi properties must have begun almost immediately. Several entries of 1255 in a *libro di ricordi* that covers the area around Empoli concern disbursements to one Rollenzo da Sovigliana 'per la rikonpera del konte Guido Novello'. See A. Castellani (ed.), *Nuovi testi fiorentini del dugento con introduzione, trattazione linguistiche e glossario*, 2 (Florence, 1952), I, 174, 178, 179. None of the entries are dated precisely, but adjacent entries are dated from August 1255, soon after Guido Novello's sale was complete. 50 O. Brattö (ed.), *Liber extimationum (Il libro degli estimi) (an. MCCLXIX)*, *Göteborgs Universitets Årsskrift [Acta Universitatis Gothoburgensis]* 62, no. 2 (Göteborg, 1956), pp 75–76 no. 398. 51 Brattö (ed.), *Liber extimationum*, pp 74–5 no. 389. 52 Brattö (ed.), *Liber extimationum*, p. 76 no. 400. The brothers were perhaps

The sale of Guidi holdings in and around Empoli and throughout the lower Arno Valley in the *contado fiorentino* should be seen in the context of at least two historical developments. First, the death of Frederick II and the consequent decline in the power and influence of the imperial household, to which the Guidi, as *comites palatini caesarii*, were nominally attached, precluded any imperial intervention or support that might have enabled the Guidi to hold onto their possessions around Empoli. Second, the Guidi alienations were part of a broader liquidation of Guidi properties both within the *contado* and in neighbouring areas that had begun at least as early as 1226, precipitated not only by the deteriorating relations between the counts and the emergence of Guelf and Ghibelline wings within the household but also by their mounting debts.[53] The divestments of 1254–5 were nevertheless of a different order of magnitude. At the same time that three of the four Guidi branches were disposing of their properties around Empoli to Florence, the same three branches were off-loading their holdings in Montevarchi in the upper Arno Valley and in Montemurlo between Prato and Pistoia, again to the Florentines, for a combined price of 12,500 *lire*.[54]

For present purposes, however, it is important only to stress that the Guidi alienations in and around Empoli strongly suggest that the counts were responsible for developing the town into the thriving commercial centre it evidently was by the middle of the thirteenth century. The conveyances show that Empoli was a market town with its own commercial measure for grain, the *staio empolese*,[55] and they suggest that it was centre of artisan activity and

---

tied to one Goccia di Filigno who lost a house with an out-building valued at 40 *lire* in Montemurlo, where the Guidi also disposed of properties and rights in 1254. For Goccia's losses, see Brattö (ed.), *Liber extimationum*, p. 76 no. 401. For the Guidi alienations at Montemurlo (and Montevarchi), see below.   53 For the alienations of comital possessions at Larciano in the Pistoiese to the commune of Pistoia for 6,000 *lire* in November 1226, see Q. Sàntoli (ed.), *Il 'Liber Censuum' del Comune di Pistoia: regesti di documenti inediti sulla storia della Toscana nei secoli XI–XIV* (Pistoia, 1906–15), pp 188–93 docc. 267–73. A group of documents dated from 1240 illustrate the measures taken by the creditors of Count Guido Guerra, son of Marcovaldo, to sieze some of his assets as a means of recovering debts. These documents, which are sewn together, were redacted over a period from late July to early December 1240. They are described in a catalogue of documents relating to the Medici and sold at auction by Christie, Manson & Woods (8 King Street, St James' Square, London SW1) on 4 February 1918, lot 2. In May 1245, one of the creditors named in the 1240 documents, Buonaccorso di Bellincione, purchased properties in Empoli and Petroio from another Guido, the son of Aghinolfo, for 612 *lire*, and in September, Buonaccorso's son Forese together with a partner acquired properties in the Sieve Valley from the same Guido di Aghinolfo for 1,000 *lire*. See ASF *Dipl.* Strozziane Uguiccioni, 1245 maggio 31, 1245 settembre 16.   54 Santini (ed.), *Documenti, Appendice*, pp 48–59 doc. 16 (31 March–29 April 1254), pp 59–62 doc. 17 (6–21 April 1254), pp 62–4 doc. 18 (6–29 April 1254). In 1219, the sons of Count Guido VII Guerra had already promised to sell their holdings in and around Montevarchi and at Montemurlo to the Florentines in 1219. See Santini (ed.), *Documenti*, pp 192–5 doc. 67 (1219 April 24).   55 Santini (ed.), *Documenti, Appendice*, p. 79 n., p. 80 nn., p. 130 n., p. 132 nn., p. 133 and nn. See also

probably small-scale manufacturing. Other evidence supports this view. A *libro di ricordi* from the second half of the thirteenth century indicates the presence of a banking sector offering financial services 'a la tavola d'Enpoli', presumably a money-changing table in the marketplace.[56] The deliberations of the communal counsels of Florence in February 1282 make it clear that Empoli was by then, and probably for a long time beforehand, one of the four or five most important secondary market towns in the *contado*, particularly in so far as concerned the provisioning of the capital with staple foodstuffs.[57] The fertile lands around Empoli might have been among the most productive in the *contado* in the thirteenth century[58] and were serviced by a network of tertiary market towns, including a number of frontier market towns such as Fucecchio, Greti, and Vinci,[59] which functioned as satellites in a hierarchical

Castellani (ed.), *Nuovi testi fiorentini*, pp 173 (1255), 197 (1273). The documents show that Vinci likewise had its own measures of capacity. See Santini (ed.), *Documenti, Appendice*, p. 79 n. e, 132 n. i. **56** Castellani (ed.), *Nuovi testi fiorentini*, pp 172–3 (1255), 183 (1256). On the guild of grain merchants and money-changers in Empoli, see below, p. 62–3. **57** Gherardi (ed.), *Consulte*, I, 66, 68–9. **58** The contribution of Empoli towards the grain supply of the beseiged town of Montalcino in 1260 was greater than anywhere else in the documented parts *contado* except for the *piviere* of San Pietro in Bossole, between the upper valleys of the river Elsa and *torrente* Pesa, and even greater when Empoli's input is considered together with that of Monterappoli. See Paoli (ed.), *Il Libro di Montaperti*, pp 103–77 esp. 104–5 and 111–13. Sixteenth-century historians of Florence referred to Empoli as the city's granary. Research on Empoli in the early modern period nevertheless suggests that the moniker stemmed more from Empoli's role as a deposit for imported grain coming into Florentine territory than local production. Locally cultivated cereals might have been insufficient to satisfy even local requirements in the sixteenth and seventeenth centuries. See L. Guerrini, *Empoli dalla peste del 1523–26 a quella del 1631: vita borghese e popolare, produzioni, commerci, trasporti, istituzioni, demografia, Documenti inediti di cultura toscana*, n.s. 2:2 (Florence, 1990), II, 429–30, 436; A.M. Pult Quaglia, 'Mercato e manifatture in una comunità del contado fiorentino: Empoli tra XVI e XVII secolo' in Claudio Lamioni (ed.), *Istituzioni e società in Toscana nell'età moderna (Atti delle giornate di studio dedicate a Giuseppe Pansini, Firenze. 4–5 dicembre 1992)*, *Pubblicazioni degli archivi di stato, Saggi* 31:2 (Rome, 1994), pp 196–8. The role of Empoli as a centre for the collection of imported cereals perhaps helps to explain agricultural rents often fixed in Sicilian grain, *grano siciliano*, presumably hard grain durum wheat. **59** Fucecchio is not explicitly attested as a market town but it had its own commercial measure for grain in the thirteenth century, which implies that it was a market town. See ASF *Dipl.* Stozziane-Uguccione, 29 ottobre 1209, 6 febbraio 1215, 17 marzo 1224, 29 gennaio 1247, 6 ottobre 1248. For Greti, see Castellani (ed.), *Nuovi testi fiorentini*, I, 192. The reference to the market town of Greti most likely concerns Cerreto Guidi, which had been called Cerreto di Greti before it came under the control of the Guidi counts certainly by the eleventh century. It is also possible, but perhaps less likely, that the reference alludes to one of the smaller nearby villages such as Sant'Ansano in Greti or San Donato in Greti. The term *greti* derived from the chalky (*cretose*) nature of the soil on the southern and southwestern escarpments of Monte Albano. See Repetti, *Dizionario geografico*, I, 664, and II, 507–8. For Vinci, see Santini (ed.), *Documenti, Appendice*, pp 78–86 doc. 22 (10 settembre 1254); C.M. de La Roncière, *Florence, centre economique regional au XIVe siècle: le marché des denrées de première nécessité à Florence et dans sa campagne et les conditions de vie des salariés (1320–1380)*, 5 (Aix-en-Provence, 1976), IV, p. 347; Day, 'The early development of the

market network centred on the more important secondary market in Empoli. The Empoli market was in fact a major centre of collection and distribution in the capital's food supply chain. It received consignments of agricultural goods from these and other tertiary market towns in the area, both within the *contado* and just outside it, and prepared them for despatch to Florence. It also functioned as a nodal point for the articulation of Florentine regional and supra-regional trade.[60] Like other important secondary market towns in the larger Florentine rural market network, in other words, it facilitated the effective co-ordination of local, regional, and supra-regional trade.

Not only Empoli and but also nearby Colle di Pietra, Pagnana, and Sovigliana, all on the right bank of the Arno, were river-ports,[61] and there is evidence of small-scale shipbuilding at the latter of these.[62] The channel below Empoli was deep enough to support larger barges that displaced more water than the small flat-bottomed *scafi* that operated upriver at least as far as Figline Valdarno and perhaps even into the lower reaches of the Casentino above Arezzo.[63] Empoli was therefore well suited to receive large shipments of imported grain, whether *grano duro* from Sicily and Apulia or soft-grained wheat from Sardinia and elsewhere to help make up for the 10 to 15 per cent annual shortfall in domestic grain production in the Florentine *contado* in the early fourteenth century, and it was equally suitable for despatching smaller shipments of locally produced soft-grained wheat to the urban market in Florence, either directly to urban river-ports or by way of the river-port at Signa.[64]

The commercial importance of Empoli is attested by the fact that it had its own merchant guilds by 1280. The guild of wine merchants and innkeepers, for example, had 31 members in 1281,[65] and there was also a guild of grain

Florentine economy', II, 477 no. 96.   **60** The importance of Empoli as a nodal point in regional and supra-regional trade is illustrated in a document of 1224 by which Florence guaranteed the safe passage of all men of Pisa, Pistoia, Poggibonsi, and Siena 'in tota fortia et districtu' of Florence, whether by way of Empoli or anywhere else, suggesting that by way of Empoli was indeed the usual route. See Sàntoli (ed.), 'Liber Censuum', pp 166–7 doc. 210.   **61** For Empoli, see Davidsohn (ed.), *Forschungen*, III, 64 doc. 284 (1297: ASF *Capitoli* 35, fol. 105r). A reference to Empoli's *porto di sopra* suggests that the town had at least two ports. See Berti, 'Vita empolese', p. 29. For the ports at Colle di Pietra (Colle Alberti, Confienti) and Pagnana, see Santini (ed.), *Documenti, Appendice*, p. 133 n. (1255); for Sovigliana, see Castellani (ed.), *Nuovi testi fiorentini*, p. 205 (1281).   **62** Berti, 'Vita empolese', p. 20.   **63** In 1421, Filippo Brunelleschi was able to transport by river the large marble blocks needed for the construction of the cupola of the Duomo in Florence only as far as Empoli, from which the rest of the journey had to be negotiated by land. Davidsohn, *Storia*, I, p. 1173 n. 1.   **64** On Empoli as the terminus of river traffic ultimately bound for Florence when conditions on the river or the size of the load did not permit travel as far as Signa, the more usual port of disembarkation, see Davidsohn, *Storia*, VI, p. 526. On the port of Signa and river transport between Pisa and Florence more generally, see Davidsohn (ed.), *Forschungen*, III, 1 doc. 1; Davidsohn, *Storia*, I, 1172–4, and VI, 526. See also F.B. Pegolotti, *La pratica della mercatura*, ed. Allan Evans (Cambridge, MA, 1936), p. 212.   **65** Davidsohn (ed.), *Forschungen*, III, 234 doc. 1188; Davidsohn, *Storia*, VI, 88; Berti, 'Vita empolese', pp 35, 36.   **66** Berti, 'Vita empolese', p. 21.

merchants and money-changers ('mercatores bladii et campsores monetarum').[66] There was in addition an active private market for short-term credit in Empoli, usually on twelve-month contracts but sometimes on shorter terms, with the rate of interest usually set at 20 per cent per annum.[67] Empoli was also a pole of attraction for immigrants. The contracts contained in the earliest surviving notarial register for Empoli, redacted by the notary Lasta di Giovanni from 1280 to 1283,[68] show that the newcomers were mostly prosperous peasants from the nearby villages in the lower Arno Valley,[69] but settlers also came from farther away, including the capital city.[70] One painter (*pittore*) originally from Florence named Ghino di Gianni even supplemented whatever income he earned through painting by selling Florentine cloth in Empoli.[71]

When Florence annexed Pisa in the early fifteenth century, Empoli might have lost something of its role as a gateway at a major nodal point of entry into and exit from Florentine territory, but it remained an important depository for both locally produced and imported grain in the urban food supply of Florence through the seventeenth century.[72] Empoli's continuing commercial importance in the Quattrocento is further reflected in the fact that its merchants were active not only in the Mediterranean but even as far afield as the Indian Ocean and southern Asia by the end of the century.[73] Empoli also had its own distinct money of account in the later fifteenth century. In 1484, the *Società di Sant'Andrea* contracted the painter Francesco di Giovanni de' Botticini to make a tabernacle of the sacrament for the sum of 40 *fiorini empolesi* at the rate of four *lire* and two *soldi* for each florin.[74] This was not a reference to gold coins of Empoli but to a distinct money of account. What is so striking here is that the rate of exchange stipulated in the contract, while greater than it could possibly be for any Tuscan silver coin, was considerably less than the usual five *lire* or sometimes even as much as five *lire* and three *soldi* given as the value of the gold florin of Florence in the moneys of account of Florence, Pisa, or Siena at the time.[75] For a provincial town such as Empoli that had never struck its own coinage to have had its own distinct money of account in the later fifteenth century is not unprecedented but it was not very common.

It is important to stress that Empoli never achieved the degree of jurisdictional and territorial independence that places like Prato, San Gimignano, San Miniato al Tedesco, or even Poggibonsi managed to obtain, and apart from its

67 Berti, 'Vita empolese', pp 15–20.   68 ASF *Notarile antecosimiano* 11550/L99; Berti, 'Vita empolese', pp 3–39.   69 For example, Pagnana Canina, Petroio, Sovigliana, Spicchio (Pagnanamina).   70 Berti, 'Vita empolese', pp 23–4.   71 ASF *Notarile antecosimiano* 11550/ L99, fol. 25r (4 novembre 1254). See also Berti, 'Vita empolese', p. 23.   72 Pult Quaglia, 'Mercato e manifatture', pp 197–9.   73 For example, M. Spallanzani, *Giovanni da Empoli: un mercante fiorentino nell'Asia portoghese* (Firenze, 1999).   74 G. Milanesi (ed.), *Nuovi documenti per la storia dell'arte toscana dal XII al XVI secolo* (Rome, 1893), pp 132–3, doc. 156. For another reference to *fiorini empolesi*, this one from 1481, see O. Pogni, *L'inventario del medioevale albergo sotto il titolo della Cervia di Empoli* (Castelfiorentino, 1930), p. 8.   75 P. Spufford, *Handbook of medieval exchange* (London, 1986), 32, 48, 57, respectively.

qualified submission to Florence in 1182, it never negotiated treaties on its own behalf. By the middle of the thirteenth century, however, Empoli had been thoroughly commercialized if not industrialized, largely under the impetus of the Guidi counts. Empoli also had its own well-defined territory. There were nevertheless three things that prevented Empoli from achieving an appreciable degree of jurisdictional and territorial independence. The first, and probably the most important, was Guidi dependence on imperial support. The collapse of imperial power first in 1197 after the death of Henry VI (1190–7, emp. from 1191), son of Frederick I Barbarossa, and then again following the death of Henry's son Frederick II appreciably weakened the Guidi and obliged them to take a more conciliatory approach line in their relations with Florence.[76] They sometimes were even compelled to depend on Florentine backing, as in fact they did at the beginning of the thirteenth century when the Pistoiese seized their stronghold of Montemurlo.[77] The second was the growing rift in the Guidi household, the partitioning of their assets in the Florentine *contado* in 1230,[78] and the further break-up of their immovable wealth.[79] The third was Guidi indebtedness, probably due in part to the debts that Count Guido Guerra VII incurred in building up Empoli and Montevarchi, which led to the dismemberment of the most important agglomerations of Guidi possessions in the Florentine *contado*,[80] with the bulk of Guidi holdings in and around Empoli ultimately winding up in the hands of some of the counts' urban creditors.[81]

---

76 Clear evidence of the Guidi counts yielding to the Florentines comes in Count Guido Guerra's subscription to the Tuscan League in February 1198, less than five months after the death of Henry VI in late September 1197. For the treaty of the Tuscan League and the Guidi subscription to it, see Santini (ed.), *Documenti*, pp 33–9 doc. 21; Davidsohn, *Storia* I, 911–31. By the end of 1198, the Florentines had consolidated their position atop the 'Tuscan League' by securing the appointment of their own representative as prior of the League. See A. Potthast (ed.), *Regesta Pontificum Romanorum inde ab A. post Christum natum MCXCVIII as A. MCCCIV* (Berlin, 1874–5), I, 39 reg. 403. The register entry does not establish the Florentine citizenship of the prior, but see Davidsohn, *Storia*, I, 930.
77 Villani, *Nuova cronica*, I, 258 (vi. 31); Davidsohn, *Storia*, I, 957–8. 78 See above, n. 44.
79 ASF *Dipl.* Riformagioni, Atti pubblici, 18 febbraio 1239 (*st. fior.*), 24 marzo 1253, 24 aprile 1263.   80 The offloading of Guidi possessions in Empoli, Montemurlo, and Montevarchi nevertheless failed to resolve the problem of Guidi indebtedness. Guido di Aghinolfo and his brothers Alessandro and Aghinolfo of the Romena branch of the family based in the Casentino in the upper Arno valley even oversaw the striking of counterfeit gold florins in their *castello* of Romena around 1280. According to Davidsohn, they did so specifically in an attempt to reduce their considerable debts. In 1281, a fire in the Borgo San Lorenzo part of Florence led to the discovery of a cache of the false florins in the house of the Anchioni family where an agent of the counterfeiters was living. The agent and the moneyer working in Romena, Adamo da Brescia, were both burned to death but the traditionally Ghibelline Guidi counts who had instigated them, after having their possessions confiscated, soon reached an agreement with the Florentine authorities by which their possessions were returned and the three brothers changed their political allegiance and entered the Guelf party. See Davidsohn *Storia*, III, 251–3.   81 See above, pp 59.

The origins of the *Signoria* in Cremona: the family background of Boso of Dovara

EDWARD COLEMAN

In the ninth circle of Hell Dante and his guide Virgil come upon a frozen lake in which are imprisoned the traitors to their kindred, traitors to their country, traitors to their guests and traitors to their lords. Amongst the last-named group the poet recognizes Boso da Dovara – 'him of Duera' – who had betrayed the Ghibelline party in Lombardy and its leader Marquis Oberto Pelavicino at the crucial moment of the invasion of Italy by Charles of Anjou in 1265. According to Dante, Boso had been bribed with 'French money' – 'l'argento dei Franceschi' – and his ambition was to replace Pelavicino as lord of the city of Cremona.[1]

Boso of Dovara's betrayal, if such it was, did indeed pave the way for him to seize Cremona. In November 1266 he was elected 'perpetual podestà and lord of the community and society of all men of Cittànova' demonstrating that he had gained control over this important and traditionally Guelf area of the city.[2] But his dominion proved to be short-lived. His opponents in the Cremona obtained the support of the Papacy and by April of the following year had forced him into exile. He made two brief comebacks: firstly in 1268, when the Ghibelline or imperial cause in Italy was revived by the arrival of Conradin, grandson of the emperor Frederick II. A decade later in 1278 he returned once more, this time with the support of King Alfonso X of Castile and Visconti Milan. He succeeded in capturing the town of Crema, near Cremona, but never managed to regain Cremona itself. He spent his remaining years in Verona under the protection of that city's *signore* Alberto della Scala until his death in 1291, ironically enough just as Dante was to live under the protection of Alberto's successor Cangrande della Scala a generation later.

Apart from his cameo role in Dante's *Inferno*, Boso's career is mentioned in several contemporary north-Italian chroniclers, including Salimbene and Rolandino of Padua.[3] Amongst modern historians of medieval Italy he is most

---

1 Dante, *Inferno*, canto xxxii, l.112–17: '"Va via" rispuose "se ciò che cu vuoi conta; / ma non tacer, se tu di qua entro eschi, / di quel ch'ebbe or così la lingua pronta. / El piange qui l'argento de' Franceschi: 'Io vidi', potrai dir, 'quel da Duera / là dove i peccatori stanno freschi'"'. Dante puts the accusation against Boso in the mouth of another traitor, Bocca degli Abbati who abandoned the Guelf side at the battle of Montaperti in 1260.   2 'Perpetuus potestas et dominus communitatis et universitatis omnium hominum Citanovae', *Codex Diplomaticus Cremonae, 715–1334*, ed. L. Astegiano, 2 (Turin, 1896), I, n.880, p. 339.   3 *Salimbene de Adam, Cronica*, G. Scalia (ed.), CCCM 125, 125a (Tumholt,

often discussed in association with his erstwhile ally Oberto Pelavicino and is portrayed, like Pelavicino and the emperor Frederick II's other lieutenant in northern Italy Ezzelino da Romano, as an early or precocious *signore*, a harbinger of the signorial age to come.[4] Boso differed from his two elder contemporaries, however, in that they controlled a shifting group of cities whilst he based himself in only one, his native city of Cremona.[5] His position was therefore deeply rooted in local society and his family background provides clues that help to explain his rise to power.

If Boso the man, *signore* of Cremona and leading exponent of the Ghibelline party in Lombardy in the mid-thirteenth century, is a familiar figure to historians, Boso's family, the da Dovara, remained relatively unstudied until recently. Now, however, thanks particularly to the research of François Menant, we know a great deal more about the da Dovara.[6] It has become clear that the da Dovara was one of the most powerful and prestigious families in Cremona long before Boso emerged on the scene.

The da Dovara emerged from the ranks of the vassals of bishop of Cremona.[7] Cremonese sources show us that bishops had begun to gather an armed following around themselves for security and protection already before the year 1000 although the social profile of this group only begins to become clearly defined in the first half of the eleventh century. The bishops were

1998–9), pp 717, 718, 723.; Rolandini Patavanini, *Cronica*, A. Bonardi (ed.), *RIS*, VIII, 1, pp 152, 161, 166; *Chronicon Marchiae Tarvisinae et Lombardiae*, ed. L.A. Botteghi, *RIS*, VIII, 3, pp 35, 47. For further chronicle references see E. Voltmer & F. Menant, 'Dovara (Buoso da)' *DBI*, 41 (Rome, 1992), p. 571.   4 J. Larner, *Italy in the age of Dante and Petrarch* (London, 1980), pp 133–7; T. Dean, 'The rise of the *signori*' in D. Abulafia (ed.), *The new Cambridge medieval history*, V, c.*1198–c.1300* (Cambridge, 1999), pp 459–64; P. Jones, 'Communes and despots: the city-states in late medieval Italy' in *Transactions of the Royal Historical Society*, 5th series, 15 (1965), 71–96, ibid., *The Italian city state, 500–1300* (Oxford, 1997), pp 341, 520, 619, 621–3, 631.   5 Cremona in the context of the political history of Lombardy during the reigns of Frederick II and his sons is amply covered in F. Menant, 'Cremona al tempo di Federico II' in *Cremona città imperiale*, Nell'VIII centenario della nascita di Federico II, Atti di Conv.int., Cremona, 27–8 ott., 1995, Annali della Biblioteca Statale e Libreria Civica di Cremona, Cremona ,1999; and *idem.*, 'Il lungo Duecento 1183–1311' in G. Andenna (ed.), *Storia di Cremona, 2, Dall'alto Medieoveo all'età comunale* (Brescia, 2004), pp 282–364.   6 E. Voltmer & F. Menant, 'Dovara (Buoso da)', *DBI* 41 (Rome, 1992) pp 569–71; F. Menant, 'Dovara (Egidio da)' *DBI*, 41 (Rome, 1992), pp 569–71; 'Dovara (Girardo da)' *DBI*, 41 (Rome, 1992), pp 571–2; 'Dovara (Isaaco da)', *DBI*, 41 (Rome, 1992), pp 572–3; 'Dovara (Oberto da)', *DBI*, 41 (Rome, 1992), pp 576–9; *idem.*, *Campagnes lombardes du moyen âge. L'économie et la société rurales dans la region de Bergame, Crémone et de Brescia du Xe au XIIIe siècle*, BEFAR, 281 (Rome, 1993); *idem.*, 'Cremona in età precomunale: il secolo IX' in *Storia di Cremona, 2, Dall'alto Medieoveo all'età comunale*, pp 166–70 et passim.   7 The first recorded da Dovara is a certain 'Samson son of Ribaldo', who appears in a document dated 987 (*Codex Diplomaticus Langobardiae*, G. Porro-Lambertenghi ed. (Turin, 1873), n. 840). The village of Dovera, from which the family derived their name, is situated on the border between the territories of Milan and Cremona, in an area that was contested between the two cities (F. Menant, 'Cremona in età precomunale: il secolo IX', 168).

effectively rulers of the city at this time but they felt the need to build up a private military force because their authority was increasingly being challenged by groups of citizens, economically empowered by involvement in commerce on the river Po (Cremona being an important port and toll point), but politically excluded from the episcopal regime. The bishop's supporters, including the da Dovara, were rewarded for their services in land, rights and privileges. In 1045/6 a certain Ribaldo da Dovara and his nephew of the same name appear in the following of the bishop of Cremona as witnesses to two acts, and from this time forwards members of the da Dovara family are regularly recorded in Cremonese documents that testify to their elevated social states and prominent political role.[8]

In terms of social rank the da Dovara belonged to the group generally known to historians as *capitanei*. Members of this class possessed very considerable lands, often spread over a wide area, and typically including rural *castelli* and rural *pievi* (baptismal churches). They had their own retinues of armed followers, or vassals (*valvassores*). They exercised a *signoria di banno* on their estates that left them free to dispense private justice and immune from external judicial interference. Although they usually did not belong to ancient noble lineages, they were the social equals of such families. In fact in the eleventh century there was a strong trend towards inter-marriage between old comital and vice-comital houses and new capitaneal families.[9] In the case of the da Dovara they made advantageous marriage alliances with the counts of Sospiro (1080) who were descended from a branch of the Carolingians (the Bernardenghi), and also with the counts Bergamo (the Gisalbertini) (1114).[10] The *capitanei* were, in short, members of a powerful and wealthy ruling elite who originated in the countryside but who also came to play a major political role in cities. Although they were not numerous – François Menant estimates that there were probably not more than twenty such families in the diocese of Cremona: they wielded power and influence that was out of proportion to their numbers.[11]

The social position of the da Dovara was underwritten by vast landed wealth. They had some estates in Dovera, the hamlet located in the north-

---

8 *Le carte cremonesi dei secoli VIII–XII*, ed. E. Falconi, 4 (Cremona, 1979–88), II, n.186. *Acta Cremonae (saec.x–xiii) quae in Academia Scientarum URSS conservantur*, 2 (Moscow, Leningrad, 1937), I, n. 10; F. Menant, *Campagnes lombardes du moyen âge*, p. 610, n. 197.
9 H. Keller, *Signori e vassalli nell'Italia delle città (secoli 9–12)* (Turin, 1995), pp 169–92, 244–51; F. Menant, 'Aspetti delle relazioni feudo-vassalitiche nelle città lombarde dell'XI secolo' in R. Bordone & J. Jarnut (eds), *L'evoluzione delle città italiane nell'XI secolo*, Atti della settimana di studio, Trento, 8–12 sett. 1986, Annali dell'Istituto Storico Italo-Germanico, Quaderno 25 (Bologna, 1988), pp 295–311, reprint in *idem, Lombardia feudale. Studi sull'aristocrazia padana nei secoli X–XIII* (Milan, 1994); J.C. Maire-Vigueur, *Cavalieri e cittadini. Guerra, conflitti e società nell'Italia comunale* (Bologna, 2004), pp 287–97. 10 F. Menant, 'Cremona in età precomunale: il secolo IX', p. 168; *idem*, 'I Gisalbertini conti della contea di Bergamo e conti palatini' in *Lombardia feudale*, pp 101–27. 11 F. Menant, 'Cremona in età precomunale: il secolo IX', p. 166.

west of the territory of Cremona from which the family took its name. But the major concentration of their property was in the *bassa pianura*, the lower reaches of the river Oglio towards the confluence of that river and the river Po: an area of extensive land reclamation through drainage.[12] Most of the family's estates here seem to have come to them originally by way of concession from the bishop of Cremona. The da Dovara, in turn, re-distributed portions of their estates as fiefs amongst their own vassals such as the da Burgo and the Dotoni.[13] Much of this ecclesiastical land also included tithe rights, an extremely lucrative source of income that was likely to increase in value in areas such as this where newly cultivated areas were becoming populated. The vast extent of their tithe farm is apparent in an extremely informative document of 1221 which in addition to listing tithes also describes services *(albergaria)* and renders in kind that were due to the da Dovara, such as the transport of wood from the river Po to their house, though whether for construction or for fuel is unclear. [14] In addition to their enormous landholding and ecclesiastical tithe rights, the da Dovara also seem to have exercised commercial toll rights on the river Po, the great trade and communications artery of the northern Italy. They controlled a stretch of the river between Cremona and the river Oglio, one the Po's tributaries.[15] Records of commercial toll on the Po go back to the eighth century and by the ninth century it had come under control of the bishop of Cremona. Thereafter toll was the subject of frequent and sometimes violent disputes between the episcopal church and the *cives* of Cremona. It is uncertain when the da Dovara acquired the right to levy toll on the river but it may be assumed that, like much else, they received it from the bishop. It would certainly have been very profitable. In Cremona itself the family were well established around the

12 According to François Menant 'Dovara (Oberto da)', p. 576, their estates were in four large concentrations in the localities of Isola Dovarese and Monticelli Ripa d'Oglio as far as Grontardo; in the area of Viadana, Pomponesco and Dosolo; in the Oltrepò cremonese around Monticelli d'Ognina and finally at Bussetto.   13 A document of 1187 reveals lands in the Oltrepò cremonese had been held in held in fief from the da Dovara by the de Burgo for two generations (*Codex Diplomaticus Cremonae, 715–1334*, ed. L. Astegiano, 2 (Turin, 1896), I, n. 444, p. 164). Around the same period in an undated document, members of the da Dovara invested members of the Dotoni family in tithe in various localities along the lower course of the river Oglio (*Codex Diplomaticus Cremonae, 715–1334*, I, n. 109, p. 215), p. 215. In 1201 a *pars curie* of the Dovara is recorded for the first time but it must certainly have been in existence at a much earlier date: *Codex Diplomaticus Cremonae, 715–1334*, I, n. 1, p. 202; F. Menant, 'Cremona in età precomunale: il secolo IX', pp 167–8, nn. 209, 210, 212.   14 *Codex Diplomaticus Cremonae, 715–1334*, I, n. 335, n. 242: *et etiam debent ducere ligna a Pado usque ad domus eorum*.   15 On commerce on the Po and controversies over toll payments see: P. Racine, 'Poteri medievali e percorsi fluviali nell'Italia padana', *Quaderni Medievali* 61 (1986), 9–32; G. Fasoli, 'Navigazione fluviale. Porti e navi sul Po' in *La navigazione mediterranea nell'Alto Medioevo*, Settimana di Studio del Centro Italiano di studi sull'Alto Medioevo, XXV (1978), pp 565–601; A.A. Settia, 'L'età carolingia e ottoniana' in Andenna, *Storia di Cremona*, pp 38–53, 65–73, 88–95; F. Menant, 'Cremona in età precomunale: il secolo IX', pp 108–11.

southern gate, the Porta Ariberti, near the city's cathedral, where they owned various properties and at least one fortified tower, which would have served them both as a secure base and as a symbol of their elevated social status.

Office-holding was a key to success for most aspiring families in this period. In eleventh-century Lombardy the offices and titles of the imperial administration – counts, viscounts and the like – ceased to have any real meaning as the imperial administration system atrophied. Some families appropriated the titles as hereditary badges of status, but they were little more than that. The only offices that were worth holding at this time were in the Church. The most important of these was obviously the bishop, a position that fell into the hands of the da Dovara at a later stage. But already by the mid-eleventh century it would seem that the family had appropriated another role which was attractive in terms of power and prestige, namely the office of archdeacon, effectively the bishop's second-in-command. In 1066 Eriberto, son of Osberto, was invested by Bishop Odelrico as archdeacon of Cremona in succession to his father. The record of the investiture makes it clear that a large benefice was attached to this office and, moreover, that it was hereditary.[16]

Despite the family's close associations with the bishop the da Dovara appear to have been relatively unaffected by the upheavals of the *Pataria* and the Investitures Contest which led to the see of Cremona lying vacant for nearly forty years (1078–1117).[17] With the establishment of the city commune, which in Cremona probably came into existence shortly before 1100, they re-emerged to hold positions of responsibility and influence in the new regime. One of the first recorded consuls of the Commune, a certain Anselmo (1130), was probably a da Dovara; several other family members – namely, Egidio, Girardo, Osberto and Alberto – also held the office of consul during the twelfth century. In 1175 another Anselmo da Dovara held the prestigious position of rector of the Lombard League and head of its army (1175), whilst Isaaco da Dovara (1187–1221) was twice consul of Cremona (1196, 1209) and six times elected *podestà* of other cities. Both Anselmo and Isaaco were clearly very high-profile figures on the political scene not only of Cremona but of Lombardy in the late twelfth century.[18] Although such prominence brought

---

16 A. Hortzchansky & M. Perlbach (eds), *Lombardische Urkunden des 11. Jahr hundert aus des Sammlung Morbio auf der Königlichen Üniversitätsbibliothek zu Halle* (Halle, 1890), n. 23, p. 49 (dated 1065). 17 These events are conveniently summarized in F. Menant, 'Da Liutprando (962) a Sicardo (1185); "La Chiesa in mano ai laici" e la restaurazione dell'autorità episcopale' in A. Caprioli, A. Rimoldi & L. Vaccaro (eds), *Diocesi di Cremona*, Storia Religiosa della Lombardia 6 (Brescia, 1998), pp 47–9. 18 F. Menant, 'Cremona in età precomunale: il secolo IX', p. 168, n. 224 lists the following office-holders in the commune: Egidio, consul 1157, 1162, 1164, 1169, podestà 1159; Osberto, consul 1163, 1170, 1174; Girardo, consul 1180, podestà 1180, member of the Credenza, 1176; Isaaco, consul 1196, 1209; Alberto, consul 1207. For Isaac's office-holding in other cities, including Bologna, Ferrara, Parma, Pavia and Reggio, see F. Menant, 'Podestats et captaines du people d'orgine crémoniase' in *I Podestà dell'Italia communale, I reclutament e circolazione*

its rewards, it also carried risks: Girardo da Dovara, elected podestà of Cremona by the nobles in 1184, was assassinated later in the same year.[19] Politically motivated murder was by no means rare in this period when in-fighting between rival families, Guelfs and Ghibellines and nobility and Popolo was the norm. Cremona was no different from anywhere else in this respect: trouble between *milites* and *popolani* is apparent in 1210 when Bishop Sicardo was called to upon to deliver a celebrated judgement – the so-called *lodo di Sicardo* – that dealt with matters such as the distribution of offices and revenues, the curtailment of violence and the treatment of prisoners and exiles.[20] Factionalism within the city, together with growing class tensions, ultimately provided the background to the rise of Boso himself.

The most outstanding member of the da Dovara family in the twelfth century was in fact not a consul or a podestà such as Anselmo or Isaaco, sig-nificant though these men were; it was a bishop of Cremona who held office between 1117 and 1162: Oberto da Dovara.[21] In an episcopate spanning more than half a century Oberto worked tirelessly to further the interests of his see and also his family. The evidence for strong land-holding connection between the episcopal church and the da Dovara family from the mid-eleventh cen-tury onwards has already been noted. These links are very apparent in a doc-ument of 1126 in which Bishop Oberto invested his brother Alberto in 'everything he holds from the bishopric as a fief'[22] Unfortunately the content of the fief is not described in detail in this text, but it is likely that it would have been similar to the package of lands and rights that can be shown to be in the family's possession in the thirteenth century records already mentioned. On occasion Bishop Oberto styled himself *episcopus et comes* (1138, 1151) in documents, the first incumbent of the see of Cremona to use such a title. It is uncertain whether the title of 'count' had been conferred on him, or even if it contained any real judicial or political content. If Oberto was self-styled it implies that he held an elevated view of his position in society perhaps as a consequence of the fact that he moved in the highest political circles; he attended the courts of the emperors Lothar III (1131, 1136)[23] and Frederick

degli ufficiali forestieri (fine sec.XII–metà sec. XIV), ed. J. Maire-Vigueur, I (Rome, 2000), 75–105. A total of nine members of the family held the office of podestà 22 times in other cities, mainly during the period when Boso was signore of Cremona, F. Menant, 'Cremona in età precomunale: il secolo IX', p. 169. For the positions held by the family in Cremona up until 1265 see also *Codex Diplomaticus Cremonae*, II, 176–92. **19** *Codex Diplomaticus Cremonae*, II 179–80, 295. **20** *Codex Diplomaticus Cremonae*, I, n. 111, 215–16; F. Menant, 'Cremona in età precomunale: il secolo IX', pp 298–300; also discussed in E. Coleman, 'Sicard of Cremona as legate of Innocent III in Lombardy' in A. Sommerlechner (ed.), *Innocenzo III. Urbs et Orbs*, Atti del Congresso Internazionale, Roma, 9–15 sett. 1998 (Rome, 2003), pp 951–3. **21** F. Menant, 'Dovara (Oberto da)', pp 576–9. **22** *Codex Diplomaticus Cremonae*, I, n. 67, p. 105: *de omnibus rebus quae tenebat per feudum ab episco-pato*. **23** *Le carte cremonesi dei secoli VIII–XII*, II, n. 317, 183; n. 352, 248. F. Menant, 'Cremona in età precomunale: il secolo IX', p. 209.

I (1159, 1161),[24] and received two popes – Innocent II (1132) and Eugenius III (1148)[25] – in Cremona. Other documents show him to have been a proud and uncompromising character, notably in a long-running dispute he had with his own cathedral canons over offerings and lodgings that required two papal judgements before it was finally settled in 1139.[26] Oberto also quarrelled with several other churches and monasteries over lands and rights; on the occasion of Pope Eugenius III's stay in Cremona in 1148, for example, he obtained a papal decree subjecting the clergy of the nearby town of Crema to his episcopal jurisdiction.[27] In this case Oberto was clearly aligning himself closely with the expansionist policy of the commune of the Cremona, which had the Crema firmly in its sights. He was more than willing to use the temporal as well as the spiritual sword. He was captured whilst defending the episcopal *castrum* of Genivolta, against the Milanese in 1136, but effected a dramatic escape. Twenty years later, by which time he must have been aged around seventy, he was still up for a fight, participating in the sieges of Crema (1160) – an operation noted for its brutality – and Milan (1161).[28] Oberto was, in short, every inch the warrior-bishop of a type later characterized by Salimbene as being 'the ... sort of man [who] with clerks was a clerk, with knights was a knight, and with barons was a baron'.[29] His long and energetic period at the helm of the Cremonese church which coincided, it should be noted, with the frequent terms of office of other da Dovara family members in the Commune – his brother Anselmo and another relative Gilio were city consuls in 1160–2 during the decisive war with Crema, for example[30] – symbolized a convergence of civic and familial interest. A full century before Boso da Dovara it would not be an exaggeration to say that the city was already experiencing the first signs of domination by a single family.

Vassalage, fiefs and ties to the episcopal church all play a key role the rise of the da Dovara family between the eleventh to thirteenth centuries. Boso da Dovara's eleventh- and twelfth-century ancestors held all the important ecclesiastical and communal offices in Cremona at various times, including the key position of bishop, archdeacon, consul and podestà. They amassed great landed wealth in the *contado* of Cremona and built fortified residences in the

24 G. Andenna, 'Le istituzioni ecclesiastiche', in G. Andenna & G. Chittolini (eds), *Storia di Cremona. Il Trecento. Chiesa e cultura (VIII-XIV secolo)* (Brestia, 2007), pp 66–7. 22. 25 *Le carte cremonesi dei secoli VIII–XII*, II, n. 339, 222. 26 *Le carte cremonesi dei secoli VIII–XII*, II, n. 288, 133 (1124); n.321 (1139). The two popes concerned were Calixtus II and Innocent II. Bishop Oberto may be judged to have won round one of this dispute over rights and privileges but he had to make significant concessions in round two. 27 *Le carte cremonesi dei secoli VIII–XII* , II, n. 339 (1148). 28 During the siege of Crema Frederick issued a grant in favour of Oberto ceding him lands confiscated from the rebellious Cremaschi: *Le carte cremonesi II*, n. 388: *in obsidione castri Crème*. 29 Salimbene, *Cronica*, 62, quoted in R. Brentano, *Two churches: England and Italy in the thirteenth century* (Berkeley, 1968), p. 204, describing Bishop Obizzo of Parma. 30 *Codex Diplomaticus Cremonae*, II, 177.

city. They gathered an impressive curia of vassals around themselves and constructed a network of clients and political allies. This combination of landed wealth, serial office-holding and influential social connections made the da Dovara a formidable force in the political life of Cremona in the twelfth century. All of this is relevant to Boso's rise to power. There can be little doubt that he aspired to the ultimate prize – lordship of the city – in part because he was an ambitious and able man who saw an opportunity in the 1260s. But he was also almost predestined to act in this way because his family background propelled him to prominence. Although no member of the da Dovara clan had exercised absolute power in the city before Boso, their wealth, political experience and social connections lent them a formidable aura of prestige and authority. An understanding the historical context of Boso da Dovara's *signoria* in Cremona thus sheds considerable light on the success of Dante's deep-frozen traitor.

Setting the prisoners free: Innocent III's papal leadership in action

BRENDA BOLTON

Christine Meek will certainly be celebrated more than once in this volume for her splendid work, not only on late medieval Lucca but also on various aspects of the lives of medieval women which she has made so much her own. Imagine then my pleasure at discovering from her research in the Archivio Archivescovile that one aspect of a complex Lucchese marriage case not only provides an appropriate starting point for this contribution in her honour but also allows the further development of a shared interest that conveniently serves to span the 200 years between us.[1]

On 17 November 1424, the Florentine Ciardo di Piero Iacobi arrived in Lucca intending to venerate the Volto Santo. Instead, he found himself giving evidence before Nuto, vicar general of the bishop of Lucca in the process of separation or divorce by Bartolomea di Matteo against her husband, Simone di Iacopo Davini.[2] Ciardo attested that some two years earlier, he had been on the Barbary Coast in the company of other envoys from Florence whose operations were centred on Tunis.[3] Whilst he was there, Simone had come to the place called the 'Fundaco' or headquarters of the Florentines on several occasions in the very real hope that the envoys and merchants there would be influential enough to help him obtain his freedom. Simone had been captured, perhaps by pirates in the Magreb, and then sold on to a Saracen. At this time he was then living like a slave. His feet were in irons and he had been unable to obtain redemption either by grace or through ransom.[4] Since, however, he failed to convince the envoys, he had reluctantly to leave them, having no recourse other than to subject himself to the power of his Saracen lord.

Following this encounter, which probably took place in 1422, Ciardo was to remain in Tunis for a considerable length of time arranging his own business affairs.[5] Some time later, it seems that Simone returned to the same

---

1 Christine Meek, '"Simone ha aderito alla fede di Maometto": la "fornicazione spirituale" come causa di separazione (Lucca, 1424)', in Silvana Seidel Menchi & Diego Quaglioni (eds), *Coniugi nemici: la separazione in Italia dal XII al XVIII secolo* (Bologna, 2000), pp 121–39. 2 Ibid., pp 125–9. 3 Ibid., p. 137: *Quod ipse fuit deputatus ad eundem in Barbariam cum ambaxiatoribus dominorum Florentinorum et transfretavit cum eis deferens certas suas merces et applicuit Tunisis …* 4 Ibid., pp 137–8: *Et quod in principio dicti temporis dum erant ibi dicti ambaxiatores superscripti Simon qui dicitur maritus dicte Bartolomee pluries venit ad dictum fundacum et ad dictos ambaxiatores ad procurandum eorum favoribus liberacionem, quia tunc portabat compedites ferreos et non valens obtinere per gratiam vel redentionem abibat et revertebatur sicut ipse dicebat sub potestate domini sui saraini.* 5 Ibid.: *… et ibidem stetit*

73

headquarters where Ciardo, the Florentine envoys and some other Italian 'cristiani' were still work. Thus they all became witnesses to the fact that he was now freed from his fetters, questioning him as to how this could have come about and demanding to know the means by which he had been able to obtain redemption. Simone replied that it was his renunciation of the Christian faith which had brought about the change in his circumstances and so he was now acting like a good Moslem observing the faith and the law of Mahomet.[6] As a result of his apostasy, he had not only been granted his liberty but was also forever exempt from having to repay the 'tallia' of 86 golden 'dobli', the amount for which he had been sold.[7] Furthermore, it seems that Simone had contracted a marriage (his second) with the daughter of a certain John of Novara, also an Italian apostate, and he announced that it was his firm intention to live and die in this new faith.[8]

The case of 1424, brought before the ecclesiastical court in Lucca at the instigation of Bartolomea, exemplifies an intractable and on-going 'prisoner problem'. Simone had clearly lacked any high status support following his capture and the system of redemption or exchange between Christian and Moslem prisoners appears to have failed him completely. Certain events of two hundred years before will show that this was not always so. In particular, the career of Innocent III (1198–1216) becomes the focus of this essay as one of the under-appreciated themes of his pontificate was a desire to assist Christian prisoners in Muslim lands.

Imprisonment and captivity, two features of human existence with the potential to present consistently worrying elements, have long required but not necessarily always commanded, strong leadership in order to ensure the protection of the weak and the salvation of souls.[9] By the turn of the twelfth

---

de anno *MCCCCXXII et MCCCCXXIIII quia remansit ibi ad expediendum eius merces post recessum dictorum ambaxiatorum et reducebat se ad locum qui dicuntur fundacum Florentinorum.* **6** Ibid.: *...dixit quod ipse annegaverat fidem cristianam et erat effectus bonus saracenus et fidem et legem Macometti colebat et servabat et inde fuerat liberatus et quod quia ipse fuerat venditus pro ottuaginta sex doblis auri per dictam annegationem erat liber a dicta tallia et contraxerat matrimonium cum quadam filia Iohannis de Novara cristiani similiter annegati.* See also Raoudha Guemara, 'La libération et le rachat des captifs. Une lecture musulmane', in Giulio Cipollone (ed.), *La liberazione dei 'captivi' tra Cristianità e Islam. Oltre la Crociata e il Ǧihād: Tolleranza e Servizio Umanitario,* [Collectanea Archivi Vaticani 46] (Vatican City, 2000), pp 333–44. **7** For contemporary redemption payments elsewhere in the Mediterranean, Nicholas Coureas, 'Christian or Muslim captives on Lusignan Cyprus: redemption or retention?', ibid., pp 525–31; Francisco Javier Marzal Palicios, 'Solidaridad islámica, negotio cristiano: la liberatión de esclavos musulmanes por mudéjares en la Valencia de inicios del Cuatrocientos', ibid., pp 777–87. **8** C. Meek, '"Simone ha aderito alla fede di Maometto"', 138: *Et quod admodum intendebat in illa fide vivere et mori.* **9** E.M. Peters, 'Prison before the prison: the ancient and medieval worlds', in Norval Morris & David J. Rothman (eds), *The Oxford history of the prison: the practice of punishment in western society* (Oxford, 1995), pp 3–47, at 23–30; Jean Dunbabin, *Captivity and imprisonment in medieval Europe, 1000–1300* (London, 2002); Guy Geltner, *The medieval prison: a*

century, it was abundantly clear that for the inhabitants of the Latin Kingdom of Jerusalem and other Christian principalities in the East as well as those in Iberia, the duty of care with regard to prisoner and captive alike was as much an obligation as an urgent necessity.[10] The imprisonment and ill-treatment of captives by non-Christians and the associated danger of apostasy threatened the Church as a living reproach to the faith. Incipient warfare between rulers and princes and spasmodic fighting between local lords both needed to be quelled and, wherever possible, a perpetual peace or lasting truce established in order to free them and their men to go to the aid of fellow Christians in the East. An inspired charismatic leadership combined with the ability to envisage and create this desired future condition being demanded of the popes of the day was met in the person of Innocent III,[11] a worthy protagonist, who stepped up to meet the extraordinary challenge!

Around 1200, a renewed emphasis on the *vita apostolica* had already begun to change attitudes, reflecting 'a complexity of social causes and real world problems for which deeply committed Christians (with Pope Innocent in the lead) sought solutions in the wellsprings of their faith and especially the Gospels'.[12] As those in captivity ran the risk of being held indefinitely, any release from prison was deeply significant since this would be seen as God's blessing and an answer to prayer – the ultimate goal of the *vita apostolica* for all in such need.[13] The proponents of this apostolic life style did not have far to look to find appropriate injunctions on the treatment of prisoners. The important link between the Old and New Testaments was revealed in Christ's visit to the Synagogue at Nazareth[14] where his remarks indicated the fulfil-ment of Isaiah 61:1 'to proclaim liberty to the captives with the opening of the prison to them that are bound' and follow Christ's exhortation in Luke, 4:19, 'to preach deliverance to prisoners and to set at liberty them that are bruised'. Innocent, the theologian would also have pondered two other rele-vant texts from the Psalms, 'to bring out of prison those which are bound in chains',[15] and to take heed of 'the sighing of the prisoner'.[16]

social history (Princeton, NJ, 2008), pp xvi–xvii.   10 G. Cipollone (ed.), *La liberazione dei 'captivi'*, pp 79–83, 329–51.   11 Giulio Cipollone, *Cristianità–Islam. Cattività e liberazione in nome di Dio. Il tempo di Innocenzo III dopo 'il 1187'*, Miscellanea Historiae Pontificiae 60 (Rome, 1992). For the suggestion that Innocent's compassion was manifest in his treat-ment of all kinds of prisoners, see Helene Tillmann, *Pope Innocent III*, trans. Walter Sax (Amsterdam, 1980), pp 298 and 310, n. 81.   12 J.M. Powell, 'Innocent III, the Trinitarians, and the renewal of the Church', in G. Cipollone (ed.), *La liberazione dei 'cap-tivi' tra Cristianità e Islam*, pp 245–54, at 246, repr. *idem*, *The Crusades, the Kingdom of Sicily, and the Mediterranean* (Aldershot, 2007), same pagination.   13 Michael Markowski, 'Peter of Blois and the conception of the Third Crusade', in B.Z. Kedar (ed.), *The Horns of Hattin* (Jerusalem, 1992), pp 261–9; Brenda Bolton, '"Serpent in the dust: sparrow on the housetop": attitudes to Jerusalem and the Holy Land in the circle of Pope Innocent III', *Studies in Church History* 36 (2000), 154–80, at 157–65.   14 Lk 4:16; Mt 13:54.   15 Ps 68:10.   16 Ps 79:11.

For the Pope, concerned to implement these injunctions, the obvious place to begin his task was in or close to Rome where a variety of prisoners or captives were in need of care and attention. Those prisoners whom he most frequently encountered were involved in transitory skirmishes or longer outbreaks of warfare between the cities of central Italy. One such was Francis of Assisi for whom imprisonment in Perugia was to prove such a life-changing experience![17] It is clear that Innocent considered the captivity of each and every individual as deeply detrimental to the maintenance of peace or truce throughout *Italia*. Other prisoners originated from within the Patrimony of St Peter or from elsewhere in central Italy. Indeed, the Pope met them wherever he and his Curia happened to be at any one time, and more than one of these meetings brought him face to face with constant reminders of the captivity and spiritual needs of Christians held in Iberia, in the Holy Land and the Magreb of North Africa.

Innocent certainly faced some serious prisoner-related issues, all of which made heavy demands on his leadership qualities. His interventions on their behalf were based on two fundamentally important virtues: humanity and religiosity. Both qualities underlay his political actions at a time of particular turmoil in Italy, and gave him a considerable personal experience of prisoners. Many of those who came to him had themselves suffered captivity or were relatives or friends of others who had suffered similarly. The experience of such meetings was to prove crucial in the formation of Innocent's views.

A passage from the *Deeds of Pope Innocent III* by his anonymous biographer[18] offers an early indication that the captivity, treatment and release of prisoners were subjects close to this pope's heart. Indeed, these were amongst those matters on which he was prepared to act most decisively, both at home and abroad.

> The Senator [of the City of Rome] sent to the Canaparia all the prisoners who were destined to be tormented with many miseries, amongst whom there were two men of greater importance, namely Napoleone, viscount of Campilia, and Burgundio, protonotary of Viterbo; the Lord Pope took pity on these two and had them taken from the Canaparia and detained for some time in his palace and finally, he held them in honourable confinement at Lariano; and taking pity on the others, he began to negotiate for peace between the Romans and the Viterbans.[19]

---

17 S. da Campagnola, 'La società nelle fonti francescane' in *Assisi al tempo di San Francesco*, Società Internazione di Studi Francescani 5 (Assisi, 1978), pp 361–92. 18 J.M. Powell, 'Innocent III and Petrus Beneventanus: reconstructing a career at the Papal Curia', in J.C. Moore (ed.), *Pope Innocent III and his world* (Aldershot, 1999), pp 51–62; Giulia Barone, 'I *Gesta Innocentii III*: politica e cultura a Roma all'inizio del duecento', in Giulia Barone, Lidia Capo & Stefano Gasparri (eds), *Studi sul medioevo per Girolamo Arnaldi* (Rome, 2001), pp 1–23. 19 J.-P. Migne, *Gesta Innocentii pp III*, in *Patrologia Latina* 214

The acclaim awarded to Innocent by this allegedly sycophantic biographer for releasing two men 'of greater importance' and giving them special treatment might seem scarcely worthy of mention in placing the Pope as one of history's leading religious humanitarians! Yet, his leadership role, reinforced elsewhere in the *Deeds* as 'the most conscientious pontiff, mercifully concerned about the liberation of captives',[20] is worth not merely a glance or two, but more serious study.

Around 1200, imprisonment, that is, apprehension and control, might mean anything on a scale from fairly minimal restraint to extreme physical restriction in tiny prisons.[21] It could certainly be used coercively, with the aim of extorting a ransom or a debt, or as an instrument of private vengeance. More often than not, however, imprisonment became a means of forcibly withdrawing from the political scene a prisoner too dangerous to let loose. The treatment of Napoleone and Burgundio, detained during one of the two wars between Rome and her then enemy, Viterbo,[22] could not be said to come into quite this category. As part of the long-standing contractual relationship existing between captive and captor whereby the prisoner was neither to be killed nor tortured and, although placed under lock and key, could not be threatened with death, it was well understood that, wherever possible, the lot of those taken in time of war should not be too harsh. Napoleone and Burgundio were first held in the Canaparia,[23] the notorious successor to the Carcer and Mamertine prisons at the foot of the Capitoline, where the miserable conditions were deemed unsuitable for men of their high status. Following their release, they were placed under house arrest in a 'palatium',[24] probably as 'guests' of the Pope in his Lateran palace, and were then transferred to Lariano, a *castrum* or fortified papal stronghold some eight miles south east of Tusculum.[25] Escaping from there, Napoleone subsequently

(Paris, 1855), cols xvii–ccxxviii, cap. CXXXIV, col. clxxxii. The only modern edition is David Gress-Wright, 'The *Gesta Innocentii III*: text, introduction and commentary' (PhD, Bryn Mawr College 1981) (Ann Arbor, MI, 1994), p. 329. An English translation of the text is available as *The Deeds of Pope Innocent III by an anonymous author*, trans. & ed. J.M. Powell (Washington, DC, 2004), p. 246. **20** *Gesta Innocentii*, cap. XXII, col. xxxii; Gress-Wright, 'The *Gesta Innocentii III*', p. 17; J.M. Powell, *The Deeds of Pope Innocent III*, p. 20: *Idem vero piissimus pontifex ad liberationem captivorum clementer intendens.* **21** J. Dunbabin, *Captivity and imprisonment*, pp 1–6. **22** *Gesta Innocentii*, caps CXXXIII–CXXXV, cols clxxvii–clxxxv; D. Gress-Wright, 'The *Gesta Innocentii III*', pp 324–30; *Deeds of Pope Innocent III*, pp 241–46. See also Niccolo della Tuccia (1417–68), *Cronache di Viterbo e di altri Città* in I. Ciampi, *Cronache e Statuti della Città di Viterbo* (Cellini, Florence, 1872), p. 11; C. Pinzi, *Storia della Città di Viterbo*, 4 (Rome, 1887–9), i, 161–72. **23** *...ad custodiam Cannapariae in qua uincti tenebantur*, A. Wilmart, 'Nouvelles de Rome au temps d'Alexandre III (1170)', *Revue Bénédictine* 45 (1933), 63–78, at 74–5, 77, line 97 and nn. 2–3, for the earliest mention of the Canaparia. **24** For the use of *palatium* to describe private residences in Rome around 1207, see E. Hubert, *Espace urbain et habitat à Rome du Xe siècle à la fin du XIIIe siècle* (Rome, 1990), p. 194. **25** *Italia Pontificia*, ii, 106, no. 2; P. Toubert, *Les structures du Latium médiéval: le Latium méridional et la Sabine*

incited the Viterbans to further violence. In the event, Innocent managed to negotiate a peace which, at the same time, maintained unimpaired the people's fealty to the Church, and so achieved a lasting settlement between the two sides. In this way, all the prisoners were eventually freed.

Napoleone and his compatriot were not the only high-status prisoners from within the Patrimony and its surrounds with whom Innocent was concerned. A few were even more noble and important! The process to reclaim those lands in the Patrimony formerly held by Philip of Swabia, brother of Emperor Henry VI,[26] and Markward of Anweiler, Henry's henchman,[27] would extend over more than ten years and throughout the capture and mistreatment of both clerical and lay prisoners provide the Pope with a telling propaganda weapon. In his famous letter of December 1200 known as the *Deliberatio*, Innocent expatiated on a list of persecutions conducted by the imperial family going back to Henry V who had so violently and treacherously taken Pope Pascal II prisoner, with a collection of bishops, cardinals and many Roman nobles.[28] Innocent cited Philip of Swabia as guilty for having held in captivity the archbishop of Salerno[29] and other innocent victims, including Gentile, bishop of Osimo (1177–1205), whose beard Philip had pulled when he was forced to confess before him to having obtained his position through papal influence.[30] Philip had also ordered another of his agents, the aptly named Conrad 'Fly-Brain', to capture and place in chains the venerable cardinal Octavian of Ostia as he returned from a legation to France.[31]

---

du ixe siècle à la fin du xiiie siècle, Bibliothèque des Écoles françaises d'Athènes et de Rome, 221:2 (Rome, 1973), ii, 1341, n. 4.   **26** Eduard Winkelmann, *Philipp von Schwaben und Otto IV. von Braunschweig*, 2 (Leipzig, 1873–8), i, *König Philipp von Schwaben, 1197–1208*, pp 10–42; Peter Csendes, *Philipp von Schwaben. Ein Staufer im Kampf um die Macht* (Darmstadt, 2003), pp 92–101.   **27** Thomas C. Van Cleve, *Markward of Anweiler and the Sicilian Regency: a study of Hohenstaufen policy in Sicily during the minority of Frederick II* (Princeton, NJ, 1937).   **28** *Regestum Innocentii III papae super negotio Romani imperii*, Miscellanea Historiae Pontificiae 12, ed. F. Kempf (Rome, 1947), pp 74–91, no. 29, at pp 83–4: *Henr(icus) enim, qui primus imperium de genere hoc accepit , persecutionem grauissimam in ecclesiam suscitauit et bone memorie Pascalem papam, qui eum coronauit, cum episcopis, cardinalibus et multis nobilibus Romanorum cepit per uioentiam et perfidiam … autem filius et successor ipsius in ecclesie persecutionem sue dominationis execrauit primitias, cum beati Petri patrimonium uiolenter ingressus, illud multipliciter deuastauit, qui etiam quosdam familiares fratrum nostrorum naso fecit in iniuriam ecclesie mutilari* and 86, n. 34.   **29** Ibid., 81: *…Salernitani archiepicopi, quem ante absolutione ipsius mandabamus ab ergastulo sue captiuitatis absolui…*   **30** Ibid., 86: *Ipse venerabilem fratrem nostrum [Gentile] Auximanum episcopum, quia confessus est coram eo quod episcopatum per sedem apostolicam obtineret, alapsis in presentia sua cedi fecit et de barba eius pilis auulsis ipsum inhoneste tractari.*   **31** Ibid., 86: *Corradus Musca-in-cerebro venerabilem fratrem nostrum [Octavian] Hostiensem episcopum cepit et in vinculis posuit et inhoneste tractauit de mandato ipsius…* See also O. Hageneder, W. Maleczek & A.A. Strnad (eds), *Die Register Innocenz' III. 2. Band. 2. Pontifikatsjahr, 1199/1200*: Texte (Rome, 1979), 166 (175), 322 and n. 1 [henceforth, *Inn. Reg.* 2]; *Gesta Innocentii*, cap. IX, col. xxv; D. Gress-Wright, 'The *Gesta Innocentii III*', p. 8; *The Deeds of Pope Innocent III*, 11–12, IX (bis); Robert Davidsohn, *Geschichte von Florenz*, 4 (Berlin, 1896–1927), i, 597.

Across the central part of the peninsula, while city fought against city in a microcosm of contemporary relations between the rulers of Christendom, the Pope struggled to re-establish peace or truce, urging that instead of fighting against one another, citizens should take the Cross and enlist for the ongoing crusade. On 17 April 1201,[32] following an outbreak of war in the Marche, Innocent wrote to inform bishop Gentile, together with the clergy, podestà and people of Osimo, that Simon, their *nuntius*, and a deputation of citizens and castellans who had come to Rome to see him in person, had sworn on the Gospels to follow his mandates in relation to all disputes. Further, the Pope ordered that all prisoners were to be handed over to his proctors and that, concerning all the disputes between a long list of cities, Civitanova against Montecosaro, Fermo against S. Elpidio, Fermo against Monterubbiano, and Osimo against Recanati, Bishop Gentile and the others were told that he (Innocent) had now taken charge.[33] After hearing the cases of both sides and having examined the documents, the Pope decreed that all ransoms, which ought to have been paid following the arrival of his order to release the prisoners, were likewise to be handed over to the proctors. This, of course, followed the principle that any procedure had to be halted once an appeal was forthcoming or if, as in this case, matters had been taken into papal hands. The very careful planning concerning the treatment of prisoners was a forerunner of things to come and displayed that even-handed approach for which Innocent was justly famous.[34] On 11 July 1207, from the by now peaceful city of Viterbo where the Pope and the Curia were staying for the summer,[35] Innocent wrote to Guifredottus Grassellus, then Podestà of

32 J.F. Böhmer, *Regesta Imperii*, V, *Die Regesten des Kaiserreichs 1198–1272*, ed. Julius Ficker-Eduard Winkelmann, I (Innsbruck, 1892–4), 1072, no. 5749; A. Theiner, *Vetera Monumenta Slavorum Meridionalium, I–II, 1198–1549* (Rome, 1863), i, 58, no. 110: *Episcopo et clero ac populo Auximanis super concordia inter ipsos et Firmanos, et ecclesiam et multas alias civitates precipue de marchia per dominum papam limitata.*; Potthast, 1429. **33** Luigi Martorelli, *Memorie historiche dell' antichissima e nobile città d'Osimo* (Venice, 1705), Bk II, cap. 1, 76–9; Carisio Ciavarini, *Collezione di documenti storici antichi inediti ed editi rari delle città e terre marchigiane* (Ancona, 1870–84), iv (1878), 117–19. **34** Thomas of Marlborough, *History of the Abbey of Evesham*, ed. & trans. J. Sayers & L. Watkiss (Oxford, 2003), pp 332–3, cap. 342: *Ex ore sedentis in throno procedit gladius bis acutus* [Rev. 19:15]. *Quoniam ex ore Romani pontificis qui presidet apostolice sedi rectissima debet exire sententia, que contra iustitiam nulli parcat set reddat quod sum est unicuique.*; *Die Register Innocenz' III.* 8, Band. 8. Pontifikatsjahr, 1205/06: Texte und indices, ed. Othmar Hageneder & Andrea Sommerlechner, with Christoph Egger, Rainer Murauer & Herwig Weigl, Publikationen des Historischen Instituts beim Österreichischen Kulturforum in Rom II. Abteilung, 1. Reihe, 10: Texte und Indices (Vienna, 2001), 205 (204), 351–7, at 351. **35** On the papal visit to Viterbo, see A.P. Bagliani, 'La mobilità della Curia Romana nel secolo XIII. Riflessi locali' in *Società e istituzioni dell'Italia comunale: l'esempio di Perugia (secoli XII–XIV)*, Atti del congresso storico internazionale (Perugia, 6–9 November 1985), (Perugia, 1988), pp 155–278, at p. 163; idem, 'La mobilità della corte papale nel secolo XIII' in S. Carocci (ed.), *Itineranza Pontificia: la mobilità della curia papale nel Lazio (secoli XII–XIII)*, Nuovi Studi Storici 61 (Rome, 2003), pp 3–78, at p.

Florence, and the citizens of Florence, following the siege of Montepulciano and the shattering victory of 20 June over the Sienese relief army at Montalto della Berardenga.[36] In his letter, *Si diligenter attenditis*, he warned the Florentines of over-confidence.[37] Neither were they to ascribe this victory to their strength, nor demand from the Sienese more than was strictly necessary in order to establish peace. And he reminded them not only that discord was responsible for the 'scattering of possessions, grave loss of lives and a huge danger to souls' but also that it was his concern to call back those in disagreement to peace.[38] In order to match his actions to these words, Innocent announced that he was sending Guala, cardinal deacon of S. Maria in Portico,[39] whose credentials of honesty and prudence would particularly qualify him to re-establish peace with Siena. And that the cardinal was charged with setting free the prisoners on both sides was made clear in no uncertain terms.[40] Innocent uses a unique metaphor to stress the need on the part of the victors for humility and equality of treatment, reminding the Florentines that while a wise father often causes a slave to be beaten by a son, he was equally empowered to order the same slave to beat that son.[41] The Pope also reminded the Podestà that a form of the peace treaty had been set down in writing and threatened that the Cardinal would promulgate the censure of ecclesiastical compulsion against any who refused to observe its terms.[42]

Two other local skirmishes involved Innocent's treatment of prisoners.[43] During the outbreak of war with Terracina in 1204, Innocent ordered his allies,

---

10. Brenda Bolton, 'A new Rome in a small place: imitation and re-creation in the Patrimony of St Peter', in Claudia Bolgia, Rosamond McKitterick & John Osborne (eds), *Rome across time and space* (Cambridge, 2010), forthcoming. **36** *Die Register Innocenz' III*. 10 Band. 10. Pontifikatsjahr, 1207/08: Texte und indices, ed. Rainer Murauer & Andrea Sommerlechner, with Othmar Hageneder, Christoph Egger, Reinhard Selinger & Herwig Weigl (Publikationen des Historischen Instituts beim Österreichischen Kulturforum in Rom II. Abteilung, 1. Reihe, 10: Texte und Indices (Vienna, 2007), pp 145–6, no. 86 and nn. 1–2 [henceforth *Inn. Reg. 10*]; Davidsohn, *Geschichte von Florenz*, 650–2. **37** *Inn. Reg. 10*, 146: *vobis in ipsorum conflictu astitisse creditor, triumphi tamen accepti gloriam viribus vestris non debetis ascribere*. **38** Ibid., *Cum ergo discordie tante causa in grande rerum dispendium, grave dampnum corporum et immane periculum animarum redundare noscatur et ad nos tanto pertineat specialius revocare discordantes ad pacem*. **39** Guala Bicchieri, cardinal deacon of S. Maria in Portico (1204), cardinal priest of S. Martino (1211–27); W. Maleczek, *Papst und Kardinalskolleg von 1191 bis 1216. Die Kardinäle unter Coelestin III. und Innocenz III*, Publikationen des österreichen Kulturinstitut in Rom. Abhandlungen 6 (Vienna, 1984), pp 141–6. See also *The letters and charters of Cardinal Guala Bicchieri, Papal Legate in England 1216–1218*, ed. Nicholas Vincent, The Canterbury & York Society, lxxxiii (1996), xxxii–ii. **40** *Inn. Reg. 10*, 146: *pro reformanda pace inter vos ac Senenses predictos et captivis liberandis utrimque curavimus destinare*. **41** Ibid., 145: *Si diligenter attenditis, quod providus pater sepe servum a filio, sepe vero filium a servo facit propter offensam utriuslibet vapulare...* **42** Ibid., 146: *Nos enim prefato cardinali dedimus in mandatis, ut ad ea, qui premisimus, peragenda prudenter insistat et diligenter intendat, in partem, si quam repererit contumacem, sub(lato) ap(pellationis) [obstaculo] dis(tricte) ec(clesiasticam) promulgando censuram*. **43** H. Tillmann, *Pope Innocent III*, p. 312, n. 81.

the Frangipani, to hand over the prisoners to him, and when he failed to obtain satisfaction from the citizens, threatened to reclaim those revenues granted to the Church by Celestine II in 1143.[44] In 1208, as the German forces were finally driven from the Marittima and Campania as well as from the Terra di Lavoro, a last stand was made by Conrad, castellan of Sorella, and the imperial forces at Rocca d'Arce, the *castrum* of Isola del Liri and at Sora, along the frontier between the Patrimony and the Regno.[45] A peaceful outcome was only finally achieved once the treacherous Conrad had been out-manoeuvred by the papal army.[46] When the garrison of imperial troops defied Conrad and refused to capitulate in defiance of his promises, Innocent ordered the commanders of the papal army to buy off the garrison with money and the release of the prisoners, thus allowing their release unharmed.[47]

While instances such as these moved the papal biographer to high praise of Innocent for his concern over the captives of war, two cases, one heard personally and informally by the Pope, the other so complex that even he could not finally adjudge on it, dramatically focussed Innocent's attention on the problem of those held in captivity by the Saracens. A certain Robert, coming to him as a penitent, *lacrimabiliter*, at the Curia on its summer retreat in 1202 at Subiaco,[48] recounted an horrific tale of capture at the hands of a Saracen prince during a period of terrible famine.[49] Having been forced to kill and share his daughter as food with starving captors and captives alike, Robert had been unable to bring himself to eat the flesh of his wife when served up to him. The penances, which Innocent placed on this sinner, were of the most severe kind, but the Pope gave Robert hope by ordering him to return to the Holy See at the end of three years to seek a merciful outcome. Robert's case vividly illustrated the need for the rehabilitation of former pris-

44 D.A. Contatore, *De Historia Terracinensi libri quinque* (Rome, 1706), p. 176. **45** *Gesta Innocentii*, cap. XXXIX, cols lxx–lxxiii; D. Gress-Wright, 'The *Gesta Innocentii III*', pp, 55–7; *Deeds of Pope Innocent III*, pp 241–6. Michele Maccarrone, *Studi su Innocenzo III*, Italia Sacra 17 (Padua, 1972), pp 189–93, for an excellent analysis of these highly complex events. **46** *Annales Casinenses 1195–1205*, *MGH SS*, xix, ed. G.H. Pertz (Hanover, 1856), pp 303–20, at 319: *Mense Februarii arx dicta noctu expugnatur a nostris, uno tantum de nostris ab hostibus audacter resistentibus caeso … Captus Corradus Sorellae cum universis qui fuerant illic inventi.* **47** *Gesta Innocentii*, cap. XXXIX, col. lxxii; D. Gress-Wright, 'The *Gesta Innocentii III*', p. 57; *Deeds of Pope Innocent III*, pp 241–6: *Qui cum ad reddendum eam non minis nec persuasionibus posset induci, ut sine mutiliatione membrorum et sanguinis effusione negotium ageretur, maxime propter summi pontifici honestatem, promissis et datis mille auri unciis et equis viginti, liberatis etiam captivis, arcem obtinuerunt in pace.* **48** *Die Register Innocenz' III.* 5 Band. 5. Pontifikatsjahr, 1202/3: Texte, ed. Othmar Hageneder with Christoph Egger, Karl Rudolf & Andrea Sommerlechner, Publikationen des Historischen Instituts beim Österreichischen Kulturinstitut in Rom (Vienna, 1993), pp 155–8, no. 79. **49** *Chronicon ignoti monachis Cisterciensis sanctae Mariae de Ferraria*, ed. Augustus Gaudenzi (Naples, 1888), pp 32–3; H.E. Mayer, 'Two unpublished letters on the Syrian earthquake of 1202', in *Medieval and Middle Eastern Studies in honour of Aziz Suryal Atiya* (Leiden, 1972), pp 295–310, at 303–5, reprinted in *idem*, *Kreuzzüge und lateinischer Osten*, Collected Studies Series, 171 (London, 1983), no. X.

oners of the Muslim enemy, who had endured conditions of hardship and depravity beyond the realms of normal human experience.

In the second case which, like that of Robert, almost certainly relates to the 1190s, Palmerius from Picciati, near Pietralunga in the diocese of Città di Castello, claimed to have been captured by a band of Tuscan knights and peasants.[50] When no ransom was forthcoming from his family, the nobles sold him to three pirates (one appropriately called Monoculus) who took him to Torres in Sardinia. From there, the unfortunate Palmerius, captured by two other pirates, was then sold on to some Saracens, consequently spending a year-and-a-half in Tunis in Moslem captivity. Palmerius' redemption 'for the love of God', together with treatment for an eye infection contracted during his captivity was effected by Matthew, chancellor of the Kingdom of Sicily, who had him freed in Trapani. This case came to Innocent's attention between 1200 and 1205 when Palmerius claimed to be still married to the Lady Gilla who, believing him to be dead, had since remarried. This peculiarly complex and intriguing case of identity and enforcement of marriage survived as a draft decretal but without any hint of possible apostasy.

Innocent's recognition that individuals could suffer great privation was important to both Robert and Palmerius but was merely the tip of the iceberg, while literally thousands more prisoners were still held in Saracen captivity.[51] The Pope, however, had already been instrumental from 1198, the first year of his pontificate, in confirming the Order of Trinitarians, the purpose of which was the redemption and rehabilitation of captives.[52] By 1210, the hospital of S. Tommaso in Formis, the first Trinitarian foundation in Rome, depicted on its facade a mosaic of Christ in Majesty, holding by the wrists two captives, one black, the other white, both in leg irons while the black captive's hands are also manacled. This dramatic visual representation in Rome itself sought to remind Christians everywhere that the preaching of deliverance to captives would indicate the time of the Lord. Innocent, insisting where the duty of deliverance lay, addressed a series of communications to the faithful throughout Christendom as well as to the patriarchs and Christian captives in the Holy Land and elsewhere.

Until the mid-twelfth century, the inevitable fate of those held captive by the Saracens was, if not death, then perpetual slavery, but by Innocent's pon-

---

50 C.R. & M.G. Cheney, 'A draft decretal of pope Innocent III on a case of identity', in *Quellen und Forschungen aus italienischen Archiven und Bibliotheken* 41 (1961), pp 29–47; Brenda Bolton & Constance M. Rousseau, 'Palmerius of Picciati: Innocent III meets his "Martin Guerre"' in *Proceedings of the Tenth International Congress of Medieval Canon Law, Syracuse, New York, 13–18 August 1996* (Vatican City, 2001), pp 361–85. 51 Elena Bellomo, '*Milites* e *captivitas* in Terrasanta agli albori del movimento crociato' in G. Cipollone (ed.), *La liberazione dei 'captivi'*, pp 439–46. 52 Giulio Cipollone, 'La redenzione e la liberazione dei captivi. Lettura Cristiana e modello di redenzione e liberazione secondo la regola dei Trinitari', ibid., pp 345–84; Melanie Vasilescu, 'Even more special sons? the importance of the Order of the Holy Trinity to Pope Innocent III', ibid., pp 721–33.

tificate the situation had somewhat improved. The payment of a ransom in money or in kind, or the exchange of a suitable captive or group of captives, had resulted in freedom for such as Palmerius. The ever-present fear of the Pope was, however, that the captives might be forced or be beguiled into converting to the religion of their captors. Innocent, therefore, sought to encourage the means by which the captives' faith could be strengthened during their imprisonment by receiving exhortatory letters, preaching and pastoral care. That he was well-informed of the spiritual suffering of specific groups of prisoners early on in his pontificate is revealed first in the surviving rubric of a consolatory letter, sent in May 1200, encouraging and sympathizing with those held in captivity by the king of Morocco.[53] In *Fraternitatem tuam*, of 23 March 1209, Innocent addressed Nicholas, the Melkite Patriarch of Alexandria (1209–35), in an attempt to console and encourage him whilst he himself was experiencing imprisonment in the midst of a 'perverse nation'. [54]

Within the space of six days in January 1212, Innocent had addressed three important letters to the East, similarly consolatory and inspiring, and destined to be received by those whose duty and those whose fate lay in the Holy Land, not only patriarchs but also captives. On 13 January, Innocent wrote to Albert, patriarch of Jerusalem (1205–14), to express his grave concern for the many prisoners languishing in Alexandria, lest 'on account of the length of time that they have been imprisoned, that they might be forced into apostasy'.[55] Albert was to make every effort to get them freed through ransom or exchange. Five days later, in a letter to Nicholas of Alexandria,[56] one of the Pope's chief informants about the plight of those under Saracen rule, Innocent replied to the petition which he had received from the Patriarch on behalf of prisoners then in Saracen hands and stressed that those being held 'as if they were the captives of Christ' had already been proved like gold in the furnace', one of his favourite phrases.[57] Given that some of these prisoners had been held for at least 20 years, ever since 1187 and the Christian defeat at Hattin, Innocent not only stressed his confidence in the strategy which he was advancing for their liberation but also made a practical suggestion to maintain their spiritual welfare in the meantime. As the captives had

53 A. Theiner, *Vetera Monumenta Slavôrum*, i, 49, no. 82: *Universis captivatis per regem de marroch consolatorie super eodem captivitate*; G. Cipollone, *Cristianità–Islam*, pp 376–8, 426–9. **54** *Fraternitatem tuam in Domino commendamus quod in medio prave ac perverse positus nationis*, Innocent III, *Opera Omnia in PL*, 214–17 (Paris, 1855), 216, col. 23; G. Cipollone, *Cristianità–Islam*, pp 527–8. **55** *PL* 216, cols 507–9, at 508: ... *ne propter acerbitatem poenarum quas longo tempore sunt perpessi, apostare cogantur*; G. Cipollone, *Cristianità–Islam*, pp 529–30, at 529. On Albert, see V. Mosca, *Alberto, Patriarcha di Gerusalemme: Tempo–Vita–Opera*, Institutum Carmelitum. Textus et Studia Historica Carmelitana 20 (Rome, 1996). **56** *PL* 216, cols 506–7; G. Cipollone, *Cristianità–Islam*, pp 531–2. **57** 1 Cor, 19.13. *PL* 216, 508; G. Cipollone, *Cristianità–Islam*, p. 532. See for the same text used in relation to the Patrimony of St Peter, *Gesta Innocentii*, cap. CXXXIII, col. clxxvii; Gress-Wright, *The Gesta Innocentii III*, p. 324; *Deeds of Pope Innocent III*, p. 241.

only an aged priest to say the divine service for them,[58] they had asked
Patriarch Nicholas to promote one of their number who was well versed in
ministry to the diaconate, to provide the sacraments for the Latin Christians.
The Patriarch, however, declared his unwillingness to do this without a spe-
cial papal licence and an order from the Pope himself to do as they desired.
This Innocent granted willingly.

The third letter sent by the Pope on 19 January was an amalgamation of
parts of his letters to both Albert and Nicholas and was addressed to all captives in Alexandria and *Babylonia*.[59] The Pope assured these unfortunates that
he had heard their groans of distress and fully intended to work for their liberation through the good offices of the Templars, Hospitallers, kings and
princes of the Eastern provinces who were all seeking to do their best to
obtain their commutation or exchange. Using scriptural texts, Innocent
reminded the miserable captives that their present suffering in this life was
transitory, encouraging them to continue manfully, *viriliter*, to the end, when
they would finally receive the crown of glory! In the following year, Innocent
issued *Vineam Domini*, a series of vital circular letters of 19 April 1213, summoning all ecclesiastical leaders and various secular rulers to the Fourth
Lateran Council to be held in Rome in November 1215.[60] An unprecedented
period of two-and-a-half years was set aside for planning, not only for the
reform of the whole Church but also to promote the Fifth Crusade. At the
same time, the Pope sent out to all Christendom with the exception of distant Norway and Iberia, still recovering from the victory of Las Navas de
Tolosa, his great crusading encyclical, *Quia Maior*.[61] Within his text, he
included the passage:

> For how can a man be said to love his neighbour as himself, in obedi-
> ence to God's commands when, knowing that his brothers who are
> Christians in faith and in name, are held in the hands of the perfidi-
> ous Saracens in dire imprisonment and weighed down by the yoke of
> the most heavy slavery, he does not do something effective to liberate
> them, thereby transgressing the command of that natural law which
> the Lord gave in the Gospel: *Whatsoever you would do that men should
> do to you, do you also unto them?*

---

58 *PL* 216, at 507; G. Cipollone, *Cristianità–Islam*, p. 532: *Ceterum, sicut nobis scripsisti,
prefati captivi non habent nisis quemdam vetulum sacerdotum qui eis possit ministrare divina,
unde fraternitatem tuam humiliter rogaverunt ut unum ex ipsis, in ecclesiasticis ministeriis eru-
ditum, in diaconum promoveres, quod tu sine nostra licentia facere noluisti.*   **59** *Universis captivis in Alexandria et Babylonia constitutis, PL* 216, cols 506–9; G. Cipollone, *Cristianità–
Islam*, pp 533–4.   **60** Alberto Melloni, '*Vineam Domini*–10 April 1213: new efforts and
traditional *Topoi* – summoning Lateran IV' in John C. Moore (ed.), *Pope Innocent III and
his world* (Aldershot, 1999), pp 63–73, and text at pp 72–3.   **61** G. Tangl, *Studien zum
Register Innocenz' III* (Weimar, 1929), pp 88–97; Louise & Jonathan Riley-Smith, *The
Crusades: ideal and reality, 1095–1274* (London, 1981), pp 119–24.

And then Innocent posed a startling question. 'Or perhaps you do not know that many thousands of Christians are being held in slavery and imprisonment in their hands, tortured by countless torments?'[62] Here, Innocent appears to be moving towards a new emphasis, revealing that he saw his task as giving a strong lead on the duties of Christendom in which the needs of captives and prisoners were not to be neglected.

Italian and particularly Roman participation in the Fifth Crusade forms a fitting postscript to Innocent's call to set the prisoners free. At Orvieto on 1 May 1216, Innocent with his own hands distributed crosses to 2,000 would-be crusaders[63] and this same enthusiasm was repeated at nearby Bagnoregio and all across central Italy. It is clear that he saw the problem of the captive as increasing throughout his pontificate. In common with secular rulers, he needed to bring peace or at least a truce to enable men to take up the Cross. In all these examples, it was also clear to Innocent III that the needs of both individuals, and the groups from which they came, could best be achieved by following the Scriptural injunction 'to set the prisoners free'.

---

62 Brenda Bolton, 'Perhaps you do not know? Innocent III's approach to the release of captives', in G. Cipollone, *La liberazione dei 'captivi'*, pp 457–63, at 461.   63 Pierpont Morgan Library, New York, MS 465, fol. 90v; M. Maccarrone, *Studi*, pp 8–9; David Foote, 'How the past becomes a rumour: the notarialization of historical consciousness in medieval Orvieto', *Speculum* 75 (2000), 794–815, at 813–14.

The sweet beloved and his legacy: a lawsuit for love and money from Lucca (1237)

ANDREAS MEYER

The story really is a short one. Marsubilia, daughter of Donatus Ughetti, married the furrier Deotisalvi, called Imbrattaferro, son of Aldebrandinus in Lucca, around the year of 1220. Although the event in itself was a happy one, it had a downside, since Marsubilia was at that time the lover of Dulcis qd. Bernardi Sciagri, who was not at all disposed to accept the bitter loss, and who therefore not only continued his affair with her, but soon also forbid the married couple to see each other. Astonishingly enough, Marsubilia had more than a little sympathy for this request, and furtheron she stayed with her sweet beloved. The duped husband, who carried the unflattering cognomen *Imbrattaferro* – *imbrattare* translates as stain, pollute, soil, contaminate, an *imbrattacarta* is a bad author – consequently filed for divorce, and after a successful separation married a daughter of Ubaldus Gonnelle, who was also a good catch. After this twist our savoury story might have had a happy ending, only that in such a case, we would not know of it. Although this reads like the plot of a novel, it is taken from real life, which is always good for a surprise. For when Dulcis died unexpectedly around Easter in 1237, his brother Quiricus qd. Bernardi Sciagri denied the former's oral provisions made for his long-term lover on his deathbed by stating that Marsubilia was in truth married to another man, and her only desire was for filling her purse (*marsupium*). Because Quiricus had a hands-on mentality, and had already created a fait accompli, the argument was on the verge of escalating. Consequently, Aldebrandinus qd. Leonardi Malagallie, a judge living in the same quarter, was called upon to arbitrate between the parties. He first heard the parties of dispute (A), then went on to hear the witnesses on both sides (B, C), and in the end, he unconditionally confirmed Marsubilia's claim (D).[1] By way of a small compensation, our thanks go to the defeated party, to whom we owe this entertaining tale, for without his avarice, his envy and his hate, this story would undoubtedly have soon been lost forever. Once again it is confirmed that whosoever aspires to fame had much better be a bad person than a good.[2]

I would like to express my gratitude to Rebekka Götting, Marburg, for the translation of my article into English.   1 ACL, LL 11 fol. 117r–118v, 120v–121v. A, B, C and D refer to the transcripts in the appendix. The arbitrator adhered to the common procedure of a church court, cf. R.H. Helmholz, *Marriage litigation in medieval England* (Cambridge, 1974), pp 13–22.   2 Arnold Esch, 'Überlieferungs-Chance und Überlieferungs-Zufall als methodisches

The uncommonly rich historical tradition in Lucca, which is of course well known to the honoree, allows us to locate the protagonists of our story more firmly. Because the entire incident took place right outside Ciabatto's door, his notarial register once again proves to be of great value.[3] Thanks to his deeds, we can locate this story in the upper circles of the Lucchese society. On the other hand, the acting personae seldom appear in the roughly 10,000 charters from the thirteenth century that are extant today, but this must not point to their former status, because tradition depends on many accidents.[4]

I want to begin the introduction of the participants with Bernardus qd. Sciagri, father to both the beloved and the plaintiff. He acted as witness when Pisternarius qd. Bernardi allocated a property *in Classo Subgruminese*, that is immediately next to San Martino, to the *dos* of his wife Dulcena qd. Gottifredi Mencalegoi in 1172 in recompensation for another one.[5] By the time his son Quiricus made his first appearance in the sources in 1208, Bernardus was already dead.[6] Living in the *Contrada S. Martini*, Quiricus was a dyed-in-the-wool banker, whose table stood in the Porticus of the cathedral – he bequeathed it to the chapter of San Martino in his testament of 1249, and he was a regular customer with Ciabattus.[7]

By contrast, we know next to nothing about Dulcis qd. Bernardi Sciagri. He lived with Quiricus on the paternal property *in Classo Sogrominesi*.[8] In 1212 he sold a parcel of land *in villa S. Cassiani a Vico prope ipsam ecclesiam*.[9] It is likely that he was a merchant, too, although this must remain a conjecture for which we have but indirect proofs. Traders were among his frequent guests: on 27 April 1237, immediately after Dulcis' death, a Bonfilius qd. Gallegani from Pistoia signed a receipt for Ubaldus qd. Orselli, a dealer in pigs from Lucca, *in domo qd. Dolcis*.[10]

Problem des Historikers', *Historische Zeitschrift* 240 (1985), 529–70.   3 Andreas Meyer, *Felix et inclitus notarius. Studien zum italienischen Notariat vom 7. bis zum 13. Jahrhundert* (Tübingen, 2000), Index s.v.; Andreas Meyer (ed.), Sar Ciabattus, *Imbreviature lucchesi del Duecento, regesti,* I: Anni 1222–32 (Lucca, 2005) [hereafter Ciabattus I]; ibid., II: Anni 1236–9 (forthcoming) [hereafter Ciabattus II].   4 On the proportions of that tradition see Meyer *Felix et inclitus notarius*, pp 235–320, and Andreas Meyer, 'Hereditary laws and city topography: on the development of the Italian notarial archives in the late Middle Ages' in Albrecht Classen (ed.), *Urban space: the experience of urban life in the Middle Ages and the early modern age. The 6th International Symposium University of Arizona, Tucson, May 1–4, 2008* (Berlin, 2009), pp 225–43.   5 ASL Dipl. Spedale di S. Luca 1172.10.16 n. 2; on the toponym see Ciabattus I, p. 49. Dulcena came from a family of merchants that maintained business relations as far as the Near East, cf. Ciabattus I, pp 25–34.   6 ASL Dipl. Archivio de' notari 1208.06.05.   7 ACL LL 23 fol. 43rs; Andreas Meyer, 'Lepra und Lepragutachten aus dem Lucca des 13. Jahrhunderts' in Andreas Meyer und Jürgen Schulz-Grobert (eds), *Gesund und krank im Mittelalter. Marburger Beiträge zur Kulturgeschichte der Medizin. 3. Tagung der Arbeitsgruppe 'Marburger Mittelalter-Zentrum (MMZ)', Marburg, 25th and 26th March 2005* (Leipzig, 2007), pp 189–191 n. 19f.; on Quiricus cf. also the works cited in note 3.   8 Ciabattus I, p. 50; Ciabattus II, n. 17.   9 ASL Dipl. Miscellanee 1228.03.28 (inserted charter).   10 Ciabattus II, n. 362 (1237.04.27); cf. also n. 718 (1238.04.23): on

The hapless temporary fiancé or husband of Marsubilia, furrier Deotisalvi qd. Aldebrandini, first appears in the sources in 1213.[11] On the 27 March 1230, Deotisalvi Imbrattaferro and his wife Ubaldesca receipted the payment of 4 lb. *de dote* to the notary Bonacingus in their house, with Iohannes f. Guidi Delpiano acting as witness. The latter was probably a relative of Johannes qd. Arrigi del Piano *calthorarius*, who acted as Quiricus' first witness in our case in 1237.[12] If in 1230 Deotisalvi was still living in the same house in which he had once married Marsubilia, that would be *in domo qd. Orlandini Berlescie* next to San Michele in Foro, namely, at the very heart of Lucca and on the main street, if in an area from which not many sources have survived.

The owner of that house, Orlandinus qd. Peregrini Berlescie *de S. Michele de Ponte ad Forum*, whom we first find mentioned in 1216, was a member of the Lucchese élite.[13] In 1221 and between 1231 and 1234 he served as proctor resp. *advocatus* for the monastery and the hospital of San Ponziano.[14] Between 1225 and 1235, he was *mensurator terrarum* resp. *mensurator publicus comunis lucani*,[15] and in 1237, he was dead, provided we believe in the testimony of Albertinus *peliciarius*. Albertinus qd. Albertini *peliciarius* was a member of the same guild as Deotisalvi, which is why he is probably trustworthy in this case. He makes several appearances as a witness in Ciabattus' deeds between 1224 and 1249.[16]

In January 1237, Deotisalvi and Corsus Sclatte[17] bore witness to Custor Nordili depositing a bag with 30 pounds of Lucchese *grossi* in the vestry of

the anniversary of Dulcis' death Ciabattus erroneously took down a legal act as having taken place *in domo qd. Quirichi*.   11 ACL Dipl. F 185 (1213), ACL Dipl. H 15 (1213): as a witness.   12 Ciabattus I, C167.   13 ACL Fondo Martini perg. 1216.08.05. The house *filiorum qd. Peregrini Berlescie*, situated *prope ecclesiam S. Michaelis*, had figured in the sources since 1181, Regesto del capitolo di Lucca 3 (Roma, 1933) No. 1643 and 1678. Jacobus Berlescie makes a repeated appearance as a witness in 1222 in the house of a merchant family situated between the Via Fillungo and the Piazza San Michele. Ciabattus I, p. 9 and also No. A47, A48 and A53; cf. also Raffaele Savigni, *Episcopato e società cittadina a Lucca da Anselmo II († 1085) a Roberto († 1225)* (Lucca, 1996), p. 501.   14 ASL Dipl. S. Ponziano 1221.05.11, 1221.12.15, 1232.12.30, 1234.01.31; ACL LL 7 fol. 5v and fol. 6r.   15 ASL Dipl. Altopascio deposito Orsetti-Cittadella 1225.04.10, ACL LL 6 fol. 28v, ASL Dipl. Spedale di S. Luca 1233.09.06, ASL Dipl. Altopascio 1235.06.11; Oliçeus Berlescie, 1277 *operarius opere S. Michaelis in Foro*, was probably a son of Orlandinus, cf. Graziano Concioni, Claudio Ferri and Giuseppe Ghilarducci (ed.), *Arte e pittura nel medioevo lucchese* (Lucca, 1994), p. 113 cr. 125; Dinus Uliçei Berlescie was a *consiliarius consilii generalis* in 1284, ASL Dipl. F. M. Fiorentini 1284.05.30.   16 Ciabattus I, A28, A43, C232 (*peliparius et sutor*), D5, D344; Ciabattus II, No. 657; ACL LL 23 fol. 26rs (1249.12.19). Galganus Tempagnini, Marsubulia's second witness, can also be found in other documents between 1213 and 1238, ASL Dipl. S. Maria Forisportam 1213.08.11, ASL Dipl. Spedale di S. Luca 1238.08.15. Lastly, Redditus qd. Aliocti *civis lucanus*, Mabilia's husband, is verifiable as a *nuntius* of the commune between 1229 and 1257, AAL Dipl. *O 21 (1229.06.12), AAL Dipl. ††D 55 n. 2 (1257.09.29), Ciabattus I and II, Index s.v.   17 Cf. AAL Dipl. *O 2 (1228.03.21): Corsus Sclate *de contrada S. Iusti de Arcu*. In 1238, Perfectus qd. Sclatte had travelled to Ceuta und Alexandria with money he had borrowed,

San Martino.[18] Custor Nordili, who likewise lived nearby the cathedral, conducted trade as far as Alexandria in the east, and Ceuta in the west.[19] Because he brought Deotisalvi in as a witness in this case, it seems likely to assume that he had a regular business relationship with him.

Lastly, there is Deotisalvi's wife Ubaldesca. According to the witness Iohannes qd. Arrigi del Piano, she was a good catch, being the daugther of Ubaldus Gonnelle, and this evaluation was doubtlessly correct, since her grandfather Gonella qd. Malagonella had been one of the *consules maiores* who led the commune of Lucca between 1183 and 1197. Like the incomparably more famous Antelminelli and Castracani families, Ubaldus was a descendant of Ugo *de S. Martino* (†1123), liegeman of the bishop of Lucca, and he conducted long-distance trade and money exchange like the Antelminelli. Bonacingus, a notary, was also a relative of Ubaldus Gonnelle, which circumstance explains the payment mentioned above.[20]

Bringing together the collected evidence, namely, that all parties concerned had not only business relations with each other, but were often tied by family bonds as well, we can conclude that Marsubilia stemmed from the same social class, even though we know nothing further about her.

The question now arises why Deotisalvi once considered marriage to Marsubilia. At the same time, we must not ignore the fact that marriages could be contracted in different ways during the Middle Ages. If, by way of example, two people had sex on a regular basis and by mutual consent, this could well be acknowledged as a marriage, even though more formal procedures – including marriage vows before witnesses, the placing of a ring on the bride's finger, the exchange of *dos*, *Morgengabe* and *antefactum* – were more common in Lucca, especially among the wealthy people.[21] Marsubilia sure

from Custor Nordili among others, Ciabattus II, No. 800; Ciabattus I, p. 64: Perfectus was married to Felicitas, a daughter of Gerardus Maghiari; the Maghiarii in turn were active in Genoa and England after 1250, and in the 1260s were counted among the partners of the Ricciardi, ibid. pp 62–4; Andreas Meyer, *Felix et inclitus notarius*, p. 303.   **18** Ciabattus II, No. 282, cf. also No. 290. Deotisalvi had made occasional appearances at San Martino before, when he bore witness to acts that Ciabattus recorded, ACL LL 6 fol. 67r (1229.06.09), ACL LL 7 fol. 15r (1230.10.18). The reason for his call was probably no longer Marsubilia, but the fact that canons have a relish for fur, too.   **19** Among his partners in the 1230ies were counted the Battosi, cf. Ciabattus I and II, Index s.v.; Ignazio Del Punta, *Mercanti e banchieri lucchesi nel Duecento* (Pisa, 2004), pp 217–265, failed to notice this connection.   **20** Cf. the genealogical tables in Ciabattus I, pp 67 and 73, and on Gonnella see also Savigni (note 14) p. 528. Ubaldus qd. Gonnelle was a brother of Inghifredus *iudex* and of Mabilia *relicta* qd. Orlandi Spiafamis, cf. Ciabattus II, No. 188. On Inghifredus *iudex et notarius romani imperii* (verifiable since 1214, †1237) cf. Andreas Meyer, *Felix et inclitus notarius*, No. 1180 and Ciabattus I and II, Index s.v.   **21** Cf. Andreas Meyer, 'Wie heiratet man richtig? Der Prozess zweier Frauen um den Luccheser Notar Bonansegna (1234–1238)' in Stephan Buchholz and Heiner Lück (eds), *Worte des Rechts – Wörter zur Rechtsgeschichte. Festschrift für Dieter Werkmüller zum 70. Geburtstag* (Berlin, 2007), pp 247–66; Andreas Meyer, 'Einleitung' in Andreas Meyer (ed.), *Kirchlicher*

seemed like a good catch to the furrier, even though her background is unfortunately unknown to us. And very likely he was ignorant of her having – or having had – an intimate relationship to Dulcis. Marsubilia herself apparently did not understand her relationship to Dulcis as a marriage, and consequently accepted Deotisalvi's offer. She proceeded to wear his ring openly on several sucessive days, and even spoke of him as of her husband to Dulcis. But her lover, just as apparently, considered her his lawful wife, since according to the witness Donetta he threatened her in broad daylight that he would cut off her nose should she refuse to return to him. According to an assize of King Roger II of Sicily, which later found its way into the constitutions of Melfi, this was the way husbands were allowed to punish their cheating wives.[22] Undoubtedly this was more humane than beating them to death, which punishment both the Roman and the Langobardic law suggested in cases of adultery.[23] In addition, Dulcis asked Marsubilia to take off Deotisalvi's ring and give it back to him, and on the same occasion he forbade the husband – or was he only the bridegroom? – to ever walk past Dulcis' house again.

After this dramatic scene that certainly damaged her honour somewhat, Marsubilia returned to Dulcis and stayed with him until his death. On his deathbed, he at last decided it would be a sin to leave her unprovided for. As if she had really been his wife, he granted her a life estate in his house and bequeathed several of his possessions to her, while he appointed Quiricus as his principal heir.

One question remains to be examined: Why did the arbitrator confirm Marsubilia's claim unconditionally? Aldebrandinus qd. Leonardi Malagalie

und religiöser Alltag im Spätmittelalter. Akten der internationalen Tagung in Weingarten, 4th–7th October 2007 (Ostfildern, 2010). Concerning marriage, the Lucchese statutes only regulated the right of confirmation of parents and legal guardians, Statutum lucani comunis an. MCCCVIII (Lucca, 1991 [1867]), pp 137f. § 5f. On the problem of the endowment cf. Julius Kirshner, 'Wives' claims against insolvent husbands in late medieval Italy' in Julius Kirshner and S.F. Wemple (eds), *Women of the medieval world: essays in honor of John H. Mundy* (Oxford 1987), pp 256–303; C.E. Meek, 'Women, dowries and the familiy in late medieval Italian cities' in C.E. Meek & Katherine Simms (eds), *The fragility of her sex?: medieval Irish women in their European context* (Dublin, 1996), pp 136–52.   22 Wolfgang Stürner (ed.), *Die Konstitutionen Friedrichs II. für das Königreich Sizilien* (Hannover, 1996), pp 438f. Loosing one's nose meant losing one's honour as well, cf. Vincenzo Cioffari (ed.), *Guido da Pisa's expositiones et Glose super Comediam Dantis or commentary on Dante's Inferno* (Albany, NY, 1974), S. 583 (Inferno 28, vv. 64–6): *Nam de nullo membro perdito faciei homi ita confunditur ut de naso. Et quia iste letabatur de confusione alterius, ideo suo est honore privatus.* The Lucchese statutes of 1308 only regulated who was allowed to file a suit in these cases, and determined the fine, cf. Statutum lucani comunis (note 21) pp 136 § 4. On the church penances of the time see Mino Marchetti, *Peccati, peccatori e penitenze nella Chiesa medioevale di Siena. Il 'Libro penitenziale' della Chiesa di Siena e la celebrazione liturgica delle ordalie o giudizi di Dio* (Siena, 2000), pp 77–9 § 23–5.   23 Friedrich Bluhme and Alfred Boretius (eds), *Leges Langobardorum, MGH* Leges 4 (Hanover, 1868), reprint 1984, pp 51f. (Rothari § 212), cf. also pp 158f. (Luitprand § 121).

iudex, who came from a genteel family himself,[24] probably decided in her favour because he also looked upon her as Dulcis' wife. With this judgement he confirmed an earlier sentence of a church court, which regarded the marriage between Marsubilia and Deotisalvi as null and void because of her earlier connection to Dulcis. Passed in the twenties, this sentence did not survive. Had she stayed with Deotisalvi back then, a strict interpretation of the canon law would have pronounced their joint children to be illegitimate, a circumstance the impolite witness Bonagrathia alluded to.

In order to attach more importance to the sentence, two judges *(iudices)* – Arrigus Sexmondi[25] und Rugerius qd. Aldibrandi Roncilliati[26] – as well as Usaccus qd. Simeonis Beraldelli, a neighbour of the contestants, attended as witnesses. Arrigus Sexmondi came from a noble family, which ruled over Castellaccio di Compito and whose houses stood on the Via della Croce between Via Fillungo and Via dell'Olivo. Peregrinus Sesmondi, whose exact position in the family remains obscure, was an active member of the *Societas Ricciardorum* in England in the 1250s.[27]

Rugerius qd. Aldibrandi Roncilliati *causidicus* served several terms as a judge at municipal courts in Lucca.[28] Other than that, the only thing we know about him and his brother Orlandus is that they reappeared before the same arbitrator to fight for two properties in Massa Macinaia with the canon of San Martino in 1241.[29]

Usaccus, lastly, was such a good client to Ser Ciabatto that the latter maintained a register solely for him during several years. When Usaccus died in November 1240, he left behind a widow and a son who was probably under age at the time. Usacco's widow carried a name that was exceedingly rare in Lucca, and it is very tempting to identify this Marsubilia, widow of Usacco, with our lady. Maybe she fell in love with her neighbour under the impression of the more than favourable sentence she had received.[30] Fact is stranger than fiction, as the saying goes.

---

24 Cf. Graziano Concioni, 'Lucani campsores: i Malagallia', *Rivista di archeologia, storia, costume* 24/3:4 (1996), 3–96, here pp 62–74 (the entry '1236 luglio 27' is actually from 1237 and can be found in LL 11 fol. 113v); Andreas Meyer, *Felix et inclitus notarius*, No. 3007. 25 Andreas Meyer, *Felix et inclitus notarius*, No. 3014: verifiable between 1202 and 1247. 26 Andreas Meyer, *Felix et inclitus notarius*, No. 3095: verifiable between 1220 and 1256. 27 Ciabattus I p. 65 n. 386. 28 ASL Dipl. Fregionaia 1227.10.29: *consul foretanorum*; ASL Dipl. S. Ponziano 1233.10.21, 1234.01.31: *consul treuguanus*; AAL Archivio del Decanato di S. Michele perg. 1236.06.04: *consul causarum et foretanorum*; ASL Dipl. Serviti 1245.12.16: *vicecomes comunis lucani*. 29 ACL Dipl. G 86 (1241). 30 On Usacccus cf. Andreas Meyer, *Felix et inclitus notarius*, pp 156, 300–2 and 343–5; Ciabattus I and II, Index s.v. Only in 1208 can we find a second Marsubilia in the documents, namely Marsubilia filia qd. Lucterii, wife of Giangus qd. Angiorelli, AAL Dipl. ††L 57.

APPENDIX

Quiricus qd. Bernardi Sciagri vs. Marsubilia (1237), in the notorial register of
Ciabatto, Lucca, Archivio Capitolare, LL 11 fol. 117r–118v, 120v–121v.

Editing Principles: Square brackets designate supplements for destroyed text
lines. Angle brackets contain parts that the notary forgot out of negligence.
Round brackets mark insertions made by the editor. // = page change within
continuous text. Contemporary orthography has been respected.

A

Marsubilia quondam Donati Ughetti consensu et auctoritate Bonagratie quondam Ugolini mundualdi sui dativi a ‹consulibus› treuguanis, ut contineri dicebant in publica scriptura manu Grathiadei notarii, litigans ab una parte et
Quiricus quondam [Ber]nardi Sciagri litigans ab altera ad invicem inter se
investitionem de[der]unt, promiserunt et convenerunt, quod ipsi et eorum
heredes omni tempore habebunt, tenebunt et observabunt firmum, [ra]tum et
incorruptum totum illud et ea omnia, quod et que Ildebrandinus iudex quondam [Le]onardi inter eos dixerit, laudaverit seu arbitratus fuerit[1] inter
suprascriptos per rationem et usum lucane civitatis et arbitrium et amicabilem
compositionem una vice tam pluribus, partes presentes vel absentes, sive una
presente et altera absente, factum vel non sacramentum calumnie,[2] de
omnibus litibus et discordiis et requisitionibus, quas inter se facere possent
usque ad hanc ‹diem›, et sic ipsas lites et discordias et requisitiones in eum
compromiserunt et eum arbitrum et laudatorem fecerunt et con‹stituerunt›.
Et sic facere et observare inter se promiserunt et convenerunt, obligando sese
et suos heredes et bona[3] sua omnia presentia et futura iure pignoris et
ypothece ad ‹penam› dupli et consulum et treuguanorum et potestatis lucanorum presentium et futurorum. Actum Luce in domo suprascripti
Aldibrandini iudicis, coram presbitero Iacobo et Aldibrando clerico ipsius,
MCCXXXVII, pridie nonas augusti, indictione X (*4 August 1237*). Lis autem,
que inter eos vertebatur, talis est: Petebat namque suprascripta Marthabilia a
suprascripto Quirico herede quondam Dulcis libras XX denariorum et totam
blavam et omnia ligna et vestimenta, que quondam Dulcis germanus dicti
Quirici reliquid tempore mortis, dicens quondam dictum Dulcem reliquisse
tempore mortis suprascripte Marsubilie, et super predictis deducit omnia iura
sibi competentia et competitura.
    Quiricus op‹p›osita exceptione et doli mali et sui ipsius, qui convenitur, et
omnibus aliis exceptionibus dilatoriis et peremptoriis sibi initio litis et usque
ad finem cause competentibus et competituris oppositis, negat se suprascrip-

---

1 *follows* p *expunged*.   2 *follows* factum vel.   3 *corrected from* bonam.

tis petitionibus teneri et dare et facere negat, et non offerendo se liti in his, que non possidet.[4] Lis contestata est pridie nonas augusti (*4 August 1237*). S[acramentum] C[alumnie] f[actum] ab utraque parte.

Dicit Marsubilia, quod remanserunt apud ipsum Quiricum tempore mortis Dulcis ipsius Dulcis libre XX denariorum et quas iudicavit suprascripte Marsobilie. Quiricus negat.

Dicit Marsubilia, quod remanserunt tempore mortis Dulcis apud ipsum Quiricum staria XX inter granum et milium et fabas et que fuera⟨n⟩t ipsius Dulcis et quem iudicavit seu reliquid suprascripte Marsubilie et que valuerunt[5] solidos L. Quiricus de iudicio negat et confitetur, quod habet staria II grani et IIII milii et II segalis, et de plus negat et de valere reliquid iudici credendum.

(fol. 117v) Dicit Marsubilia, quod tempore mortis Dulcis remanserunt[6] duos currus lignorum,[7] que fuerunt suprascripti Dulcis et que reliquerat seu iudicaverat suprascripte Marsubilie et que valuerunt solidos XII. Quiricus confitetur[8] de lignis, que habet, que fuerunt quondam Dulcis, et de valere confitetur de solidis VIII et de plus negat et de iudicio negat.

Dicit Marsubilia, quod suprascriptus Dulcis reliquid tempore[9] mortis[10] unam guarnachiam[11] vermiliam fodratam[12] de cunicolo[13] valentem solidos XVI.[14] Item unam guarnachiam persam[15] novam cum tunica valentem solidos LX.[16] Item unam tunicam panni cammelis valentem solidos IIII.[17] Item duo paria de serrabulis[18] novis. Item unam bonam interulam[19] valentem solidos X.[20] Item unum mantellum blavettum valentem solidos VIII.[21] Qui panni fuerunt suprascripti Dulcis, et quos[22] reliquid dicte Marsubilie, et[23] qui panni[24] valuerunt libras IIII et solidos IIII. Quiricus, quod quondam Dulcis reliquerit unam guarnachiam vermiliam et quam ipse non habuit, confitetur et alia negat, nisi viderit legiptimam probationem, et negat aliquod de predictis ad ipsum pervenisse.

Dicit Quiricus, quod Marsubilia fuit, iam sunt anni X et plus, et est nunc uxor Deotisalvi pelliparii. Marsubilia negat.

Dicit Quiricus, quod ipse Deotisalvi anulavit eam per suam sponsam et ipsa consensit in eum sicut in sponsum et virum suum, iam sunt anni X et plus. Marsubilia negat.

Dicit Quiricus, quod ipsa Marsubilia precepto vel timore quondam Dulcis Sciagri post dictam anulationem apud V vel VIII dies, dum ipse Deotisalvi

---

4 et non – possidet *interlinear.* **5** *ms.* valuit. **6** *follows* apud suprascriptum Quiricum *expunged.* **7** lignorum *and an illegible word interlinear.* **8** *follows* et di *expunged.* **9** *corrected from* temporem. **10** *follows* suprascripto Quirico *expunged.* **11** Long cloak. **12** *corrected from* fodrandam. **13** *ms.* cunicunicolo. **14** valentem – XVI *interlinear.* **15** Dark blue. **16** valentem – LX *interlinear, follows* persam. **17** valentem – IIII *interlinear.* **18** Pants, underpants. **19** Shirt. **20** valentem – X *interlinear.* **21** valentem – VIII *interlinear, follows* quos *expunged.* **22** quos *interlinear.* **23** qui *corrected from* que. **24** panni *interlinear.*

transiret per oram, in qua morabatur Marsubilia cum ipso Dolce amasio suo, et suprascripta Marsubilia videret suprascriptum Deotisalvi ire inde, extraxit sibi anulum de digito et proiecit ipsum post dictum Deotisalvi. Marsubilia negat.

Dicit Quiricus, quod post hec dictus Dolce minatus fuit ipsi Deotisalvi et fecit ipsum iurare, quod non peteret ipsam Marsobiliam ulterius et non inquietaret eam per suam uxorem. Marsubilia negat.

Dicit Marsubilia, quod[25] Quiricus est heres quondam suprascripti Dulcis. Quiricus confitetur.

Inquisitio testium facta est VIII idus augusti (6 August 1237).

Folcus nuntius ex parte domini Ildebrandini iudicis dixit et precepit Quirico, ut hodie post commestionem sit coram eo ad publicationem testium, X kalendas novembris (23 October 1237).

Dicit Quiricus, quod Galganus debet habere partem de his,[26] de quibus petitionem facit Marsubilia. Marsubilia negat.

B

(fol. 118r) Testes Marsubilie in causa cum Quirico.

Presbiter Iuncta capellanus Sancti Sensii, iuratus XVI kalendas septembris (*17 August 1237*), dixit: Recordor, quod in proxima preterita die lune pasce resurrectionis Domini (*20 April 1237*) ivi ad domum Dulcis Sciagri, qui erat infirmus, pro penitentia ei danda et fuit mane ante missam maiorem, et recordor, quod tunc inter alia iudicia seu legata, que fecit suprascriptus Dulcis, dixit ita hec mulier, dixit de Marsubilia, que causam facit et que presens erat: 'Multo tempore servivit michi, si ego non facerem sibi bonum, facerem peccatum lassale, quod debeat habere omnes pannos meos et libras XX et godimentum domus', in qua ipse Dulcis iacebat, donec dicta Marsubilia staret ibi; et his interfuerunt Benvenutus clericus, qui tunc erat serviens domini Pauli lucani canonici, qui tunc mecum venerat, et Galganus et quidam alius, qui dicebatur nepos suprascripti Dulcis, de nomine cuius non recordor, et aliquantulum patitur in manu, et quedam mulier, que pregnans erat, cuius nomen ingnaro;[27] et dixit, quod suprascriptus Dulcis erat[28] tunc in bono sensu et de predicta infirmitate obiit apud V vel VI dies et tunc iacebat in lecto Marsubilie, quia, quando Dulcis dixit: 'Relinquo lectum meum malatis', et hic testis dixit: 'Ubi est ille[29] lectus, et de quo lecto[30] loqueris?', et Marsubilia dixit: 'Iste est meus lectus', et dicebat de lecto, in quo iacebat Dulcis in cammera, et alius erat extra. Item dixit hic testis, quod ipse dixit Dulci propter legata, que fecerat piis locis multis: 'Vis, Dulce, quod isti sint testes de his

---

25 *follows* quondam *expunged.* **26** *follows* que *expunged.* **27** *sic.* **28** erat *corrected from* erant. **29** ille *interlinear.* **30** *follows* diceris *expunged.*

omnibus', et ipse respondit 'Sic' et dixit, quod volebat mittere pro Oddo notario, sed pro sollempne festo non poterat facere moram. Interrogatus de omnibus aliis secundum formam tituli et contratituli dixit se nichil scire.

Galganus Tempagnini, iuratus XV kalendas septembris (*18 August 1237*), dixit: Recordor, quod in illis tribus vel quattuor diebus post pasca resurrectionis ⟨Domini⟩[31] ante mortem Dulcis interfui in domo Dulcis, qui iacebat infirmus in domo sua in camera, ubi ipse Dulcis sua spontanea voluntate inter alia iudicia, que fecit, iudicavit Marsubilie, dicens 'Iudico Marsubilie libras XX denariorum et omnes pannos meos mei dorsi et totam blavam, que erat[32] in domo, et etiam ligna, que erant in suprascripta domo', et dixit mihi Dulcis in illa infirmitate, quod habebat staria XVI blave in suprascripta domo inter granum et milium et segale, et vidi ligna, que erant in suprascripta domo et erant duo carra et plus et valebant solidos XII et plus, et ego darem modo inde XV. Et tempore mortis habebat Dulcis unam guarnac⟨h⟩iam vermiliam fodratam pelle[33] cuniculorum et valebat solidos XV et aliam guarnachiam novam blavettam de Mostaruolo[34] incisam et non sutam, que valebat solidos XXX et plus, et gonellam eiusdem pan⟨n⟩i sutam et valebat totidem. Item et unam gunellam[35] veterem et unum mantellum et valebant solidos VIII; et hec omnia videbam sepius et credo, quod Quiricus habuerit omnia predicta, et dictus Dulcis erat tunc in bono sensu, et fuit in die lune pasce resurrectionis mane ante missam maiorem, et interfuerunt ibi presbiter, qui modo moratur apud Sanctum Sensium, qui tunc erat capella⟨nus⟩ ecclesie Sancti Martini, qui dedit sibi penitentiam, et etiam quidam clericus, qui venit cum eo, de cuius nomine non recordor, et Bernardus filius Orlandi Belli et Maria, que moratur in vicinia quondam Dulcis, uxor Pieri, et uxor Redditi erat extra, et dicta Marsubilia erat presens in domo, quando suprascripta fuerunt, et suprascriptus Dulcis dixit nobis, qui eramus presentes: 'Sitis[36] testes, quia ego ita iudico et volo, quod Quiricus[37] // (fol. 118v) debeat[38] bene facere.'[39] Et in eodem die dictus Dulcis fecit alia legata, que fuerunt scripta manu Oddi notarii, et volo, quod obtineat, qui ius habet. Interrogatus de omnibus secundum formam tituli et contratituli dixit nichil.

Bernardus filius Orlandi Belli de Picciorano, iuratus suprascripta die (*18 August 1237*), dixit idem per omnia, quod dictus Galganus de iudicio facto Marsubilie,[40] et tanta plus, quod venit ipse cum dicto presbitero ad domum[41] dicti Dulcis, et quod ipse dixit Dulci, ut recordaret se de Marsubilia, que bene servierat ei et bene laboraverat, et quod quasi illud, quod habebat Dulcis, habebat bonitate Marsubilie. Et tanta plus dixit, quod iudicavit ei omnes massaritias[42] et habiturium domus. Et dixit de testibus, qui presentes erant, et loco et die et ⟨h⟩ora ut suprascriptus Galganus, et quod Dulcis dixit:

---

31 *follows* pant *expunged.* **32** *follows* i. **33** *ms.* pena. **34** *Montreuil*, France. **35** *sic, follows* et. **36** *follows* rebus *expunged.* **37** *follows* debeat. **38** *sic.* **39** *reading doubtful.* **40** de iudicio – Marsubilie *interlinear.* **41** ad domum *ms.* a domo. **42** *follows* et de *expunged*

'Volo, quod sitis testes de istis iudiciis.' Interrogatus de aliis, que continentur in titulo et contratitulo, dixit se nichil scire.

Mabilia uxor Redditi nuntii lucani comunis, iurata III nonis septembris (*3 September 1237*), dixit: Recordor, quod ea die, quando presbiter Iuncta dedit penitentiam dicto Dulci ‹in› infirmitate, de qua mortuus fuit, sed de mense vel die non recordor, eram in domo ipsius Dulcis extra cameram, ubi dictus Dulcis iacebat, et tunc audivi ipsum Dulcem dicentem 'Ego reli‹n›quo Marsubilie domum et omnes massaritias, donec vixerit Marsubilia, et omnes pannos meos et libras XX', et dictus Dulcis habebat tempore mortis unam guarnachiam vermiliam et aliam guarnac‹h›iam blavettam non sutam et unam clamidem albaseum, et que omnia habuit Quiricus et etiam res alias scilicet cultram et res alias, quas nescit nominare; et hoc credo, quod Quiricus habuerit ea et res, quia guarnachiam Dulcis vidit post mortem D‹ulc›is in dorso uxoris Quirici et clamidem ad collum ipsius Quirici; et quando dictus Dulcis fecit iudicium, era‹n›t ibi Galganus et Bernardus, ut mihi videtur, et dictus presbiter et quidam clericus, de cuius nomine non recordor. Interrogatus de aliis omnibus secundum formam tituli et contratituli et valere rerum dixit se nichi‹l› scire.

Maria uxor quondam Alberti Galletti, iurata suprascripta die (*3 September 1237*), dixit: Recordor, quod ea die, qua Dulcis recepit penitentiam ‹in› infirmitate, de qua obiit, eram iuxta hostium camere, in qua iacebat Dulcis, et tunc dictus Dulcis iudicavit Marsubilie domum et stivilias, donec viveret Marsubilia, et omnes pannos sui dorsi et totam blavam, quam habebat in domo, et ligna, que habebat in domo, sed de die vel mense non recordor, et in dicta camera[43] erant tunc Galganus, Bernardus et presbiter, qui dedit penitentiam ei et qui vocatur, ut mihi videtur, presbiter Iuncta, sed cuius modi pannos vel quantam blavam vel ligna haberet, nescio. Interrogata de omnibus aliis secundum formam tituli et contratituli dixit se nichil scire plus.

Donetta, iurata suprascripta die (*3 September 1237*), dixit: Recordor, quod post mortem Dulcis apud VIII dies vel circa Quiricus dedit mihi ad portandum ad domum suam, ubi moratur, in domo, que fuit quondam Dulcis, duo staria grani, quod erat in quodam sacco, et duo staria milii alia vice in continenti et duo ‹staria› segalis, et quod milium et segale extraxit de arca, que erat in domo suprascripti Dulcis. Item portavi de dicta domo ad domum Quirici tot ligna[44] mala[45] in VI vicibus, que valuerunt denarios VI. Item pro parte Quirici dixit: Recordor, quod, iam sunt XV ‹anni› vel circa, quod vidi dictam Marsubiliam anulum deferentem, quia dicebat, quod Deotisalvi peliparius acceperat eam in uxorem, sed ego non interfui desponsationi, et portavit anulum bene per XIII dies, et recordor, quod iusta domum Bonvillani Dulcis dixit in illis diebus Marsubilie, quod incideret sibi nasum, nisi proiceret. Et Marsubilia dixit: 'Ex quo tu abstulisti mihi virum et honorem, ego reddam ei'. Et alii ibi interfuerunt, de quorum nominibus non recordor pre‹ter› de

---

43 ms. *camerar*.   **44** *follows* que val *expunged*.   **45** *load*.

quondam Bonvillano, et antequam me separarem[46] [a] suprascripta Marsubilia, venit suprascriptus Deotisalvi et recepit anulum a suprascripta Marsubilia, et Dulcis recesserat. De aliis omnibus interrogata secundum titulum et contratitulum dixit se nescire plus.

Lectus est unus pro omnibus.

C

(fol. 120v) Testes Quirici in causa cum Marsubilia.

Iohannes quondam Arrigi del Piano calthorarius,[47] iuratus XI kalendas septembris (*22 August 1237*), dixit: Sto iuxta clavicam[48] Sancti Georgii et recordor, quod iam sunt XX anni[49] et plus satis, quod ego utebar cum Deotisalvi pellipario prenominato[50] Inbrattaferro, qui habuit pro uxore filiam Ubaldi Gonelle, et eo tempore, quo utebar cum eo, dixit mihi, quod anulaverat Marsubiliam, quam bene congnosco, que consuevit morari in Classo Segrominensi, et dixit mihi, qui minabatur a quodam, qui tenebat eam, sed quis esset vel quo nomine vocaretur, nescio, et quidam noster socius, qui vocatur Bonfiliolus similiter mihi dixit, quod Deotisalvi acceperat illam Marsubiliam in uxorem, et pluries dixerunt mihi in civitate et in pluribus locis, sed coram quibus non recordor nec ego interfui alicui desponsationi facte de ea, et ego predictum classum Segrominensem veni cum eodem Deotisalvi et Bonfiliolo pluries, quia Deotisalvi ducebat nos et volebat loqui cum suprascripta Marsubilia,[51] quandoque fuit locutus[52] cum ea, sed quod ei diceret, nescio. De aliis interrogatus secundum tituli et contratituli dixit se nichil scire

Benetta uxor quondam Iuncte magistri, iurata suprascripta die (*22 August 1237*), dixit: Audivi, iam sunt XII vel XIII anni, cum essem infirma in lecto cum viro meo, et habitabam[53] in curia Fralminga, quod Dulcis expellebat per contradam Classi Segrominensis Deotisalvi, qui fuit gener Ubaldi Gonelle, quem Deotisalvi audivi, quod ceperat in uxorem Marsubiliam et quod eam volebat, et quod Dulcis ideo expellebat eum, quod eam volebat, sed non congnovi homines, qui hec dicebant, quia ego eram in lecto et illi homines ibant[54] per curiam. De aliis interrogata secundum titulum et contratitulum dixit se nichil scire.

Albertinus peliciarius, iuratus XI kalendas septembris (*22 August 1237*), dixit: Iam sunt XVIII anni et plus, quod audivi, quod Deotisalvi Inbrattaferri, qui moratur in domo quondam Orlandini Berlescie, ac‹c›eperat in uxorem Marsubiliam, que[55] morabatur cum Dulce, sed a quibus audivi et ubi, non

---

46 *following word illegible.* **47** calthorarius *with signs for place of insertion after* septembris. **48** *small channel.* **49** ms. *annis.* **50** ms. *prenominatus.* **51** *follows* et. **52** *corrected from* locuta. **53** *corrected from* habitambam. **54** ms. Inbant. **55** *corrected from* qui

recordor, et audivi a Bonasengna de Cerreto eo tempore, quo accepit dictus[56] Deotisalvi filiam Ubaldi Gonelle in uxorem, quod idem Deotisalvi coram episcopo Ruberto[57] receperat sententiam separationis seu divortii a dicta Marsubilia, et etiam mihi dictus Deotisalvi dixit idem: 'Quia nolebam', quod haberet dictam filiam Ubaldi, et nullus alius interfuit, quando dixit mihi Deotisalvi nisi Bonansegna, et non recordor, ubi hec mihi dixerit. De omnibus aliis interrogatus dixit se nichil scire.

Mardora[58] uxor Lanfranchi, iurata suprascripta die (*22 August 1237*) dixit interrogata secundum formam tituli[59] se nichil scire.

(fol. 121r) Ricca mulier, iurata pridie idus septembris (*12 September 1237*) dixit: Steti cum Quirico annis X[60] ad serviendum sibi et, quod non steti, sunt anni XVI, et tunc audivi, quod Deotisalvi ceperat in uxorem Marsobiliam, que causam facit, et eam anulaverat,[61] ut audivi, sed anulationi vel desponsationi non interfui, sed postquam Dulcis scivit, fecit dictum Deotisalvi iurare, quod non repeteret eam ex tunc in antea pro sua uxore, et anulum extraxit sibi dicta Marsubilia de digito et proiecit eum post ipsum precepto Dulcis[62], et etiam iuravit non transire per contradam Dulcis, videlicet ante domum suam ab inde in antea, et hoc fuit apud domum quondam Bonvillani vinacterii me presente, et eam vidi verberari a Dulce ob hoc,[63] et minatus fuit eundem Deotisalvi dictus Dulcis. Et non odio, non amore, non prece, non pretio.

Bo⟨n⟩filiolus custor quondam Martini, iuratus XIIII kalendas octubris (*18 September 1237*), dixit interrogatus, si scit Marsubiliam esse uxorem Dolcis, dixit, quod non, nisi quod audivit, quod erat eius uxor, et audivit a Maria fusaiola[64] et Verde. De proiectione anuli, que in titulo continetur, dixit se nichil scire. Item dixit, quod minatus fuit ipsum Deotisalvi dictus Dulcis in Classo Segrominensi, dicendo: 'Non sis ausus transire per istam oram, quia vis mihi auferre amicam meam', et sic recessimus, sed, quod fecisset ipsum Deotisalvi iurare, nescio, sicut in titulo continetur. De allis nichil.

Mabilia uxor Redditi, reversa XII kalendas novembris (*21 October 1237*) ad testationem red⟨d⟩e⟨n⟩dam pro Quirico, interrogata secundum formam tituli suprascripti Quirichi dixit se nichil scire et de facto Galgani interrogata similiter dixit se nichil scire.

Maria testis uxor quondam Alberti reversa suprascripta die (*21 October 1237*) ad testationem red⟨d⟩endam pro Quirico, interrogata dixit: Quod audivit, quod Marsubilia post mortem Dulcis vendidit fabas, sed nescio quantas vel cui, et hoc audivi in vicinia a vicinis, et etiam dicta Marsubilia dixit me audiente, quod vendiderat fabas, sed non dixit de quantitate vel cui. De aliis interrogata secundum formam tituli dixit se nichil scire.

---

56 *follows* filius *expunged.*   57 † *21 September 1225,* cf. Raffaele Savigni, *Episcopato e società cittadina a Lucca da Anselmo II († 1085) a Roberto († 1225)* (Lucca, 1996), p. 409. 58 *follows* relicta *expunged.*   59 *follows* dixit.   60 *follows* iam *expunged.*   61 *corrected from* anulaverant.   62 precepto Dulcis *interlinear.*   63 et eam – ob hoc *interlinear.*   64 *woman who spins*

Adalansea mater Marie testis suprascripte, iurata suprascripta die (*21 October 1237*), dixit: Scio, quod Marsubilia post mortem Dulcis vendidit fabas[65] cuidam lograiolo[66], sed de nomine non recordor, sed quantas nescio. De aliis nichil.

(fol. 121v) Bonagrathia, iuratus suprascripta die (*21 October 1237*), dixit: Recordor, quod post inceptionem huius cause ivi ad apothecam Orlandi peliciarii, in qua laborabat Deotisalvi, sed non studiose et tra‹n›seundo, cum vidi ipsum, dixi[67]: 'Ei, Deotisalvi malaguarto[68], quare mittis te in istis verbis, vis tu filios tuos facere adulterinos? Tu habes uxorem de magno hospitio', sed non specificavi, de quo dicerem, et ipse respondit: 'Frater, vade in bona hora, nescio, quid dicas, nec videtur mihi, quod sis sapiens vel cortese.' De facto Galgani dixit se nichil scire. De aliis nichil.

Lectus est unus pro omnibus.

D

Statutus est terminus ad dicendum supradictis et personis testium[69] proxima[70] die veneris mane et de hinc ad dictum terminum ap‹p›ortent prima solidos XXV pro unaquaque parte.

Statutus fuit terminus suprascripto Quirico per nuntium die martis mane ad sententiam peremptoriam, VI kalendas novembris (*27 October 1237*).

E

Quas lites[71] diligenter examinatas atque discussas, visis quoque petitionibus, responsionibus, allegationibus utriusque partis et testibus in causa productis diligenter inspectis, habita quoque diligenti deliberatione, in Dei nomine amen, ego Ildebrandinus Malagalie iudex arbiter et laudator et amicabilis compositor a partibus electus taliter per laudamentum et arbitrium et amicabilem compositionem diffinio videlicet suprascriptum Quiricum, ut de hinc ad IIII proximos mense‹s› det et solvat suprascripte Marsubilie libras XX, condepmno. Item et, ut de hinc ad unum proximum mensem det et restituat suprascripte Marsubilie staria duo grani et staria IIII milii et staria II segalis, similiter condempno suprascriptum Quiricum. Item et, ut det et restituat suprascripte Marsubilie ligna, que dictus Dulcis reliquid tempore mortis et que valeant solidos VIII, de hinc ad tres dies[72], similiter dictum Quiricum

---

65 *follows* seu de *expunged.* **66** *trader.* **67** *corrected from* dixim. **68** Cf. Carlo Battisti & Giovanni Alessio, *Dizionario etimologico italiano* 3 (Firenze, 1952), 3, 2324: *malagurato = unhappy.* **69** *follows* de hinc ad *expunged.* **70** *corrected from* proximam. **71** quas lites *corrected from* quam litem. **72** de hinc – dies *interlinear*

condempno[73]. Et dat⟨i⟩um solvant per medium. Et notario solva⟨n⟩t pro quoli-
bet solidos VI denariorum lucanorum. Actum Luce iusta ecclesiam Sancti
Martini, coram Arrigo Sexmondi et Rugerio iud⟨icibus⟩ et Usacco Beraldelli,
MCCXXXVII, VI kalendas novembris, indictione X (*27 October 1237*).[74]

(S. N.) Ciabattus iudex et notarius hec scripsi.

---

73 *follows, cancelled by a wavy line,* Item et, ut de hinc ad unum proximum mensem reddat
et restituat suprascripte Marsubilie unam guarnachiam vermiliam, quam Dulcis Dulcis (!)
reliquid tempore mortis, similiter condempno.   **74** *on the left margin at the level of the subscription* FCC Mar

Debito pubblico e fiere di Champagne: un inedito documento lucchese di fine Duecento

IGNAZIO DEL PUNTA

A hitherto unpublished document in the Fondo Diplomatico of the Archivio di Stato di Lucca sheds new light on the relationship between the merchant-banks of Lucca and the Commune. This document, currently listed as of the fourteenth century, but which internal evidence clearly shows is thirteenth century, shows how prestigious banking companies such as those of the Battosi and Ricciardi requested repayment of their loans to the Commune at the fair of Provins St Ayoul, thus benefiting from a profitable rate of exchange. The document shows how Lucchese companies were working in financial activities in north-western Europe from the 1280s, and that the fairs of Champagne were in fact used as a favourable site for the repayment of loans contracted by the Commune. The value of this source is in the way it demonstrates the level of complexity in the public finance and fiscal systems of Lucca by the late thirteenth century.

Tra le pergamene del Diplomatico dell'Archivio di Stato di Lucca si conserva un documento di estremo interesse per la storia della fiscalità in età comunale e, più in generale, per la storia economica delle città italiane, in particolare per quanto concerne le compagnie mercantili-bancarie, i commerci a lunga distanza e le attività finanziarie. Questo documento è non solo inedito, ma del tutto ignoto agli studiosi che finora si sono occupati della storia di Lucca nel Basso Medioevo. Io stesso non l'ho mai menzionato nel mio libro 'Mercanti e banchieri lucchesi nel Duecento', che pur riguarda specificamente la storia commerciale di Lucca di quel periodo.[1] Il documento è tanto più interessante perchè attesta direttamente una pratica che – almeno a mia conoscenza – non è certificata per altre città che pure intrattenevano intensissimi rapporti commerciali e finanziari con le fiere di Champagne.[2] Non che si debba perciò

---

1 I. Del Punta, *Mercanti e banchieri lucchesi nel Duecento* (Pisa, 2004). 2 Per Siena si veda: W.M. Bowsky, *The finance of the commune of Siena, 1287–1355* (Oxford, 1970); *idem, A medieval Italian commune: Siena under the Nine, 1287–1355* (Berkeley, 1981); *Banchieri e mercanti di Siena*, a cura di C.M. Cipolla (Roma, 1987), in particolare i saggi di Michele Cassandro, 'La banca senese nei secoli XIII e XIV', pp 107–60; e di Marco Tangheroni, 'Siena e il commercio internazionale nel Duecento e nel Trecento', pp 21–105. Per Firenze: R.A. Goldthwaite, *The economy of Renaissance Florence* (Baltimore, 2009); A. Sapori, *Studi di Storia Economica 3 (Secoli XIII–XIV–XV)* (Firenze, Sansoni, 1955–67), passim. Per Piacenza: P. Racine, 'L'expansion commerciale de Plaisance au Moyen Age', in *Corpus Statutorum Mercatorum Placentie*, a cura di P. Racine e P. Castignoli (Milano, 1967), pp liii–lxxxviii; *idem*, 'I banchieri piacentini ed i cambi sulle fiere di Champagne alla

inferire dall'assenza di fonti che solo a Lucca avvenissero certe transazioni finanziarie tra il Comune e le compagnie mercantili-bancarie, chè anzi è del tutto probabile che anche a Piacenza, Siena, Firenze e altre città italiane operazioni del tipo documentato a Lucca fossero comunemente praticate.[3] L'assenza di testimonianze analoghe altrove è da imputare semplicemente, a mio parere, alla casualità con cui il patrimonio documentario medievale si è conservato negli archivi di ciascuna città.[4] Tuttavia, il fatto che solo la pergamena lucchese sia rimasta ad illustrare questo genere di operazioni finanziarie nel Duecento dà senz'altro ad essa un valore particolare.

E veniamo quindi al documento in questione. Si tratta di una pergamena, un bifolio, privo di data per quanto riguarda l'anno, mentre disponiamo del giorno e del mese: 18 agosto. La pergamena è conservata nel fondo 'Disperse' del Diplomatico sotto la data '18–08– sec. XIV'.[5] L'ultima indicazione è senz'altro sbagliata, perchè da elementi interni si può datare il documento senza tema d'errore alla seconda metà del Duecento, più precisamente in tutta probabilità agli anni 1280. Infatti, le compagnie mercantili-bancarie citate nella pergamena erano tutte attive nella seconda metà del XIII secolo e all'apice degli affari negli anni 1280, mentre alcune di esse erano già in grave crisi, se non praticamente fallite, nel decennio seguente. Mentre nel Trecento le stesse compagnie non erano più operanti sui mercati, se non sotto ragioni sociali differenti e sotto il 'management' di altri soci, parenti più o meno stretti dei precedenti mercanti-banchieri titolari delle compagnie nominate nella pergamena.

Il documento è un atto di natura pubblica e fu rogato da Leonardo di Ruggerone, notaio e cancelliere del Comune di Lucca. Il contenuto è relativo

---

fine del Duecento', in *Studi storici in onore di Emilio Nasalli Rocca* (Piacenza, 1971), pp 475–505; *idem, Storia della banca a Piacenza dal Medioevo ai nostri giorni* (Piacenza, 1974). 3 Per le pratiche fiscali e la gestione del debito pubblico nelle città italiane del Duecento e della prima metà del Trecento: M. Ginatempo, *Prima del debito. Finanziamento della spesa pubblica e gestione del deficit nelle grandi città toscane (c.1200–1350)* (Firenze, 2000). Per le città dell'Italia settentrionale cfr. il volume a cura di Patrizia Mainoni: *Politiche finanziarie e fiscali nell'Italia settentrionale (secoli XIII–XV)* (Milano, 2001). Per Milano si veda in particolare P. Grillo, 'L'introduzione dell'estimo e la politica fiscale del comune di Milano alla metà del secolo XIII (1240–1260)', in *Politiche finanziarie e fiscali*, pp 11–37; *idem, Milano in età comunale (1183–1276). Istituzioni, società, economia* (Spoleto, 2001), pp 522–35. Per Lucca gli unici studi riguardanti la fiscalità sono relativi al Trecento, in particolare al periodo del dominio pisano: C. Meek, *The Commune of Lucca under Pisan rule, 1342–1369* (Cambridge, 1980), pp 63–85; C. Meek, 'Public policy and private profit: tax farming in fourteenth-century Lucca', in *'The other Tuscany': essays in the history of Lucca, Pisa and Siena during the thirteenth, fourteenth and fifteenth centuries*, ed. T.W. Blomquist & M.F. Mazzaoui (Kalamazoo, MI, 1994), pp 41–82; C. Meek, 'Finanze comunali e finanze locali nel quattordicesimo secolo: l'esempio di Montecarlo', in *Castelli e borghi della Toscana tardomedievale* (Pescia, 1998), pp 141–51. Cfr. anche Ginatempo, *Prima del debito*.   4 La documentazione di natura commerciale resta, però, in parte ancora inesplorata negli archivi delle città italiane e dunque non si può escludere che in futuro altri studiosi possano trovare fra le pergamene del Diplomatico o fra le carte notarili documenti simili a quello lucchese.   5 ASL, Diplomatico, *Disperse*, 18–08–sec. XIV.

ad un prestito pubblico contratto dal Comune presso alcune compagnie mercantili-bancarie lucchesi per importi successivamente rimborsati dal Comune a rappresentanti delle stesse compagnie alle fiere di Champagne. Di fatto il documento è composto da due parti: la prima, che è anche la più lunga, contiene tutti i dettagli relativi al prestito contratto dal Comune tramite i suoi rappresentanti: Coscione, 'preco Lucani comunis et sindicus ad hec infrascripta facienda constitutus', e il notaio-cancelliere Leonardo di Ruggerone. Mancano purtroppo le ultime righe di questa prima parte, la pergamena essendo mutila alla fine. Ecco perchè non disponiamo della data esatta e neppure della *datatio loci*. La seconda parte è un'appendice della prima e contiene il testo dell'accordo stipulato fra le autorità comunali e le compagnie per il rimborso delle somme prestate con l'indicazione dei proventi da utilizzare per tale rimborso.

La prima società ad essere nominata nel documento è quella dei Battosi, rappresentata da Custore Battosi, che agiva a nome dei suoi fratelli e degli altri soci. A quel tempo Custore era il direttore della compagnia, che aveva grossi interessi e un vasto giro di affari in Italia meridionale, a Roma, a Genova e presso le fiere di Champagne.[6] La società Battosi aveva versato al Comune 2000 lire lucchesi in denari piccoli di moneta locale. Da questa somma il Comune procedeva quindi a detrarre una contribuzione fiscale pari a 12 denari per lira, ovvero al 5% dell'imponibile calcolato per i Battosi in base alle loro ricchezze. Tale contribuzione si rendeva necessaria per il finanziamento dell'esercito comunale che si stava preparando per un'*oste*, per una spedizione militare.[7] Il contributo che i Battosi dovevano pagare ammontava complessivamente a 469 lire e 1 soldo. Detraendo tale somma dalle 2000 lire che i Battosi avevano precedentemente dato in prestito al Comune, quest'ultimo risultava debitore nei confronti della compagnia di 1530 lire e 19 soldi in denari piccoli. Nel documento si specifica poi che tale somma sarebbe stata pagata in fiorini d'oro, più precisamente 712 fiorini più un aquilino d'argento, equivalenti a 1370 lire, 14 soldi, 8 denari di buona moneta ('ad bonam monetam') secondo un tasso di cambio di 38 soldi e 6 denari per ciascun fiorino d'oro.[8] La somma totale dovuta dal Comune ai Battosi (ovvero 1530 lire

---

6 Sulla società Battosi si veda Del Punta, *Mercanti e banchieri lucchesi*, pp 217–65. 7 '... occasione presentis futuri exercitus'. Un resoconto generale su questo tipo di finanziamento delle spedizioni militari nel mondo comunale tramite imposte *ad hoc* è disponibile in Ginatempo, *Prima del debito* e P. Jones, *The Italian city-state: from commune to signoria* (Oxford, 1997), pp 396–8. 8 Questo tasso di cambio di 1 fiorino d'oro = 38 soldi 6 denari lucchesi in buona moneta, è attestato a Genova nel 1287 e ancora nel 1291. Cfr. P. Spufford, *Handbook of medieval exchange* (London, 1986), p. 40. S'intende che la moneta lucchese oggetto del cambio era 'nuova moneta', ovvero quella che aveva subìto nel corso della seconda metà del Duecento una svalutazione importante rispetto alla 'vecchia moneta', che aveva un contenuto di fino considerevolmente maggiore. Per intenderci, il tasso di cambio tra fiorini d'oro e 'vecchia moneta' lucchese era: 1 fiorino = 20 soldi. La differenza messa in evidenza continuamente nel documento oggetto di questo articolo non

e 19 soldi di denari piccoli) era quindi convertita in denari di Tours, i cosid-
detti tornesi (*turonenses*), di valore equivalente ai denari di Provins o provesini.
Il tasso di cambio applicato in questo caso era il seguente: 44 denari lucchesi
di buona moneta per ciascun soldo di tornesi. A questo tasso la somma dovuta
dal Comune alla società Battosi ammontava a 373 lire e 18 soldi di tornesi,
che i rappresentanti delle autorità comunali avrebbero versato a Custore
Battosi in persona o ai suoi soci alla prossima fiera di Provins St Ayoul,
'seguendo le abituali procedure di pagamento usate dai mercanti lucchesi presenti alle fiere oltremontane'.[9]

Inoltre Custore Battosi aveva agito anche come procuratore per un consorzio formato da alcuni mercanti-banchieri, per conto dei quali aveva prestato
al Comune la somma di 834 lire e 10 soldi di denari lucchesi piccoli. I
banchieri rappresentati per l'occasione da Custore Battosi erano: *dominus*
Forteguerra di Arrighetto, *dominus* Aliotto de Rocca, *dominus* Guglielmo
Malaspina, *dominus* Giovanni Oddi, Tore di *dominus* Ubaldo, Iacopo
Normannini e Nicolò di Pontadore Notti. Gli stessi dovevano al fisco comunale un contributo di 87 lire e 19 soldi in moneta piccola per il finanziamento
dell'esercito cittadino, contributo equivalente al 5% dell'imponibile.
Sottraendo quest'ultima somma dal prestito che i banchieri rappresentati dal
Battosi avevano fatto al Comune, il loro credito residuo risultava essere di 746
lire e 11 soldi di denari lucchesi piccoli ('parve monete'). In pratica, la somma
era stata pagata con 346 fiorini d'oro e 4 guelfi grossi, equivalenti a 668 lire,
8 soldi e 6 denari in buona moneta lucchese. A sua volta tale somma era
equivalente a 182 lire e 7 soldi di denari tornesi, secondo il tasso di cambio
applicato in questo e in tutti gli altri prestiti di 44 denari lucchesi di buona

era dunque tra 'vecchia' e 'nuova moneta', ma solo – all'interno della nuova moneta – tra
denari piccoli (o moneta piccola) e denari 'buoni' (o 'buona moneta') ovvero denari che non
avevano subito un'ulteriore svalutazione rispetto alla nuova moneta.   9 '... secundum
modum et consuetudinem solutionum que fiunt per mercatores civitatis lucane. com-
morantes in feris ultramontanis'. La fiera di St Ayoul era la seconda fiera, quella autun-
nale, che si teneva a Provins nell'arco dell'anno. Iniziava il 14 settembre, giorno dell'e-
saltazione della Croce, una ricorrenza religiosa particolarmente importante per la comunità
lucchese, dal momento che la festa principale a Lucca era ed è ancor oggi appunto quella
di Santa Croce, in onore del Volto Santo. L'altra fiera di Provins era la cosiddetta 'Provins
di maggio', che si teneva nei mesi di maggio-giugno. Le fiere in totale erano sei ogni anno:
la fiera di Lagny sur Marne cominciava il 2 gennaio e terminava a fine febbraio, seguita in
marzo dalla fiera di Bar sur Aube; quindi vi era la prima fiera di Provins, poi la 'Troyes
San Giovanni', che apriva i battenti quindici giorni dopo la festa di San Giovanni (24
giugno); a metà settembre toccava alla 'Provins St Ayoul' e infine alla fiera di 'Tresetto' o
'fiera fredda' o 'Troyes St Remy', che aveva luogo nel borgo di St Remy, adiacente alla
città di Troyes nei mesi di novembre e dicembre. Ogni fiera durava in media circa sette
settimane. Cfr. T.W. Blomquist, 'Some observations on early foreign exchange banking
based upon new evidence from XIIIth–century Lucca', in *Journal of European Economic
History* 19:2 (1990), 353–75: 364 n. 31; F. Bourquelot, *Études sur les foires de Champagne*,
in *Mémoires présentées par divers savants à l'Academie des Inscriptions et Belles-Lettres*, 2
(Paris, 1865–6).

moneta per ciascun soldo di tornesi. Tale cifra sarebbe stata versata da procuratori del Comune a Custore Battosi nella prossima fiera di Provins St Ayoul.

Va subito detto che apparentemente le cifre non tornano. Innanzitutto il lettore meno esperto in questioni monetarie potrà rimanere disorientato dal fatto che in questo come in tutti gli altri prestiti elencati nel documento si riportano due cifre diverse in moneta lucchese per l'ammontare del debito residuo che il Comune deve pagare alle fiere di Champagne. Ad esempio, prendiamo il primo prestito contratto dal Comune con la società Battosi: si parla di un debito residuo di 1530 lire e 19 soldi di denari lucchesi piccoli. Quindi si fa riferimento a 712 fiorini d'oro e 1 aquilino, che sono le monete con cui di fatto è stato pagato il prestito: questa somma è pari alle 1530 lire e ai 19 soldi di cui sopra.[10] Infine, si dice che tale somma in fiorini è equivalente a 1370 lire, 14 soldi e 9 denari in buona moneta. A questo punto lo stesso debito è rappresentato da due somme, entrambe in lire lucchesi: 1530 lire e 19 soldi e 1370 lire, 14 soldi e 9 denari. La chiave di volta per capire questa differenza e per capire invero tutti i prestiti riportati nel documento sta nella distinzione tra somme in 'denari piccoli' o 'moneta piccola', da un lato, e somme 'in buona moneta', dall'altro. I denari piccoli erano naturalmente di minor valore rispetto alla 'buona moneta', rispetto a denari meno svalutati, ovvero con maggiori percentuali di fino, di argento. Chiaramente la stessa somma calcolata nei due tipi di moneta, nei denari lucchesi piccoli e nei denari lucchesi 'buoni' (con maggior intrinseco) è espressa da valori diversi. Anzi, proprio l'equivalenza tra le due cifre menzionate in tutti i casi di prestito citati nel documento ci dà il rapporto, il tasso di cambio corrente in quel periodo tra denari lucchesi piccoli e denari lucchesi 'buoni'. Riepilogando, dunque, per ogni prestito innanzitutto si dà la cifra in lire tornesi che il procuratore del Comune avrebbe versato alla società creditrice alla fiera di Provins St Ayoul, cifra pari al debito residuo del Comune, quindi si dichiara la stessa somma calcolata in denari lucchesi piccoli, poi si fa riferimento alla somma equivalente in fiorini d'oro e eventuali altre monete correnti con cui di fatto il prestito era stato effettuato, successivamente si indica il valore di questa somma in buona moneta lucchese, precisando il tasso di cambio tra fiorini d'oro e buona moneta lucchese (sempre 1 fiorino d'oro = 38 soldi e 6 denari), infine si fa riferimento alla somma dichiarata all'inizio in lire tornesi, precisando la sua equivalenza alle somme citate precedentemente

---

10 La formula con cui s'introduce questa equivalenza in fiorini d'oro o in altre monete utilizzate dai mercanti-banchieri per i pagamenti di cifre consistenti è 'in qua summa intrant ... 'È una formula di fatto un po' ambigua, che può dare adito a fraintendimenti e far credere che la cifra enumerata in fiorini o altre monete sia solo una parte della somma dichiarata prima in lire lucchesi, ma in realtà dal seguito si capisce chiaramente che si tratta di un modo per introdurre l'equivalenza tra una cifra calcolata in moneta di conto (le lire e i soldi lucchesi) e la stessa somma calcolata nelle monete concretamente usate per pagamenti di questo tipo (fiorini d'oro, aquilini, grossi d'argento).

sulla base di un altro preciso tasso di cambio (sempre 1 soldo di tornesi = 44 denari lucchesi in buona moneta). I conti tornano tutti, con alcune piccolissime, ininfluenti discrepanze, dovute probabilmente ad aggiustamenti forfeittari che i finanzieri della Camera comunale adottavano e in parte forse anche al valore esatto di alcune monete incluse nei pagamenti insieme ai fiorini d'oro, valore che ci sfugge: ad esempio gli aquilini e i grossi guelfi. Per maggiore chiarezza ho incluso al termine dell'articolo una breve appendice che riassume tutte le equivalenze relative a ciascun prestito.

Ma vi è un aspetto forse ancora più interessante ed è il fatto che dalla quota versata da ciascuna compagnia nelle casse comunali per il 'datum', per la tassa diretta e proporzionale che serviva a finanziare l'esercito comunale, si può ricavare l'imponibile fissato nell'estimo per le compagnie citate nel documento. Nel testo si afferma che la tassa era pagata in ragione del 5% dell'imponibile. Vale a dire che se la società Battosi, ad esempio, pagava 469 lire e 1 soldo, come si afferma nel testo, il suo imponibile nell'estimo era fissato a 9381 lire, evidentemente solo una frazione della ricchezza mobile di cui la compagnia poteva disporre.[11] Per maggior comodità, ho allegato all'appendice un elenco degli imponibili calcolati per ogni società.

La seconda compagnia ad essere annoverata nella pergamena fra i creditori del Comune è quella dei Ricciardi, rappresentati da Adiuto Rosciompelli, che agiva per conto di Paganuccio Guidiccioni, Giovanni Sismondi, Labro Volpelli e altri soci della compagnia.[12] I Ricciardi avevano dato in prestito al Comune ben 6000 lire in moneta lucchese, esattamente il triplo della cifra prestata dai Battosi, il che riflette la differente disponibilità di capitali liquidi tra le due compagnie e, più in generale, le diverse dimensioni delle stesse.[13] In cambio del denaro prestato, il cancelliere comunale aveva promesso di pagare alla società Ricciardi 1200 lire, 14 soldi e 3 denari in buoni denari 'forti' di Tours.[14] Anche in tal caso una certa somma doveva essere detratta dal debito del Comune, somma pari al contributo che i Ricciardi dovevano versare nelle casse comunali per finanziare l'esercito che si accingeva appunto a partire per una campagna militare. Il contributo dovuto dalla società Ricciardi era di 1084 lire e 6 denari lucchesi in piccola moneta. Il debito

---

11 Le cifre sono da intendere in denari lucchesi piccoli. Anche se non è esplicitamente detto nel testo, è sottinteso dal fatto che si sottrae quindi il contributo per il 'datum' dal credito dei Battosi verso il Comune, pari a 2,000 lire di denari lucchesi piccoli. La somma residua è di 1,530 lire e 19 soldi di denari lucchesi piccoli.   12 Per il personale della società Ricciardi e le famiglie presenti nel *board* direttivo cfr. I. Del Punta, 'Capitalismo' familiare. Un esempio dalla Lucca del tardo Medioevo', *Actum Luce*, 35:2 (2006), 83–127. Ad effettuare il prestito a nome della società era stato Paganuccio Guidiccioni, direttore della stessa.   13 Per la storia della società Ricciardi: R.W. Kaeuper, *Bankers to the crown: the Riccardi of Lucca and Edward I* (Princeton, 1973); Del Punta, *Mercanti e banchieri lucchesi*, pp 141–215. Cfr. anche *Lettere dei Ricciardi di Lucca ai loro compagni in Inghilterra (1295–1303)*, a cura di A. Castellani – I. Del Punta (Roma, 2005).   14 'Mille et ducentas libras et XIIIIcim soldos et tres denarios bonorum denariorum turonensium fortium de Francia'.

residuo del Comune nei confronti della compagnia ammontava dunque a 4400 lire, 10 soldi e 6 denari, che, convertiti in moneta di Tours, davano la suddetta somma di 1200 lire, 14 soldi e 3 denari, che i Ricciardi avrebbero incassato anch'essi alla prossima fiera di Provins St Ayoul.

Inoltre Adiuto Rosciompelli aveva prestato a titolo personale al Comune altre 4997 lire e 14 soldi di denari lucchesi in moneta piccola. Questa somma era stata pagata di fatto con 2324 fiorini d'oro e ½, equivalenti a 4474 lire, 13 soldi e 6 denari lucchesi in buona moneta.[15] Applicando il consueto tasso di cambio di 44 denari lucchesi in buona moneta per soldo di tornesi, tale cifra era pari a 1220 lire e 13 soldi di tornesi, che le autorità comunali avrebbero pagato ad Adiuto Rosciompelli in Champagne alla fiera di Provins St Ayoul.

Infine, Adiuto doveva riscuotere un terzo credito in Champagne per un altro prestito fatto al Comune per conto di alcuni colleghi: Orlando Malaprese, Guicciardino di Giovanni, Coluccio Volpelli e *dominus* Cione d'Arco, a nome dei quali Adiuto aveva prestato al Comune 358 lire e 3 soldi di denari lucchesi in buona moneta. In pratica il prestito era stato effettuato con 186 fiorini d'oro e 2 soldi di denari piccoli, pari a 97 lire e 14 soldi di tornesi, che i procuratori del Comune avrebbero versato ad Adiuto alla prossima fiera di Provins St Ayoul insieme agli altri crediti, secondo i soliti tassi di cambio di 1 fiorino d'oro per 38 soldi e 6 denari lucchesi di buona moneta e 1 soldo di tornesi per 44 denari lucchesi di buona moneta.

Il debito successivo riguardava la compagnia di Ughetto Onesti, rappresentata in questa circostanza alla stessa fiera di Provins St Ayoul da Custore Battosi e Adiuto Rosciompelli, ovvero dalle compagnie Battosi e Ricciardi. Chiaramente in tal caso le società lucchesi coinvolte in questo prestito straordinario al Comune agivano come una sorta di consorzio di creditori. Era pratica comune, del resto, fra le compagnie mercantili-bancarie di una stessa città, e anche di città diverse, collaborare e aiutarsi reciprocamente in alcune circostanza, sempre che, naturalmente, esse fossero in buoni rapporti fra di loro. La somma data in prestito da Ughetto Onesti al Comune era più modesta delle precedenti: 502 lire e 10 soldi in denari piccoli di Lucca.[16] In cambio il cancelliere comunale s'impegnava a versare alla compagnia 122 lire, 14 soldi

15 Secondo il tasso di cambio applicato in tutti i casi relativi a questa operazione, ovvero 1 fiorino d'oro = 38 soldi e 6 denari lucchesi in buona moneta, la somma esatta risultante dai calcoli è di 4,474 lire, 13 soldi e 6 denari. La differenza con la cifra dichiarata nel documento è dunque di appena 3 denari. 16 La società di Ughetto Onesti era senz'altro di dimensioni assai più piccole rispetto a quella dei Ricciardi e dei Battosi, ma non in senso assoluto. Nel 1283 la compagnia Onesti compare in Inghilterra fra i depositari della decima per la Terrasanta a fianco di numerose altre compagnie italiane: fiorentine, lucchesi, senesi, pistoiesi e piacentine. Gli Onesti avevano nelle loro casse £372 2s. 8d. dei proventi della decima. Cfr. Del Punta, *Mercanti e banchieri lucchesi*, p. 154. Nonostante la cifra sia piccola rispetto ai depositi delle altre compagnie, il fatto che gli Onesti fossero tra le banche presenti in Inghilterra e in rapporti finanziari con la Camera Apostolica testimonia in favore della dimensione internazionale del loro giro d'affari.

e 8 denari in buoni tornesi 'forti' di Francia. Titolari di questo credito erano Ughetto Onesti, suo fratello, i suoi nipoti e gli altri soci della compagnia.[17] Nella somma erano inclusi 233 fiorini d'oro, 12 grossi d'argento del tipo 'Guelfo' ('XII Guelfi crossi de argento') e 12 denari, complessivamente equivalenti a 449 lire, 18 soldi e 5 denari di buona moneta ('ad bonam monetam').

Al termine di questa prima parte del documento, insieme al cancelliere è nominato anche il tesoriere comunale come garante responsabile del rimborso da parte del Comune delle suddette somme ai rispettivi creditori. Si trattava di *dominus* Giusto da Guamo, un monaco proveniente dal monastero di San Michele di Guamo, a pochi chilometri di distanza dalla città.[18] Ecco un monaco agire nella veste di tesoriere comunale: può sembrare strano, ma in realtà era una prassi piuttosto frequente nel contesto della civiltà comunale italiana del Duecento e del Trecento. Del resto, a Lucca alla fine del Duecento una parte dei libri di conto della società Ricciardi era custodita presso la sacrestia del convento di San Francesco.[19] Spesso erano per l'appunto frati degli ordini mendicanti, domenicani e francescani e monaci cistercensi o benedettini in particolare, a ricoprire cariche di direzione finanziaria, mansioni che richiedevano per l'appunto una conoscenza approfondita degli studi di calcolo e aritmetica, nonchè una certa confidenza con le monete in corso nelle varie aree monetarie italiane ed europee.[20]

Nella seconda parte della pergamena sono enumerati i vari cespiti fiscali da cui le autorità comunali lucchesi intendevano trarre le risorse finanziarie per rifondere i debiti contratti. Innanzitutto, si fa riferimento ai proventi della 'Tallia', un'imposizione straordinaria che a quel tempo era divenuta ormai una tassa regolare. Si trattava di una imposizione fiscale diretta e proporzionale, calcolata in base ad un estimo, che fissava l'imponibile per ciascun cittadino lucchese e per ogni comunità del contado. Generalmente la 'Tallia' serviva a finanziare una spedizione militare, un'oste. In seconda istanza, i liquidi per rimborsare il prestito comunale dovevano venire dalle multe e dalle pene pecuniarie comminate nei tribunali locali, nelle varie corti presiedute dal Capitano del Popolo, dal Podestà o dai loro ufficiali. In terzo luogo, bisognava attingere ai capitali derivanti da ogni altro genere di imposte, dirette e indirette, vecchie

---

17 Nel testo si afferma che Ughetto Onesti agiva anche per conto di *dominus* Nicolao di Macone, Bonagiunta di Macone, Salamone Isfacciati, Bonoste di Boninsegna, *dominus* Opizzo Malaspina 'miles', *dominus* Ghiddino Simonetti e il notaio Iacopo Sismondi. Per il personale della compagnia di Ughetto Onesti v. T.W. Blomquist, 'Commercial association in thirteenth-century Lucca', in *Business History Review* 45:2 (1971), 157–78.   **18** Sul monastero di San Michele di Guamo si veda la monografia di D.J. Osheim, *A Tuscan monastery and its social world: San Michele of Guamo (1156–1348)* (Roma, 1989).   **19** Del Punta, *'Capitalismo' familiare*, pp 97–8. Cfr. anche I. Del Punta, 'Il testamento di un banchiere lucchese alla fine del Duecento: Paganuccio Guidiccioni', *Actum Luce* 34:2 (2005), pp 7–47.   **20** See Frances Andrews, 'Regular observance and communal life: Siena and the employment of religious' in Frances Andrews, Cristoph Egger and C.M. Roussea (eds), *Pope, Church and city. Essays in honour of Brenda M. Bolton* (Leiden, forthcoming).

e nuove, imposte dal Comune. Infine, le autorità comunali avrebbero fatto ricorso, se necessario, alle entrate provenienti dal monopolio statale sul commercio e sulla vendita del sale, ovvero dalle entrate della dogana del sale.[21]

Inoltre, il Comune avrebbe ipotecato parte del suo patrimonio fondiario ad ulteriore garanzia del rimborso delle somme dovute. Nell'ipoteca erano incluse case e terre che le autorità comunali avrebbero sequestrato nel prossimo futuro a famiglie locali che si fossero macchiate di reati passibili della confisca di beni patrimoniali.

Per concludere, questo documento è senz'altro di grande interesse non solo perchè mostra come l'uso delle 'prestanzie', di prestiti straordinari appoggiati sull'élite mercantile-bancaria della città come pratica corrente ad una data piuttosto alta, quando ancora le fonti in proposito sono relativamente scarse, ma anche perchè attesta uno stretto collegamento a Lucca tra prestiti pubblici e fiere di Champagne. Nessun preciso tasso d'interesse è menzionato in questo documento pubblico, ma il pagamento di eventuali 'danni, costi e spese' ('dampnis, inprontibus, gostis et expensis') è esplicitamente citato più di una volta. Si può essere certi, peraltro, che nei tassi di cambio cui si è fatto riferimento più sopra era celata una certa percentuale d'interesse che i contemporanei potevano facilmente riconoscere. A quella data l'applicazione di tassi d'interesse su prestiti era assolutamente normale, ammessa perfino dalle autorità ecclesiastiche (che la mettevano in pratica a loro volta nella Camera Apostolica), a patto che i tassi fossero moderati e non superassero una certa soglia, fissata talora al 12%, altre volte anche su valori più elevati, il 14 o il 16%, al di sopra dei quali i prestiti erano considerati usurari. Grazie ad una documentazione relativamente abbondante ho potuto in altra sede raccogliere e confrontare i dati relativi alle operazioni di cambio condotte dalle società mercantili-bancarie lucchesi tra Lucca e le fiere di Champagne. Proprio la società Battosi, ad esempio, era fra le più attive in questo genere di transazioni finanziarie. Ebbene, nel 1284 la società Battosi concluse un gran numero di contratti di cambio sia per l'acquisto che per la vendita di provesini sulle fiere di Champagne. In media i Battosi acquistavano provesini al tasso di cambio di 1 soldo di provesini per 44 denari lucchesi, e li vendevano a tassi più alti: 45, 45 e ½, perfino 46 e ¾ e 47 denari lucchesi per soldo di provesini.[22] Sulla fiera di Provins St Ayoul, nella fattispecie, la compagnia lucchese acquistava provesini per lo più al tasso di 44 denari per soldo di provesini, ma anche a tassi meno favorevoli 44,875 per esempio (il 13 luglio), o a tassi più bassi all'approssimarsi della fiera (43 e ½, 43 e ¾ e 42 e 3/8 rispettivamente il 7, l'11 e il 20 settembre).[23] Poichè questi

---

21 'Item introytus et proventus omnes et singulos qui habebuntur et haberi et percipi debebuntur et consueti sunt haberi et percipi pro douana et occasione douane salis Lucani comunis et dependentibus ex ea'. Per la gestione della gabella del sale nelle città dell'Italia settentrionale nel Duecento e nel Trecento v. P. Mainoni, *La gabella del sale nell'Italia del Nord (secoli XIII–XIV)*, in *Politiche finanziarie e fiscali*, pp 39–85. Più in generale: Ginatempo, *Prima del debito*. **22** Del Punta, *Mercanti e banchieri lucchesi*, pp 240–2. **23** Ibid., p. 241.

contratti di cambio erano in realtà operazioni di mutuo a breve termine, nel tasso di cambio era sempre incluso un tasso d'interesse variabile a seconda della data del contratto. Nei contratti di cambio più ci si avvicinava alla data di apertura della fiera e più il tasso di cambio era favorevole al 'prenditore di cambio', ovvero al debitore, a colui che aveva preso denaro a Lucca promettendo di restituirlo alle fiere di Champagne in valuta diversa. Viceversa, più il contratto di cambio era stipulato in anticipo rispetto alla fiera e più il tasso di cambio era favorevole al 'datore di cambio', ovvero al creditore, a colui che dava denaro a Lucca per riaverlo in Champagne. Questa variazione nei tassi di cambio è facilmente comprensibile alla luce del fatto che il contratto di cambio era una forma di mutuo in cui il fattore tempo giocava un ruolo fondamentale, come in tutti i prestiti. Più il denaro anticipato a Lucca, per fare un esempio, restava nelle mani del debitore e più era alto il tasso di interesse che questi doveva pagare. Al contrario, meno era il tempo per il quale il debitore o 'prenditore di cambio' poteva usufruire del denaro ricevuto a Lucca e più basso era il tasso di interesse previsto, vale a dire che il tasso di cambio con il quale stipulava il contratto gli era più favorevole.[24]

Il dato interessante relativo ai contratti di cambio conclusi a Lucca nel 1284 dalla compagnia Battosi è che quando essa agiva come 'datrice di cambio', ovvero quando anticipava denaro a Lucca per acquistare somme corrispondenti in provesini alle fiere di Champagne, lo faceva spesso ad un tasso di 44 denari lucchesi per soldo di provesini, vale a dire esattamente lo stesso tasso applicato nel debito pubblico contratto dal Comune con le varie società mercantili-bancarie che è oggetto del presente studio. Come si è già osservato, quando i Battosi acquistavano provesini lo facevano ad un tasso di cambio basso, a loro conveniente, un tasso che prevedeva per loro un buon margine di interesse, dal momento che anticipavano denaro a Lucca, quindi di fatto agivano come creditori. Per maggior esattezza, grazie ad un cartulario notarile particolarmente ricco di contratti commerciali, sono documentate 43 operazioni di acquisto di provesini nel solo 1284 stipulate dalla società Battosi. La media del tasso di cambio con cui la compagnia acquistò provesini sulle fiere quell'anno è di 44,56 denari lucchesi per soldo di provesini, un tasso più alto (quindi meno favorevole) rispetto a quello concordato dal Comune con le compagnie creditrici nel caso di prestito pubblico qui esaminato.[25] Ciò significa che quest'ultimo tasso (44 denari) era senz'altro largamente vantaggioso per le compagnie creditrici, prevedeva una buona percentuale d'interesse per quelle società private che avevano agito nei confronti del Comune come 'datrici di cambio', anticipando capitali a Lucca.

Concludendo, si potrà osservare che la particolarità di questa fonte lucchese non sta nell'attestare un caso di prestito straordinario finanziato da soci-

---

24 Per una spiegazione più dettagliata del sistema dei cambi cfr. Del Punta, *Mercanti e banchieri lucchesi*, p. 118 sgg. e bibliografia ivi citata.   25 Ibid., pp 240–1.

età mercantili–bancarie – pratica comune in tutte le città commercialmente più sviluppate dell'Italia centro-settentrionale –, bensì nell'indicare le fiere di Champagne come sede del rimborso dei debiti contratti dal Comune. Nessun altro documento analogo è stato trovato – a mia conoscenza – negli archivi di Siena, Firenze o Piacenza, per citare alcune delle città italiane maggiormente coinvolte in rapporti di affari con le fiere di Champagne. Di fatto questa pergamena, databile come si è detto agli anni '80 del Duecento, dimostra a quale profondo livello le compagnie mercantili-bancarie lucchesi fossero coinvolte in attività finanziarie su un piano internazionale un po' in tutta Europa, ma in particolare nelle aree nord-occidentali del continente. A quella data i Ricciardi erano divenuti già da più di un decennio i banchieri della Corona inglese, mentre la compagnia dei Battosi era al servizio di Carlo d'Angiò in Italia meridionale nel ruolo di primi banchieri del Regno, ruolo che sarà successivamente ricoperto dalle più note società fiorentine dei Bardi, Peruzzi e Acciaiuoli. Il documento lucchese qui di seguito pubblicato mostra il grado di complessità che la finanza pubblica e i sistemi fiscali dei comuni italiani avevano raggiunto nella seconda metà del Duecento.

APPENDICE

Imponibile calcolato per ciascuna compagnia in base al datum o tallia che esse dovevano pagare per finanziare l'esercito comunale (tassa diretta pari al 5% dell'imponibile).[26]

– Battosi: 9381 lire di denari lucchesi piccoli
– Ricciardi: 21680 lire e 10 soldi di denari lucchesi piccoli
– consorzio formato da *dominus* Forteguerra Arrighetti, *dominus* Aliotto de Rocca, *dominus* Guglielmo Malaspina, *dominus* Giovanni Oddi, Tore di *dominus* Ubaldo, Iacopo Normannini e Niccolò di Pontadore Notti:[27] 1759 lire di denari lucchesi piccoli

Le somme relative al credito di ciascuna compagnia.

Battosi.
– Credito da incassare alla fiera di Provins St Ayoul:

26 Mancano i dati relativi ad Adiuto Rosciompelli, al consorzio formato da Orlando Malapresa, Guicciardino di Giovanni, Coluccio Volpelli e *dominus* Cione d'Arco (rappresentati da Adiuto Rosciompelli) e alla società di Ughetto Onesti. Nel primo caso la circostanza si spiega facilmente perchè Adiuto aveva già pagato il *datum* come membro della società Ricciardi e l'ulteriore prestito che effettuava al Comune era puramente a titolo personale ('et ipsi Adiuto, recipienti pro se et suo nomine proprio'), mentre negli altri casi la particolarità era probabilmente dovuta ad una ridotta disponibilità di denaro liquido da parte dei soggetti contribuenti, che già aiutavano il Comune con un prestito volontario, o forse ad una loro esenzione dal *datum* per ragioni particolari che ci sfuggono. 27 Rappresentati nel prestito al Comune da Custore Battosi.

373 lire e 18 soldi di tornesi.

– Somma prestata al Comune:

2000 lire di denari lucchesi piccoli.

– Somma da pagare al Comune per il *datum*:

469 lire e 1 soldo di denari lucchesi piccoli.

– Credito residuo dei Battosi (derivante dalla detrazione del *datum* dalla somma prestata al Comune):

1530 lire, 19 soldi di denari lucchesi piccoli

– Tasso di cambio tra denari lucchesi e tornesi:

1 soldo di tornesi= 44 denari lucchesi di buona moneta

– Credito residuo dei Battosi in buona moneta lucchese:

1370 lire, 14 soldi, 9 denari[28]

pari a:

373 lire, 18 soldi di tornesi

e pari a:

1530 lire, 19 soldi di denari lucchesi piccoli.

– Somma versata in prestito dai Battosi al Comune usando le seguenti monete:

712 fiorini d'oro e 1 aquilino d'argento,

al tasso di cambio di 1 fiorino= 38 soldi e 6 denari di buona moneta lucchese

pari a: 1370 lire, 12 soldi + 1 aquilino,

pari a: 1370 lire, 14 soldi e 9 denari,

quindi: 1 aquilino= 2 soldi e 9 denari di buona moneta lucchese.

Consorzio formato da *dominus* Forteguerra Arrighetti, *dominus* Aliotto de Rocca e altri, rappresentato da Custore Battosi.

– Credito da incassare alla fiera di Provins St Ayoul:

182 lire, 7 soldi di denari tornesi.

– Somma prestata al Comune:

834 lire, 10 soldi di denari lucchesi piccoli.

– Somma da pagare al Comune per il *datum*:

87 lire, 19 soldi di denari lucchesi piccoli.

– Credito residuo del consorzio (derivante dalla detrazione del *datum* dalla somma prestata al Comune):

---

28 È la somma equivalente dichiarata nel documento. Dai calcoli nostri, tuttavia, 373 lire e 18 soldi tornesi – ad un tasso di cambio di 1 soldo di tornesi=44 denari lucchesi in buona moneta – sono equivalenti a 1,370 lire, 19 soldi e 4 denari lucchesi in buona moneta. La discrepanza è molto lieve: appena 5 soldi e 4 denari in meno nella somma dichiarata nel documento. È probabile che tale differenza andasse a far parte dell'interesse riscosso dalla compagnia Battosi al termine dell'operazione di credito. Un'altra possibilità è che il redattore del documento abbia confuso le cifre relative a soldi e denari, scrivendo 14 soldi e 9 denari anzichè 19 soldi e 4 denari. Ma quest'ultima ipotesi mi pare meno probabile.

746 lire, 11 soldi di denari lucchesi piccoli.

– Somma versata in prestito dal Custore Battosi (a nome del consorzio) al Comune usando le seguenti monete:

346 fiorini d'oro e 4 guelfi grossi d'argento,

pari a:

668 lire, 8 soldi, 6 denari in buona moneta lucchese,

pari a:

182 lire, 7 soldi di denari tornesi.

Tasso di cambio fiorni/buoni denari lucchesi:

1 fiorino d'oro= 38 soldi, 6 denari

quindi:

346 fiorini e 4 guelfi grossi= 666 lire, 1 soldo in buona moneta lucchese e 4 guelfi grossi

se ne deduce che:

4 guelfi grossi= 2 lire, 7 soldi e 6 denari,

1 guelfo grosso= 142 denari= 11 soldi, 10 denari e ½

Ricciardi.

– Credito da incassare alla fiera di Provins St Ayoul:

1200 lire, 14 soldi, 3 denari di tornesi.

– Somma prestata al Comune:

6000 lire di denari lucchesi piccoli.

– Somma da pagare al Comune per il *datum*:

1084 lire, 6 denari lucchesi piccoli.

– Credito residuo dei Ricciardi (derivante dalla detrazione del *datum* dalla somma prestata al Comune):

4915 lire, 19 soldi, 6 denari lucchesi piccoli,

pari a:

4400 lire, 10 soldi, 6 denari lucchesi in buona moneta.

– Somma versata in prestito dai Ricciardi al Comune usando le seguenti monete:

2286 fiorini d'oro e 7 aquilini d'argento,

al tasso di cambio di 1 fiorino= 38 soldi, 6 denari lucchesi di buona moneta,

la suddetta somma è pari a:

4400 lire, 11 soldi di buoni denari lucchesi e 7 aquilini.[29]

Al tasso di cambio di 1 soldo di tornesi= 44 denari lucchesi in buona moneta,

29 Somma risultante dai calcoli. La discrepanza con la somma dichiarata nel documento relativa al credito residuo dei Ricciardi (4,400 lire, 10 soldi e 6 denari in buona moneta lucchese) c'è, ma è lieve: appena 6 denari e 7 aquilini in più (nella somma derivante dai calcoli). Ma tale discrepanza si giustifica con il risultato del successivo calcolo relativo alla somma in tornesi che i Ricciardi dovevano riscuotere in Champagne. Cfr. nota seguente.

1200 lire, 14 soldi, 3 denari di tornesi
sono equivalenti a:
4402 lire, 12 soldi, 3 denari lucchesi in buona moneta.[30]

Adiuto Rosciompelli.
– Credito da incassare alla fiera di Provins St Ayoul:
1220 lire, 13 soldi di tornesi.
– Somma prestata al Comune:
4997 lire, 14 soldi di denari lucchesi piccoli.
– Somma versata in prestito dai Adiuto al Comune usando le seguenti monete:
2324 fiorini d'oro e ½,
pari a:
4474 lire, 13 soldi, 6 denari lucchesi in buona moneta.[31]
Al tasso di cambio di 1 fiorino= 38 soldi, 6 denari lucchesi in buona moneta,
2324 fiorini d'oro e ½ equivalgono a:
4474 lire, 13 soldi, 3 denari.[32]
Al tasso di cambio di 1 soldo di tornesi = 38 soldi, 6 denari lucchesi in buona moneta,
1220 lire, 13 soldi di tornesi equivalgono a:
4475 lire, 14 soldi, 4 denari lucchesi in buona moneta.[33]

Consorzio formato da Orlando Malapresa, Guicciardino di Giovanni, Coluccio Volpelli e *dominus* Cione d'Arco, rappresentati da Adiuto Rosciompelli.
– Credito da incassare alla fiera di Provins St Ayoul:
97 lire, 14 soldi di tornesi.
– Somma prestata al Comune:
400 lire …[34] di denari lucchesi piccoli.
– Somma versata in prestito da Adiuto al Comune (a nome del consorzio) usando le seguenti monete:
186 fiorini d'oro e 2 soldi di denari lucchesi piccoli,
pari a:
358 lire, 3 soldi di denari lucchesi in buona moneta.[35]

---

30 Somma superiore di 2 lire, 1 soldo, 9 denari rispetto al credito dei Ricciardi dichiarato nel documento. Ecco spiegata la discrepanza di 6 denari e 7 aquilini di cui sopra.   31 Somma dichiarata nel documento.   32 Anche in questo caso c'è una piccola discrepanza tra la somma dichiarata nel documento e la somma derivante dai calcoli, ma si tratta di appena 3 denari.   33 Anche qui una leggera differenza rispetto alle cifre enumerate nel documento: 1 lira e 10 soldi in più rispetto al credito dichiarato. Si tratta probabilmente di una parte dell'interesse che il creditore doveva incassare a conclusione dell'operazione di credito.   34 Illeggibile a causa di un guasto nella pergamena.   35 Somma dichiarata nel documento.

Al tasso di cambio di 1 fiorino= 38 soldi, 6 denari in buona moneta,

186 fiorini d'oro e 2 soldi di denari lucchesi piccoli equivalgono a:

358 lire, 1 soldo di denari lucchesi in buona moneta + 2 soldi di denari lucchesi piccoli.[36]

Al tasso di cambio di 1 soldo di tornesi= 44 denari lucchesi in buona moneta, 97 lire, 14 soldi di tornesi equivalgono a:

358 lire, 4 soldi, 8 denari lucchesi in buona moneta.[37]

Società di Ughetto Onesti.

– Credito da incassare alla fiera di Provins St Ayoul:

122 lire, 14 soldi, 8 denari di tornesi.

– Somma prestata al Comune:

502 lire, 10 soldi di denari lucchesi piccoli.

– Somma versata in prestito da Ughetto Onesti al Comune usando le seguenti monete:

233 fiorini d'oro, 12 guelfi grossi d'argento e 12 denari lucchesi piccoli, pari a:

449 lire, 18 soldi, 5 denari lucchesi in buona moneta.[38]

Al tasso di cambio di 1 fiorino= 38 soldi, 6 denari lucchesi in buona moneta,

233 fiorini equivalgono a:

448 lire, 10 soldi, 6 denari,

quindi 12 guelfi grossi= 1 lira, 7 soldi, 11 denari lucchesi in buona moneta.[39]

Al tasso di cambio di 1 soldo di tornesi= 44 denari lucchesi in buona moneta,

122 lire, 14 soldi, 8 denari di tornesi sono pari a:

450 lire, 5 denari e 1/3 di denari lucchesi in buona moneta.[40]

---

36 Qui la discrepanza tra la somma dichiarata nel documento (358 lire, 3 soldi in buona moneta) e quella derivante dai calcoli è ancora più lieve che negli altri casi. La differenza sta tutta in 2 soldi di buoni denari lucchesi, da una parte, e 2 soldi di denari lucchesi piccoli, dall'altra.   37 Leggermente di più rispetto alla somma dichiarata nel documento. Si tratta di appena 1 soldo, 8 denari lucchesi in buona moneta, facenti parte dell'interesse che il creditore avrebbe dovuto incassare al termine del prestito.   38 Somma dichiarata nel documento.   39 Vale a dire che 1 guelfo grosso d'argento valeva poco meno di 2 soldi, 4 denari lucchesi in buona moneta.   40 La differenza tra questa somma derivante dai calcoli e la somma dichiarata nel documento è di appena 2 soldi e 1/3 di denaro. Anche tale differenza doveva far parte dell'interesse che spettava al creditore a conclusione del prestito.

Flying across the Alps: 'Italy' in the works of Petrarch

JENNIFER PETRIE

This essay is concerned with the significance of Italy in Petrarch's works, and so, by implication, with what Italy may have meant to literate people in the late Middle Ages. It therefore raises the question of what at that time may have counted as 'Italian identity', and suggests that this is by no means an empty concept, at least from a literary and cultural point of view.

Petrarch refers to himself on occasions as a Florentine, although he never lived in Florence, and also as a Tuscan: he speaks of his 'native Tuscan air'.[1] His family was Florentine and had owned property in Florence before the poet's father was sent into exile in the political turbulence in that city at the beginning of the fourteenth century. Petrarch had Florentine friends: Francesco Nelli, Zanobi della Strada and Boccaccio for example. He visited the city for the first time as a man in his forties in the Jubilee year of 1350, and in the next year or two he did consider living in Florence but nothing ever came of this. He was in fact born in exile near Arezzo in 1304: when he was still a child his family moved to papal Avignon, where his father obtained a post as a notary. Avignon would always be significant for the poet's own particular perspective on Italy. Petrarch studied at Bologna, though chose the church rather than law, always however remaining in minor orders. This did not prevent him having a number of benefices, several in Italy. While based in Avignon under the patronage of the Colonna family, he was free to travel extensively (though this could involve various diplomatic missions). His travels included visits to Rome, and then Naples, where he enjoyed the patronage of Robert of Anjou, under whose sponsorship he was crowned poet lau-

---

1 For biographical information, see E.H. Wilkins, *Life of Petrarch* (Chicago, 1961); also U. Dotti, *Vita di Petrarca* (Bari, 1987). For references to Petrarch's works I have drawn especially on Francesco Petrarca, *Prose*, ed. G. Martellotti et al. (Milan–Naples, 1955) and Francesco Petrarca, *Rime, Trionfi e poesie latine*, ed. F. Neri et al. (Milan–Naples, 1951); for the complete *Familiares*, ed. V. Rossi & U. Bosco, E. Bianchi (trans.): Francesco Petrarca, *Opere*, 2 various eds (Florence, 1975), I, 239–1285; for the *Seniles*, for which there is not a modern Latin edition, I have used the English version, Francis Petrarch, *Letters of old age: Rerum Senilium Libri*, 2, trans. A.S. Bernardo et al. (Baltimore, 1992). For the Italian poetry I have used Gianfranco Contini's text: Francesco Petrarca, *Canzoniere* (Turin, 1964). This is the basis for most of the more recent editions, whether entitled *Rime* or *Rerum vulgarium fragmenta*: I shall (for brevity) use the title *Rime*. For Petrarch's references to himself as a Florentine, see for example, his letter to Boccaccio, *Familiares*, XXI. 15. 1 (*Prose*, p. 1002), where he refers to Dante as a fellow-citizen: *in con-terranei nostri [...] laudibus*; see also *Rime*, 166. 3: *Fiorenza avria forse oggi il suo poeta*, and, speaking of himself as Tuscan, 194. 6: *fuggo dal mi' natio dolce aere tosco*.

reate in Rome in 1341. This, as well as his presence in Avignon, led to a huge network of contacts and possibilities of support and patronage, such as that of the Correggio family in Parma, where he acquired a house, and which was to be his main base in Italy in the 1340s. Subsequently, navigating the Po, or possibly travelling overland, which he seemed to prefer, allowed for further explorations and such treasure troves for a humanist as the cathedral library of Verona, where he discovered Cicero's letters.

Disappointments in Avignon, the Black Plague, the death of friends and patrons (and if we take him literally, his lady Laura), led Petrarch to decide to settle permanently in Italy. He changed residence, but always in the north: Milan, Venice, Padua, Pavia briefly, and the village of Arquà where he died. No doubt general accessibility, the navigability of the Po and the large number of acquaintances, as well as opportunities as they presented themselves came to suit this restless but now aging traveller.

Did he understand this as living in Italy? In some of his letters he in fact refers to this area, classically, as Cisalpine Gaul.[2] However this should not, I think, be taken as an anticipation of the Celtic leanings of the present day *Lega lombarda*. For Petrarch, once you crossed the Alps you were in Italy. There are two Latin poems, 'Ad Italiam' and 'Linquimus Italiam' marking the crossing of the Mont Genèvre pass.[3] In each case, this pass is unmistakably the boundary. Entering Italy he sees a fresh clear sky, leaving it, appropriately, he faces snow and mist. The Alps provide the demarcation; indeed nature itself ensures that Italy is protected by them. *Gentibus hic fuerat terminus, est et erit*, this was and always will be the boundary between peoples, he says in the concluding line of the epigram 'Linquimus Italiam'. In his Italian poem 'Italia mia' he speaks of the Alps provided by nature to keep out the German fury, the *tedesca rabbia*.[4] This protective boundary of the Alps is part of what makes Italy special, privileged, chosen providentially it might even seem.

So what, we may wonder, did Petrarch understand by Italy? Undoubtedly there is the primary sense of a geographical entity, bounded by the Alps and the sea. He produces eulogies of its favoured position, as well as of it as a place of abundance and variety, protected yet accessible, by sea and mountain passes. But clearly there is more than that. It is also a question of a people, *gens*. The Alpine boundary separates peoples, the Romans and the barbarians. The poem 'Ad Italiam' greeting Italy from the Mont Genèvre pass hails the *tellus sanctissima*, marked by nobility and abundance, fertility and beauty, arms, law, the Muses and by the role of teacher, *magistra* over the world given by art and nature.

2 For Cisalpine Gaul, see for example the dating of the letter to Seneca, *Familiares*, XXIV. 5: *apud superos, in Gallia Cisalpina*; also V. 6. 6; V. 7. 12; VII. 10. 3.   3 *Epistole Metrice* III. 24, *Ad Italiam*, and the epigram *Linquimus Italiam*, both edited by E. Bianchi in *Rime, Trionfi e poesie latine*, p. 804 and 850.   4 *Rime*, 128.35.

cuius ad eximios ars et natura favores
incubuere simul mundoque dedere magistram.

[Art and nature worked together to give you their greatest favours and
they made you the schoolmistress of the world.][5]

The Roman past and the present are evidently seen as one. For if the Italy of
Petrarch's day can be a *magistra*, it must be on the strength of its classical
past, or perhaps too on the strength of the heritage of Christian Rome, now
disgracefully abandoned by the popes.

The idea of Italy as expressed in Petrarch's works is almost always, as in
the above text, bound up with its classical and Roman past. The letters of the
young humanist show his enthusiasm for the relics of ancient Rome, or for
the Virgilian associations of Naples. In later life one of Petrarch's invectives,
Contra eum qui maledixit Italie, is far more a defence of the historical significance of Rome and the greatness of her achievements than a defence of Italy
as such.[6] But it is written against what he saw as a French tendency to belittle Rome. His 'Gallus' has invoked for preference Alexander the Great (*furio-
sus adolescens*, Petrarch calls him) or Greek philosophy: Aristotle rather than
Cicero or Seneca.[7] The barbarian Gauls clearly still resent Julius Caesar!

A second significant factor (not unrelated) is Petrarch's opposition to the
Avignon papacy, the church leadership exiled to the Babylon of the West.[8]
He was energetically in favour of a return of the papacy to Rome, and he was
eloquent in the defence of both Rome and Italy against the French cardinals
who, possibly with good reason, felt that such a move would take them into
a thoroughly dangerous, lawless and violent place. The debate is well known,
conducted especially in two long letters to Pope Urban V (the pope who did
briefly return to Rome), and in the subsequent invective *Contra eum qui
maledixit Italie*, already mentioned.[9] In the letters Petrarch praises Italy's
beauty and abundance, its favoured location, its accessibility by land and sea,
even, by implication at least, its commercial prosperity and maritime strength,
as well as the historic greatness of Rome, that city now tragically widowed.
He speaks angrily of French hostility to Italy. Notoriously, much space (a dis-
proportionate amount, one might think) is given to the French cardinals'
attachment to the wines of Burgundy.[10] In Petrarch's polemic this perhaps
serves a number of functions, some of them contradictory. In one way, his

---

5 *Ad Italiam, Epistole Metrice*, III. 24. 1; 8–9; *Rime, Trionfi e poesie latine*, p. 804.   6
Invectiva contra eum qui maledixit Italie, ed. P.G. Ricci in *Prose*, pp 768–807.   7 *Prose*, p.
792.   8 'Babilonia' for Avignon is used particularly frequently in Petrarch's *Sine nomine*
letters: see Petrarca, *Sine nomine: Lettere polemiche e politiche*, ed. & trans. Ugo Dotti (Bari,
1974); see also *Rime*, 137.1 and 138.3.   9 The letters to Pope Urban V are *Seniles*, VII.1
(the letter comprising the entire book) and IX. 1.   10 See *Letters of old age*, I. 251–4 and
307–10.

making such an issue of the wine plays down the more real objections to law-lessness, violence, banditry, kidnappings and so on. (Is this all the cardinals have to worry about?) It can also clearly be a way of satirizing the cardinals' gluttony, and by contrast praising the frugality and asceticism of Pope Urban, a former Benedictine abbot, and associating this pontiff's self-denying ideal with the return to Christian Rome: the red wine is contrasted with the blood of the Roman martyrs. On the other hand, Petrarch is anxious to praise the abundance and fertility of Italy, and therefore to assure the cardinals of excel-lent Italian wines!

Italy and Rome, then, are all the more closely linked through opposition to France and to Avignon. Indeed the sense of Italy as a significant place grows through the need to defend it. There is a strong personal note here. 'Italia *mia*' [my italics] is the opening of one of Petrarch's best-known Italian poems (*Rime*, 128). In the Latin letters the poet comes across as intensely sensitive to the various jibes at Italy's expense uttered by non-Italians: he seems to take them personally, remembers them, is eager to produce rejoin-ders, have the last word. To comments like 'it is a beautiful country but we have better government' he wants to reply with 'whose fault is that?'[11] Beauty is permanent, a gift of Nature he says, good government a matter of human choices. His experience of living in Avignon and his wide travels in Italy together served to give a sense of emotional identification that was not local in the narrow sense of attachment to one's city. Indeed as a moralist, Petrarch advocates citizenship of the world (being *mundanus, omne solum forti patria est*: for the strong every soil is a fatherland), and it is only fair to say that many of his letters reflect such an attitude, along with an eagerness for travel and for geography.[12] He saw himself indeed as a man with no *tellus: peregrinus ubique*.[13] He is also however interested, in a somewhat unsystematic way, in the phenomenon of attachment to one's native place. This is the source of an appeal to the warring Italian lords in 'Italia mia': the land 'where I grew up, my nest, where my parents are buried, trustworthy patria, benign tender mother' (*non è questa la patria in ch'io mi fido,/ madre benigna e pia,/ che copre l'un e l'altro mio parente*: 128. 84–6). Writing to Urban V he notes the way in which people prefer the things or the food from their own place of origin (to that extent the French cardinals are not to be blamed for liking the wines of Burgundy).[14] But Petrarch lays claim to a certain objectivity in his attitude to Italy, deriving from the historical greatness of Rome.

Italy and Rome then, Italy as a geographical entity surrounding Rome, Italy as *patria* and source of personal identification, Italy as opposed to

---

11 See *Seniles* VII.1: *Letters of old age*, I. 242.   12 *Familiares*, IX. 13. 10: *omne solum forti patria est*; also *Seniles*, VII. 1, *Letters of old age*, p. 246.   13 For *peregrinus ubique*, see *Metrice*, III. 19, lines 15–16, in F.P. *Rime, Trionfi e poesie latine*, p. 798.   14 See *Seniles*, VII. 1, *Letters of old age*, I. 251–2.

France, or Gaul, that land of the barbarians conquered by Julius Caesar. For
Petrarch, doubly exiled from Tuscany and from Italy, loathing Avignon,
smarting at what were perceived as put-downs on the part of the French,
classical scholar and humanist, all these came together. This close association
of Italy and Rome can appear in small ways, typical of Petrarch's blending of
past and present. In a letter to Pope Urban V at one point he commends the
pontiff's favouring of decorum and simplicity of dress, this in a world of
outré fashions, long pointed shoes, doublets which would choke the wearer
and so forth. Such fashions are regrettably particularly prevalent in Italy, so
inappropriate to the *gravitas* of the toga.[15] One could say indeed that dignity
is a major issue: it is bound up with identification with Roman greatness,
shame, refusal to be outdone culturally by France. Petrarch saw his own role
as providing the link between past and present, Roman culture and that of his
own day. In a somewhat obscure Latin eclogue (*Bucolicum Carmen* IV,
'Dedalus'), there is a dialogue between Tirrenus and Gallus: an Italian and a
Frenchman.[16] Gallus is envious of Tirrenus' lyre, and wants to buy it. But
no, says Tirrenus, it was a gift at birth from no less a person than Daedalus,
the master of all craftsmen (who appeared at the door like a sort of fairy godfather). It cannot be sold or given away. In the ongoing debate between Italy
and France, the poetic arts (here represented by Daedalus) evidently favour
Italy rather than France. And since Tirrenus can most probably be identified
with Petrarch (at least they seem to have the same birthplace between the
Tiber and the Arno), his role is to maintain Italy's literary greatness, the
greatness of Virgil, Horace and Ovid. The same idea is to be found in Book
IX of Petrarch's epic poem the *Africa*, in which the Roman poet Ennius, cel-
ebrator of the poem's hero Scipio, foresees a remote poetic successor in
Petrarch himself.[17]

Unlike Dante, Petrarch does not discuss the question of language. For
Dante, the *lingua di sí* was something which defined Italy. Indeed, Dante,
whose attitude to Italy in many ways anticipates Petrarch's, was interested in
a vernacular writing in Italy which could rival the vernaculars of France and
Provence. But Petrarch, ostensibly at least, played down his vernacular works
as a sort of second string, a hobby as it were. His use of Latin was another
link with Rome.

The question then remains of how far the idea of Italy, its cities, its rivers,
its geography can be separated in Petrarch's works from the idea of Rome.
Certainly for Petrarch, the geographical reality in itself seems significant,

15 Ibid., I. 220–30.   16 See *Petrarch's Bucolicum Carmen*, ed. & trans. T.G. Bergin (New
Haven, 1974), pp 49–56.   17 On Ennius and Petrarch in the *Africa*, see F. Galligan,
'Poets and heroes in Petarch's *Africa*: classical and medieval sources' in Martin
McLaughlin et al. (eds), *Petrarch in Britain: interpretations, imitations and translations over
700 years*, Proceedings of the British Academy, 146 (Oxford, 2007), pp 85–93; also in the
same volume, J. Usher, 'Petrarch's second (and third) death', pp 61–82.

something worthy of eulogy. There are many passages on the beauty of various parts of Italy: the Ligurian coast for example, where the sailor can forget to row in stunned astonishment at its beauty.[18] (In this case the beauty is also a sign of Genoese wealth: much of the wonder of the place lies in the splendid houses and palaces.) But then Petrarch would also write of the beauty of Vaucluse in Provence, his *transalpina solitudo*, where, *exul ab Italia*, as he begins one poem, he pursues a life of solitary study.[19] In 'Italia mia' (*Rime*, 128) he mentions rivers, the Tiber, the Arno and the Po, from where he is writing, and bewails the damaging wars between the *signori*, and of course, the presence of foreign mercenaries. The Rome of his own day is not mentioned but the Roman past is (once again) invoked in the victories of Marius and Caesar over the ancestors of these unwelcome barbarian soldiers of fortune. Italy itself is seen as a unity through the initial personification of this country as a beautiful but wounded woman. But there is also the implied unity of *Romanitas*, made all the more apparent, in imagination at least, by the presence of the barbarian 'other' in the mercenaries.

Petrarch was not alone in this ideal of *Romanitas* as a unifying force in Italy. Here one may mention Cola da Rienzo's abortive attempt to restore the ancient role of tribune, in which he had the enthusiastic support of Petrarch, whether or not it is true that, as Petrarch claimed, his efforts made all Italy wake up.[20] Certainly one of Cola's proposals was granting liberty and Roman citizenship to all peoples of Italy, with all the ancient privileges of the *populus romanus*. It was a form of ideal Italian political unity under a restored Rome that made perfect sense to Petrarch: he was disgusted when Avignon declared such proposals inexpedient. After Cola's failure, Petrarch was to look to the Emperor, Charles of Bohemia, with completely fruitless requests to him to make Rome and Italy his base.[21]

In general in the fourteenth century, Rome would be significant mainly as the Christian capital. Cola was intensely aware of the Christian as well as the classical significance of contemporary Rome, and attempted to blend the two. But after his failure, there remained the importance of Rome as a place of pilgrimage, the practice that would associate Italy and Rome in the minds of Petrarch's contemporaries. In *Familiares*, XIII 9, Petrarch describes the itinerary of Cardinal Gui de Boulogne in the Jubilee year of 1350 (Petrarch had been one of those who petitioned for 1350 to be declared a Jubilee year).[22] The Cardinal has already crossed the Alps in the path of Hannibal and arrived in Milan, moving on to Brescia, Verona, Padua, Venice and Treviso.

---

18 See *Familiares*, XIV. 5. 24; also IX. 13. 40.   **19** For 'Exul ab Italia', see *Francisci Petrarchae poemata minora*, ed. Domenico Rossetti, 3 (Milan, 1829–34), II. 60–66; see also Dotti, pp. 136–40; for *transalpina solitudo* (accompanying a drawing by Petrarch in his volume of Pliny), see Wilkins, pp. 63–73. Vaucluse features a great deal in Petrarch's correspondence in both prose and verse, and is the setting of many of his Italian love-lyrics. **20** On Cola, see Wilkins, pp 63–73; Dotti, pp 176–90.   **21** See *Familiares*, X. 1.   **22** See

He has then visited Austria and returned to Padua for the translation of the body of St Antony. (It was this cardinal who, admiring the beauty of Lake Garda remarked to Petrarch that Italy was more beautiful than France, but France was better governed.) His itinerary will then take him to Ravenna, Rimini, Perugia and Rome, where he will venerate the holy relics but also perhaps admire the ruins of classical Rome. On his return route, Petrarch continues, the Cardinal plans to visit Viterbo, Orvieto, Siena and Florence; then across the Apennines to Bologna, then to Milan, then back again across the Apennines to Genoa, and finally back to France enjoying the beauties of the Riviera. One feels a whiff of the Grand Tour. Petrarch himself travelled to Rome for the Jubilee, but had to curtail his own plans because of a leg injury.

Petrarch also composed an itinerary for a pilgrimage to Jerusalem, which entailed sailing from Marseilles to Genoa and then down the West coast of Italy, across to Puglia and then across the Mediterranean.[23] Classical interests accompanied religious ones, and there was plenty in Italy to awaken the pilgrim's interest. He declined to go on this pilgrimage himself, he said, because he disliked sailing. It seems that as a child, sailing from Genoa to Marseilles, he had the terrifying experience of a storm which almost prevented the ship arriving in port. In his Italian poetry the image of sea travel is often an intensely negative one: it can represent anxiety, fear, or despair.[24] Mountains on the other hand have generally a more positive significance: an aspiring poet climbs Mount Parnassus, the journey up Mont Ventoux leads to Augustinian self-knowledge; mountains can represent thoughts, reflections, moral stocktaking.[25] Italy for Petrarch is ideally entered not by sea, but across the Alps. Hence the somewhat frivolous title of this paper, which leads us back to the mysterious Daedalus. According to one of Petrarch's verse letters (III. 22), written when he finally decided to leave Avignon for good, Daedalus, the great craftsman, having made himself wings, flew away from Crete to Provence, and created a labyrinth at Avignon, darker and more terrible and harder to escape from than the Cretan one. Horrified at his own work, he flew away again: to Italy. And I, says Petrarch, disgusted at the Babylon of the West, will follow him, *similisque volanti*, [and] like that flying man.[26] However his path, it seems, more modestly, was across the Mont Genèvre, to greet the sacred, beautiful land of Italy, destined by nature and art to be the *magistra* of the world.

Wilkins, pp 93–5. **23** *Itinerarium in breve de Ianua usque ad Ierusalem et Terram Sanctam*, ed. G. Lumbroso, in *Atti della Reale Accademia dei Lincei*, 4th series, Rendiconti, 4 (1888); Francesco Petrarca, *Itinerario in Terra Santa*, ed. F. Lo Monaco (Bergamo, 1990); see also Wilkins, pp 159–60. **24** Poems such as *Rime* 189 and 272, 11–14 use the image of the sea voyage to express distress and spiritual anxiety. **25** See *Familiares*, IV. 1 for Petrarch's account of his climbing Mont Ventoux; see also *Rime* 129. **26** See *Epistole Metrice*, III. 22, *Poemata minora*, II. 256.

A dialogue of power: the politics of burial and commemoration in fourteenth-century Italy

WILLIAM CAFERRO

The English mercenary John Hawkwood was fourteenth-century Italy's most successful soldier. He fought on Italian soil for 33 years (1361–94), serving numerous employers. He rode at the head of armies during times of war and led marauding 'free' companies during times of peace. His military achievements included the great tactical victory at the battle of Castagnaro on behalf of Padua, a feat which the noted military historian Charles Oman viewed as one of the most impressive of the era.[1] Hawkwood gained considerable renown during his career, and his life intersected with those of other outstanding personages of the day. He sat with Petrarch at a wedding banquet in Milan, met Chaucer on an embassy on behalf of King Richard II of England, and received angry letters from the saintly Catherine of Siena, who demanded that he give up his military career, leave Italy and go on crusade.[2] Hawkwood did not comply with Catherine's request, but stayed in Italy until he died in 1394. The Florentines, his last employer, honoured him with an elaborate funeral, described by contemporaries as one of the great events of the age. The ceremony was followed by the commission of a fresco in Hawkwood's honour in the cathedral, later repainted by Paolo Uccello in 1436.

Uccello's work remains in the Florentine cathedral, and is Hawkwood's most enduring legacy to the modern world. It depicts the captain atop his horse, baton at his side. It is the portrait not of a fearsome warrior at the head of his army, but a captain moving about his brigade, inspecting his troops. The pose emphasizes Hawkwood's role as Florentine employee, performing one of his most basic tasks. It is this image of Hawkwood that has served as the basis for subsequent biographies and popular works on the man. Modern authors have extended and amplified it, portraying Hawkwood's life wholly in terms of his Florentine employment, and stressing personal virtues such as faithfulness, loyalty and even honesty.[3] According to Richard Gough (one of Hawkwood's first biographers) Hawkwood's relationship with Florence was

---

1 Charles Oman, *Art of war in the Middle Ages*, 2 (London, 1924), II, pp 296–7. 2 For details on Hawkwood's personality and military feats, see William Caferro, *John Hawkwood, an English mercenary in fourteenth-century Italy* (Baltimore, 2006). 3 John Temple Leader & Giuseppe Marcotti, *Sir John Hawkwood* (London, 1889). Recent restatements of the orthodoxy are in Philippe Contamine, *War in the Middle Ages*, trans. Michael Jones (Oxford, 1984), p. 159 and Denys Hay & John Law, *Italy in the age of the Renaissance, 1380–1530* (London, 1989), pp 86–7.

characterized by 'irreproachable fidelity'.[4] As a result, our current understanding of Hawkwood, the greatest soldier of the age, has curiously centered not on his military abilities, but on his moral qualities. He is the 'exception to the rule,' an honest man in a profession known for the opposite.

There is no point here rehearsing the vagaries of this scholarly construct. But what has not been adequately acknowledged is that it is in fact a construct.[5] Hawkwood's persona is a fashioned persona, fashioned, as I will argue here, by the most skilled of all fourteenth-century propagandists, the Florentines. Hawkwood was not a particularly faithful or loyal soldier; nor was he a dutiful or honest employee of Florence, for which he worked for a relatively small part of his career. He passed most of the time in the service of others, with whom he often forged closer relations. Hawkwood's Pisan employer, Giovanni dell' Agnello, chose him as godfather to his son; Hawkwood's Milanese employer, Bernabò Visconti, gave him his illegitimate daughter in marriage. Florence's own relations with Hawkwood were contentious and problematic, characterized by angry exchanges back and forth, over issues relating to money, priority, service and performance. Florence's ambivalent attitude toward its most difficult employee is perhaps best expressed in an extant ambassadorial dispatch from 1378 in which city officials counseled their envoys to Hawkwood 'to proceed cautiously' in dealing with him and his fellow English soldiers. To 'anger' or upset them in any way was to induce them to 'do things to the commune that we will not like.'[6] The letter makes clear that Hawkwood's character was defined also by its independence and vindictiveness, traits confirmed repeatedly in the sources. Hawkwood played his Florentine employer against others and maintained his 'faith' only when promptly and generously paid. Hawkwood's character combined brutality with duplicity, qualities that were in fact critical to his success on the battlefield. The latter trait won for Hawkwood his Italian nickname, *acuto* (Giovanni Acuto), which has erroneously been taken by some scholars as a clumsy rendering of his English name, but was in fact a conscious appellation that paid tribute to his 'keenness' and 'craftiness.'[7]

But whatever the reality, John Hawkwood's character has been lost in layers of Florentine propaganda. His last service to the city, and his death, occurred during bitter and protracted war with Milan and Siena, a conflict that ultimately lasted for 40 years. The struggle involved intense propagandizing, a feature that has been amply noted by scholars. Hans Baron and

---

4 Richard Gough, *Memoirs of Sir John Hawkwood* (London, 1776), p. 2.   5 The vicissitudes of the construct are in William Caferro, 'John Hawkwood, Florentine hero and faithful Englishman' in Donald Kagay & Andrew Villalon (eds), *The Hundred Years War: a wider focus* (forthcoming).   6 Biblioteca Riccardiana di Firenze, MS 786, fol. 72r; see also Caferro, *John Hawkwood*, p. 198.   7 See, among others, Philip Morant, *History and antiquities of Essex*, 2 (London, 1768), p. 288. For a fuller discussion see Caferro, *John Hawkwood*, pp 9–11.

others have famously shown how the city fashioned itself as a bastion of liberty against Milanese tyranny. For Baron, and later P.G.A. Pocock, the discourse brought the beginnings of modern republican ideology.[8] There exists, however, no counterweight to this Florentine construct on the Milanese side, owing to the loss of archival records in that Lombard city and to the general scholarly preference for the Florentine point of view and for accepting at face value Florence's opinion of itself. This last tendency has affected our understanding of Hawkwood, whose career has been extrapolated almost wholly from Florentine sources. The presence of the Uccello fresco in the Duomo has fixed for posterity the connection between the city and captain.

The argument here is that Hawkwood's funeral rites constituted a critical moment in the construction of his public persona, a sort of domestication post-mortem of the warrior. The funeral occurred in the context of war, amid posturing and propagandizing among the participants. It provided a means by which the Florentines co-opted Hawkwood for themselves and made him their own. It not only honoured the man, but also formed part of an inter-state discourse, what I call here a dialogue of power.

This interpretation stresses the role of Hawkwood's funeral as a species of ritual, as were all public events. The role of ritual and representation in late medieval Italy is well known and has been studied by Richard Trexler, Edward Muir, Ronald Weissman and others.[9] Edward Muir, in particular, has emphasized how rituals were used to 'make power visible' and render it noticeable to the eye.[10] David Kertzer, in more general terms, has shown how political rituals often involved construction of symbolic meanings around great men.[11] Sharon Strocchia has examined the rituals attendant on late-medieval Italian burials and has unpacked the Hawkwood ceremony in particular. She has argued that it was the most elaborate of an already 'flamboyant' post-plague Florentine funerary style. City officials used the ceremony in didactic ways, as a 'tool' to celebrate civic pride and to emphasize important political themes. Hawkwood's funeral conveyed images of 'civic loyalty' and 'communal power' as well as a 'striking picture both of the triumph of flamboyance and of the commune triumphant'.[12]

Strocchia's analysis is sensitive and suggestive, but stresses only the domestic function of the ceremony and the projection of images at Florence's

8 Hans Baron, *The crisis of the early Italian Renaissance*, 2nd ed. (Princeton, 1966); J.G.A. Pocock, *The machiavellian moment: Florentine political thought and the Atlantic republican tradition* (Princeton, 1975). For reappraisals of this view see now James Hankins (ed.), *Renaissance civic humanism, reappraisals and reflections* (Cambridge, 2000). 9 Edward Muir, *Civic ritual in Renaissance Venice* (1982); Richard Trexler, *Public life in Renaissance Florence* (New York, 1981); R.F.E. Weissman, *Ritual brotherhood in Renaissance Florence* (New York, 1982). 10 Edward Muir, 'Representations of power,' in J.M. Najemy (ed.), *Italy and the age of the Renaissance* (Oxford, 2004), p. 226. 11 D.I. Kertzer, *Ritual, politics and power* (New Haven, 1988), pp 12–13. 12 S.T. Strocchia, *Death and ritual in Renaissance Florence* (Baltimore, 1992), pp 55, 79–82.

own citizens. Hawkwood's funeral, however, also had an external function, intended to send those same images of civic loyalty, pride and triumph out-side of the city, to other states, which kept careful watch on such ceremonies and judged their actions in terms of each other. The funerals themselves may be understood as an extension of the rituals attendant warfare. The current scholarly emphasis on mercenaries, 'bloodless' battles and lack of civic virtue has obscured the fact that war was highly ritualistic, characterized by coded behaviour in the field. This included choreographed insults in front of enemy town walls and defamatory paintings (*pitture infamante*) of enemy captains, placed in public areas.[13] Honour and shame were, as Richard Trexler has argued, intrinsically linked in the military sector. Opponents 'sacralized' that which was anathema to the other; the 'greatest honour' was that which was 'most disgraceful' to the enemy.[14]

Hawkwood's funeral occurred on 20 March 1394. The several extant accounts recall a spectacular event.[15] The Florentine diarist Naddo da Montecatini wrote that 'neither citizen nor foreigner has ever received such a tribute'. The Minerbetti chronicle claimed that in all of Italy 'at no time had any person been honoured so magnificently'.[16] The whole city participated in the funeral, including politicians, magistrates, guildsmen, priests, monks and ordinary citizens. Local shops were closed by communal decree. The com-mune and guilds supplied caparisoned horses, candles and torches. The cer-emony began in the Piazza della Signoria, where Hawkwood's bier was placed, dressed opulently in vermilion velvets and cloths brocaded with gold. It was then transferred to the Baptistery of San Giovanni, laid out on the baptismal font for public viewing. Sharon Strocchia has stressed the unique-ness and importance of this act, which symbolized both the city's 'loss' and 'cyclical renewal'.[17] The act was likewise one of appropriation, making the erstwhile Englishmen an adoptive Florentine, baptized anew, in death, by the city. Hawkwood's corpse was transferred to the cathedral, put on a catafalque in the central choir, eulogized and then buried in the cathedral.

---

13 Richard Trexler, *Pubic life in Renaissance Florence*, pp 4–5 and '"Correre la Terra": col-lective insults in the late Middle Ages', *MEFRM* 96 (1984), 857–60, 864–5. On *pitture infamante*, see S.Y. Edgerton, *Pictures and punishment: art and criminal prosecution during the Florentine Renaissance* (Ithaca, 1985), and Gherardo Ortalli, *Pingatur in palatio. La Pittura infamante nei secoli XIII –XVI* (Rome, 1979).   14 Trexler, '"Correre la Terra"', p. 871. 15 The published primary accounts include *Cronica volgare di Anonimo Fiorentino* (Piero di Giovanni Minerbetti), ed. Elina Bellondi, *RIS*, 17, part 2 (Bologna, 1937) and Naddo da Montecatini, *Memorie storiche dal anno 1374 al anno 1398*, ed. Ildefonso di San Luigi, Delizie degli Eruditi Toscani, vol. 18 (Florence, 1784) and G. Aiazzi (ed.), *Ricordi storici di Filippo di Cino Rinuccini dal 1282 al 1460 colla continuazione di Alemanno e neri suoi figli fino al 1506* (Florence, 1840). The standard secondary account, with documents, is A. Medin, 'La morte di Giovanni Aguto,' *ASI* 17–18 (1886), 161–71.   16 Naddo da Montecatini, *Memorie storiche*, p. 141; Medin, 'La morte di Giovanni Aguto,' p. 173.   17 Strocchia, *Death and ritual*, p. 81.

That the city sincerely mourned the loss of Hawkwood is beyond question. He had performed well in the war against Milan and Siena, a conflict that Florentine officials viewed as a threat to the very existence of the commune. Florence fought on two fronts, both north (against Milan) and south (against Siena). Hawkwood headed efforts in the north. His success lay not in major victory in the field, but in keeping his army from defeat and returning safely from deep within Milanese territory. Florentine officials had intended to link Hawkwood's army with a force descending from France under the count of Armagnac for a major assault on Milan. Hawkwood advanced as far as the territorial space of Bergamo, to the banks of the Adda River, within 25 kilometers of Milan. But Armagnac was greatly delayed, by a combination of lack of money and difficulties assembling his force. This left Hawkwood isolated and overextended, short on supplies, and facing the full weight of the Milanese army. Hawkwood had little recourse but to retreat, an option rendered all the more difficult by the work of Milanese engineers, who ruptured the banks of the Adige, flooding the plain. But Hawkwood escaped, largely by means of ruse. He sent a challenge to battle to the Milanese army and then, under the cover of night, ordered a full retreat, leaving his banners hoisted high on his now abandoned camp and the bonfires burning, so that the enemy would believe he was still there. The ruse was worthy of Hawkwoood's nickname 'acuto'.[18] The retreat was arduous and involved crossing three major rivers (Oglio, Adige, Mincio), swollen by rains. The rigors of the action likely exhausted Hawkwood, who was then nearly 70 years old. He became ill soon after a truce was signed, and died shortly thereafter.

Hawkwood died a hero. His performance in the war was one of the few positives in a conflict of little real result and no resolution of the basic issues. The Minerbetti chronicle praised Hawkwood's retreat as emblematic of his 'wisdom' and 'skill' as a captain.[19] Soon after his death, an unknown author composed a song (*cantare*) in *rima ottava* honouring Hawkwood's deeds. It circulated throughout the city, and the chronicler Benedetto Dei claimed to know it by heart.[20] Leonardo Bruni in his Histories of the Florentine People, begun in 1415, praised Hawkwood's war service and claimed that 'no other captain ... would have been able to save the army from such difficulty'.[21]

The dimensions and details of Hawkwood's funeral were, however, not as unique as Florentine sources would have them appear. Hawkwood's death rites occurred between two elaborate state funerals for military captains in Siena: one for Giovanni D'Azzo degli Ubaldini, who died three years before the Englishman, and another for Giovanni 'Tedesco' da Pietramala, who died

18 Minerbetti, *Cronica volgare*, pp 131–2; *Chronicon Estense*, ed. Giulio Bertoni & Emilio Paolo Vicini (eds), *RIS*, 15, part 3 (Bologna, 1933), col. 523.   19 Minerbetti, *Cronica volgare*, p. 132.   20 Medin, 'La morte di Giovanni Aguto', p. 173.   21 Leonardo Bruni, *Istoria fiorentina*, trans. Donato Accaiaouli (Florence, 1861), p. 539.

almost exactly a year after Hawkwood. Both men served Siena as captains in
the war against Florence in 1390. Both were from prominent feudal clans,
whose patrimonies lay within the confines of the Florentine state.[22] The
Ubaldini family held lands in the Mugello region, north of Florence, near the
Appenines, where Florentine territory gave way to that of Bologna. Their possessions formed an important passageway, used by armies to enter and leave
Tuscany. This strategic importance engendered very tense relations between
the family and the state, which flared on several occasion into open war.
Giovanni 'Tedesco' Pietramala came from the Tarlati clan, which had formerly
been lords of Arezzo, and held important castles in the environs of that city.
They were effectively disenfranchized, however, when Florence bought Arezzo
in 1384. Florentine officials demanded that they give up their properties, a
request that led to armed confrontation, in which Giovanni took part (1385/6).
But Florence prevailed and the Pietramala family, in the estimation of the
Minerbetti chronicle, emerged embittered and severely damaged.[23]

Both men were thus well-known in Florence, where their service was perceived as treacherous. Giovanni d'Azzo degli Ubaldini's behaviour was seen
as particularly treacherous, since Florentine officials had made an accommodation with him just a few years earlier, which involved paying him substantial sums of money. In the end, both Ubaldini and Pietramala died by means
of Florentine poison, the former dispatched by a tainted bowl of cherries; the
latter by corrupted wine.[24] Their funerals in Siena did not go unnoticed in
Florence. Indeed, an anonymous diarist claimed that there was widespread
rejoicing in Florence at the news of Pietramala's death.[25]

The dislike of the men in Florence was proportional to the intensity of the
conflict with Siena. The long-standing cultural, economic and military competition between the two states is well known to scholars. By the middle of
the decade of the 1380s the conflict became especially intense. The point of
departure was the purchase by Florence in 1384 of Arezzo, a city that the
Sienese had also bid on. Florence then embarked aggressively on building a
territorial state, extending its authority beyond its usual local sphere of influence.[26] The expansion came at the direct expense of Siena. Several key

---

22 On the Ubaldini, see Laura Magna, 'Gli Ubaldini del Mugello: una signoria feudale nel
contado fiorentino' in *I ceti dirigenti del eta comunale nei secoli xii e xiii* (Pisa, 1982), pp 13–
66; Samuel K. Cohn, *Creating the Florentine state: peasants and rebellion, 1348–1434*
(Cambridge, 1999), pp 19, 21, 81. 23 Minerbetti, *Cronica volgare*, p. 6. 24 The charges
of poison relating to Ubaldini are recorded by Montauri in *Cronache senesi*, ed. Alessandro
Lisini & Fabio Iacometti, *RIS*, n.s., 15, part 4 (Bologna, 1931–7), p. 735. The charges
relating to Pietramala are in a Florentine account, by an anonymous diarist; ed. Anthony
Molho & Franek Sznura, *Alle bocche della piazza (diario di anonimo fiorentino, 1382–1401)*
(Florence, 1986), p. 176. 25 *Alle bocche*, p. 176. 26 Gene Brucker, *The civic world of
early Renaissance Florence* (Princeton, 1977), pp 105–6. On the Florentine territorial state,
see Andrea Zorzi, 'The "material Constitution" of the Florentine dominion' in W.J.
Connell & A. Zorzi (eds), *Florentine Tuscany: structures and practices of power* (Cambridge,

Sienese satellite towns, notably Montepulciano and Lucignano, rebelled against the city, for which officials held Florence responsible.[27] By the late 1380s a *de facto* but as yet undeclared state of war existed between the two. In 1389 Siena signed a ten-year alliance with Milan, essentially placing itself under Milanese protection, in return for military aid.[28] When war broke out a year later, the Sienese front became the most bitter theater of activity. The standard conventions of fourteenth-century warfare – capture rather than murder, manoeuver rather than battle – were largely ignored. 'For every one of ours killed,' wrote a Sienese ambassador stationed at the front, 'we killed one of theirs ... for no one wants prisoners.'[29]

Giovanni d'Azzo degli Ubaldini had been Siena's most effective captain until he died suddenly on 26 June 1391. His funeral occurred on 28 June. The description of his funeral by the Sienese chronicler Paolo di Tommaso Montauri is strikingly similar to contemporary descriptions of Hawkwood's funeral. Montauri claimed that 'no man, not pope nor emperor', had ever received such consideration. The particulars are similar to those of Hawkwood's funeral. As with Hawkwood, the Sienese chronicler stressed the participation of the whole city in the ceremony: politicians, clergy and the populace at large. The guilds supplied caparisoned horses, candles and torches – the latter flooding the cathedral with light. Stores and shops were closed. Ubaldini's bier was draped with ornate cloths. He was eulogized in the cathedral and then buried there.[30]

The Sienese chronicler's account is less detailed than the Florentine sources regarding Hawkwood, thus hampering further comparison of motifs and symbolism. But the Sienese account is sufficient to make clear the grandness of the ceremony and that it occurred in the most sacred space of the city. The scale is itself significant since ostentatious funerals, as Robert Munman has pointed out, were uncommon at the time in Siena, owing to prohibitive sumptuary legislation.[31] Philippa Jackson has recently suggested that the number of wax torches used in funerals served as a measure of the status of the deceased. By this index, the Ubaldini funeral ranked above all others of the era. The 500 double-branched candles (*doppieri*) and 800 torches which Montauri claimed the city supplied for the service dwarfs the outlay for Pandolfo Petrucci (40 torches and 10 *doppieri*), the famed Sienese tyrant of the sixteenth century, whose funeral scholars have viewed as the period's

2000), pp 6–31.   **27** William Caferro, *Mercenary companies and the decline of Siena* (Baltimore, 1998), pp xvi–xvii, 19, 24, 33–5, 165; Brucker, *Civic world*, pp 106–12.   **28** Caferro, *Mercenary companies*, pp 165–6.   **29** Archivio di Stato di Siena, Concistoro 1829, 57; Caferro, *John Hawkwood*, p. 290.   **30** *Cronache senesi*, pp 735–6.   **31** Robert Munman, *Sienese Renaissance tombs* (Philadelphia, 1993), pp 4–8. For Sienese sumptuary legislation and funerals, see A. Liberati, 'Un funerale a Siena nel XV secolo', *Bulletino senese di storia patria* 46 (1939), 53–9; Patrizia Turrini, 'Le ceremonie funebri a Siena nel basso medioevo', *Bulletino senese di storia patria* 110 (2003), 53–104.

most conspicuous.[32] Ubaldini appears to have received greater consideration in this regard than John Hawkwood, for whom the Minerbetti chronicle claimed the city supplied 140 *doppieri* and an undisclosed number of torches.[33]

As in Hawkwood's case, there is little doubt that the ceremony reflected a sincere love for Ubaldini. But the Sienese knew well the effect of the ceremony on its neighbor and enemy, Florence. The funeral occurred in the middle of war. The chronicler estimated its cost at 2–3,000 florins, a figure that constituted fiscal negligence given the desperate financial state of Siena, whose armies were by now wholly paid for by Milan. The city did not have sufficient revenue to meet the cost of the basic governmental functions.[34] In honouring Ubaldini there was the unmistakable feature of 'sacralizing' that which was anathema to the opponent.

If the Ubaldini funeral helped set the terms for Hawkwood's funeral that followed it, then the funeral of Giovanni Pietramala, Siena's other prominent captain, makes sense only in terms of the Hawkwood funeral that preceded it. Pietramala had, like Ubaldini, been a hero in the Milanese war. But just prior to his death, he fell into disfavor with the Sienese authorities. According to the chronicler Montauri, Pietramala had angered officials by aiding a band of Breton mercenaries, who were at odds with the city. He in fact joined with the Bretons against the Sienese army, defeated the Sienese force and took prisoners. Nevertheless, when Pietramala died he received a lavish funeral, on the model of those of Ubaldini and Hawkwood.

Like both the Ubaldini and Hawkwood ceremonies, Pietramala's funeral was a spectacular public affair in which the whole city participated. Pietramala's funeral occurred February 1395 and laid bare the pointed interstate dialogue embedded in the ceremonies.[35] It was attended by politicians, clergy and monks as well as local citizens. Montauri decribes a highly emotional scene, with much weeping and lamentation. A rainstorm occurred in the middle of the ceremony, which, for Montauri, seemed as 'if the skies too were crying'.[36] As in the other funerals, Pietramala's corpse was taken to the cathedral, eulogized and then buried there. The chronicler again gave hyperbolic statement of the significance of the ceremony. 'There was no one at this time who remembers having seen or heard of such magnificence and honour bestowed on a man.'[37] The line recalls the description of the Hawkwood ceremony in the Minerbetti chronicle, as well as Montauri's own earlier statements about Ubaldini. The declaration is clearly disingenuous, however, because in the very next paragraph Montauri gives a dramatic disclaimer. He says that Pietramala's funeral would have been grander still had

---

32 Philippa Jackson, 'Pomp or piety?: the funeral of Pandolfo Petrucci', *Renaissance Studies* 20 (2006), 240–52; G.A. Johnson, 'Activating the effigy: Donatello's Pecci tomb in Siena's cathedral', *The Art Bulletin* (1995), 445–59.   33 Minerbetti, *Cronica volgare*, p. 183.   34 On the fiscal condition of Siena at this time see Caferro, *Mercenary companies*, pp 156–71.   35 *Cronache senesi*, p. 747.   36 Ibid., p. 748.   37 Ibid., p. 748.

he not betrayed the city, something which, he writes, the Sienese were 'unable to forgive'.

The statement raises the question, why celebrate Pietramala at all? His funeral makes little sense apart from its role as part of a continuing dialogue with Florence, as a means of portraying images of power and civic loyalty as a counter to the Hawkwood rite, an opportunity to heap scorn on Florence, to sacralize that which was anathema to the opponent.

The funerary dialogue involved more than just Florence and Siena, and historians still need to sort out the details. Mercenary captains received state funerals and burials in cathedrals elsewhere in Italy in the fourteenth century.[38] Tibertino Brandolino, an Italian mercenary, who fought both for and against Hawkwood, was laid to rest in the church of San Francesco in Venice; Jacopo de' Cavalli, who had fought along with Hawkwood outside Verona in 1379, was interred in the same city at SS Giovanni e Paolo; and Paolo Savelli, who had opposed Hawkwood on the Sienese border during the Milanese war, was buried at the church of the Frari in Venice.[39]

For the most part, the death rites of these men were less spectacular than those for Hawkwood, Ubaldini and Pietramala. Cavalli, for one, paid for his own funeral. We possess no evidence of such ceremonies in Milan, but this was because its leading captains remained alive for the duration of the war with Florence. Siena, Milan's ally, already provided a venue for this behaviour. Nevertheless, we do see a posturing and competition with respect to living military men. During their wars, Florence and Milan, vied with each other in bestowing honours on their captains. Here again Hawkwood is a key figure. Prior to his great offensive into Milanese territory, Florentine officials granted Hawkwood citizenship (April 1391). The decision probably came not as a reward for meritorious service, but to match a similar grant given by the Milanese to their main captain, Jacopo dal Verme, who opposed Hawkwood. Dal Verme received Milanese and Veronese citizenship of, as well as landed estates in both places. Hawkwood, for his part, was granted an increase in his lifetime pension and dowries for his unmarried daughters. The gifts were intended to tie the captains more closely to their employers, in the hope of minimizing the risk of desertion and disaffection.[40] Hawkwood's Florentine citizenship thus had little to do with any affection for the city, but was wholly utilitarian.

A similar discourse can be detected in the efforts to commemorate Hawkwood with a monument, which culminated in Uccello's great work in

38 Eve Borsook, *The mural painters of Tuscany* (Oxford, 1980), pp 75–6; Michael Mallett, *Mercenaries and their masters* (Totowa, 1974), pp 94–5; W. Valentiner, 'The equestrian statue of Paolo Savelli in the Frari', *The Art Quarterly* 16 (1953), 280–93. 39 Reinhold Mueller, 'Veronesi e Capitali Veronesi', in Gian Maria Varanini (ed.), *Gli Scaliger, 1277–1387* (Verona, 1988), p. 371; Borsook, *Mural painters*, pp 75–6. 40 ASF, Capitoli, registri, 1 fols. 160v–163v; ASMi, Registri, Panigarola, n. 1. fols. 150r–150v. See Caferro, *John Hawkwood*, p. 299.

the Florentine Duomo in 1436.[41] Such honours were, along with public burials, becoming increasingly common in the late *trecento* and would become
even more so in the next century.[42] The art historian H.W. Janson, among
the first to study these monuments, stessed their role as 'public enterprises'
and expressions of public sentiment.[43] More recently, Sarah Blake McHam
has made clear the role played by public statues in Florence in representing
power and political purpose.[44] Randolph Starn, Diane Zervas, Charles M.
Rosenberg and others have emphasized more generally the political function
of art and architecture of the period.[45]

In the case of Hawkwood, the events in neighboring Siena again appear
most important. After the funeral and burial of Ubaldini, the Sienese undertook to make a memorial in his honour. According to Giorgio Vasari, who
describes it in detail, this was an equestrian statue, in wood, done by Jacopo
della Quercia.[46] Recent scholarship has, however, shown, on the basis of documentary evidence, that the memorial was in reality a painting, by an artist
who remains unknown.[47] Nevertheless, all sources agree that a work was made
in Ubaldini's honour and placed in the cathedral of Siena, where it was at the
time Hawkwood died.

The efforts in Florence to commemorate Hawkwood with a monument of
his own followed not long after. Florence initiated the project as early as
1393, while Hawkwood was still alive, though most likely infirm. The plans
called for a marble tomb. The project was, however, delayed, though it is not
certain why. In the meantime, Pietramala died and the Sienese now commissioned a monument on his behalf. The precise timing of this is unclear, as are
all the details relating to the Pietramala commission. Like the Ubaldini painting, it has not survived into the present day. This appears, however, to have
been the work of della Quercia and took the form of a statue made of wood,
which was placed in the cathedral.

While the della Quercia statue honouring the Sienese Pietramala was being
considered or perhaps already undertaken, the plans for Hawkwood's memo-

---

41 Hugh Hudson, 'The politics of war', *Parergon* 23 (2006), 1–34.   42 Stephan Selzer,
Deutsche Söldner im Italien des Trecento (Tübingen, 2001), pp 173–5.   43 H.W. Janson,
'The equestrian monument from Cangrande della Scala to Peter the Great' in *Sixteen
Studies* (New York, 1965), pp 159–68.   44 Sarah Blake McHam, 'Public sculpture in
Renaissance Florence' in Sarah Blake McHam (ed.), *Looking at Italian Renaissance sculp-
ture* (Cambridge, 1998), pp 149–89.   45 Randolph Starn, 'Reinventing heroes in
Renaissance Italy, the evidence of art: images and meaning in history', *Journal of
Interdisciplinary History* 17 (1986), 67–84; Diane Zervas, *The Parte Guelfa, Brunelleschi and
Donatello* (New York, 1987); C.M. Rosenberg, *The Este monuments and urban development
in Renaissance Ferrara* (New York, 1997); Andrew Butterfield, 'Monument and memory in
early Renaissance Florence' in Giovanni Ciapelli & Patricia Lee Rubin (eds), *Art, memory
and family in Renaissance Florence* (Cambridge, 2000), pp 135–60.   46 Giorgio Vasari, *The
lives of the Artists*, trans. Conaway Bondanella & Peter Bondanella (Oxford, 1998) pp 58–
9.   47 James Beck, *Jacopo della Quercia*, II (New York, 1991), pp 334, 341.

rial were revived in Florence. The new proposal called for reworking an older wooden statue already in the cathedral and dedicated to Piero Farnese, an Italian mercenary captain who served the city in its war against Pisa (1362–4). Both Hawkwood and Farnese would be sculpted in marble and placed in the north aisle of the cathedral, facing the high altar. This project, however, gave way to a still larger design to erect a series of monuments in the cathedral commemorating men of action and men of letters, including Dante, Boccaccio, Petrarch and the humanist theologian Luigi de' Marsigli.[48]

The ever-escalating scheme delayed the completion of the Hawkwood project. In 1396 a committee of experts chose Agnolo Gaddi and Giuliano Arrighi (known as Pesello) to sketch the Hawkwood and Farnese tombs. But for reasons that are again unclear, officials decided to leave Farnese in wood, and reduce the Hawkwood project to a wall painting, done by the above-named artists. Scholars have speculated that the decision was due to a lack of funds resulting from plague and war or perhaps even to Florentine superiority with respect to painting technique.[49] The loss of all the memorials – those of Ubaldini, Pietramala, Farnese and Hawkwood – renders impossible any comparison of motifs and styles and the ways that these may have affected each other.

This could well have been the end of the story, but the plan for a marble tomb in Hawkwood's honour was revived 37 years later, in 1433. The original painting by Gaddi and Pesello appears to have become damaged by then; and scholars note the coincidence between the renewed plans and the refurbishing of the cathedral owing to its rededication as Santa Maria del Fiore in March 1436 by Pope Eugenius IV.[50] But the decision to honour Hawkwood anew so long after his death raises questions, most notably why did the city remained so devoted to him after so much time? The choice seems all the more perplexing since the plans for the Uccello fresco were initiated by one government, the Albizzi in 1433, and then effected by another, the Medici in 1436 – two regimes that had little in common.[51]

The decision makes sense, however, in terms of a continuing dialogue among states regarding military men. Florentine governments had changed since Hawkwood's death, but the military situation had not. Florence remained at war with Milan and Siena, and the survival of the city was still in doubt. This, in conjunction with the uncertain service of recent mercenary captains, provided fertile ground in Florence for the propagation and projec-

48 Alessandro Parronchi, *Paolo Uccello* (Bologna, 1974); Borsook, *Mural painters*, p. 76. 49 Borsook, *Mural painters*. p. 75 and 'The power of illusion: fictive tombs in Santa Maria del Fiore' in Margaret Haines (ed.), *Santa Maria del Fiore, the Cathedral and its Sculpture* (Florence, 2001), pp 59–78; Temple-Leader & Marcotti, *Sir John Hawkwood*, p. 294. 50 Borsook, *Mural painters*, p. 76. 51 Borsook, *Mural painters,* p. 75; Leader & Marcotti, *Sir John Hawkwood*, p. 294; Giovanni Poggi & Margaret Haines (eds), *Il duomo di Firenze*, 2 vols (Florence, 1988) II, pp 94–5; Ulisse Forni, *Manuale del pittore restauratore* (Florence, 1866), p. 23.

tion of Hawkwood's legend. Officials again sought to convey images of civic loyalty and communal triumph to the outside world. The art historian Wendy Wegener has shown that Uccello's commission followed the painting of a fresco in 1430 in the city of Lucca honouring the Italian captain Niccolò Piccinino. Lucca was then at war with Florence and allied with Milan and Siena. The memorial to Piccinino drew much attention in Florence, for which the captain had recently worked, leaving under suspicious circumstances.[52] In 1428, after Piccinino's departure from Florentine service, city officials had a *pittura infamante* of him drawn on the walls of the Signoria, depicting him upside down and in chains.[53] Uccello's portrait of Hawkwood followed afterward, presenting the image of what a mercenary captain should be. Piccinino was the image of what a mercenary ought not be.

The pose Uccello gave his Hawkwood confirms this larger political agenda. Hawkwood is depicted in the manner of a captain conducting an inspection of his troops. The gait of the horse is an *ambio* or amble, consistent with a commander slowly moving about his brigade. The movement of the legs confused Giorgio Vasari, who thought it a technical mistake.[54] But the depiction was intentional and didactic. Uccello and his Florentine employers wanted an idealized Hawkwood, in a stance suggestive of a loyal communal servant. The epitaph affixed to the bottom of the fresco was taken from the eulogy of Fabius Maximus, the great Roman general of the third century BC who through his patience and commitment to the state had defeated the great Carthaginian captain Hannibal.[55]

Further support for this interpretation comes from a recent study using ultraviolet rays on the extant design (*modello*) that Uccello submitted to earn the Hawkwood commission. It shows that the painter originally intended to depict Hawkwood in a more bellicose manner, in armor from head to toe, with his baton slightly raised and his horse at the ready. This was Hawkwood the warrior, an image that Florentine officials specifically did not want. This design was rejected, and he was asked to do it again.[56]

It was an idealized, domesticated John Hawkwood that Uccello ultimately portrayed, and it is this image that has been passed down to posterity. But it

---

52 Wendy Wegener, '"That the practice of arms is most excellent declare the statues of valiant men": the Luccan War and the Florentine political ideology in paintings by Uccello and Castagno', *Renaissance Studies* 7 (1993), 142–58.   53 Mallett, *Mercenaries*, p. 94.   54 Vasari, *Lives*, p. 80.   55 Eve Borsook, 'L'Hawkwood d'Uccello et le Vie de Fabius Maximus de Plutarque', *Revue Art* 55 (1982), 44–51.   56 Lorenza Melli, 'Nuove indagine sui disegni di Paolo Uccello agli Uffizi: Disegno sottostante, tecnica, funzione', *Mitteilungen des Kunsthistorischen Institutes in Florenz* 42 (1998), 6. The decision of the *operai* of the cathedral to make Uccello redo the painting has elicited much discussion among art historians, who have cited, among other things, problems with perspective and colors. See D. Gioseffi, 'Complementi di prospettiva di Apollodor d'Atene, di Filippo, di Paolo e d'atre cose', *Critica d'arte* 5 (1958), 131; B. Degenhart & A. Schmitt, *Corpus der Italienische Zeichnungen, 1300–1450*, 2 vols (Berlin, 1960) II, p. 382; Parronchi, *Paolo Uccello*, p. 31.

was an image consciously fashioned in the context of war, and bears little resemblance to the 'real' John Hawkwood. For the sake of Florentine propaganda Hawkwood needed to be a loyal communal employee. And so he was. The funeral and memorial became a means of co-opting the great captain's image, announcing to other states that so skillful a soldier had chosen to ally himself for posterity with the city. The placing of Hawkwood's body on the baptismal font of San Giovanni during his funeral, the most novel feature of the ceremony, was a symbolic act that effectively made Hawkwood a Florentine. What Uccello has given us – and what biographers have trumpeted – is therefore little more than a mask, a vestige of Florentine propaganda, that has impeded a proper understanding of the man.

Community and country life in
late medieval Tuscany

DUANE OSHEIM

Christine Meek's studies of Lucchese politics and society have concentrated on the role of government and the problems of the commune. But in doing so she has also noted the importance of relations with the countryside. It is to the country that I would like to return today. Although the Lucchese countryside suffered terribly in the wars, famines and plagues of the fourteenth century, its basic social and economic structure remained resilient, and interestingly different from the situation elsewhere in Tuscany.

In northwestern Tuscany the late Middle Ages was a golden age for independent farmers. Since early in the thirteenth century, servile status (whatever it actually meant in Tuscany) was little more than an excuse for a landlord to collect an occasional *servitium*, or payment in lieu of services. Yet independence was not simply a matter of legal status. As Frank McArdle noted, seventeenth-century Tuscan peasants were legally free, but because of economic and social structures, they behaved in a manner quite like that of the legally bound peasantry of Eastern Europe.[1]

Thus it was economic and social factors and not legal status which made for independent farmers in what are now the modern provinces of Lucca and Pisa. Farmers in the districts of Pisa and Lucca were really an exception in the late Middle Ages. For it was here that farmers held out most effectively against the formation of unified farms and transformation of landlord–tenant relations with the introduction of sharecropping contracts.

In order to better understand what was unusual about the farmers of north-west Tuscany, it would be well to consider for a moment the transformation which was changing agriculture in much of the rest of Tuscany. Both the formation of unified farms and sharecropping depended on a level of landlord supervision and control highly unusual before about 1250. *Appoderamento*, that is, the process of the creation of farms, involved the gathering together of sufficient quantities of land so that a tenant could rent all he needed, lands, gardens, house, well, threshing floor perhaps even an oven from a single landlord. In some cases all these properties would be a compact whole separated from the lands of others in the same neighborhoods. More commonly however, they were pieces of land scattered among the holdings of

1 Francis McArdle, 'Another look at peasant families east and west', *Peasant Studies Newsletter* 3:3 (1974), 11–14.

others living in the same area. In this last case farmers continued to live in small communities, sometimes centered on a single *corte* or courtyard where they could share a well, threshing floor and oven. But what whatever its form, *appoderamento* meant that a tenant was holding virtually all his land from a single landlord.

The reorganization of the land market around relatively large, compact farms was often the first step in the transformation of the landlord tenant relationship. Simply put it was a matter of control. Students of Tuscan agriculture agree that for the landlord, the introduction of sharecropping agreements, specialization in products highly valued in the urban markets like wheat, wine, or oil and intensive methods of fertilization and cultivation depended on the ability of the landlord to control tenants. The nature of landlord control is most evident in the *mezzadria classica*, the Tuscan sharecropping arrangement.[2]

In the classic sharecropping agreement, the landlord can be expected to provide the equipment, farmstead, land, up to half the necessary seed or fertilizer and even short-term loans to get the farmer through the year. Landlords could define the crops to be raised, plowing and fertilizing techniques, and the times for pruning and harvesting. Tenants provided the labour. It was understood that the sharecropper and his family should devote all their labour to the farm unless they were given permission to work elsewhere by the landlord. Landlords preferred that the sharecropper live on an isolated farmstead, cut off from the surrounding community. Indeed at Siena, city statutes required that except in times of war, sharecroppers of townsmen should not be required to assume any of the fiscal or personal burdens of the village.[3]

While contracts dividing wine or olive harvests can be found from the eleventh century, the classic sharecropping contract only appeared in significant numbers in the second half of the thirteenth century. First around Siena and later in the Florentine countryside, sharecropping contracts appeared in the fertile valleys closes to towns in those districts where townsmen preferred to invest their money. The last areas to get sharecropping contracts were in what are now the modern provinces of Pisa and Lucca. In those districts, independent farmers generally managed to avoid sharecropping arrangements until the very late fifteenth or sixteenth centuries and around Pisa, where they were much more common, they were one of the effects of Florentine conquest. Thus, the independent farmers of northwest Tuscany offer an interesting counter example to the growth of landlord power in the late Middle Ages.

2 For recent work on the mezzadria see Gabriella Piccinni, 'In merito a recenti studi sulla mezzadria nella Toscana medievale', *Bulletino senese di storia patria* 89 (1982), 336–82. 3 Gabriella Piccinni, '*Seminare, fruttare, raccogliere': mezzari e salariati sulle terre di Monte Oliveto Maggiore (1374–1430)* (Milan, 1982), pp 50, 103 n. 4.

Lucca's *districtus* which is comprised of the band of territories directly under communal jurisdiction since the late eleventh century and covering most of the plain between the Serchio and Arno Rivers is exactly the sort of area which should be most appealing to landlords. Yet independent farmers continued to predominate throughout most of the fifteenth century. The plains and foothills in the parishes of San Paolo and Compito to the south of the city included vineyards, grain fields, olive groves and woodland areas. They are, in a sense, a fertile microcosm of the agrarian lands of the Lucchese plain. And in certain respects they resemble parts of the Pisan plain. If we analyse a series of precise portraits of various parts of these two parishes, we can appreciate why independent farmers in this area long resisted the *mezzadria* contracts which were increasingly popular in other parts of Tuscany.

In this context, the first surviving *Estimo* (1284) declarations of the village of Santa Margarita in the Parish of San Paolo make very interesting reading.[4] As one would expect in a village located only a few miles from Lucca, the town had a significant influence on tenant relations. In the first place, even by 1284 townsmen made up a significant proportion of the landlords or others who could claim a share of the harvest. The 52 villagers who made declarations listed some 490 payments of which over half were made to townsmen or urban ecclesiastical institutions. And of those payments almost exactly three-quarters (75.6 per cent) were to laymen, mostly to men associated with Lucca's commercial elite. The landlords claimed their rents almost exclusively in wheat and millet; only a small fraction accepted any lesser grains or legumes like broad beans. While many of the pieces of land in the *estimo* were noted as including grape vines, trees and even orchards, landlords do not seem to have found these crops of a sufficient quality or market value to make them worth collecting. What is interesting about these urban landlords is that in terms of rents, commodities required, size of fields, or even contractual relationships, these urban landowners behaved no differently than other landlords in the village. The reason may be the complex of economic, and probably social, relationships which bound the villagers, their families and their lands together in such a way that it would have been extremely difficult for any single landlord monopolize a farmer's economic relations. Thus even in the areas closest to the city, precious commercial products like wine and oil were not preferred, that is, the landlord could not make the switch in rent commodities.

On an average, each villager held about just under five acres (4.7) of land in the village or in nearby parts of the parish. These five acres would have been divided into about six fields, usually described simply as *campus* by which they meant arable. Of these pieces, the villager probably owned one, usually with a house, shack or other buildings.[5] On the remaining five pieces,

4 ASL, Estimo 24.   5 Ibid., e.g., s. n. Bonaiunctius Arimanni: *Item dixit quod habet alodium qua est capanna.*

the villager owed about eight (8.4) payments to townsmen, other countrymen, or ecclesiastical institutions. Many of the payments were traditional sorts of rent, but may others were secondary rents, or perpetual loans created when a tenant sold his share of the improvements in the land, or *melioramentum*, to a third party. As if matters were not complex enough, 15 per cent of the villagers acknowledged that they too were collecting rents from neighbors, for perpetual loans '*pro melioramento*'.

The land market was extremely volatile in Santa Margarita. In several cases the scribe was forced to add a marginal notation that the piece of land in question had been transferred to another, often within a year of the composition of the register. At times the tenant declared that he was making a payment to the landlord in the name of another who apparently was the tenant of record in the inventory of the landlord. And one other tenant specifically confessed that he had no written proof of his right to farm the land.[6] It seems from these entries and other documents that much of the land circulated within families and between friends who often made no formal agreement about rents and terms. One tenant for example, 'confessed that ... he holds the above mentioned pieces of land from Luttero Simi of Santa Margarita and accordingly pays twenty-three staia, half of wheat and half of millet to the Hospital of Altopascio'.[7] But what is interesting is that while he acknowledged Luttero's right to the land, he did not include any annual payment in recognition of that right. It is very likely that here, as elsewhere in the document, a whole series of unwritten transactions and agreements were successfully hidden from the eyes of the government.

The *Estimo* of Santa Margarita shows that while urban speculators indeed held a significant amount of land in the village, the web of loans, purchases and trades between the villagers and others of the same and neighboring parishes was probably just as significant. The money lending for casual credit, in fact, probably was done by local residents, for almost all the payments listed as being '*pro melioramento*', the typical way to make small loans, were being made to the countrymen of Santa Margarita or of neighboring villages.

What the document does not show is the presence of livestock in the village. It may well be that on holdings of five or six acres there was little need of draft animals. Yet later in the fourteenth and fifteenth centuries, there is evidence that there were some. Much more common however in the Parish of San Paolo and even more so in Compito was the existence of meat animals: sheep or goats in San Paolo and more often pigs in the Compito. Most families had only a few pigs or goats which probably grazed on common lands

---

6 Ibid., s.n. Landorus Bonaiuncte: ... *de qua terra non habet cartam tenementis.* 7 Ibid., s.n. Bonasaltus Galli: ... *quas duas suprascriptas petias terrarum dictus Bonasaltus suo jure dixit tenere a Lucterio Simi de Sanct Margarita ad reddendum exinde pro dicto Lucterio Mansioni Altopassus starias viginti tres grani et milli per medium.*

until after harvest. Some few of them were held by *soccida* contracts with townsmen, but as late as the early fifteenth century pigs and goats – even cows, horses and donkeys – were usually owned outright by the farmer.

It is difficult to evaluate the size of the rents. It seems likely that if good land could produce about three staia of wheat or millet for each staia of seed, landlords claimed less than half the crop, perhaps as little as one third. Rents were usually paid in a combination of wheat and millet. Other grains, legumes and wine, which it is apparent from the descriptions of the lands and from other documents were produced by most of these farmer, do not appear in the declared rents.

A farmer on only about five acres who surrenders one third to one half of his crop would be in a perilous position unless there were other sources of income. We can get a glimpse of the possibilities if we move from the pieve of San Paolo to the nearby parish of Compito. Compito is not perfectly analogous to San Paolo however. San Paolo was on the plain with a number of waterways and drainage ditches, but most of the land was arable. There were several wooded areas, where farmers harvested poplars, willows and some varieties of reeds, but for the most part pieces of land were described as arable fields, perhaps with vineyards. Compito, on the other hand, stretched from the shores of the marsh and lake of Bientina/Sesto to the summit of the Monti Pisani. The parish had a great number of grain fields, but there were also groves of olive trees and large tracts of forests where oaks, poplars, and chestnuts predominated. Landlords in the Compito, like their peers in San Paolo, preferred whenever possible to collect rents in grains, primarily wheat and millet. They did collect large amounts of olive oil, a product for which Compito is still rightfully famous. Because of the hilly nature of large parts of the parish plots tended to be smaller than in San Paolo and thus the average farmer held more and smaller plots than his neighbor in San Paolo, but otherwise the dynamics of the landlord–tenant relationship tended to be similar to that elsewhere.

A surviving book of gabelle payments, however, allows us to view something of economic activities which are otherwise unrecorded. The book records gabelles collected on wood and other products sold in or imported into the parish of Compito for a single semester of 1383. While books of gabelle receipts seem to offer a snapshot of economic activity, we find that it offers considerably less. Any products carried to Lucca for sale, of course, would pay city gabelles and therefore would not be noted here. Crops, animals, products sold by Lucchese or imported from Lucca would not be included. Thus the snapshot has considerable distortion. Nonetheless because of Compito's location, the problem is not so great as it would be if the parish were closer to Lucca. Although Compito is located on the Lucca side of the Monti Pisani, travel to Pisa was quite simple because boats could move across the lake of Sesto, down one of a number of canals leading to the Arno and hence to Pisa. As many entries indicate, it was an ideal way to travel.[8]

Although farmers were enjoined from exporting most produce from the Lucchese district, forest products were not covered. And wood was a major product in the district. The Compitesi sent boatloads of construction timber, barrel staves and firewood down the river to Pisa. Even whole chestnuts (a cheap and popular source of flour) and other nuts were sold. Farmers produced straw, wicker baskets, rope and flax for the Pisan market. Given the waterways, marsh, and lake itself, it is not surprising that nets, fishtraps, and devises for capturing eels also were imported from Pisa and its district. In addition farmers traveled to Pisa for linen cloth, iron pots, sickles and knives. Given the woods and common lands in the parish, it is not surprising that farmers raised and sold large numbers of sheep and goats. While certainly most found their way to Lucca (and hence were unrecorded here), numerous sales of goats are recorded in the book. Most local sales were to soldiers garrisoned in Castelvechio di Compito, but farmers also bought and sold among themselves, in one case for local wedding feasts.[9] What is surprising about this local trade is not its variety – we ought to have expected as much – it is the fact that nearly 90 per cent of the commerce was in the hands of villagers themselves (it must be recalled that Lucchese merchants and peddlers would have been exempt from the gabelle. Further, in many cases payments must have been made only because the debtor had been denounced to the gabellarius by a third party. In that was it would have been easier for outsiders to leave the parish quickly and thus avoid paying the tax than for locals). This trade makes clear the variety of interests local farmers had. They were not entirely dependent on the major crops which interested either the ecclesiastical or lay landlords.

Had the taxbook from Compito dated from the early fourteenth century, the mix of activities noted in it might have been even greater. By the 1380s, the Lucchese plain, and especially the districts of San Paolo and Compito, had suffered a series of shocks which shattered the communities of independent farmers. Internal political tumult, wars with Pisa and Florence, occupying armies, and finally plague had a profound impact on village life. It began a process of impoverishment of the kind which had been evident in the Sienese countryside a century earlier. The effects are evident in a number of ways. Villages lost so much population that they often were without any communal organization to represent them. For administrative purposes many of the villages of Compito were joined together.[10]

8 ASL, Gabelle del Contado e delle Vicarie 90 (Valle di Compito 1383), 1v: ... *conductus pisae per aquam laci sexti.* 9 Ibid., 10v: ... *quos macellavit pro se et de suis pro nuptiis in domo sua celebratis.* 10 For a discussion of broken communes in a similar Tuscan context, see W.M. Bowsky, *The finance of the commune of Siena, 1287–1355* (Oxford, 1970), pp 250–320.

An analysis of the *estimo* of 1412 for the village of Santa Margarita makes clear some of the changes which had occurred. Because of the effects of war and plague, there were many fewer residents in the village – 16 heads of households were previously there had been 52. On the average each held about nine pieces of land in the village – and sometimes more land in other places about which we know nothing. Instead of holding about five acres (4.6), they now held just under eight. Fields tended to be about the same size as earlier, but in 1412 more were described as being with vines and trees: sometimes including fruit trees. These would have been planted along the edges of the fields, probably with the vines tied to the trees.

Profound differences appear in the patterns of landownership. Only eight of the pieces were listed as alodial. The pattern of rental payments also changed in interesting ways. More of the payments were to religious institutions (both urban and rural) than was true earlier. Townsmen did not register any gain: in fact, they claimed a lower percentage of the payments than they had in 1284. Thus, the impact of death and charitable bequests may have reduced the influence of townsmen.

Most significant in the *Estimo* of 1412 is what seems to be the destruction of the rural network of credit, trades and associations between neighbors and kin. The effects are evident in a number of ways. First, the fine tissue of local loans, recorded as rent payments '*pro melioramento*' has disappeared. And where previously a tenant made payments to several people for a single property, in 1412 the tenant was more likely to list a single payment for a number of properties – some even outside the village of Santa Margarita. Missing as well were the notes indicating that fields were being traded among villagers. The *estimo* has a sleek, transparent quality which seems to indicate that, in this case at least, the rural inventories of churches and monasteries accurately reflect the situation. The village population was also much more mobile. Of the 16 heads of households one was a silvan citizen of Lucca, two were from Florentine territories and at least one had moved in from a neighboring village. According to Franca Leverotti's analysis, mobility is a characteristic of most of the villages recorded in the surviving portions of the *estimo*.[11] And finally, much of the land was in the possession of non-residents of the village: Lucchese as well as villagers from across the Lucchese plain.

The village revealed by the *estimo* of 1412 is smaller and simpler than the thriving village of 1284. And although there are no signs of compact farms or of sharecropping contracts, it seems that the age of the independent farmers was coming to an end. There are a series of phenomena, some better documented in other parts of the district than in Santa Margarita and Compito, which support the conclusions drawn from the *estimo*. In a previous study I

---

11 According to Franca Leverotti's analysis, mobility is a characteristic of most of the villages recorded in the surviving portions of the *estimo*.

argued that on occasion relatives and neighbours aided farmers when they were cited in communal courts. This solidarity, however, was less evident in the late fourteenth century than it had been previously.[12] And Sandte Polica's study of Michele Guinigi's land transactions in the fifteenth century indicate that, although he had not created any compact farmsteads or offered *mezzadria* contracts, he did manage to control his tenants by ensnaring them in a web of gifts, loans, and short-term leases.[13] And finally, through the fifteenth century, there was a concerted attack on the rights of individuals to use public lands. They became, in Massimo Montanari's phrase, land of the commune instead of common lands.[14] The net effect was that a farmer no longer could depend on friends and neighbours for help, credit or land. Farmers also lost access to firewood, nuts, or grazing space. The independent farmers still may have attempted to make their way through a variety of products and economic strategies available to them, but increasingly they had few alternatives to the expensive and dangerous help of the patrician speculators who would reorganize Lucchese agriculture in the years after 1500.

12 D.J. Osheim, 'Countrymen and the law in late medieval Tuscany', *Speculum* (April, 1989), 313–37. 13 Sante Polica, 'An attempted "reconversion" of wealth in XVth century Lucca: the lands of Michele di Giovanni Guinigi', *Journal of European Economic History* 9 (1980), 655–707. 14 Massimo Montanari, *Contadini e città fra 'Langobardia' e 'Romania'* (Florence, 1988), pp 121–2.

The countryside and rural life in the fifteenth-century Lucchesia

M.E. BRATCHEL

Franca Leverotti has calculated that the adult population of the Lucchese countryside fell by perhaps 30 per cent between 1413 and 1451, with the first signs of demographic recovery in the Lucchese plain (the Sei Miglia) dating only from the late 1440s.[1] High mortality rates – and the higher incidence of · flight – can be attributed, in part, to the wars of the first half of the fifteenth century and, more specifically, to the depredations of the *compagnie di ventura*. The grand narrative is familiar from the writings of Lucchese chroniclers, who, from an urban perspective and characteristically of their genre, give meticulous attention to inter-state relations and to the movement and pillagings of troops. A more intimate picture can be gleaned from the legal records, even though record-keeping itself was severely dislocated by the wars of the 1430s.

The years 1429 to 1433 are covered in a volume of civil cases heard before the court of the bishop of Lucca and recorded by the notaries ser Francesco di Gabriele Gonnella and ser Giovanni Teri.[2] The register, haphazardly put together, is prefaced with a rare contemporary account of the invasion of Lucchese territory by the troops of Niccolò Fortebraccio in November 1429, the subsequent Florentine siege of Lucca, and the saving arrival in December 1430 of 'an angel sent by God' in the person of the *condottiere* Niccolò Piccinino. From this source we know of the parishioner of S. Quirico in Licciano di Moriano who, at the beginning of the wars, had taken into safe-keeping a chalice, paten, and chasuble belonging to his local church, but whose own impoverishment had then forced him, shortly before his death, to pledge the sacred items at usury with the Jews of Lucca.[3] Within Lucca, the presence of armed men posted for the defence of the city resulted in the frequent disruption of court proceedings; in the wider diocese, there are repeated references to the impossibility of movement because of the likelihood

1 Franca Leverotti, 'La crisi demografica nella Toscana del Trecento: L'esempio delle Sei Miglia Lucchesi', in Sergio Gensini (ed.), *La Toscana nel secolo xiv: Caratteri di una civiltà regionale* (Pisa, 1988), p. 97. The figure relates to *teste* (able-bodied males aged 16–70). The Sei Miglia was an area of perhaps 250 square kilometres around the city, consisting of an alluvial plain surrounded by low hills though rising in places to more rugged terrain. 2 ASDL Tribunale Ecclesiastico, 103. 3 ASDL Tribunale Ecclesiastico, 103, fo. 29v. The pledges were later redeemed by presbyter Arrigo Bartolucci, rector of the church of S. Michele di Villaorbana, whose benefice was united to the church of S. Quirico.

of death, injury, capture, and robbery at the hands of Florentine forces.[4] The direct (and perhaps indirect) consequences of capture are illustrated in the melancholy story of Iacopo del fu Martino of Moriano, ransomed with the aid of a loan of nine florins from the rector of S. Stefano of Moriano, but soon thereafter – along with his brother Benedetto – dead of the plague.[5] The most graphic description relates not to the misfortunes of a native of the Lucchese state but to Giovanni Pardi of Ripafratta (Librafatta) in the territory of Pisa.[6] Giovanni had been captured with many others in a cross-border sortie from Lucca,[7] and had ended up in the hands of the man who had been delegated by his companions to handle the ransoming of prisoners, a Lucchese citizen (and stipendiary) named Iacopo del fu Giovanni da Bologna. In a theme common to many of these cases, the captive became infirm, and his anxious brother arrived in Lucca to try to arrange his release. Unable to pay the ransom of 40 florins, Giovanni's brother appealed to the Lucchese priest, and *pievano* of Montuolo, Iacopo Pieroni.[8] Giovanni was given into Iacopo Pieroni's custody, the latter promising to pay the ransom as a condition of freeing the prisoner. The promise was not honoured, and Iacopo del fu Giovanni demanded (successfully, at least in the court judgment) either the return of his captive or payment by Iacopo Pieroni of the agreed ransom.

Evidence for the disruptive impact of armed conflict on rural life is clustered, unsurprisingly, in the early decades of the fifteenth century, though more localized skirmishes continued throughout the century with a range of consequences both for the economy of the countryside and for the security of its inhabitants.[9] Tenants not infrequently protested that they were unable to work land occupied by enemy troops.[10] Livestock were particularly vulnerable.

---

4 For example, ibid., fos. 31r–34r.   5 Ibid., fo. 43v. For a closely parallel but much grander case, involving not humble country-dwellers but the Lucchese citizen messer Filippo del fu Paolino de' Salamoni and his brother Giovanni, see ibid., fos. 110r–114v. 6 Ibid., fos. 116r–117v.   7 For reflections on the characteristics of a *cavalcata* (drawn from a somewhat earlier period): Jean-Claude Maire Vigueur, *Cavalieri e cittadini: Guerra, conflitti e società nell'Italia comunale* (Bologna, 2004), pp 66–8.   8 Presbyter Jacobus olim Pieronis coriarii is here described as one of the castellani of Ponte S. Pietro. For his later, colourful career, see M.E. Bratchel, *Lucca 1430–1494: the reconstruction of an Italian city-republic* (Oxford, 1995), pp 54, 55, 62.   9 In October 1468 a band of 41 men of Pietrasanta allegedly rampaged through the countryside around Monteggiori plundering and stealing sacks of chestnuts and supplies of firewood in a raid clearly provoked by cross-border tensions: ASL Sentenze e bandi, 181, first case, no visible foliation. Much of the correspondence of the Anziani and Gonfaloniere di Giustizia of Lucca with Giovanni Marco de' Medici vicar of Castiglione in 1491–2 related to sheep carried off, beaten, or killed in cross-border raids by the men of Fontanalúccia and Miscoso in the *podesterìa* of Monte Fiorino: ASL Anziani al tempo della libertà, 654 (1) (1491–2).   10 Particularly in border areas, as in 1403 in the case of land belonging to the church of S. Bartolommeo of Collodi: ASL Vicario di Valleariana, 71, fo. 8r. In January 1419 a commission was established to hear disputes relating to losses, unpaid rent etc. following the 'inestimable damage' caused

In a lawsuit of 1447, that harks back to the traumatic appearance in Lucchese territory of Niccolò Fortebraccio, witnesses told of the 100 goats belonging to messer Iacopo da Santa Giulia, together with an unspecified number of cows, goats, and other animals belonging to the inhabitants of Massarosa, hidden in a wood near Massarosa called 'del debio del peccia', that failed to escape the notice of the Florentines. Others, including Meo Benettoni and Parduccio Cecolini, more foresighted than their neighbours, had managed to lead their animals to the safety of Camaiore and Pietrasanta.[11] Animals were often leased *in soccida*, and the responsibility of lessees for stock losses incurred at time of war was at the centre of a number of lawsuits of the period.[12]

The insecurities of life in the countryside were not limited to the relatively brief periods of open warfare. Against the background of the fractured political geography of the region, robber bands (themselves, no doubt, often the detritus of the wars) preyed on peasants, local notables, and Lucchese citizens alike. The criminal proceedings of the late fourteenth and early fifteenth centuries are rich in instances of peasants who were seized with their livestock and personal goods by itinerant robber bands, and who were then carried beyond Lucca's jurisdiction for purposes of ransom.[13] In this context we find sundry references to 'private prisons', particularly in territories to the north under the theoretical control of the various branches of the Marchesi Malaspina. Many of the armed bands were composed of *banniti*: local men sheltering across political borders beyond the reach of the Lucchese courts. In the middle years of the rule of Paolo Guinigi, Bartolomeo di Antonio Franchutii alias Passarino, recently resident in pieve S. Paolo, collected a group of fugitives at Caprona in Pisan territory in order to launch an attack on his former neighbours: *contadini* (comitatinos) living around pieve S. Paolo.[14] Such personal ventures were particularly dangerous at time of war, when they become inextricably entangled with the movement of armies.[15] Again, much of the best evidence coincides both with the wars and with the

by the incursion into Lucchese territory of Braccio da Montone: ASL Governo di Paolo Guinigi, 2, p. 459.   11 ACL B+3 (ser Giovanni Folchini), fos. 9r–12v, 14r–v. Events in the wood involved the capture of both men and their animals.   12 The details are obscure, but a dispute over obligations and responsibility at time of war clearly lies at the heart of a case before the *podestà* of Casoli oltre Giogo brought in the early 1430s by Giorgio di Francesco of Aiola against Pietro di Martino of Sermezzana: ASL Podestà di Casoli oltre Giogo, 30, fos. 15r–16r.   13 See, for example, ASL Vicario di Pietrasanta, Atti Criminali (1370), 101, fo. 26v; Sentenze e bandi, 121, fos. 59v–60v.   14 ASL Sentenze e bandi, 122, fos. 181r–182r; Capitano del contado, 32, no foliation, sentence dated 23 December 1412. More than 55 years later Antonio di Bartolomeo alias Passarino, resident in S. Margherita, was involved in a brawl outside the walls of Lucca with a man from neighbouring Tassignano (both villages in the *piviere* of S. Paolo): ASL Sentenze e bandi, 181, fos. 16v–17v.   15 See, for example, ASL Sentenze e bandi, 137, no foliation, case against Antonio di Nicolao of Empoli and Angelo di Lorenzo of Pistoia.

demographic crisis that mark the first half of the fifteenth century. But on the permeable and fractious border with Pistoia local security remained fragile throughout the fifteenth century as a whole.

Disease, like warfare, was as pervasive a scourge of the fifteenth- as of the late fourteenth-century countryside. The familiar motif of citizens fleeing from fourteenth-century pestilences to the relative safety of their country villas has perhaps obscured the degree to which plagues in the century after the Black Death impacted upon both town and countryside alike. Within the Lucchesia the illusion of rural security is shattered most famously by the death in May 1400 of Bartolomeo Guinigi, brother of Paolo, who had sought refuge in Castiglione from the plague then raging in the city.[16] It has been argued that over the course of the fifteenth century, plagues (whether or not 'true' plagues) were becoming more distinctly an urban scourge.[17] But in the Lucchese countryside, following the repeated visitations that characterized the first three decades of the fifteenth century, there were widespread epidemics in the late 1440s and again throughout the period 1476–80.[18] The legal and notarial records are rich in the details of individual experience. A cluster of illustrative cases relate to life in the far northern reaches of Lucca's state that stretched from Minucciano to Pugliano. In 1423 Iacopo di Geptino of Albiano claimed a florin from Bertone Albertini of Pugliano: in part for Iacopo's labour at the grape harvest, but also for the custody and burial of Bertone's daughter Antonia – the father having fled Pugliano to escape the plague.[19] A more vivid picture emerges from events in Albiano during the plague of 1429 when Ottolino (di Ursone?) of Pugliano was entrusted with the care of the dying mother and servant of Bartolomeo di Lorenzo de' Nobili di Albiano. Following the death of his wife, Bartolomeo gave his infant daughter into the care of Ottolino's daughter-in-law as wet-nurse, and then fled his plague-stricken household for the safety of his property in neighbouring Pugliano. Meanwhile, Ottolino was to guard the Albiano property (presumably against theft); we see him burying the dead in the garden and threatened with death by the men of

16 *Le Croniche di Giovanni Sercambi Lucchese*, Sercambi Bongi (ed.), 3 (Rome, 1892), III 4–5. Sercambi notes specifically that *la morìa* of May 1400 struck both city and *contado*, so that wealthy citizens were forced to seek shelter as far away as Bologna and the Genoese Riviera. 17 A.G. Carmichael, *Plague and the poor in Renaissance Florence* (Cambridge, 1986), p. 1. 18 For the measures taken in July 1479 by the men of Gignano (one of the nine *popoli* of the *piviere* of Brancoli) to prevent the spread of plague into their commune (essentially limiting all contacts with the outside world): ASL Archivio de' Notari, parte 1, 1014 (ser Domenico Domenici), fo. 63r–v. As late as 1496 the men of Pedona di Camaiore were claiming that they had been greatly reduced by pestilence (*mortalitas*) and illness (*infirmitas*), and that Pedona was 'likely soon to be completely deserted', clearly a reference to the incidence of malaria in the marina di Viareggio: ibid., 1342 (ser Giovanni Medici), fos. 164r–175r. 19 ASL Podestà di Casoli oltre Giogo, 29, Atti Civili (1421–6), p. 154.

the village should he risk spreading the plague by departing from Bartolomeo's house until a month or two after the plague had abated. The testimony of witnesses suggests that it was not unusual to hire men to tend the sick at time of plague, and that this perilous work might be remunerated at a monthly wage of two florins.[20] A third exemplar from the same period and the same region shows another plague victim, Michele di Pietro of Casoli oltre Giogo, chased from his home by his neighbours after exhibiting signs of *aposteme pestilenziose*. Michele died at a place called 'alla lama', in the company of men who probably shared his condition, perhaps a pointer to the existence in the countryside of small quarantined communities during plague years.[21]

As in the history of the city, it is not difficult to link plague epidemics to the dramatic political events of the period. In the first Florentine war, Argigliano fell to the Florentines after being abandoned by the greater part of the men of the territory because of the *morbo*.[22] Minucciano itself rebelled against the Malaspina and returned to Lucchese obedience in 1449 at time of serious plague. The precise impact of epidemic disease on the demography, family fortunes, and productive relationships of the countryside is more difficult to assess. For Florentine Tuscany a series of peasant biographies has been constructed on the basis of notarial records and those of the *catasti*.[23] Sometimes it has been possible to link a number of deaths within the same family to a plague epidemic, particularly during the first three decades of the fifteenth century and again after 1469. It is entirely plausible that disease was a major factor in the declining vitality of individual families, though it might present others with new opportunities for self-enrichment and land acquisitions. Clearly a cluster of deaths of productive males prejudiced a family's ability to work its lands, leaving behind too many unproductive mouths and often widows with dowries to be repaid by vulnerable survivors. But any number of factors might explain the decline of some family fortunes (and the rise of others): progressive indebtedness resulting from bad harvests or unwise investment decisions; inter-family conflicts; the machinations of ruthless neighbours; a disequilibrium between men and women, young and old; the irrational attachment to family lands that allegedly characterizes all peasant societies; bad luck. Even in the best documented case-studies we can do little more than chronicle plague deaths and speculate on the long-term consequences of recurrent epidemics.

Whilst mortality rates from plague remain speculative,[24] there can be no doubt of the dislocating impact of warfare, plague, and the (probably dimin-

20 ASL Podestà di Casoli oltre Giogo, 31, Atti Civili (1436), fos. 3r–v, 9v–10v, 19r–v, 25r–v, 47r–48v. 21 ASF Notarile AnteCosimiano, N 115 (ser Nicolao di Coluccio di Pellegrino da Pietrasanta, 1432–4), fos. 3r–6r, 30v–31v. 22 ASL Podestà di Casoli oltre Giogo, 31, Atti Civili (1436), fo. 51r–v. 23 Maria Serena Mazzi & Sergio Raveggi, *Gli uomini e le cose nelle campagne fiorentine del Quattrocento* (Florence, 1983), pp 239–315. 24 M.S. Mazzi,

ishing)[25] incidence of harvest failures on Italian rural society. Notably, in the Lucchesia as elsewhere, the first half of the fifteenth century was marked by very visible peasant mobility. The *estimo* returns of 1412 for the communes of the *piviere* of pieve S. Paolo on the Lucchese plain to the east of Lucca (the *corpo* of the *piviere*, Carraia, Mugnano, Paganico, Parezzana, S. Margherita, Tassignano, Toringo) show the presence of 18 resident foreigners with their families.[26] Most were from Pisa (presumably signifying Pisan territory), with a scattering from Cascina, Castelfiorentino, Empoli, Florence, Novara, Parma, Perugia, and Vinci. Only Nanni Dinucci had translocated from within the Sei Miglia (from nearby Capannori),[27] though many other men (and women) from neighbouring communities held or owned land within the *piviere*. The list of resident foreigners does not include Cecco Pacini of Fucecchio, who rented land in Tassignano whilst living just outside the *piviere* in Capannori.[28]

Although the Lucchese *estimi* or *catasto* of 1411–13 (and that of 1451) are supposed to have listed even fiscally exempt new arrivals, the fiscal sources are static, geographically limited, and unlikely to have captured *forestieri* who were less solidly entrenched. A more comprehensive (though haphazard) impression can be gleaned from legal sources. Surveying for illustration the criminal court records of 1446 as collected in the series *Sentenze e bandi*,[29] miscellaneous references attest to the widespread presence of natives of Pontremoli and its surrounding villages like Gróndola in the vicariate of Camaiore and throughout the villages of the Sei Miglia – specifically in Farneta, Formentale, Maggiano, Orbicciano, pieve S. Stefano, S. Macario, Vecoli, and further east in Lammari. In S. Macario, both the custodian of *danno dato*, Franceschino di Agostino, and the man that he accused of stealing chestnuts from the lands of the monastery of S. Giustina of Lucca came from Pontremoli.[30] Casual references from 1446 suggest some movement

Salute e società nel Medioevo (Florence, 1978), pp 41–4. **25** Food shortages did not cease with the release of population pressures after 1348: Giuliano Pinto, 'Le colture cerealicole', in *La Toscana nel tardo medio evo: Ambiente, economia rurale, società* (Florence, 1982), pp 149–55. For the Lucchesia: Franca Leverotti, *Popolazione, famiglie, insediamento: Le Sei Miglia Lucchesi nel xiv e xv secolo* (Pisa, 1992), pp 71–6. **26** ASL Estimo, 116. The number of foreigners increases if we add servants and dependants listed under the households of both local men and immigrants. For a more complete survey of the numerical presence of *forestieri* within the communes of the Sei Miglia, see Franca Leverotti, 'La famiglia contadina lucchese all'inizio del' 400', in Rinaldo Comba, Gabriella Piccinni, & Giuliano Pinto (eds), *Strutture familiari epidemie migrazioni nell'Italia medievale* (Naples, 1984), pp 237–68. **27** ASL Estimo, 116, fo. 95v. Also in Paganico, Landuccio di Michele may likewise have arrived from a neighbouring commune. **28** Cecco leased two fields in Tassignano from the monastery of S. Martino in Colle, itself situated about 3 miles east of Capannori: ASL Estimo, 116, fos. 284r, 334v. **29** ASL Sentenze e bandi, 164. **30** Ibid., fo. 154v.

between the communes of the Sei Miglia; others, like the two men from Pisan Ripafratta now living in Cerasomma and Montuolo,[31] though having crossed state borders, also had not moved very far from their place of birth. But many (besides the Pontremolesi) reached the Sei Miglia from much further afield: from the northern Garfagnana; 'Lombards', sometimes explicitly described as coming from Modena, Reggio, or Parma; others from the Genoese Riviera. For political and geographical reasons it is hardly surprising that many migrants to the Sei Miglia came from lands under the political control of Florence: mostly from Pisa and Pistoia, but also from as far afield as S. Miniato.

Turning from the Sei Miglia to the vicariates,[32] it is not always easy to distinguish men who had established themselves with a degree of permanence from more transient visitors and litigants. The civil court records of the vicariate of Gallicano in the upper valley of the Serchio for the period 1454–64 provide, nevertheless, a clear indication of migrants resident within Gallicano in the decade after it was restored to Lucchese rule.[33] Many were drawn to Gallicano from the hill-top villages of its vicariate (and of its former vicariate, now under the rule of the Estensi). As in the previous century (though on a smaller scale) Gallicano attracted a number of individuals from across the river Serchio from the Florentine enclave of Barga, and also from the Estense *piviere* of Fosciana. Others came to Gallicano from the northern Garfagnana, from the Lucchese vicariate of Coreglia, and from the much more distant *podesterìa* of Villa Basilica. And a significant number of migrants came from even further afield: from Bergamo, Milan, Parma (particularly Tizzano), Bologna, Reggio, Modena (specifically Barigazzo), and Genoa. Immigrants were particularly attracted to Gallicano itself, a settlement of some size in the valley of the Serchio. But higher up in the mountain village of Verni we find Antonio from Olina (Modena), and numerous references to Cristoforo di Domenico of Pontecosi (a village then under the rule of the Este situated on the Serchio a little to the north of Castelnuovo di Garfagnana).

The high incidence of peasant mobility in the century after the Black Death has been widely attributed to the impact of taxation on populations reduced by war, famine, and plague.[34] There were, of course, various possible responses to mounting fiscal oppression. One was defiance, as in the case of a native of Ceserana (vicariate of Castiglione) who, in 1393, in the very presence

---

31 Ibid., fo. 62r–v. 32 The Lucchese state, beyond the Sei Miglia, was divided into a number of vicariates. These were ruled by a vicar who was a Lucchese citizen appointed by Lucca. 33 ASL Vicario di Gallicano, 129–43. 34 S.K. Cohn, *Creating the Florentine state: peasants and rebellion, 1348–1434* (Cambridge, 1999). For Siena: Giuliano Pinto, 'L'immigrazione di manodopera nel territorio senese alla metà del Quattrocento', in *La Toscana nel tardo medio evo: Ambiente, economia rurale, società* (Florence, 1982), p. 443, n. 69.

of the Anziani of Lucca, protested against Lucca's abusive treatment of his commune.[35] Resentment might lead to rebellion and to the permanent loss of Lucchese territory, as happened in the case of the *quasi-città* of Pietrasanta in the 1430s.[36] More likely and more pervasive were the evasion of dues and the falsification of assets. Obligations to maintain roads, water courses, and bridges went unheeded – the dereliction justified, perhaps, by the dangers posed by troop movements.[37] The records of the *gabelle* of the *contado* and vicariates of Lucca contain numerous cases of attempts to defraud the customs. Sometimes the fraud was effected by the simple undervaluing of the goods carried or false declarations of destination; sometimes there are stories of mules laden with contraband merchandise led at night along the network of mule trails that criss-crossed the mountains; often there are protests that tax had (or should have) been paid elsewhere – perhaps by a third-party.[38] Many of the most spectacular incidents of smuggling relate to breaches of the salt monopoly. Nine men of Vico Pancellorum were apprehended in September 1469 carrying salt into Lucchese territory (presumably from Pistoia) on two mules, one horse, and five donkeys.[39] Supplies of wheat and barley (for consumption or sowing) were periodically demanded from the vicariates by the city authorities, resulting in negotiations when the quantities were said to exceed local resources. And the court records are full of cases of individuals who tried to lessen their tax burden by failing to declare some part of their holdings.[40] In all these ways the inhabitants of the countryside attempted passively (and sometimes less than passively) to escape burdens imposed by the state and by the village officials charged with their collection.[41]

The most obvious remedy for a peasant burdened with private debts and unbearable public obligations was the anonymity offered by flight. In 1384 representatives of Castiglione di Garfagnana, claiming that their land had lost

35 'Lo mio comune é fforzato et inghanato da questo collegio': ASL Sentenze e bandi, 86, fo. 7r–v.   36 M.E. Bratchel, *Lucca 1430–1494: the reconstruction of an Italian city-republic* (Oxford, 1995), pp 234–50.   37 ACL B+2 (Giovanni di Francesco da Montecatini), no foliation. See also: ASL Sentenze e bandi, 164, fos. 62v, 67r.   38 ASL Gabelle del contado e delle vicarie, 30, Gabella di Coreglia (1427–42), 1st foliation, fos. 42r–43v; 3rd foliation, fos. 4r–15v, 20r–24v; 36, Gabella di Coreglia, 1st foliation, fo. 34r; 77, Gabella di Pietrasanta (1425–6), 2nd foliation, fos. 91r–92r; 5th foliation, fo. 91r–v; 91, Gabella di Villabasilica (1343–1408), 4th foliation, fo. 33r; 5th foliation, fo. 20r; 93 (1422–53), 8th foliation, fo. 40r; 11th foliation, fo. 24r.   39 ASL Sentenze e bandi, 181, fos. 19r–v, 32v–34r. 40 More generally, individuals both from the Sei Miglia and the vicariates might attempt to escape the *estimo* by handing over their property to churches and religious institutions, a device tackled in a decree of Paolo Guinigi of November 1401: ASL Governo di Paolo Guinigi, 1, p. 89.   41 Failure to perform services and pay dues could, of course, pit a man against his neighbours rather than against the state: ASL Sentenze e bandi, 119, fos. 32r–33r; Capitano del contado, 32 (1412–13), no foliation, case against Giovanni Vianucii of Torre. Very many civil cases against local officials relate to assessments for the *estimo*. Tax assessments were also a frequent source of conflict between neighbouring communes.

90 per cent of its inhabitants since 1348 as a result of the plagues of the past four decades, and protesting that it was no longer possible for the remaining men to bear tax and military burdens that had been assessed when Castiglione was a much larger community, threatened the abandonment of the territory and a mass migration into the Sei Miglia.[42] The threat was self-evidently a negotiating ploy, but clearly represented a plausible option for the more desperate, and was lent credence by reference to a recent exodus from neighbouring Sassorosso.[43] At the beginning of the fifteenth century changes to the tax regime resulted, allegedly, in the departure of many whose livelihood derived from the plaster mines of Stazzema and Pomezzana in the vicariate of Pietrasanta.[44] And it was not only peasants and artisans who threatened to leave. Still in 1403, there was the warning that nobles and Lucchese citizens ('cittadini salvatichi') living in the vicariates of Castiglione, Camporgiano, and the *podesteria* of Casoli oltre Giogo would be forced to leave (presumably from Lucchese territory) unless they received some relief from their very considerable tax arrears.[45] Short-term leases made geographical mobility perhaps a less traumatic experience for the tenants of the plains than for the peasant owner-cultivators and impoverished minor nobility of the mountains. The men of Nozzano spoke in 1403 of the departure of some families, and the likely departure of others, because of the intolerable burden of guarding the *castello* borne by a community depleted by war and plague.[46] It is easier to count the threats of departure than to illustrate their fulfilment. But when the three remaining inhabitants of Paganico (pieve S. Paolo) said in October 1403 that all the other men of their commune were either dead or had fled from the Lucchese state,[47] they were clearly identifying plague deaths and refuge across political borders as the twin ingredients that had led to the depopulation of their commune.[48] In an effort to counter the latter eventuality, a decree of 1415 imposed a fine of 200 gold florins (or the amputation of a foot) on countrymen leaving Lucchese territory without express permission.[49]

Admitting the impact on population mobility of specific crises within and beyond Lucca's borders, it would be mistaken to see all migrants as perenni-

---

42 ASL Capitoli, 10, pp 128–30.   43 In 1403 the vicar of Coreglia confirmed the claim of the men of Motrone that 24 *bocche* (persons of more than 5 years) had left to settle in other communes (mostly, clearly, within the Lucchese state): ASL Governo di Paolo Guinigi, 1, p. 194.   44 Ibid., 168.   45 Ibid., 172–3, 433, 591.   46 Ibid., 165.   47 Ibid., 193. Two years earlier ten men had been assessed in the commune, for a total *estimo* of 19s. 6d. In 1312 the communal parliament of Paganico had been attended by between 73 and 81 men: M.E. Bratchel, *Medieval Lucca and the evolution of the Renaissance state* (Oxford, 2008), p. 98. For a similar case from Palmata (*piviere* of S. Pancrazio): ASL Governo di Paolo Guinigi, 1, pp 269, 329.   48 Attempts were made to enforce the obligations of those who had translocated within the Lucchese state, but nothing could be done about those who had departed Lucca's jurisdiction: ASL Governo di Paolo Guinigi, 1, 269, 329.   49 Ibid., 2, 319.

ally mobile escapees from unpaid rents and fixed fiscal obligations – abandoning their holdings 'andarsene con Dio'.[50] In the proceedings of the court of *danno dato* of the vicariate of Camaiore for the second semester 1455,[51] 22 men and women are described as *terrigeni* – meaning, in this context, not native-born residents ('nato o generato dalla terra') but immigrants who had been present for a long time, who paid local taxes, and who had assumed local obligations. They came from the Lunigiana (particularly Pontremoli and its environs), from the northern Garfagnana, and from all parts of Florentine Tuscany. It would be perilous to draw statistical data from casual references in the criminal court records, but in 1455 *terrigeni* made up 46 per cent of the immigrants making their appearance as litigants and witnesses before the court of Camaiore.[52] Whether described as *terrigeni* or residents, we find immigrants owning land: throughout the first half of the fifteenth century the political records are full of petitions requesting exemption from the laws that prohibited foreigners from owning land within the Lucchese state. More often they appear as the tenants of Lucchese citizens and local notables, lessees of public lands, and as the custodians of animals.[53] In the first half of the fifteenth century, against a background of depopulation and chronic labour shortage, mobility might result as much from a search for new opportunities as from a flight from penury.[54] In 1384 the men of Castiglione themselves (though anticipating no takers) requested that foreigners of good condition should be exempted from guard duty and other personal obligations if they came to settle in Castiglione.[55] In 1404, since plague and war had left the greater part of both the vicariates and the Sei Miglia depopulated and uncultivated, the government of Paolo Guinigi freed from all taxes and obligations (excluding the salt tax) any tenant or cultivator of the land who came into Lucchese territory with the intention of living honestly and working hard.[56] Similar offers were proffered by the rulers of the restored republic after 1430.[57]

50 The 1391 statute of Fagnano (*piviere* of Montuolo/Flesso) instructed the consuls and councillor of the commune to assess for taxation all foreigners after they had been resident for one year: ASL Archivio de' Notari, 179 (II) (ser Conte Puccini), p. 6. The period of residence is named in other late fourteenth-century statutes.   **51** ASL Vicario di Camaiore, Atti Criminali (Danno Dato), 2087.   **52** Piero di Martino of Ballone appears as both *terrigeno* of and resident in Corsanico. There is no reason to assume that the distinction was recorded with any degree of rigour. Names are often given without patronymics, so the same individual may have been counted twice. The relevant point is that a large number of immigrants were stable residents displaying a measure of commitment to the communities in which they had settled.   **53** Note in particular a number of cases against the Lombard Lorenzo Neretti, *terrigeno* of Camaiore, for damage done to wheat fields by his horses.   **54** There is some indication of concentrations of immigrants bound by family ties and by village of origin, but the trend seems less pronounced than among the artisans studied by Pinto, 'L'immigrazione di manodopera', p. 440.   **55** ASL Capitoli, 10, p. 129.   **56** ASL Governo di Paolo Guinigi, 1, p. 266.   **57** Comparable efforts might be made by

The distinction must always have been chimerical between those attracted to the fertile valleys and plain of Lucca in search of productive employment and the vagabonds (those found without work) whose apprehension and expulsion became a constant of Lucchese policy.[58] Some immigrants certainly eked out their precarious existence by turning to petty crime. Antonio di Masino of Succisa in the district of Pontremoli came to Farneta in the *piviere* of Arliano having already broken out of prison in his home territory, where he had been accused of many acts of theft. Employed as a day-labourer in the threshing of wheat, Antonio continued his activities in the communes of the Sei Miglia and suburbs of Lucca – stealing mainly wheat, but also a horse and woollen tunic – for which, in February 1443, he was sentenced to death by the court of the Podestà.[59] Even in the depopulated countryside of the first half of the fifteenth century large numbers of immigrants generated tensions. The 1404 statute of the commune of Bergiola in the *podesterìa* of Casoli oltre Giogo is very largely concerned to prevent the transfer of land to men who might claim exemption from communal taxes and services.[60] In Camaiore in 1428 it was unanimously agreed, out of respect for the commune and its preservation, to impose a fine of £25 *buona moneta* on anyone daring to elect any foreigner to communal office or honours (a *forensis* or *advena* being defined as anyone from outside the territory and *distretto* of Lucca).[61] Attitudes seem to harden with the first signs of population recovery from mid-century. Perhaps to a changing demographic environment (as well as to political vicissitudes) we can attribute the measures in 1458 to recover pastures and chestnut woods in the vicariate of Castiglione di Garfagnana that had been illegally sold to foreigners from the *podesterìe* of Minozzo and Montefiorino.[62] By the late fifteenth century, the rural statutes are full of restrictions on the presence and role of immigrants.[63]

the larger centres of the vicariates to attract permanent residents. In Camaiore, for example: Andreolo di Simone of Beduzzo (1428), Archivio Comunale, Camaiore, Deliberazioni, 112, fo. 8r; Honorato Vernaccini of Pietrasanta (1428), ibid., fos. 9v–10r; maestro Iacopo di Domenico of Como (1428), ibid., fo. 16r–v; Guglielmo, Lombard (1431), ibid., 113, fo. 9r–v; Andrea Copinelli del Cavallaio da Berreto (1432), ibid., 28v; Nocco di Giunto of Pisa (1438), ibid., 107v.   **58** One duty of the new *podestà* appointed in the Sei Miglia in 1411 was 'discacciare li vagabundi': ASL Governo di Paolo Guinigi, 2, p. 106.   **59** ASL Sentenze e bandi, 163, fos. 1r–v, 27r–v. Though described as resident in Farneta, Antonio clearly slept wherever he was employed. In stealing 3 staia of wheat in the contrada of S. Concordio he had an accomplice whose name, as so often, is concealed.   **60** Including a clause prohibiting anyone of the commune of Bergiola from leasing or working the land of any foreigner not sustaining 'onera realia et personalia': ASL Archivio de' Notari, 208 (III) (ser Lorenzo da Barga), fos. 289r–291v.   **61** Archivio Comunale, Camaiore, Deliberazioni, 112, fo. 17r. The intention was explicitly that the territory should not be overrun or trampled under foot by foreigners.   **62** ASL Capitoli, 10, pp 158–60.   **63** See, for example, ASL Archivio de' Notari, 1115(I) (ser Pietro Berti), fo. 65r–v (S. Pietro a Valdottavo,

Many of the men drawn into the Lucchesia from the mountains of Modena and the Emilia[64] were custodians or owners of livestock. In 1445 the procurator of Giuliano di Giovanni of Acquabona (Emilia) claimed wages of 199 bolognini (of which 65 remained unpaid) for the 5 months and 7 days when Giuliano looked after the cows and pigs of the men and commune of Carsciana in the vicariate of Valdilima.[65] Frequently, though perhaps not disproportionately, men from the north appear as the accused in cases of *danno dato*. Some had clearly taken up permanent residency in the villages of the vicariates and of the Sei Miglia. Martino di Duccio of Dalli in the northern Garfagnana, described as 'living in' Maggiano in the *piviere* of Arliano, may well have been a winter visitor. Accused in 1444 of entering the pastures of Arliano with flocks of sheep and goats on many occasions between the months of February and April, Martino's profile is compatible with that of the shepherds and *guardiani* who brought their animals down to the plain in autumn, returning to the mountains in spring. Alternatively, Martino may have been in the employ of the Lucchese citizen and butcher Domenico di Iacopo, who had sub-leased the meadows, and with whose consent Martino claimed (successfully) to have pastured his flocks.[66] The prominence of foreigners in animal husbandry, whether as the salaried shepherds of local men and communities, as the transient custodians of transhumant flocks, or as newly settled tenants and owner-cultivators, points to the attraction of the Lucchesia for men bred and skilled in the poorer regions to the north of the Lucchese state. It raises the question how far Lucca conforms to the pattern of an expansion of pastoralism that characterized much of Europe after the mid-fourteenth-century crisis.

There can be no doubt that animal husbandry impacted significantly on fifteenth-century agriculture and agricultural practices.[67] The inherent ten-

1477); 1240 (ser Iacopo Donati), fos. 21r–28v (Corsagna, vicariate of Coreglia). Alternatively, measures against leasing land to foreigners might be prompted rather by continued emigration and high mortality through disease–as in the case of Pedona di Camaiore in 1493 (where the 'foreigners' seem to have been primarily men of Camaiore and Lucchese citizens): ibid., 1226 (ser Pietro Lupardi), fos. 121r–124v.   **64** Clearly the provenance of most of those described as 'Lombards' in the Lucchese sources.   **65** ASL Vicario di Valdilima, 111, fos. 13v–14r.   **66** ASL Sentenze e bandi, 163, fo. 201v. Luchesino di Cola of Borsigliana, vicariate of Camporgiano, living in the Sei Miglia in the commune of S. Lorenzo in the *piviere* of Massa Pisana, caused damage in March and April 1395 to various lands within the *piviere* with a flock of perhaps 150 small animals (sheep and/or goats), 2 oxen, 2 cows, and a horse. In this instance, at least some of the sheep were unambiguously the property of a Lucchese citizen, Gherardo Anguilla (who later paid the fine): ASL Podestà di Lucca, 7236, fos. 5r–7v. For subsequent accusations against Luchesino, extending into May (when his sureties were two men of Camporgiano): ibid., fos. 25r–26r.   **67** For comparison see Alfio Cortonesi, 'Microanalisi di un conflitto: Allevamento stanziale e "danno dato" nelle campagne di Ferentino (secolo xv)' in *Ruralia: Economie e paesaggi del medioevo italiano* (Rome, 1995), pp 69–103.

sions are well described in a case against Lorenzo Neretti 'Lombard', a *ter-rigeno* of Camaiore. Lorenzo was accused of causing damage with his horses, grazing in June 1455 on wheat planted on an assart ('roncho') leased from the commune of Camaiore in a place called 'a precchia'. The case revolved around whether the cultivators – a number of men from Pescaglia – had adequately fenced the land (as all cultivators were bound to do). Evidence was presented by various local men regarding what they had seen, both before and after the alleged offence, when they led their sheep and wethers past the field on their way to pastures in the local alps. Despite many testimonies in his favour, Lorenzo was fined and condemned to pay damages.[68] In May 1471 the canons of the cathedral of S. Martino complained that men of the commune of Massarosa (within the secular jurisdiction of the canons) were taking large and small animals to pasture in the olive groves and other prohibited places, to the grave damage both of the canons themselves and of other men of the commune. Officials were ordered to denounce offenders within four days. The subsequent denunciations, whilst not necessarily providing a comprehensive list of the animals kept by the men of Massarosa, give an interesting pointer to patterns of livestock holdings. Most men were accused of causing damages with a single cow, an ox, a pair of oxen, or a few sheep. In terms of the number of animals involved and the size of the fine imposed, the most serious offender was Cristoforo del Chiericho with his 40 sheep and his pair of oxen.[69] The statutes of rural communes, both within the Sei Miglia and the vicariates, are full of attempts to limit the kind and number of animals kept by individual villagers.[70] The 400 sheep and goats of the men and commune of Silicagnana (della Garfagnana) accused (unsuccessfully) in 1434 of pasturing in a meadow belonging to the commune of S. Romano may well represent the bulk of the village stock.[71]

68 ASL Vicario di Camaiore, 2087, fos. 29r, 38r, 40r–41r. For further charges against the horses of Lorenzo Neretti: ibid., fos. 37r, 39r, 43v. 69 ACL B+15, fos. 35v–38r. Other large-scale offenders were Bartolomeo del Bologno with 30 sheep and one ox, Simone Mei with 25 sheep, and Matteo Thomuccii with 20 sheep. 70 Within the Sei Miglia, the 1444 statute of Capannori permitted every family to keep in the commune and within its jurisdiction up to three pairs of oxen for working the land, a pair of cows with their bull-calves (though females could be kept for no longer than a year), two pigs for domestic consumption, together with an unlimited number of riding animals and beasts of burden: ASL Archivio de' Notari, 552 (ser Ciomeo Pieri), fos. 34r–v, 68r, 303r, 304v. See also Lammari (1495) ibid., 941 (ser Bartolomeo Guarguaglia), fos. 25r–27v. Pigs and goats were especially destructive and measures were taken to limit the number that could be kept by individuals–particularly when they were not under the controlled custody of the village *vicenda*: Spulizano (S. Romano di Coreglia) (1386), Archivio de' Notari, 202 (ser Lorenzo da Barga), fos. 220v–223v; Lugliano (1445) 504 (XIII) (ser Antonio Nuccorini), fos. 17v–19r, 28v; Menabbio (1479), 1277 (ser Pietro Piscilla), fos. 175r–178v. 71 ASL Vicario di Camporeggiana, 289, fos. 5r–6v. The accusation was brought against Giovanni Satti as 'custos' of the animals of the commune and men of Silicagnana.

Alongside the pervasive incidence of peasants owning or leasing small numbers of animals, many villages both within the Sei Miglia and the vicariates possessed extensive communal pastures. These (together with privately owned meadows) were leased to local men and to herders and shepherds from outside. The men of Capannori, limited in the number of animals that they could keep within the territory of Capannori, clearly pastured a significant number of pigs (and presumably flocks of sheep and goats) in Porcari on the fringes of the Sei Miglia.[72] In 1422 the pastures of Matraia (*piviere* of S. Pancrazio) were leased for three years to Piero di Giustino of Corsagna in the vicariate of Coreglia for a total rent of 14 florins. As so often, the lease reserved the right of the men of Matraia to pasture their own animals in the communal pastures.[73] The right to winter his sheep (and those of others) in the territory of S. Quirico a Petroio (*piviere* of Segromigno) was purchased in December 1406 by Giovanni di Paolo of Limano (vicariate of Valdilima) – and subsequently sold to Piero di Bertolo of Pariana (vicariate of Valdriana).[74] In the vicariates, communal pastures were often auctioned annually – as was the case in Menabbio (Benabbio) in the vicariate of Valdilima (again reserving the right of local men to pasture their animals in the communal pastures).[75] A border dispute involving the lands of the communes of Camaiore, Schiava (Stiava), and Ponte Mazzori (in the vicariate of Camaiore) provides details of some of the men who allegedly leased the pastures and chestnut woods between 1424 and 1455. The majority of the lessees were local men from communes of the vicariate or from the neighbouring lands of the cathedral chapter of Lucca. The inevitable 'Lombards' were probably also resident locally, as, perhaps, was Lorenzo di Simone 'de Vallisnera'.[76] The chestnut woods of Castiglione di Garfagnana, leased both for the collection of chestnuts and for the pasture of goats and pigs, were an important source of communal revenue in this northern extension of the Lucchese state.[77]

It has often been argued that significant changes stemmed from the expansion of transhumance in Italy (and specifically in Tuscany) after the mid-fourteenth-century crisis, with the regular movement of large numbers of animals from summer to winter grazing. The records of the *gabella* of Pietrasanta show large flocks of 'small animals' (sheep, lambs, and goats),

---

72 ASL Archivio de' Notari, 552 (ser Ciomeo Pieri), fo. 34v.   73 ASL Archivio de' Notari, 416 (ser Giannino Nocchi), fo. 372r. In 1441 these same pastures ('del monte di Matraie') were leased to Piero di Stefano of Pontito (Valdriana) for the pasture of his sheep, goats, and other animals – but this time explicitly excluding pigs: ibid., 507 (II) (ser Francesco Pini), fo. 72r–v.   74 ASL Podestà di Lucca, 7241, fos. 42r–47r.   75 ASL Archivio de' Notari, 1277 (ser Pietro Piscilla), fos. 175r–178v. The pastures were those of 'Ciuciana di Siri et del monte di dicto comune'.   76 ASL Vicario di Camaiore, 2087, fos. 68v, 90r–v, 94r–95v, 97r–99v.   77 For example, ASL Archivio de' Notari, 408(I) (ser Federigo Nardi), fo. 114r. Many regulations and many disputes relate to the collection of chestnuts by Lombards in the vicariate of Castiglione.

sometimes numbering more than 500 animals, passing annually through the territory of Pietrasanta to and from summer grazing in the *Maremma* (the pastures of the coastal region).[78] But Pietrasanta was lost to Lucchese rule in 1436. The 1402 statute of Camaiore provided for animals that were just passing through its territory, presumably to and from the marshes and coastal pastures around Viareggio ('la pastura di Marina').[79] Impressionistically, the traffic involved was on a smaller scale than in the case of the vicariate of Pietrasanta.[80] The statutes of some communes of the Sei Miglia also regulated the passage of animals in transit – as in the case of Gragnano in the *piviere* of Segromigno (1468).[81] There can be no doubt of the frequent movement of animals, and of the value of this movement to the fisc. Much movement remained within the context of geographically circumscribed socio-economic micro-regions (whether or not crossing administrative or political boundaries): from plain or river valley to alpine pastures.[82] The right to pasture animals on Monte di Gragno was a source of conflict between the men of Gallicano and those of Barga throughout the fifteenth century and beyond: exacerbated by the fact that Barga now constituted an enclave of Florentine territory within the traditional boundaries of the Lucchese state.[83] There is abundant testimony of men from the communes of the Valdilima bringing their animals into the Sei Miglia, particularly to the area around Sesto.[84] Clearly there was a considerable movement of animals between the high and the middle valley of the Serchio: to the communal pastures of Cune, for example.[85] At the

---

78 Bratchel, *Medieval Lucca*, pp 183–4. **79** Andrea Roncoli, 'Le istituzioni camaioresi alla luce dello statuto comunale del 1402', *Campus Maior: Rivista di studi camaioresi*, 1 (1988), pp 106–8. **80** I have not worked systematically on the registers of the *gabella* of Camaiore: ASL Gabelle del contado e delle vicarie, 5–19 (1339–1467). Those of Coreglia occasionally mention small flocks passing from Reggio to pasture in the vicariate of Camaiore. Cases of *danno dato* in 1478 suggest that men of Vico Pancellorum were bringing sheep for winter pastures in the plain of Camaiore: ASL Sentenze e bandi, 183, fo. 71v. **81** ASL Archivio de' Notari, 929 (ser Bartolomeo Guarguaglia), fos. 14r–16r, where such animals were not to remain for more than a day. **82** For example the 250 'small animals' taken for pasture until September in the alps of Coreglia and Barga by Gaspare di Stefano, Piero di Lorenzo, Antonio di Iacopo, and Giovanni di Bartolomeo, all of Anchiano: ASL Gabelle del contado e delle vicarie, 31, 30 June 1464. See also ibid., 28 July 1467, for a flock of 140 animals taken by Giuliano di Antonio of Anchiano to the alps of Barga. **83** Archivio Storico, Gallicano, MS 13, fos. 42r, 179v, 182r, 225v, 227v–228r. **84** Two men of Limano were reported to the Podestà of Lucca for causing damage to the pastures of Lammari (bordering those of Segromigno) with a flock of sheep in December 1443: ASL Sentenze e bandi, 163, fo. 145r. In 1445 we find Marco di Domenico of capella S. Casciano di Controne paying *gabella* of £4 0s. 8d. for 80 'small animals' taken for pasture from Controne to the lands of the abbey of Pozzevoli near Lago di Sesto: ASL Vicario di Valdilima, 111, unfoliated at the back of the volume. **85** Where foreigners were charged 3 quattrini per month for the pasturing of each large animal, 1½ quattrini for each small animal: ASL Archivio de' Notari, 1267 (ser Pietro Piscilla), fo. 229v. Many more

beginning of the fifteenth century, men of Montignoso travelled seasonally with their flocks of sheep and goats to the pastures of Camaiore and to those around Vagli[86] and they presumably continued to do so when Montignoso became an isolated enclave of Lucchese territory following the loss of Pietrasanta in 1436.

Often the number of animals was very small: the five pigs (three large and two suckling-pigs) brought into the territory of Vico Pancellorum in 1445 by two men of Limano.[87] Sometimes the number was greater: the flocks of between 125 and 216 'small animals' (*bestie minute*) conducted in the same year from the vicariate of Valdilima to that of Valdriana, and into neighbouring territories.[88] Professor Meek draws attention to 283 animals belonging to Menabove Landucci, a butcher of Villa Basilica, that were taken to distant pastures 'in alpibus Fiumalbi'.[89] She also cites the 248 lambs, sheep, and goats belonging to Michele di Giovanni of Casoli in the vicariate of Valdilima, that wintered in 1398 in the territory of Montecarlo before passing also to summer pastures in the territory of Fiumalbo.[90] But where the long-distance migrations of large numbers of animals are recorded in the books of the *gabelle*, the flocks were often not the property of men resident within the Lucchesia, and were likely to be in the custody of shepherds and herders coming from north of Lucca's borders – some passing through Lucchese territory; others coming to pastures within the Lucchese state (to the southern vicariates and not infrequently to the pastures of Valdottavo). They came from places like the Cinque Terre; from Bismantova, Costabona, Ligónchio, Minozzo, Nismozza, Piolo, Roncaglio, and Secchio (Reggio); from Scurano (Parma); and from Fiumalbo (Modena). Some of the larger flocks passing through, or wintering within the Lucchesia belonged to men from the Florentine territories of Pescia and the mountains of Pistoia.[91] Even so – always excluding the early

animals came from the upper valley of the Serchio and from the Valdilima to the pastures of Anchiano and Decimo.   86 ASL Gabelle del contado e delle vicarie, Pietrasanta, 70, first foliation, fos. 80v–81v; 77, fifth foliation, fos. 83r, 86r, 87r.   87 ASL Archivio de' Notari, 504(XIII) (ser Antonio Nuccorini), fo. 43r.   88 Ibid., fo. 70r.   89 Christine Meek, 'Finanze comunali e finanze locali nel quattordicesimo secolo: L'esempio di Montecarlo', in *Castelli e borghi della Toscana tardo medioevale: Atti del Convegno di Studi, 28–29 maggio 1983* (Pescia, 1985), pp 139–53, here p. 146. Menabove appears very frequently in the *gabella* accounts as a butcher and also as a taverner retailing bread and wine; as an importer of wheat, millet, wine, olive oil, wool, and iron; as an exporter of wool, wine, salted meat, fish, chestnut flour, leather, rough woollen cloth, and swords; as a seller of pigs; and as a purchaser of charcoal. Later references are to Bartolomeo and Giovanni di Menabove, his sons. Among the men of Villa Basilica pasturing their animals in the alps of Fiumalbo at the end of the fourteenth century, one might add Nicolao di Coluccio.   90 Meek, 'Finanze comunali', p. 146. The *gabella* of Coreglia shows Antonio Giannelli of Tereglio later taking a (not particularly large) flock of 45 *bestie minute* for pasture from the alps of Coreglia to the alps of Fiumalbo: ASL Gabelle del contado e delle vicarie, 31, 5 August 1460.   91 For example the 250 'small animals' conducted by Lippo Mei of Vellano

fifteenth-century records of Pietrasanta – it is rare to find references to flocks of more than 200 animals.

The Lucchese *estimi* of the late fourteenth and early fifteenth centuries testify to lands in the Sei Miglia that had passed out of cultivation at a time of declining population and – perhaps – of neglected drainage works.[92] In Tofari in 1395 goats were grazing on uncultivated land (with vines and olives), abutting other land that had not been worked or cultivated for eight years.[93] In Greco in 1406 there is reference to a piece of land, formerly vineyard, 'quod nunc est boschiva'.[94] The examples can be multiplied. In the plain and low hills of the Sei Miglia, the retreat of arable and the economic opportunities offered by pasturage potentially favoured the keeping of larger herds and flocks. In the vicariates, freed from subsistence constraints, there was probably a finer balance between pasture and arable. Rural village statutes everywhere were concerned to protect arable land from grazing animals (and to encourage local self-sufficiency through the growing of vegetables);[95] they were concerned to protect pastures by preventing the penetration of arable and by regulating usage and access (sometimes prohibiting completely their use by 'foreigners').[96] These measures to defend rural microcosms were far from unsuccessful. In many parts of the Lucchesia, peasants – tenants and owner-cultivators – combined small-scale stockholding with the cultivation of their fields and the usufruct of their woods. In July 1490, Biagio di Piero of Cardoso in the vicariate of Coreglia, in his testament, bequeathed to his wife a vineyard; to his son Giovanni eight pieces of land – fields, olive groves, vineyards, and woods; to his son Domenico six pieces of land – meadows, fields, vineyards, and woods; to his son Piero six pieces of land – fields, woods, and gardens (and half undivided of two other pieces of woodland); to his son Antonio six pieces of land – fields, woods, meadows, and vineyards (and half undivided of the above two pieces of woodland); and to his son Iacopo five pieces of land – fields, woods, meadows and vineyards (all in Cardoso).[97] Promiscuous agricultural pursuits characterized the vicariates – particularly the Garfagnana and the Versilia – and can be endlessly illustrated from the notarial protocolli and the court records.[98]

There is no parallel in the Lucchesia to the thousands of sheep descending every year from the Appennino romagnolo both towards the shores of the

from S. Pellegrino in Alpe to Vellano through the vicariate of Coreglia: ASL Gabelle del contado e delle vicarie, Coreglia, 31, 18 October 1449.   92 Notably in the eastern regions of the Lucchese plain: ASL Archivio de' Notari, 632 (ser Bartolomeo Martini), fos. 67v–68r, 83r–84r.   93 ASL Podestà di Lucca, 7236, fo. 22r.   94 ASL Podestà di Lucca, 7241, fo. 6v.   95 For example in Corsagna, vicariate of Coreglia: ASL Archivio de' Notari, 1240 (ser Iacopo Donati), fos. 21r–28v.   96 Vico Pancellorum: ASL Archivio de' Notari, 504(XIII) (ser Antonio Nuccorini), fo. 37v.   97 ASL Archivio de' Notari, 1577 (ser Giuliano Granucci), fos. 154v–156v. I have not recorded the division of houses in Cardoso or of *capanne* (huts/sheds/cottages).   98 Bratchel, *Medieval Lucca*, pp 187–8.

Adriatic and to the Maremma toscana.[99] Even less can we draw comparisons with the millions of sheep that passed in the late sixteenth century from winter pastures in Apulia to summer pastures in the Abruzzi. No-one would wish to minimize the constant (and often very erratic) flow of animals within and through the Lucchese state – not least from places like Borsigliana in the northern Garfagnana to the Sei Miglia. There are occasional references to flocks in transit from the Garfagnana and the Valdilima to the *Maremma* (apparently to the Maremma pisana).[100] But, after the loss of Pietrasanta, the great transhumance highways could (and often did) by-pass Lucca's highly fragmented political dominions. Passage to and from Castelnuovo and Barga was largely through portions of Lucca's state; for the rest, Lucchese legislators were only too aware how easily shepherds and herders could avoid Lucchese territory altogether.[101] The fifteenth-century court records of Lucca contain a very large number of cases of *danno dato*. Most pasturing offences were committed by near neighbours from the same or from proximate villages; most involve damage caused by individual animals or small flocks. Village statutes were concerned (perhaps increasingly preoccupied) with cases of *danno dato*. But none reveal what has been called 'il tono catastrofico' in the face of overwhelming numbers of transhumant animals that has been identified in the Florentine rural statutes, specifically the 1421 statute of Pontedera.[102] In the fifteenth-century Lucchesia there may well have been a shift in the balance between arable and pasturage. The shift seems to have been less dramatic and less transformative than in Siena or in the former *contado* of Pisa.

Insofar as there was a heightened pastorality, attention has often been drawn to the interests and investment decisions of citizens. There is little evidence of investment by Lucchese citizens in the flocks and pastures of the mountains, though newly arrived citizens were likely to retain vestigial interests in the territories from which they originated. The shepherds that we meet are in the employ of local men and communities. The larger flocks can be linked to local notables (in the larger settlements more especially to men who are labelled as butchers). The lease of animals *in soccida* (whereby animals were leased to a peasant, who tended them in return for half the progeny and half the produce) was customarily contracted between countrymen – indeed village statutes often prohibited the introduction of foreign animals into the communal pastures through partnerships *in soccida* formed with out-

---

99 Giuliano Pinto, 'Attraverso l'Appennino: Rapporti e scambi tra Romagna e Toscana nei secoli xiii–xv', in *Toscana medievale: Paesaggi e realtà sociali* (Florence, 1993), pp 25–36. 100 ASL Gabelle del contado e delle vicarie, Coreglia, 31, 11 October 1460; Villabasilica, 91, fourth foliation, fo. 24r. 101 ASL Consiglio Generale, Riformagioni Pubbliche, 15, pp 243, 294, 400–1. 102 Lorenzo Tanzini, *Alle origini della Toscana moderna: Firenze e gli statuti delle comunità soggette tra XIV e XVI secolo* (Florence, 2007), pp 126–7. The

siders. Pastureland in the mountains was divided between the meadows of local individuals and the common pastures of the commune. It would be rash to deny any investment by citizens in livestock farming. There is some evidence of flocks kept in the early fifteenth century around Castiglione by the Guinigi. But, in the keeping of animals as in the cultivation of fields, the interests of Lucchese citizens in the mountain vicariates seem to have been very limited indeed. Things were, of course, different further south in the vicariate of Camaiore where Piero de' Guidiccioni, merchant and citizen of Lucca, owned pastures (probably chestnut woods) in Castelvecchio abutting lands (pastures) of the commune of Schiava; pastures that in 1455 were leased to Giovanni di Giannino of Mommio.[103] There is no difficulty in collecting examples of the ownership and leasing of woods and pastures by Lucchese citizens in the vicariate of Camaiore;[104] examples of Lucchese citizens owning or leasing herds and flocks are rather less easy to find.

The picture is not altogether dissimilar in the Sei Miglia: the area *par excellence* of citizen landholding and investment. The *estimi* records of 1411–13 show citizens owning numerous tracts of woods, brushwood, and meadows – leased to local men in return for fixed rents in wheat (sometimes millet); occasionally for half the fruits. In Tassignano, *piviere* of S. Paolo, the commune itself held 18 pieces of land – 17 described as woodland (*boscus*); 1 as meadowland (*pratum*) – leased in perpetuity from the heirs of Nicolao di Ceccorino di Poggio, of Stefano di Iacopo di Poggio, of Giovanni Turchi, and from Giovanni di Michele Guinigi for fixed rents in wheat and millet.[105] The neighbouring commune of Parezzana held in perpetuity from the wife of Giovanni Vannuccori of Lucca 6 pieces of land – 4 of woodland and 2 meadows – for an annual rent of 24 staia of wheat.[106] This area around pieve S. Paolo was characterized by a great fragmentation of landholding, and by the retention – in some areas more than others – of small patches of woodland and pastureland in the hands of peasant owner-cultivators. Elsewhere in the Sei Miglia there is evidence of citizens owning more extensive areas of pastureland: the pastures and hills in the *piviere* of S. Pancrazio disputed between Nicolao di Dino Avvocati and the commune of Matraia in 1442;[107] the pastures in Balbano and in the *piviere* of Massacciùccoli leased by Giusfredo di Pietro Cenami from October 1460 until the following May for

1494 statutes of Tassignano seem to envisage damage to cultivated land primarily in terms of disputes between local men–though goats were likely to belong to outsiders: ASL Archivio de' Notari, 1644 (ser Lorenzo di Poggio), fos. 34r–39v.   103 ASL Vicario di Camaiore, 2087, fo. 60v.   104 Notably the leasing of the coastal pastures of the communes of Camaiore and Mommio by Cristoforo di ser Bartolomeo Orsucci in 1455: ASL Vicario di Camaiore, 2087, fos. 45v, 52v.   105 ASL Estimo, 116, fos. 319r–320v.   106 Ibid., fo. 261r.   107 ASL Podestà di Lucca, 1180, fos. 14r–16v. Nicolao claimed that his family held the pastures by ancient imperial grant and that he had leased them to a native of Reggio presently living in Segromigno.

10 florins to Giuliano di Nicolao of Vico Pancellorum.[108] Citizens and urban churches retained some woods (and less frequently pastureland) in their own hands. And, at a time of population decline and declining income from rent, we might expect an expanded investment of capital in livestock by citizens – as appears to have happened elsewhere in Tuscany.[109] Certainly there are examples enough of herds of cows and flocks of sheep and goats belonging to citizens: like the 25 ill-custodied sheep belonging to Gherardo Anguilla.[110] But when citizens leased animals *in soccida* very many of the contracts relate only to individual animals; in the Sei Miglia as in the mountains most leases *in soccida* seem to be between countrymen. Where citizens do appear as the owners of large numbers of animals they were almost invariably butchers: Andrea di Lotto Schiactini who did damage with his flock of 'small animals' in 1395 to meadows in the suburbs of Lucca;[111] Nicolao di Giovanni similarly in 1406;[112] Giovanni di Piero Orsuccori who offended, again just outside the city walls, with his pigs in 1437.[113] The list of cases of *danno dato* involving the butchers of Lucca is endless; even in the Sei Miglia evidence for large-scale stockholding by other Lucchese citizens remains rather more elusive.

Whilst much attention has been focused on the expansion of pastoralism, many other changes to rural life and agrarian organization have been attributed, at least in part, to the insecurities and labour shortages of the century after the Black Death – and to the gradual recovery taking place in the decades from the 1450s. The posited changes include the expansion of citizen landholding and the associated rationalization and consolidation of landed possessions; more marked gradations of wealth within peasant society; a transformation in residential patterns from a countryside in which most peasants lived in nucleated settlements to one of isolated farmsteads; and a growing diversification and specialization in crop production. As with the expansion of pastoralism, the Lucchesia was not unaffected by these trends. But, as with animal husbandry, the impact of change in the Lucchesia seems to have been both distinctive and muted. Perhaps because fifteenth-century Lucca was not characterized by the spread of *mezzadria*, urban investment in the countryside, in particular, seems to have followed a rather different trajectory

Around Camaiore a great deal of land was in the possession of Lucchese citizens (including local notables of Camaiore who enjoyed Lucchese citizenship). The lands of Lucchese citizens extended northward up the valley of the Serchio as far as Anchiano.[114] In the mountains there is little sign of citizen

108 ASL Archivio de' Notari, 704 (ser Benedetto Franciotti), p. 180. For the pastures of the Cenami around Balbano: Biblioteca Statale di Lucca, MS 1110, G. Vincenzo Baroni, 'Notizie genealogiche delle famiglie lucchesi', fos. 43r–v, 63r. 109 Giuliano Pinto, 'Le strutture ambientali e le basi dell' economia rurale', in *La Toscana nel tardo medio evo: Ambiente, economia rurale, società* (Florence, 1982), pp 63–4. 110 ASL Podestà di Lucca, 7236, fo. 5v. 111 Ibid., fo. 12r. 112 ASL Podestà di Lucca, 7241, fo. 33r. 113 ASL Sentenze e bandi, 161, fo. 117r. 114 In the fifteenth century one might add the lands a

investment – a theme common to the Florentine literature. Some qualification needs to be made for families of recent rural origins, and for others who remained only very imperfectly committed to urban life. The civil court records of the *podestà* of Casoli oltre Giogo provide rich details of the houses, fields, vineyards, and animals held, and of the (sometimes usurious) landed transactions contracted around Renzano, Albiano, and Pugliano at the beginning of the fifteenth century by ser Gilio, ser Pietro, and Lorenzo, sons of the late ser Nantino de' Nobili of Pugliano – and later by Lorenzo's own sons.[115] In this instance we are speaking of men who claimed Lucchese citizenship but who were accustomed to live very far from the city (a likely source of grievance when local men invoked citizen privileges). In 1472 a general assembly of Castiglione (attended by 59 men) decided that the tenants of Benedetto del fu ser Iacopo da Castiglione, citizen of Lucca, should be freed from the payment of local taxes (excepting the *herbaticus* due for the pasturing of their animals) – this out of consideration for the great benefits that the community received every day from Benedetto and his house, and because of the great affection in which Benedetto was held by the men of Castiglione. Interestingly Benedetto's tenants are described as his 'mezadros seu colonos' (in a region that was not characterized by share-cropping), and they worked Benedetto's estate – 'praedium' – in a place called 'a Campori' (which carries implications of an unusual degree of land consolidation).[116] Further south there were the continued land purchases around Gallicano by the Bertini, a family from Gallicano that was establishing itself in Lucca during the course of the fifteenth century. But with due regard for (easily explained) pockets of citizen landholding, and excepting always Camaiore, the evidence of the notarial protocolli is quite unambiguous. In the vicariates the great bulk of land purchases and leases (and of petty loans and commercial dealings too) were contracted between countrymen. The impression is consolidated by the detailed description of abutting property that accompanied all landed transactions.

The owner-cultivators of the mountains were engaged in a wide range of agricultural and artisanal pursuits. They held a mix of arable land and pasture; of woods, chestnut trees, vineyards, and – in many areas – olive-groves. The pattern seems to remain stable throughout the fifteenth century, though – with demographic recovery – there is some evidence by the 1450s (at least from Camaiore) of attempts to encourage the conversion (or reconversion) of woodland into arable.[117] It has been argued that demographic decline accen-

little further north around Ghivizzano and Vitiana belonging to the da Ghivizzano family in the area of their origin.   **115** ASL Podestà di Casoli oltre Giogo, 29, pp 89–95, 429 (relating to *herbaticus* owing, and to damage caused by 2 cows and an ass belonging to Lorenzo); 30, fos. 30r–31v; 31, fos. 3r–v, 9v–10v, 13r.   **116** ASL Archivio Diplomatico, Archivio di Stato, 28 October 1472.   **117** ASL Vicario di Camaiore, 2087, fo. 32r; Archivio de' Notari, 1268 (ser Pietro Piscilla), fos. 147r–148r. One would add the drainage works and land improvement schemes around Viareggio driven by the city authorities in

tuated the pattern of men working both their own land and that of others.[118] Whether or not this was a distinctively late medieval phenomenon, the civil court records of Gallicano show everyone performing some work (ploughing fields, pruning vines, cutting hay) for their neighbours in return for day wages ('a opera'). There is no evidence in the mountains of a rural proletariat, though the Lucchese authorities might require the vicariates to send a specified number of men to Lucca to scythe wheat at harvest-time.[119] At a time of population decline, with the failure of families and the opportunities offered to the enterprising, it would be unsurprising if the fifteenth century saw sharper gradations of wealth within the peasant communities of the mountains. Certainly there is no difficulty in identifying village élites – men identified by their land- and stock-holding, often engaged in local commerce and manufacture, prominent in the representative assemblies of their communes, frequently offering small subsistence loans to their less fortune neighbours.[120] But peasant societies were never egalitarian, disparities of wealth can be a product of growth as well as contraction, and it is far from clear that the social profiles of villages were significantly transformed during the century after the Black Death.

The same holds true for residential structures. Villages were, of course, much smaller in 1450 than at the beginning of the fourteenth century, but the pattern remained one of clustered settlements – with, in the surrounding countryside, some dispersed houses, *capanne*, and shepherds' huts.[121] Sometimes we are given glimpses of men sallying forth from fortified villages to tend their fields. The incidence of clustered dwellings emerges from the records of the *estimi* and from descriptions of landed property in the notarial *protocolli*. But a more vivid picture of neighbourhood life can be gleaned from the narratives of the criminal court proceedings. Thus in February 1460 in Fiattone (vicariate of Castiglione) a quarrel between cousins in the church of S. Pietro resulted in Cristoforo di Bartolomeo rushing to his house, situated next to that of the heirs of Antonio di Michelino, where he collected a bill-hook (*falcinello*) from an upstairs room; there then followed a general affray between the parties in the street outside Cristoforo's house.[122] In January 1476 in the evening when Domenico di Antonio was returning

the last decades of the century.   **118** Mazzi and Raveggi, *Gli uomini e le cose*, p. 249.   **119** 'Per comandamento alla sega del grano': R. Archivio di Stato in Lucca, *Regesti*, iii, pt ii, *Carteggio di Guido Manfredi, Cancelliere della Repubblica di Lucca, Segretario della signoria di Paolo Guinigi MCCCC–MCCCCXXIX* (Pescia, 1933), no. 484; ASL Archivio de' Notari, 504 (XIII) (ser Antonio Nuccorini), fos. 47v–48r.   **120** For Gallicano and its vicariate: M.E. Bratchel, 'Usury in the fifteenth-century Lucchesia: images of the petty moneylender', *Journal of European Economic History*, 32 (2003), 257–62.   **121** For example, the temporary dwellings of the shepherds from Casabasciana tending a flock of sheep in the territory of Carsciana in 1413, who attacked and held captive a traveller from the mountains of Pistoia and raped his daughter-in-law: ASL Sentenze e bandi, 124, fos. 67r–69r; Capitano del contado, 32, no foliation.   **122** ASL Vicario di Castiglione, 733, fos. 1r–4r.

through the woods to his house in Villa Roggio he was attacked by the brothers Nicolao and Pellegrino sons of Domenico di Giovanni – though they claimed that he was injured by a falling chestnut tree. The mortally wounded Domenico was taken to Nicolao's house in Villa Roggio (apparently in an attempt to suppress news of the attack). But when they reached the door of Nicolao's house, Domenico refused to enter and sought refuge in the bed of a neighbour, Iacopo di Benedetto. The following day Domenico was carried by various men of Villa Roggio to his own house, where a few days later he died.[123] Particularly illuminating is the testimony of women regarding what they had seen and heard in the streets and in adjoining houses from behind their doors and windows. The stories are endless; the evidence from villages large and small points unambiguously to the cramped housing of men and women seeking neighbourliness and a measure of security in the shadow of the parish church.

By contrast with the mountain vicariates, the Sei Miglia (and the wine and olive belt that stretched from Camaiore to Pieve Elice) was a region of extensive citizen landholding – and had been for centuries. The *estimo* of 1411–12 for the *piviere* of Segromigno, situated to the north-east of Lucca, shows that 61.33 per cent of the land was in the hands of ecclesiastical institutions (churches, monasteries, altars); 24.2 per cent belonged to Lucchese citizens; 14.5 per cent to countrymen (*comitatini*). The equivalent figures for the neighbouring *piviere* of S. Gennaro are: ecclesiastical institutions 34.6 per cent; citizens 41.2 per cent; country dwellers 24.2 per cent.[124] In both *pivieri*, therefore, at the beginning of the fifteenth century there were substantial pockets of land that were owned and cultivated (directly or indirectly) by residents of the *contado* – more than in comparable areas of the countryside around Florence or Siena. For the most part the best land was not owned by *comitatini*, as is suggested by the dominance of ecclesiastical landholding in the rich wheat-lands of the Campi di Rucchi. A similar (if unquantified) picture emerges to the south in the *piviere* of S. Paolo.[125] Most of the land was owned by Lucchese citizens and ecclesiastical institutions (notably S. Iacopo of Altopascio), but there was also a scattering of lands owned by local men. In Tassignano Pasquino di Martino (head of a family of 7)[126] owned a field with vines and trees measuring 301 *pertiche* (about a third of a hectare); Tottoro Nucchini (a man of 66 years of age, with a wife aged 55) owned jointly with the church of S. Stefano of Tassignano a field measuring 231 *per-*

123 ASL Podestà di Lucca, 2132, fos. 14r–21r. The story is recounted in more detail in M.E. Bratchel, 'Lucca and its subject communities (1430–1494)', in Ilaria Zilli (ed.), *Fra spazio e tempo: Studi in onore di Luigi de Rosa*, 3 (Naples, 1995), I, 188.   124 Alessandra Potenti, 'Proprietà cittadina e comitatina nelle Sei Miglia lucchesi attraverso gli estimi del 1411–1413: I pivieri di S. Gennaro e Segromigno', *Quaderni Lucchesi di Studi sul Medioevo e sul Rinascimento* 4 (2003), 138–9.   125 ASL Estimo, 116.   126 Or six. In the *estimo* assessment very young children are excluded.

tiche, another of 85 *pertiche* which was his own, and a wood 'de prunis et quercibus' measuring about 2 *quarre* (230 *pertiche*) and worth 10s.; Lando di Giovanni (head of a household of 8 mouths comprising his son, his daughter-in-law, and 5 grandchildren) owned a meadow measuring 115 *pertiche*, another meadow 'cum albagattis' measuring 1 *coltra* and 315 *pertiche* (775 *pertiche*), a wood 'de ontanis prunis et quercibus' measuring 1 *coltra*, and another wood 'de prunis et quercibus' measuring 3 *quarre*. Some land in Tassignano (fields, vines, meadows and woodland) was owned by Luporino Damuccii, a Lucchese citizen resident in S. Margherita; fragments of fields and woods in Tassignano were owned by Puccinello Luporini of S. Margherita, by Puccinello Dinuccii of Paganico (both communes in the *piviere* of S. Paolo), and by men from neighbouring Capannori. The pattern is repeated throughout the *piviere*, with perhaps rather more land owned (both locally and throughout the whole *piviere*) by *comitatini* who were resident in the *corpo* of the *piviere*.[127] Local men were more likely to own woods and meadows than arable land;[128] instances of the latter often refer to fields of very small dimensions. On occasion local residents said that they did not know who owned the land (and that therefore they paid no rent) – testimony to the dislocations of the previous half-century.

Common to the *pivieri* of Segromigno, S. Gennaro, and S. Paolo was the highly fragmented nature of landholding. It was not uncommon for a lessee to hold pieces of land from between 9 and 16 different proprietors.[129] Pasquino di Martino of Tassignano held 38 pieces of property: a house, fields, fields with vines and trees, meadows, and pieces of woodland. The house and one field he owned; the rest were leased from 20 different proprietors – Lucchese citizens, the bishop of Lucca, Altopascio, local and urban churches and the commune of Tassignano.[130] The degree of landed fragmentation can be shown from the perspective of urban landowners as well as their peasant lessees. Sante Polica has described the haphazard accumulation of lands throughout the Sei Miglia in the mid-fifteenth century by Michele di Giovanni Guinigi.[131] There seems to have been little attempt to rationalize the properties (except perhaps around Matraia); the aim was the acquisition of land – often through usurious transactions – which was then handed over to peasant tenants on short-term leases (usually for a fixed rent in wheat, though for rents in money in some cases of woodland and grassland, and in return

127 For example, the extensive meadows owned in the commune of Parezzana by Coluccino di Michele.   128 For example, the ten pieces of woodland owned by Ciufforo Tinori of Paganico. A great deal of the land in the communes of Paganico and Mugnano is described as 'boscus'.   129 Potenti, 'Proprietà cittadina', pp 153–8.   130 ASL Estimo, 116, fos. 287r–290r. Foreigners were more likely to hold their pieces of land from a single proprietor, and normally, of course, owned no land of their own.   131 Sante Polica, 'An attempted "reconversion" of wealth in XVth century Lucca: the lands of Michele di Giovanni Guinigi', *Journal of European Economic History* 9 (1980), 655–707.

for half the fruits in areas of olive and vine cultivation). All this might represent a step towards the building up of an estate, but we are very far removed from the Sei Miglia of the sixteenth century as described by Marino Berengo: an area now entirely in the hands of citizens and organized into neat consolidated farmsteads (*poderi*).[132]

Certainly there are references to *poderi* in the fifteenth-century Lucchese countryside (indeed there are references to the *poderi* of residents of the Sei Miglia throughout the notarial records from the early fourteenth century). It is perilous, without supporting evidence, to endow words with the precise technical meanings that they have come to assume in the historical literature. But where the word *podere* appears in the Lucchese documents it does seem to carry connotations of a compact agricultural unit. In the 1440s there are references to the *podere* of Michele Giordani in Mammoli (*piviere* of Sesto a Moriano) with its fields, vineyard, olive grove, and woodland;[133] to that of the heirs of Gherardo Vellutelli in Tofari (*piviere* of S. Gennaro);[134] and to that of Alessandro Rapondi in Vecoli (*piviere* of S. Macario).[135] Sometimes there is mention of a house where, presumably, the tenant lived. The 'Podere Grande' of Roberto Guinigi in Segromigno was clearly in the classic mould – with the lord's palace situated next to the house of the tenant, within walled gardens, and set amidst arable land, vines, olives, and fruit trees.[136] Similarly – though on a less grand scale – the *podere* of Domenico Agostini in Casteldurante (*piviere* of Compito).[137] But there is no mention of houses in the detailed description of fire-damage caused in August 1406 to the *poderi* of the heirs of Alderigo degli Antelminelli and of Bendinello Salamoni in Mommio (vicariate of Camaiore).[138] Sometimes the tenant of a *podere* clearly lived elsewhere, in one of the villages of the Sei Miglia or on another piece of land, as was the case – more characteristic of the fifteenth-century Sei Miglia – with owner-cultivators and lessees of fragments of land from numerous proprietors. The *estimi* of the early fifteenth century show that houses figured quite prominently amongst the pieces of property that were likely to be owned by *comitatini*. The evidence does not always point towards nucleated settlements; indeed, as today, in the eastern part of the Lucchese plain it must often have been difficult to determine where one village ended and the next began. There remains little sign that depopulated villages were coming to be converted into

---

132 'L'abitante della piana che circonda la città è quasi sempre un *salano*, l'affittuale cioè di un proprietario lucchese cui è legato da contratti di locazione ricchi di elementi parziari; e non ha, al di fuori del podere che conduce, altre fonti di sussistenza': Marino Berengo, *Nobili e mercanti nella Lucca del Cinquecento* (Turin, 1965), p. 301. The description has been cited as authoritative in studies of Tuscan agriculture for more than four decades; it is perhaps time for it to be revisited.   133 ASL Sentenze e bandi, 164, fo. 49r–v.   134 Ibid., fo. 58v.   135 Ibid., fo. 78r. For further references see Bratchel, *Lucca 1430–1494*, p. 189.   136 Potenti, 'Proprietà cittadina', pp 148–9.   137 ASL Sentenze e bandi, 164, fo. 54r.   138 ASL Podestà di Lucca, 7241, fos. 24r–27v.

isolated farmsteads as seems to have happened in the contemporary Florentine countryside. Villages shrank to a handful of inhabitants, disappeared and reappeared, were united with neighbouring villages for administrative purposes. But the settlement pattern of the Sei Miglia remained remarkably resilient throughout all the trials of the fifteenth century.[139]

We need therefore to identify the changes that were taking place in the Sei Miglia during the half-century of continuing population decline (or stagnation) up to 1450 and in the period of gradual demographic recovery in the half-century thereafter. If Berengo is to be believed, patterns of landholding had changed radically by the sixteenth century as compared with the picture given in the *estimi* accounts of 1411–13. Citizens continued to purchase tracts of land from residents of the *contado*. But transformation was marked less by the gradual whittling away of the property of small owner-cultivators (present but of limited extent throughout the entire period) than by the reorganization and consolidation of the lands held by citizens themselves. References to *poderi* with a house for the tenant seem to become more plentiful from the mid-fifteenth century.[140] This change may have been facilitated by the engrossment of lands of the Church.[141] It was certainly connected with a heightened interest by citizens in the social benefits and economic returns from land posited in the various and disparate contributions to the 'return to the land' debate.[142] Recognition of the profits to be gleaned from land is attested by the numerous 'improvement leases' whereby citizen landowners sought to bring wasteland into cultivation. These fill the notarial *protocolli* from the mid-fifteenth century, and coincide with the beginnings of renewed population growth.

In the Lucchese countryside neither the challenges of labour shortage nor the later opportunities offered by demographic growth heralded the appearance of *mezzadria*. Contracts *ad medium* were the norm in areas of vine and olive cultivation, but *mezzadria* – with rare exceptions – was largely absent from the grain-producing regions of the Lucchese plain.[143] In this respect the Lucchesia – and more particularly the Sei Miglia – can be contrasted with dominant patterns of agrarian organization elsewhere in Tuscany (Pisa excepted). The absence of *mezzadria* does not signify the absence of the kind of controls over peasant tenants that are usually seen as synonymous with *mez-*

---

139 Leverotti, *Popolazione, famiglie, insediamento*, pp 173–83.   140 Bratchel, *Lucca 1430–1494*, pp 187–8, 189, 195.   141 As suggested by Potenti, 'Proprietà cittadina', pp 140–53.   142 The literature is enormous, but see in particular David Herlihy, 'The problem of the "return to the land" in Tuscan economic history of the fourteenth and fifteenth centuries', in *Civiltà ed economia agricola in Toscana nei secc. xiii–xv: Problemi della vita delle campagne nel tardo medioevo: Centro italiano di studi di storia e d'arte Pistoia, Ottavo Convegno Internazionale, Pistoia 21–24 aprile 1977* (Pistoia, 1981), pp 401–16, and the works there cited.   143 In fourteenth-century leases rent in millet was often specified *ad medium*; that in wheat in fixed quantities.

zadria – which were often incorporated into Lucchese short-term leases (perhaps increasingly after mid-century). Nor did the absence of *mezzadria* mean that the structure of Lucchese peasant families differed significantly from that of peasant families elsewhere in Tuscany (despite attempts to associate the growing complexity of peasant families with the specific dynamics of *mezzadria*).[144] The *estimi* of 1411–13 show a marked growth in the proportion of complex families in the early fifteenth-century Sei Miglia that seems to have resulted from a tendency to cohere around the paternal head of family against a background of plague, war, and harvest failure (and from the increased power by statute conferred upon the father).[145] The tendency was more pronounced among richer rural families. It characterized the families of local families much more markedly than those of immigrants, though even among *forestieri* there are instances of two co-resident brothers with their families.[146]

The distinctiveness of the Lucchesia has long been recognized in the historical literature. The distinctiveness does not preclude the possibility of establishing common themes or of making meaningful comparisons with other parts of north-central Italy. There was the common background of mortality, dislocation, mobility in the century after the Black Death; of gradual recovery from the 1450s. There was an (unquantifiable) growth of pastoralism that provoked tensions, though local and transhumant flocks never seem to have posed a real threat to settled agriculture. There may have been a growing diversification in crop-production. But the Lucchesia had always been an area of promiscuous agriculture. Reading the notarial *protocolli* from the late thirteenth to the end of the fifteenth centuries, it is difficult to believe that there was any very revolutionary change in land use. Maybe in the Sei Miglia the pattern of fields with vines and olives was giving way in places to the appearance of vineyards and olive groves[147] – not to mention (in the mountains) sporadic but increasing references to mulberry cultivation. Change is most visible in the Sei Miglia, where the dispossession of peasant owner-cultivators continued, where there are increasing references to the *poderi* of Lucchese citizens, and where, by the 1460s, there seem to be more frequent cases of the summary termination of the leases of unsuitable tenants.[148] But change lagged far behind comparable developments in the Florentine or Sienese state and

---

144 A point recognized long ago by Christiane Klapisch and Michel Demonet, '"A uno pane a uno vino": La famille rurale toscane au début du XVe siècle', *Annales, ESC*, 27 (1972), 873–901. The households of share-croppers do seem to have contained more children.   **145** Leverotti, *Popolazione, famiglie, insediamento*, particularly pp 120–7.   **146** The *Tuccius*, 'nepos' of Manuelle Dinelli of Empoli, living with Manuelle, his wife, and their three young children in the commune of Tassignano, was clearly a nephew rather than a grandson: ASL Estimo, 116, fo. 283v.   **147** Potenti points out that in 1411–13 relatively small areas were devoted to vine and olive cultivation in her two sample *pivieri* of Segromigno and S. Gennaro: 'Proprietà cittadina', pp 125–8. Wine and oil production does not seem to have attained the importance that it was later to assume.   **148** See, for example, ASL Podestà di Lucca, 1412, passim.

was unaccompanied by the introduction of *mezzadria*. The absence of *mezzadria* may help to explain why settlement patterns in the Sei Miglia remained very largely unchanged;[149] though by the same token *mezzadria* cannot be invoked in the Lucchesia to explain the growing complexity of peasant families, which seems to be characteristic of Tuscany as a whole. Wage-labour does not appear prominently in the sources.[150] Clearly there were men who depended entirely – or almost entirely – on their labour 'a opera'. My impression remains that wage-labour in the vicariates was usually provided by men who appear elsewhere as owner-cultivators: the quintessential figures of the mountains. In the Sei Miglia seasonal wage-labour was likely to be provided by men drafted from the vicariates, and by tenants on short-term leases (or their sons): the quintessential figures of the Lucchese plain. Personal traumas, continuing mobility, evolutionary changes rather than radical structural transformation remain the most distinctive features of rural life in the fifteenth-century Lucchesia.

149 For the link between *mezzadria* and dispersed settlement patterns: David Herlihy and Christiane Klapisch-Zuber, *Les Toscans et leurs familles: Une étude du catasto florentin de 1427* (Paris, 1978), p. 232.   **150** See the brief but pertinent comments of S.R. Epstein, 'The peasantries of Italy, 1350–1750', in Tom Scott (ed.), *The peasantries of Europe from the fourteenth to the eighteenth centuries* (London, 1998), pp 97–8.

Conversio and conversatio in the Life of Herluca of Epfach

I.S. ROBINSON

Among the extensive literary productions of the papal reform movement and the conflict of papacy and empire known as 'the Investiture Contest', there are numerous saints' lives. These differ in a characteristic way from traditional works of hagiography[1] in that they use the opinions of the saint and the incidents of the saint's life as propaganda in support of the religious reform movement. An interesting case study is the series of *Vitae* of Pope Leo IX (1048/9–54), the central figure in the early history of the reform papacy, beginning with the anonymous Lotharingian *Life* of c.1060. Here the pope's conduct towards the faithful, the reforming initiatives in his papal councils but above all his visions and the miracles associated with him are used to promote the papal campaign to eradicate simony from episcopal appointments.[2] The principal theme of the biography of Leo IX composed by Bishop Bruno of Segni in the late 1090s is again the campaign against simony, the author interpolating in the *Life* a lengthy polemic on the validity of the orders of clergy ordained by simoniacs.[3]

Of a similar character is the *Life of Pope Gregory VII* composed by Paul of Bernried in 1128, six years after the settlement of the Investiture Contest by the concordat of Worms of 1122 and five years after Pope Calixtus II celebrated the First Lateran Council of 1123, which confirmed the Gregorian reform programme of the preceding half century with its condemnation of simony and clerical marriage.[4] Paul of Bernried composed the *Life* so that 'this man's example, if stored in a retentive memory, becomes a prop for holy Church and an ornament of Christ's faithful and brings defeat for impious

1 F. Lotter, 'Methodisches zur Gewinnung historischer Erkenntnisse aus hagiographischen Quellen', *Historische Zeitschrift* 229 (1979) 298–356, especially 309–12, identified three separate forms of hagiographical writing in the early and central Middle Ages: the 'aretalogical-hagiographical' works, the 'rhetorical-idealizing biographies of prelates and rulers' and the 'prose obituaries'. The saints' lives of the Investiture Contest present a distinct variant of these conventional forms. 2 *Die Touler Vita Leos IX*, H.-G. Krause (ed.), MGH, *Scriptores rerum germanicarum in usum scholarum separatim editi* 70. On the hagiographical tradition of Leo IX see H. Tritz, 'Die hagiographischen Quellen zur Geschichte Papst Leos IX. Eine Untersuchung ihres Überlieferungs- und Entstehungsgeschichte', *Studi Gregoriani* 4 (1952), 191–364; I.S. Robinson, *The papal reform of the eleventh century: lives of Pope Leo IX and Pope Gregory VII* (Manchester, 2004), pp 17–35, 88–94. 3 Bruno of Segni, *Libellus de symoniacis*, MGH *Libelli de lite* 2, 543–62. 4 I.S. Robinson, *The Papacy, 1073–1198* (Cambridge, 1990), pp 134–5.

heresies'.[5] Drawing on oral tradition but also on impressive documentary evidence – papal letters, synodal decrees, narrative works – Paul presented a portrait of Gregory VII as a legislator whose decrees must be obeyed by the faithful because he was also a saint and a focus of miraculous activity. In a second hagiographical work composed two years later, this time drawing entirely on oral tradition, Paul presented another figure of great sanctity, whose example was likewise 'a prop for holy Church': not a holder of high ecclesiastical office but a lay woman whose life was spent in humble domestic work. This was *The Life of the blessed Herluca*, an account of a visionary who was Paul's close friend and adviser. 'It is more than twenty years,' wrote Paul in the prologue of the *Vita beatae Herlucae*, 'since my mind began to discover and examine certain signs of holiness in the way of life (*conversatio*) of the blessed virgin Herluca, being bound by a vow to write them down.' 'Now at last in the third year since her death' he fulfilled his vow to write the *Vita*.[6]

The *Vita Herlucae* offers the most precise extant evidence for the career of the author himself. When Paul became acquainted with Herluca, he was a priest in the city of Regensburg, whose bishops – Gebhard IV (1089–1105) and Hartwig (1105–26) – were loyal adherents of the imperialist party and enemies of the Gregorian papacy during the Investiture Contest.[7] Paul became the object of 'the hostility of the clergy of Regensburg'. 'They hated me,' he wrote in the *Vita*, 'as the cause of their uneasiness by virtue of my irreproachable life and my willingness to speak the truth.'[8] He mentioned the name of only one likeminded supporter of the Gregorian party in Regensburg: Walter, probably a member of the cathedral clergy, the distinguished reformer who in 1118 would become archbishop of Ravenna.[9] During these troubled years Paul paid a number of visits to Herluca in Epfach (in the diocese of Augsburg), where she lived in a circle of pious women, performing deeds of charity, from c.1085 to 1121.[10] On his third visit to Epfach in 1107 Paul confided in Herluca his intention of leaving hostile Regensburg but (prompted by a vision of St Laurence) she persuaded him to remain.[11]

5 Paul of Bernried, *Vita Gregorii VII papae* cap. 44, J.M. Watterich (ed.), *Pontificum Romanorum Vitae* 1 (Leipzig, 1862), p. 498.   **6** Paul of Bernried, *Vita beatae Herlucae*, prologue, *Acta Sanctorum Aprilis* 2 (Antwerp, 1675), 552A. The most important study of Herluca is R. Schnitzer, *Die Vita B. Herlucae Pauls von Bernried. Eine Quelle zur gregorianischen Reform in Süddeutschland* (dissertation: Munich, 1967), pp 55–78. See also A. Schnitzer, 'Die selige Herluka von Bernried: Persönlichkeit und Zeitlage', *Jahrbuch des Vereins für Augsburger Bistumsgeschichte* 3 (1969), 5–15.   **7** E. Boshof, 'Bischöfe und Bischofskirchen von Passau und Regensburg' in S. Weinfurter (ed.), *Die Salier und das Reich* 2 (Sigmaringen, 1991), pp 141–2, 148–50.   **8** Paul, *Vita Herlucae* cap. 43, p. 556C.   **9** Ibid., prologue, p. 552B. See G. Schwartz, *Die Besetzung der Bistümer Reichsitaliens unter den sächsischen und salischen Kaisern mit den Listen der Bischöfe, 951–1122* (Berlin, 1913), p. 160; R. Schnitzer, *Die Vita B. Herlucae*, p. 29.   **10** On the dating see R. Schnitzer, *Die Vita B. Herlucae*, pp 67–72.   **11** Paul, *Vita* cap. 43, p. 556C. See below p. 186.

Fourteen years later Paul left Regensburg, 'expelled by the persecution of [Emperor] Henry V'.[12]

Paul took refuge in Bernried (in the Augsburg diocese) on the western shore of the Starnbergersee, where he may have participated in the foundation of the house of regular canons established in Bernried around the time of his arrival.[13] There is evidence suggesting that it was Paul who travelled to Rome to obtain from Pope Calixtus II the privilege of 12 November 1122 for 'the brethren professing the regular life in the church of St Martin ... in the place called Bernried'.[14] There is no evidence, however, that Paul ever became a regular canon of Bernried. The name 'Paul of Bernried', bestowed on the author by his first editor, Jakob Gretser in 1610, is misleading.[15] Paul identified himself in the prologue of the *Vita Herlucae* only as 'brother Paul, unworthy to be called priest'.[16] After his completion of the *Vita*, probably in 1130,[17] nothing certain is known of Paul's career. A letter of uncertain date written by Paul and his pupil Gebhard to a Milanese correspondent states that they now resided in a religious house dedicated to St Magnus.[18] This has been identified as the house of regular canons of St Mang (Magnus), founded in 1138 in Stadtamhof near Regensburg, with Gebhard, canon of Regensburg as its first provost – perhaps that same Gebhard who was the pupil of Paul.[19] It was presumably here that Paul died at an unknown date.

12 Paul, *Vita* cap. 44, p. 556C. Henry V was in Regensburg on 25 March 1121: G. Meyer von Knonau, *Jahrbücher des Deutschen Reiches unter Heinrich IV. und Heinrich V.*, 7 (Leipzig, 1909), p. 168. See J. May, 'Leben Pauls von Bernried', *Neues Archiv* 12 (1887), 339–40. **13** Paul, *Vita* cap. 44, p. 556C. On the foundation of Bernried see O. Hartig, *Die oberbayerischen Stifte* 1 (Munich, 1935), pp 183–8; J. Mois, *Das Stift Rottenbuch in der Kirchenreform des XI.–XII. Jahrhunderts* (Beiträge zur altbayerischen Kirchengeschichte, series 3, 19: Munich, 1953), pp 207–10. The most recent study is W. Scherbaum, *Das Augustinerchorherrenstift Bernried. Studien zur Stiftsentwicklung und zu Problemen sozialen, wirtschaftlichen und kulturellen Lebens in einer geistlichen Hofmark* (Miscellanea Bavarica Monacensia 168: Munich, 1997). **14** Calixtus II, *JL* 6993, *Patrologia Latina* 163, col. 1257D–1258C. See M. Herrmann, 'Paul und Gebhard von Bernried und ihre Briefe an Mailänder Geistliche', *Neues Archiv* 14 (1889), 570. A trace of this visit to Rome survives in *Vita Herlucae* cap. 35, p. 555E: 'when in Rome a few years ago', Paul met a 'Roman collector' of miracles wrought by St Laurence 'that had happened in modern times in various regions of the world' and promised him an account of Herluca's visions of St Laurence. On the cult of St Laurence in the period of the reform papacy see C.H. Brakel, 'Die vom Reformpapsttum geförderten Heiligenkulte', *Studi Gregoriani per la storia della 'Libertas Ecclesiae'* 9 (1972), 252, 257, 267, 280, 281, 287, 290, 292, 301, 302, 307, 311. **15** J. Gretser, *Commentarius Pauli Bernriedensis, antiqui scriptoris, de vita Gregorii VII pontificis maximi* (Ingolstadt, 1610). **16** Paul, *Vita*, prologue, p. 552A. **17** Ibid. The *Vita* was composed 'in the third year since her death', which perhaps occurred in 1127. See M. Herrmann, 'Paul und Gebhard von Bernried' (as n. 14), pp 573–4; J. Mois, *Das Stift Rottenbuch*, p. 210; M. Maier, 'Ein schwäbisch-bayerischer Freundeskreis Gregors VII. nach der Vita Herlucae des Paul von Bernried', *Studien und Mitteilungen zur Geschichte des Benediktinerordens* 74 (1963), 330. **18** Letter to Martinus Corvus, treasurer (later provost) of S. Ambrogio in Milan: J. May, 'Leben Pauls von Bernried' (as n. 12), pp 341–2; M. Herrmann, 'Paul und Gebhard von Bernried' (as n. 14), p. 580. **19** A. Hauck,

Paul of Bernried's stated object in the prologue of his *Vita Herlucae* was 'to search out and investigate certain signs of holiness in the way of life (*conversatio*) of the blessed virgin Herluca, which have hitherto been preserved and gathered together in my heart'.[20] His purpose, therefore, was purely that of the hagiographer: not to write a biography but to record the *signa sanctitatis* during his subject's life. Nevertheless he incidentally provided some biographical information, which indicates that Herluca died in 1127 (or perhaps in 1128) at an advanced age.[21] Her date of birth has been calculated as *c*.1060.[22] Herluca was 'born of the race of the Alemannians or Swabians'.[23] The *Vita* says nothing of her family, even though Paul undoubtedly knew something of it,[24] which suggests that she was of non-noble rank. For a hagiographer rarely lost the opportunity to apply to a saint of noble origin the formula 'noble by birth, more noble in sanctity' (*nobilis genere, nobilior sanctitate*), which perhaps originated with Jerome.[25] A more precise indication of Herluca's birthplace is perhaps suggested by her biographer's account of her miraculous healing in early life: her temporary blindness was cured after she made a votive offering of a waxen eye to St Cyriacus.[26] If Herluca made this offering in a church dedicated to St Cyriacus, it is possible that she was living in the territory of the Swabian family of Helfenstein, the lords of Geislingen on the River Steig, who had particularly promoted the cult of the saint in the churches of their territory.[27]

Herluca's temporary blindness brought about her 'conversion'. The *Vita* says of this event only that, 'touched by the finger of God, she completely changed her mind together with her clothing'.[28] Henceforward Herluca wore distinctive clothing, which was the outward sign of her *conversio*. This change of clothing did not involve entry into monastic life. The *Vita* states that the

Kirchengeschichte Deutschlands 3, 8th ed. (Berlin, 1954), p. 1021; W. Wattenbach, R. Holtzmann & F.-J. Schmale, *Deutschlands Geschichtsquellen im Mittelalter. Vom Tode Heinrichs V. bis zum Ende des Interregnum* 1 (Darmstadt, 1976), p. 245.   20 Paul, *Vita Herlucae*, prologue, 552A.   21 Ibid., cap. 43, p. 556C.   22 R. Schnitzer, *Die Vita B. Herlucae* p. 56.   23 Paul, *Vita* cap. 1, p. 552F.   24 Ibid., cap. 33, p. 555B, names her father as *Baldebertus*; cap. 30, p. 555A, identifies a niece, *Luikardis*.   25 Jerome, *Epistola* 108 *ad Eustochium* cap. 1, *Corpus Scriptorum Ecclesiasticorum Latinorum* 55 (1912), 306. See, for example, the *Life* of Herluca's contemporary Paulina, the founder of Paulinzella, in which the protagonist's noble birth figures in the title: *Vita beatae Paulinae nobilis feminae*, *MGH Scriptores* 30/2, 910. See below p. 180. The formula was not confined to hagiography: cf. Bernold of Constance, *Chronicon* 1084, *MGH Scriptores rerum germanicarum, nova series* 14, 445–6, on Bishop Gebhard III of Constance: *nobilem quidem genere sed nobiliorem in monachica conversatione*. See F. Lotter, 'Methodisches zur Gewinnung historischer Erkenntnisse' (as n. 1), p. 325.   26 Paul, *Vita* cap. 3, p. 553A.   27 The Helfensteiner were the advocates of the monastery of Wiesensteig, which had been dedicated to St Cyriacus in 861: G. Hoffmann, *Kirchenheilige in Württemberg* (Darstellungen aus der württembergische Geschichte 23: Stuttgart, 1932), p. 27; R. Schnitzer, *Die Vita B. Herlucae* pp 58–9. On the cult of Cyriacus in the Gregorian period see C.H. Brakel, 'Die vom Reformpapsttum geförderten Heiligenkulte' (as n. 14), pp 246, 247, 252, 120 and n. 113, 261 and n. 115, 262 and n. 125, 264, 281–2, 289, 295.   28 Paul, *Vita* cap. 2, p. 553A.

conversion was immediately followed by charitable work in the world: 'thenceforward she began to undertake the care of infants ... washing their heads and sewing their garments and supplying their other needs.'[29] Not only is there no evidence during Herluca's career of an entry into a convent. At the time of her conversion it would hardly have been possible for her – if she was indeed of non-noble birth, as her biographer's silence on the matter seems to suggest – to enter a convent. Female religious houses in Germany in the later eleventh century were relatively few in number and aristocratic in their membership.[30] Instead the *Vita* depicts Herluca soon after her conversion living in a castle and assisting the devotions of a circle of pious noble-women. 'Adelaide, wife of the count palatine Manegold, of the castle that is called *Moropolis* ... chose Herluca to help her when she spent the night in praying to God.' This help took the form of driving out the Devil, who sought to terrify the countess while she was praying by extinguishing her candle.[31] The *Vita* adds that Herluca was also acquainted with Countess Adelaide's sisters, Wielica and Hiltiburgis, 'virgins pledged to Christ', whose piety Adelaide sought to imitate. After their deaths Herluca saw a vision of all three women in heaven.[32] This count palatine Manegold has been convincingly identified as a member of a collateral branch of the family of the counts of Dillingen that held the office of count palatine in Swabia in the later eleventh and early twelfth century.[33]

Herluca's presence in the castle of count palatine Manegold has prompted the conclusion that at this early stage in her career she belonged to the *familia* of Manegold, as his servant.[34] The *Vita*, however, says nothing as precise as this when introducing Herluca's connection with Countess Adelaide, stating only that the latter *Herlucam sibi assumpsit in adiutorium pernoctandi in oratione Dei*.[35] The biographer was equally vague about Herluca's connection with another aristocratic couple, Rutpert and Hadewig (who are known only from

---

29 Ibid., cap. 4, p. 553A. On the text of this chapter see H. Fuhrmann, 'Zur handschriftlichen Verbreitung der Vita b. Herlucae des Paul von Bernried', *Analecta Bollandiana* 74 (1956), 367; R. Schnitzer, *Die Vita B. Herlucae* p. 67. **30** Ibid., p. 62; K.J. Leyser, *Rule and conflict in an early medieval society* (Oxford, 1979), pp 63–73. Cf. R.W. Southern, *Western society and the Church in the Middle Ages* (London, 1970), pp 229–30, citing the tradition in the *Annals of Quedlinburg*, MGH SS 3, 54, that Queen Matilda, widow of Henry I, in founding Quedlinburg, insisted on receiving only novices of the highest nobility 'because those who are well-born can scarcely ever become degenerate'. **31** Paul, *Vita* cap. 5, p. 553AB. **32** Ibid., cap. 5, 10, pp 553A, 553CD. **33** P. Classen, *Gerhoch von Reichersberg. Eine Biographie* (Wiesbaden, 1960), p. 25; R. Schnitzer, *Die Vita B. Herlucae* pp 59–61, arguing against the identification (e.g. by A.M. Zimmermann, article 'Herluka', *Lexikon für Theologie und Kirche* 5, 2nd ed. [1960], col. 249) of count palatine Manegold with Count Manegold of Altshausen (-Veringen), who was well known to Paul of Bernried (*Vita Gregorii VII* cap. 89, 91, pp 526–7, 527–9) but who was never count palatine in Swabia. On the identity of the Latin-Greek place-name of *Moropolis* ('city of the dead') see M. Maier, 'Ein schwäbisch-bayerischer Freundeskreis' (as n. 17), pp 315–16; R. Schnitzer, *Die Vita B. Herlucae*, pp 60–1.

the *Vita*). It was in their company that she first arrived in Epfach on the River Lech, where she was to reside 'for about 36 years'. 'Accompanying her noble pupils (*alumni*), Rutpert and Hadewig, she arrived by chance on the bank of the River Lech.' These 'noble pupils' evidently regarded Herluca as their spiritual mentor. It was perhaps similarly as an *alumna* that Countess Adelaide sought Herluca's help against the Devil. The chapter of the *Vita* concerning Rutpert and Hadewig also calls them Herluca's *alitores*, those who supported, sustained, nourished her, and her *carnales patroni*, her worldly protectors.[36] The *Vita* records that the travellers found in Epfach a church dedicated to St Laurence and the tomb of the eighth-century Bishop Wikterp of Augsburg. Rutpert and Hadewig may indeed have been accompanying Herluca on a pilgrimage when they reached this holy 'place of great antiquity'.[37] On arrival in Epfach Herluca 'immediately tasted so great a sweetness in the patronages (*patrocinia*) of the most blessed deacon Laurence ... and of the holy Wikterp ... that, when her supporters (*alitores*) were returning to their own land, she would by no means consent to return with them. The worldly protectors were angry and no provisions were arranged for her who remained behind.' Herluca's *spiritualis consolator* Bishop Wikterp, however, appeared to her, urging her to stay with him and promising his protection.[38] The biographer clearly intended here to contrast the superior value of this spiritual *patrocinium* to that worldly protection that depended on human whim. Paul of Bernried's account of the anger of Rutpert and Hadewig and their apparent refusal henceforward to provide her with the necessities of life perhaps suggests that Herluca had been their servant, a member of their *familia*, until she parted company from them in Epfach.[39]

Paul's account of the relationship of Herluca with her 'noble pupils' is, however, confusing. Having departed in anger from Epfach 'to their own land' in chapter 12 of the *Vita*, Rutpert and Hadewig are found in chapter 27 residing in Epfach and attentive to the spiritual counsel of Herluca. 'The aforementioned Rutpert, the husband of Hadewig, at length converted by [Herluca's] frequent exhortations to the celibate life, together with his wife, did not hesitate to declare that, except for St Mary, no woman had ever been so useful to himself and to his own people as Herluca.'[40] In this section of the *Vita* Paul's theme was Herluca's 'grace in converting and in winning souls for God' and his most striking case-study was that of Judith, the daughter of

34 P. Classen, *Gerhoch von Reichersberg*, p. 25.   **35** Paul, *Vita* cap. 5, p. 553A.   **36** Ibid., cap. 12, p. 553D. On the meaning of the terms *alumni, alitores, carnales patroni* see *Acta Sanctorum Aprilis* 2, p. 553, footnote 'h'; M. Maier, 'Ein schwäbisch-bayerischer Freundeskreis' (as n. 17), p. 317.   **37** Paul, *Vita* cap. 12, p. 553D. See R. Schnitzer, *Die Vita B. Herlucae*, pp 65–6, 78–82; J. Werner, '*Abodiacum*. Die Ausgrabungen auf dem Lorenzberg bei Epfach' in *Neue Ausgrabungen in Deutschland* (Römische-Germanische Kommission des archäologischen Instituts: Berlin, 1958), pp 409–24.   **38** Paul, *Vita* cap. 12, p. 553DE.   **39** R. Schnitzer, *Die Vita B. Herlucae*, p. 66.   **40** Paul, *Vita* cap. 27, p. 554E.

Rutpert and Hadewig. Judith 'was converted to the resolution to preserve her virginity' and, despite her mother's hesitation, received 'the sacred veil' from Bishop Udalric of Passau (1092–1121). Judith died the following year and her companion in her last sickness was Luikardis, the niece of Herluca, who had taken the same vow of virginity. 'A pleasant dispute was heard between them about which of them was to depart first to the heavenly kingdom.' Judith appeared in a vision to Herluca after her death 'in great glory'.[41]

The account of Herluca's arrival in Epfach in the *Vita* is framed by two chapters that identify Herluca's own spiritual advisers and explain the reason for her decision to settle in Epfach. 'At that time' – Paul's phrase seems to refer to the period immediately after her conversion, when she was the associate of Countess Adelaide, wife of the count palatine Manegold, and was still living in Swabia – 'she had most excellent advisers on her holy purpose, namely the blessed William, abbot and father of the monastery of Hirsau, and his pupil Theoger, whom we know afterwards to have enlightened the abbey of St Georgen and the bishopric of Metz with his holiness and learning'.[42] Herluca thus consulted the great monastic reformer William of Hirsau, perhaps at a moment in his abbatiate (1069–91) when his pupil Theoger was still a monk of Hirsau, that is, before he became the first prior of the Hirsau priory of Reichenbach in 1085.[43] Paul of Bernried had already celebrated the achievements of William of Hirsau in the appendix of his *Life of Pope Gregory VII* that identified those disciples of Gregory VII who had loyally continued the pope's reforming measures: that same appendix in which Paul had first recorded some of the visions of Herluca.[44] William of Hirsau was revered by Gregorians as a pioneer of the late eleventh-century monastic reform movement in south-west Germany. That movement was founded and supported by secular princes, whose number included prominent opponents of King Henry IV, and it established a monastic reform independent of the traditional monasticism of the early eleventh century, imposed and promoted by the king-emperors.[45] The abbey of Hirsau indeed served as a refuge for adherents

41 Ibid., cap. 28–31, pp 554E–555A. See M. Maier, 'Ein schwäbisch-bayerischer Freundeskreis' (as n. 17), pp 319–20, 321, 324–5; R. Schnitzer, *Die Vita B. Herlucae*, pp 68, 71–2. 42 Paul, *Vita* cap. 11, p. 553D. 43 *Vita Theogeri abbatis S. Georgii et episcopi Mettensis* I.10, *MGH Scriptores* 10, 451. On the attribution of the *Vita* to Wolfger of Prüfening see H. Fichtenau, 'Wolfger von Prüfening', *Mitteilungen des Instituts für Österreichische Geschichtsforschung* 51 (1937), 348–9. See H. Jakobs, *Die Hirsauer. Ihre Ausbreitung und Rechtsstellung im Zeitalter des Investiturstreites* (Cologne, 1961), p. 37. Theoger was subsequently abbot of St Georgen (1088–1118) and bishop of Metz (1118–20). 44 Paul of Bernried, *Vita Gregorii VII* cap. 113, 118, pp 542, 543. 45 H. Jakobs, *Die Hirsauer*, pp 152–89; H. Jakobs, *Der Adel in der Klosterreform von St Blasien* (Cologne, 1968), pp 271–90; K. Schmid, 'Adel and Reform in Schwaben' in J. Fleckenstein (ed.), *Investiturstreit und Reichsverfassung* (Vorträge und Forschungen 17: Sigmaringen, 1973), pp 295–319; K. Schreiner, 'Hirsau und die Hirsauer Reform. Lebens- und Verfassungsformen einer Reformbewegung', *Germania Benedictina* 1: *Die Reformverbände und Kongregationen der Benediktiner im Deutschen Sprachraum* (St Ottilien, 1999), 89–124.

of the papal party and as a centre for the dissemination of Gregorian propaganda throughout the Investiture Contest.[46]

Paul's statement that the illustrious abbot of Hirsau personally gave spiritual advice to a woman of non-noble origin has a parallel in the biography of William composed by Haimo, prior of Hirsau soon after the abbot's death. Two chapters describe William's influence outside his abbey. He

> so abounded in kindness and charity that among those desiring to deliver themselves up completely to the divine service he despised none because of their poverty and he rejected none because of their ignorance. He inspired the noble and the non-noble, the rich and the poor, men and women, with contempt for the world and by his word and example he incited individuals to love the heavenly life ... As rumour spread abroad the account of his praiseworthy deeds, the faithful flocked to him from all sides, as if to *the good aroma of Christ* (II Corinthians 2:15), some of them undoubtedly wishing to make use of his most salutary advice, others commending themselves to his prayers, while very many who had cast off the burden of this world submitted to him as their master ... He instructed laymen in conversion and subjection; he educated virgins, widows and women in cleanliness and chastity.[47]

To illustrate how 'forgetful of his dignity' William could be, his biographer recounted how, on a visit to a newly founded priory, the abbot stopped at a hut in the forest, where he found 'an extremely poor woman' and her husband, a peasant barely able to earn the means of subsistence. When he discovered that they knew nothing of the catholic faith, William, sitting next to them by their fireside, 'briefly expounded the faith to them, as far as they could comprehend'.[48]

Paul of Bernried himself in his *Life of Gregory VII* identified the 'four ways of life' devised by William of Hirsau and the other leading reformers in southern Germany for those individuals who experienced a *conversio*. Among the men he distinguished carefully between the religious life of 'the tonsured servants of Christ' and 'that of the bearded brethren faithfully serving them'.[49] The distinction here was between the monks living according to the *Rule* of Benedict and the 'lay brethren', the *conversi*, bearded laymen who did not take the monastic profession. Haimo of Hirsau wrote of William's monastic innovation: 'he ordained ... that the monks should use the faithful service

---

46 H. Jakobs, *Die Hirsauer*, pp 190–223. **47** Haimo, *Vita Willihelmi abbatis Hirsaugiensis* cap. 6, *MGH SS* 12, 213; cf. cap. 21, p. 218: 'Individual members of the faithful of Christ took refuge with him, as if to their mother's breast, and through him they made great progress towards God.' **48** Ibid., cap. 17, p. 217. **49** Paul, *Vita Gregorii VII* cap. 118, p. 543.

of lay *conversi* in carrying out external functions and that these laymen should imitate the monastic discipline in correcting their morals, as far as they were able outside the cloister'.[50] Among the women who experienced a *conversio*, Paul distinguished between the religious life 'of virgins living the enclosed life of perpetual devotion and that of virgins governing their life according to the *Rule* and guarding their comings and goings'.[51] Here the distinction was between the life of nuns following the Benedictine Rule in their convent and that of the *inclusa*, the religious recluse.[52] The *Life* of Theoger, the pupil of William of Hirsau, echoes the language of William's biographer in describing the impact of the Swabian monastic reform on the local inhabitants. Theoger's 'care and great zeal was to incite the faithful by his word and example to contempt for the world' and 'from persons of both sexes and all ages he prepared a perfect people for the Lord'.[53] In his short biographical study of Theoger Mabillon referred specifically to Theoger's influence on Herluca, whom 'he moulded to the spiritual life by his salutary counsels', placing the encounter in Reichenbach during Theoger's years as prior (1085–8).[54]

The role of the Swabian monastic reformers in giving spiritual advice to the laity is also emphasized in another biographical work, the *Vita* of Paulina, the noble founder of the monastery of Paulinzella, composed by Sigeboto, monk of Paulinzella in the mid-twelfth century.[55] Paulina, a contemporary of Herluca, was a *nobilis femina*, 'born of the most illustrious lineage' in Thuringia, the daughter of Moricho, a prominent royal official, and niece of Bishop Werner of Merseburg, a distinguished supporter of the papal party in the conflict with Emperor Henry IV.[56] The *Vita* describes the stages of Paulina's gradual conversion, beginning with pilgrimages undertaken with her second husband, Udalric, to Rome and Compostella.[57] On the death of Udalric

50 Haimo, *Vita Willihelmi* cap. 23, p. 219. See H. Jakobs, *Die Hirsauer*, pp 23–6.   **51** Paul, *Vita Gregorii VII* cap. 118, p. 543.   **52** Cf. H. Grundmann, *Ausgewählte Aufsätze* 1: *ReligiöseBewegungen* (Schriften der MGH 25/1: Stuttgart, 1976), pp 114–15.   **53** *Vita Theogeri* I.29, p. 463. Cf. I.25–7, pp 459–63, on Theoger's provision for nuns. See H. Jakobs, *Die Hirsauer*, pp 197–8; M. Parisse, 'Die Frauenstifte und Frauenklöster in Sachsen vom 10. bis zur Mitte des 12. Jahrhunderts' in S. Weinfurt and F.M. Siefarth (ed.), *Die Salier und das Reich* 2 (Sigmaringen, 1991), pp 485–6.   **54** J. Mabillon, *Annales ordinis sancti Benedicti occidentalium monachorum patriarchae* 5 (Paris, 1713), 277. No evidence is offered for placing the encounter in Reichenbach. Mabillon's account also causes confusion by referring to the saint as 'Herluca, virgin of Bernried', since Herluca sought refuge in Bernried only in 1121 (after Theoger's death): see below p. 186.   **55** Date and authorship of the *Vita Paulinae*: L. Fenske, *Adelsopposition und kirchliche Reformbewegung im östlichen Sachsen* (Veröffentlichungen des Max-Planck-Instituts für Geschichte 47: Göttingen, 1977), p. 273. The most recent study is C. Badstübner-Kizik, *Die Gründungs- und Frühgeschichte des Klosters Paulinzella und die Lebensbeschreibung der Stifterin Paulina* (Hochschulschriften 41: Münster, 1993).   **56** Sigeboto, *Vita Paulinae* cap. 1, *MGH SS* 30/2, 911: Moricho was 'brought up in the court of Emperor Henry IV' and became 'steward of the royal table' (*regalis mensae dapifer*). See L. Fenske, *Adelsopposition und kirchliche Reformbewegung*, pp 280–2.   **57** Sigeboto, *Vita Paulinae* cap. 8, p. 914.

(*c*.1100) Paulina undertook a second journey to Rome, where 'she received advice from the pope [Paschal II] about the condition of her past, present and future life'. Returning to Germany, 'she came with a papal letter to the monastery of St Blasien in the Black Forest, which is in Swabia, but she found the abbot dead and could not fulfil the intention which she had in mind'.[58] The biographer's account suggests that Paschal II had provided Paulina with a letter of recommendation to Abbot Udo of St Blasien and a request for help with her plans for a spiritual life.[59] Those plans at first took the form of establishing a hermitage in Langwizza in the Thuringian Forest, where Paulina's son Werner joined her after undergoing a *conversio* and where Swabian monks also settled.[60] By *c*.1106 Paulina was making her third journey to Rome to obtain papal approval for the foundation on this site of a monastery. This was eventually to become the double monastery of Paulinzella with separate establishments for monks and nuns (Paulina's son Werner and her daughters Engelsint and Bertrad forming part of the original member-ship).[61] Paulina adopted for her foundation the monastic customs of Hirsau, where her father Moricho had 'thankfully accepted the yoke of the Lord' in old age.[62] She and her son obtained as the first abbot of Paulinzella a monk of Hirsau, Gerung, the pupil of Abbot William.[63] *The Life of Paulina* celebrates the monastic reform movement in language more extravagant than that of Paul of Bernried. 'Swabia illuminated the whole world, always adding new disciplines to the disciplines of the earlier Fathers'; 'the monastery of Hirsau shone forth in those days like the morning star and harbinger of the coming day'.[64]

William of Hirsau's advice to Herluca should be seen particularly in the light of the conversion experience in Swabia towards the end of the eleventh century, as described in the eyewitness account of Bernold of Constance. The chronicle of Bernold, successively monk of St Blasien and (from 1091) of Schaffhausen, championed the reformed monasteries of Swabia[65] and the achievements of William of Hirsau, 'most ardent in the cause of St Peter and most zealous in monastic piety, … the father of many monasteries'.[66] In his annal for 1091 Bernold recorded that laymen

renounced the world and most faithfully took themselves and their property into congregations both of clergy and of monks living accord-

---

58 Ibid., cap. 14, 15, p. 917.   **59** L. Fenske, *Adelsopposition und kirchliche Reformbewegung*, p. 274 and n. 317. J. Dieterich, 'Über Paulinzeller Urkunden und Sigebotos Vita Paulinae', *Neues Archiv* 18 (1893), 473, 475–6 suggested that Abbot Udo of St Blasien died on 24 September 1105; but see H. Jakobs, *Der Adel in der Klosterreform von St Blasien*, pp 10, 77.   **60** Sigeboto, *Vita Paulinae* cap. 23–5, pp 920–2.   **61** Ibid., cap. 27, p. 922; cap. 10, p. 915; cap. 47, p. 933. See L. Fenske, *Adelsopposition und kirchliche Reformbewegung*, pp 275–9.   **62** Sigeboto, *Vita Paulinae* cap. 16, p. 918.   **63** Ibid., cap. 30–1, pp 924–5.   **64** Ibid., cap. 29, p. 923.   **65** Bernold of Constance, *Chronicon* 1083, pp 436–7: St Blasien, Hirsau and Schaffhausen, 'excellently founded on the basis of the disciplines of the *Rule*, were held in high esteem in the kingdom of the Germans'.   **66** Ibid., 1091, p. 484.

ing to the *Rule* in order to be worthy to live the common life there in obedience to them and serving them … An innumerable multitude not only of men but also of women entered a way of life of this kind at this time so that they might live in common under the obedience of clergy or monks and might most faithfully perform the duty of daily service like maidservants. Also in the villages innumerable peasants' daughters strove to renounce marriage and the world and to live under the obedience of some priest. But even the married people never ceased to live devoutly and to obey the religious with the greatest devotion. Such zeal blossomed with particular decorum, however, everywhere in Swabia. In that province many villages dedicated themselves wholly to religion and ceaselessly strove to surpass each other in the holiness of their morals.[67]

This development is also recorded in the sources for the reform of the monastery of Ottobeuren through the intervention of Theoger, now abbot of St Georgen in 1102, when the saintly Rupert became abbot of Ottobeuren. 'He associated with the monks laymen fearing God and included honourable and noble women in the service of God and through their donations the monastery's possessions were very much enlarged.'[68]

The secondary literature has broadly accepted the view of Albert Hauck, that this conversion of 'an innumerable multitude not only of men but also of women' was the work of wandering preachers from the abbey of Hirsau.[69] The evidence for the existence of Hirsau monks as wandering preachers derives entirely from hostile polemics,[70] most importantly the satirical poem of the monks of Lorsch against the Hirsauer, prompted by the attempt to impose the Hirsau observance on Lorsch in 1105–7 by Gebhard, abbot of Lorsch and former abbot of Hirsau. One passage in the poem specifically

---

67 Ibid., 1091, p. 491. See H. Grundmann, *Religiöse Bewegungen im Mittelalter*, 2nd ed. (Hildesheim, 1961), pp 505, 509–10; H. Jakobs, *Die Hirsauer*, pp 23–5.   **68** *Chronicon Ottenburanum*, *MGH SS* 23, 617. (The chronicle is at this point an early thirteenth-century compilation.) Cf. *Vita Theogeri* I.28, p. 462. See H. Feierabend, *Die politische Stellung der deutschen Reichsabteien während des Investiturstreites* (Historische Untersuchungen 3: Breslau, 1913), p. 30; H. Jakobs, *Die Hirsauer*, pp 58–9.   **69** A. Hauck, *Kirchengeschichte Deutschlands* 3, pp 872–6; H. Jakobs, *Die Hirsauer*, pp 25–6, 198–201; P.G. Jestice, *Wayward monks and the religious revolution of the eleventh century* (Cologne, 1997), pp 249–65.   **70** *Annals of Augsburg* 1075, *MGH SS* 3, 128: 'Wandering monks (*girovagi*) running to and fro under the pretext of religion sow the greatest discord everywhere.' (The term *girovagi* is an allusion to the *Rule* of Benedict cap. 1.) Cf. the polemic of the anonymous Hersfeld monk (*c.*1090), *Liber de unitate ecclesiae conservanda* II.38, 39, *MGH Libelli de lite* 2, 266, 267 against 'the monks of the *scola* of Hirsau', who 'not only through their writings but through all their labours defend those evil deeds'; 'who send out in all directions angels of their word, preaching that the Church of God and the righteousness of God and the holy priesthoods of God are only to be found among them and their followers'; who 'create and institute their heresies and schisms'. See H. Jakobs, *Die Hirsauer*, pp 198–200.

mentions Hirsau monks preaching to the laity and has an obvious relevance to the issue of *conversio*. The satirist wrote that monks of Hirsau 'run to and fro through the provinces as if they are teachers (*doctores*), cunningly deceiving the minds of simple people. They rashly presume to teach this schismatical idea: that neither a married man, even possessing a chaste spouse, nor a woman united to a lawful husband may ever attain salvation unless they first separate and, being parted, abandon all that they possess.'[71] The *Poem of the monks of Lorsch* cited this example – a breach of the divine commandment (Matthew 19:6; Mark 10:9) that those joined by God 'could not be separated by any man' – as proof of the 'novelties, dogmas, heresies' taught by the Hirsauer, 'mixing poison with the honey' of their preaching and destroying the norms of Christian domestic life. This was the Lorsch satirist's version of the conversion experience described by Bernold of Constance: laymen and women renouncing the world and taking 'themselves and their property into congregations', 'so that they might live in common', that is, without personal property, 'under the obedience of clergy or monks'. Similarly the Lorsch monks denounced monks of the Hirsau observance as 'plunderers and ravagers' when, like Abbot Rupert of Ottobeuren, they recruited laymen and women 'in the service of God and through their donations the monastery's possessions were very much enlarged'.[72]

The element of truth contained in the satirist's taunt about the hostility of the Hirsau preachers towards marriage was the emphasis on celibacy and the exaltation of the state of virginity by the reformers. The crucial evidence that supports the claims of the Lorsch poet is found in the passage of the *Vita* of Herluca, the pupil of William of Hirsau, describing Herluca's influence on her own *alumni*, the married couple Rutpert and Hadewig. 'Rutpert, the husband of Hadewig, [was] at length converted by [Herluca's] frequent exhortations to the celibate life, together with his wife.'[73] Subsequently their daughter Judith 'was converted to the resolution to preserve her virginity' after 'Herluca had for a long time coaxed her to keep herself unstained from this world and to marry Christ'.[74] Herluca similarly converted her own niece Luikardis to a life of perpetual virginity.[75] Herluca in her own conversion resembled those contemporaries described by Bernold of Constance in his annal of 1091, the 'innumerable peasants' daughters' who 'strove to renounce marriage and the world'.[76] Thereafter the thought-world of Herluca was dom-

71 *Carmen Laureshamensium monachorum* in: *Chronicon Laureshamense, MGH SS* 21, 431. See A. Hauck, *Kirchengeschichte Deutschlands* 3, 872; H. Jakobs, *Die Hirsauer*, pp 200, 213–14; P.G. Jestice, *Wayward monks*, pp 258, 261.   72 The *Carmen* is accompanied in the Lorsch chronicle by an appeal of the monks of Lorsch (1111) addressed to Pope Paschal II and Emperor Henry V against 'the plunderers and ravagers of Hirsau' (p. 433).   73 Paul, *Vita Herlucae* cap. 27, p. 554E. See above p. 177.   74 Ibid., cap. 28, p. 554EF.   75 Ibid., cap. 30, p. 555A. See above p. 178.   76 Bernold, *Chronicon* 1091, p. 491. See above p. 182.

inated by the ideal of virginity, as is clear from the evidence of the visions recorded in the *Vita*. For example, Herluca saw a vision of her first secular patron, Countess Adelaide in heaven, together with her sisters, Wielica and Hiltiburgis, who were 'virgins pledged to Christ'. In the vision Adelaide inhabited 'a beautiful region' of heaven but that region lacked the bright splendour of the habitation of her sisters, 'for a little cloud seemed to darken her dwelling-place, to mark out the worldly way of life (*conversatio*) that she had led'.[77]

The spiritual advice given by Abbot William of Hirsau to Herluca is recorded briefly by Paul of Bernried in chapter 13 of the *Vita*, immediately following the account of Herluca's arrival in Epfach. 'The aforesaid Abbot William had given her the counsel that in whatever place she had the greater experience of divine sweetness, there she should establish the most enduring possible stability of life. Following such guides [as William and Theoger], therefore, she continued her residence in Epfach for more than 36 years.'[78] In using the phrase 'stability of life' (*conversandi stabilitas*) in his report of the counsel given to Herluca, Paul evoked the language of the monastic 'yoke of regular discipline', the *stabilitas loci* required by the Rule of Benedict,[79] demanding of lay 'converts' a similar 'stability'. William's advice has been interpreted as a rebuke to Herluca for having previously led an unstable, wandering life.[80] It is well known that during Herluca's lifetime wandering preachers in France attracted large numbers of laymen and women, who renounced their property and followed their wandering spiritual mentors. The preaching both of Robert of Arbrissel in the mid-1090s and of the young Norbert of Xanten two decades later drew to them a considerable following of 'the poor of Christ'.[81] There were certainly wandering preachers in southern Germany in Herluca's lifetime – as we have seen, they were monks of Hirsau – but there is no evidence that they were followed by wandering laymen and women.[82] The only evidence for supposing that Herluca had adopted such a way of life is the *Vita*'s account of the circumstances of her arrival in Epfach: 'accompanying her noble pupils Rutpert and Hadewig, she arrived by chance on the bank of the River Lech' and angered her companions by her refusal to continue travelling with them. Since, however, Herluca's companions at once returned 'to their own land', it is more likely that the three travelling companions were not wanderers but were engaged on a specific journey, perhaps indeed a pilgrimage, when they came 'by chance' to Epfach.[83] William of Hirsau's advice to Herluca – that she should establish

---

77 Paul, *Vita* cap. 10, p. 553CD. See above p. 176.   78 Paul, *Vita* cap. 13, p. 553E.   79 *Benedicti Regula* IV.78, LVIII.17, *Corpus Scriptorum Ecclesiasticorum Latinorum* 75, 35, 136. 80 K. Schmid, 'Bischof Wikterp in Epfach. Eine Studie über Bischof und Bischofssitz im 8. Jahrhundert' in J. Werner (ed.), *Studien zu Abodiacum-Epfach* (Munich, 1964), pp 100–1 and n. 12.   81 H. Grundmann, *Religiöse Bewegungen*, pp 16–17.   82 R. Schnitzer, *Die Vita B. Herlucae* p. 65.   83 Paul, *Vita* cap. 12, p. 553D. See above p. 177.

a permanent residence 'in whatever place she had the greater experience of divine sweetness' – could be interpreted precisely as a recommendation to undertake a pilgrimage to find that place in which she found the divine grace most accessible to her.[84]

Paul of Bernried indeed recorded William's advice in order to explain Herluca's instant decision to settle in Epfach. 'She immediately tasted so great a sweetness in the patronages of the most blessed deacon Laurence, whose church is there, and of the holy Wikterp, the former bishop of Augsburg, whose body rests in the same place, located under the altar in the oratory of the holy Mother of God, Mary', that she could not be induced to leave Epfach.[85] Herluca had thus fulfilled the mission imposed on her by William of Hirsau. During the course of her pilgrimage it was only here in Epfach that Herluca experienced the *divina dulcedo* of which William had spoken. The principal emphasis in the *Vita* is on the sacred landscape of Epfach and the protection offered by its patron saints, Laurence and especially Wikterp of Augsburg. When Herluca faced the anger of Rutpert and Hadewig at her refusal to leave Epfach, 'the spiritual comforter Wikterp appeared and soothed her, saying, "Remain here with me, daughter, and I shall remove whatever might offend you".'[86] Four further chapters of the *Vita* record visions of Wikterp in which the saint gave advice and warnings to Herluca and a further chapter records a miracle wrought by Wikterp and witnessed by Herluca.[87] In chapter 47 Paul wrote: 'Now our pen is to be directed particularly to the blessed Wikterp so that I can perhaps compensate to some extent for the neglect of our forefathers.' For the author could find no record of this saint and had known nothing of his existence until Herluca had described her visions of Wikterp, except that there had been an attempted translation of the saint's body, 'which old men, who had seen it, were accustomed to report to Herluca herself'. Bishop Henry II of Augsburg (1047–63) had attempted to translate the saint to Augsburg but 'it was suddenly fixed by so great a weight that it could not be moved by the great multitude that was present'.[88] The remainder of the *Vita Herlucae* is concerned with miracles of Wikterp and visions in which he appeared: Herluca becomes merely an onlooker in her own *Vita*.[89]

Paul indeed ceased to record Herluca's experiences once she left the sacred landscape of Epfach and the patronage of Wikterp. Paul's account of her departure is singularly terse. He reported that when (in 1121) he himself

---

84 So R. Schnitzer, *Die Vita B. Herlucae* p. 65.   85 Paul, *Vita* cap. 12, p. 553D.   86 Ibid., p. 553E.   87 Ibid., cap. 22, 43, 46, 52, 53, pp 554D, 556C, 556D, 557CD (visions); cap. 52, p. 557B (miracle). Cf. cap. 41, p. 556B (unspecified visions); cap. 54, p. 557D (vision seen by 'a certain virgin').   88 Ibid., cap. 47–9, pp 556F–557A. On the date of the attempted translation see R. Schnitzer, *Die Vita B. Herlucae*, p. 81 and n. 151.   89 She is mentioned only in cap. 47 and 53, pp 556F, 557CD. Hence the editors of the *Acta Sanctorum* gave this section of the *Vita* the title *Vita et translatio S. Wicterpi* (p. 556E).

and his pupil Gebhard were 'expelled from Regensburg by the persecution of Henry V and Herluca [was] cast out from Epfach by the rage of the wicked peasants', they 'met in Bernried'.[90] There the friends seem to have taken refuge in the new house of regular canons. The *Vita* refers only to a single incident in Herluca's life in Bernried. 'A few years ago', when one day she was walking alone to church, she was thrown into a mill-race by the Devil.[91] The absence of any further information about Herluca's life in Bernried and above all about her death and burial led both the editors of Paul's work and more recent scholarship to conclude that the *Vita* was an 'incomplete work'.[92] The *Vita* was, however, addressed to 'the very small congregation of the monastery of Bernried' in the third year after Herluca's death, that is, to an audience that had been close witnesses of Herluca's way of life during her sojourn in Bernried. Paul may well have decided, therefore, that it was super-fluous for him to include in the *Vita* an account of what was already well known to the congregation.[93]

Herluca seems to have chosen Bernried as her new residence in 1121 not because her friend Paul of Bernried had also taken refuge there. The *Vita* makes only a passing reference, in the middle of an account of a vision, to Paul and Herluca's simultaneous presence in Bernried. Encountering her there, Paul recalled that when he had consulted her 14 years before in Epfach, she had 'strongly dissuaded' him from leaving hostile Regensburg but 'had given no explanation' of her advice. Now in Bernried she explained that her advice to him in 1107 had been prompted by a vision of St Laurence, who had said, 'I do not yet wish you to advise departure' and on a second occasion, 'He ought to suffer more.'[94] There was, therefore, no concerted plan by the two friends to take refuge in Bernried. They met there by chance (Paul's term is *convenit*) after Paul had eventually been compelled to disobey her exhortation not to leave Regensburg. It has been suggested that what brought Herluca to Bernried was the appointment of Sigeboto as the first provost of the congregation of Bernried.[95] Sigeboto is characteristically intro-duced in the *Vita* only in passing, during an account of Herluca's prophetic

---

90 Paul, *Vita* cap. 44, p. 556C. J. May, 'Leben Pauls von Bernried' (as n. 12) p. 340 sug-gested that the peasants had been incensed against Herluca by the supporters of the mar-ried priests against whom she had spoken. There is, however, no evidence in the *Vita* for this conjecture. See R. Schnitzer, *Die Vita B. Herlucae* p. 74. For Herluca and unchaste priests see below p. 193.   91 Ibid., cap. 6, p. 553B. The anecdote is appended to that of the Devil disturbing the prayers of Countess Adelaide some forty years before: 'A similar thing happened to her in Bernried a few years ago.'   92 *Acta Sanctorum Aprilis 2*, 557 note f (repeating the opinion of Jakob Gretser in 1610); J. May, 'Leben Pauls von Bernried' (as n. 12), p. 335; W. Wattenbach, R. Holtzmann & F.-J. Schmale, *Deutschlands Geschichtsquellen*, p. 248.   93 J. Greving, *Pauls von Bernried Vita Gregorii VII. papae* (Münster, 1893) p. 1 n.3; M. Maier, 'Ein schwäbisch-bayerischer Freundeskreis' (as n. 17), p. 330.   94 Paul, *Vita* cap. 43–5, p. 556CD.   95 R. Schnitzer, *Die Vita B. Herlucae* pp. 77, 111.

powers. The visionary accurately predicted Paul's arrival on a visit to her in Epfach. This occurred 'once when I lived for more than a year with the venerable Sigeboto, then a priest in Epfach but subsequently provost in Bernried'. The *Vita* adds: 'For my host then lived on the Bavarian bank of the river [Lech] because there he suffered less insolence from attackers.'[96] It was with Sigeboto that Paul stayed when seeking respite from the hostility of the clergy in Regensburg and when visiting his friend Herluca.

Sigeboto was 'a priest in Epfach' but not the parish priest: that office was held during Herluca's residence in Epfach by Richard (who was revealed to Herluca in a vision to be unchaste).[97] Scholars have conjectured that Sigeboto had been driven from his own church by opponents of reform and lived a quasi-eremitical life in exile in Epfach:[98] hence perhaps Paul's reference to his host's having taken up residence in Epfach where 'he suffered less insolence from attackers'. Peter Classen (1960) drew attention to a passage in a small collection of visions of Herluca, compiled by her younger contemporary, the theologian Gerhoch of Reichersberg. In one of these visions (not included in Paul's *Vita*) Herluca and her companion, an unnamed priest, were rebuked for receiving as a member of their circle (*socius chori*) 'a certain wandering scholar' (*gyrovagus scholaris*) whose reputation was unknown to them. Classen identified Herluca's priest companion as Sigeboto.[99] Such an association seems likely, given that as soon as Sigeboto assumed the office of provost of Bernried, Herluca placed herself for the rest of her life under the protection of the congregation of Bernried. The life-long relationship of Herluca and Sigeboto is indeed reminiscent of the phenomenon recorded by the chronicler Bernold of Constance in 1091: 'in the villages innumerable peasants' daughters strove to renounce marriage and the world and to live under the obedience of some priest.'[100]

Paul of Bernried's occasional allusions to the life of Herluca and her circle in Epfach suggest a round of humble domestic and charitable work, as in his account of a vision that begins when 'the blessed Herluca was sitting one day

---

96 Paul, *Vita* cap. 40, p. 556A. Cf. Paul, *Vita Gregorii VII* cap. 115, p. 542: 'that neighbourhood, that is, the frontier of the lands of the Bavarians and the Swabians that are separated by the River Lech'. **97** Paul, *Vita* cap. 22, p. 554D: see below p. 193. See K. Schmid, 'Bischof Wikterp in Epfach (as n. 80) pp 101–2. **98** P. Classen, *Gerhoch von Reichersberg*, p. 25; R. Schnitzer, *Die Vita B. Herlucae*, pp 28, 120. It was certainly not unusual in contemporary France for individuals to move from the eremitical life to a congregation of regular canons like that of Bernried: see C. Dereine, 'Vie commune, règle de St Augustin et chanoines réguliers au XIe siècle', *Revue d'histoire ecclésiastique* 41 (1946), 403. **99** Gerhoch of Reichersberg, *Expositio super canonem missae* (*Opus 5*), *Gerhohi praepositi Reichersbergensis Opera inedita* 1, ed. D. Van den Eynde and P. Rijmersdael (Spicilegium Pontificii Athenaei Antoniani 8: Rome, 1955), 43–4. See P. Classen, *Gerhoch von Reichersberg*, p. 25 n. 31. D. Van den Eynde, 'Un nouveau complément à la Vita beatae Herlucae', *Analecta Bollandiana* 71 (1953), 323–5 had identified the *presbyter* as Paul of Bernried. **100** Bernold, *Chronicon* 1091, p. 491. See above p. 182.

as usual among her companions, virgins and widows, and they were busily occupied with manual work, according to their custom'.[2] This circle included Herluca's 'noble pupil' Hadewig, mother of Judith (whom Herluca converted to a life of virginity),[102] together with a woman to whom the *Vita* pays particular attention. This was 'a native of the place named Douda, striving for a most excellent piety and chastity, since she was the niece and disciple of Sigeboto, a hermit in Rottenbuch'.[103] Douda's uncle, the hermit living near the congregation of regular canons of Rottenbuch (and not to be confused with Sigeboto of Epfach and Bernried) wished her to remain a virgin but knew that her family would never tolerate such a decision. He therefore advised her that on first becoming pregnant, she should observe 'seven years of celibacy'. This Douda did 'with the consent of her husband'. At the end of these seven years she became pregnant with a son, after which 'she never again returned, so it is believed, to her husband's bed'.[104] This intervention of Sigeboto of Rottenbuch in the married life of Douda of Epfach is reminiscent of Herluca's role in 'converting' her 'noble pupils' Rutpert and Hadewig 'to the celibate life' – and reminiscent also of the Lorsch satirist, who attributed to the preaching monks of Hirsau the doctrine that a married couple can never 'attain salvation unless they first separate'.[105] Douda's daughter, to whom Paul gave the Latin-Greek name Charopolis, achieved the ambition denied to her mother of becoming 'a virgin devoted to Christ'. Paul recorded that Charopolis was still alive at the time of the composition of the *Vita* and living in Bernried: she 'now walks tearfully around the grave of her spiritual mother Herluca by day and night'.[106] Charopolis had thus accompanied or followed Herluca from Epfach to Bernried and now *c.*1130 continued her way of life under the protection of the congregation.

Douda, who was instructed in the spiritual life by Sigeboto, 'a hermit in Rottenbuch', was also visited on at least one occasion by 'the brother Adalbert of Rottenbuch'.[107] The latter is not specifically identified as a hermit associated with the foundation. He was perhaps, therefore, a regular canon of the congregation, founded *c.*1070 by the staunch Gregorian and 'excellent renewer of the canonical life' Bishop Altman of Passau in Rottenbuch (in the diocese

---

101 Paul, *Vita Gregorii VII* cap. 115, pp 542–3.   102 Paul, *Vita Herlucae* cap. 24, p. 554D, repeating the anecdote in *Vita Gregorii VII* cap. 115, states that Herluca saw the vision 'in the presence of the lady Hadewig'.   103 Paul, *Vita* cap. 14, p. 554A. This Douda of Epfach is to be distinguished from a second Douda, 'a most pious and most religious widow ... whose son was Udalric *de Corninga*, a man of a notable birth, courage and stature', who appears only in *Vita* cap. 29, pp 554F–555A. She provided Judith with the sacred veil when Hadewig was reluctant to do so. On the identity of Udalric *de Corninga* (Hurningen or Horningen?) see M. Maier, 'Ein schwäbisch-bayerischer Freundeskreis' (as n. 17), p. 324; R. Schnitzer, *Die Vita B. Herlucae*, pp 71–2.   104 Paul, *Vita* cap. 14, p. 554A.   105 See above p. 183.   106 Paul, *Vita* cap. 14, p. 554B. R. Schnitzer, *Die Vita B. Herlucae*, p. 145 n. 80 suggested that the Old High German name rendered by Paul *Charopolis* was perhaps *Liafburg* or *Liasburg*.   107 Paul, *Vita* cap.18, p. 554B.

of Freising).[108] Like Hirsau and the other monasteries of the south German reform movement, Rottenbuch served as a refuge for members of the Gregorian party exiled from their own churches. Thus Gerhoch of Reichersberg fled to Rottenbuch (*c*.1120) from Augsburg after the excommunication of Bishop Herman by the pro-papal party in Germany.[109] It was perhaps here in Rottenbuch that Gerhoch obtained the account of Herluca's visions that he later included in his *Expositio super canonem missae* (composed between 1135 and 1140), using them to elucidate his discussion of the Eucharist.[110]

A notable refugee in Rottenbuch was Bishop Udalric of Passau, commended for his 'many struggles in defence of Gregorian doctrine' by Paul of Bernried, whom he had ordained to the priesthood.[111] Udalric 'was a guest in Rottenbuch, avoiding the Henrician persecution', that is, the hostility of Emperor Henry IV, probably within the period 1103–5. It was at this time that Herluca's pupil Judith, daughter of Hadewig, 'was fortified with the sacred veil by Bishop Udalric of Passau', consecrating her to a life of virginity.[112] That Udalric was personally acquainted with Herluca herself has been confidently stated[113] and is likely enough, the acquaintance being made either during this stay in Rottenbuch or during his years as provost of the cathedral chapter of Augsburg before his election as bishop of Passau in 1092.[114] There is, however, no direct evidence in the *Vita Herlucae* of a meeting between Udalric and Herluca.

Confusion has been caused by chapters 122 and 123 of Paul's *Life of Gregory VII*, where, in the appendix devoted to the disciples obedient to the pope's reforming measures, there is an account of Bishop Udalric's 'special pupil, a virgin dedicated to God', who 'saw heavenly visions and received insights that did much to encourage Gregorian obedience'. 'Bishop Udalric of blessed memory loved this virgin above all the other virgins because of her innate goodness but no less because of the honourable widowhood of her holy mother and the praiseworthy virginity of her aunts, all of whom educated her in Christ.'[115] This virgin visionary has been identified as Herluca[116] but Paul gave her no name, although in the preceding chapters 114–15 he had given

---

108 Paul, *Vita Gregorii VII* cap. 118, p. 543. See J. Mois, *Das Stift Rottenbuch*, pp 28, 34, 37.   109 A. Hauck, *Kirchengeschichte Deutschlands* 3, 911; P. Classen, *Gerhoch von Reichersberg*, pp 19–24.   110 Gerhoch of Reichersberg, *Expositio super canonem missae* (as above n. 99) pp 43–4. Gerhoch cited the vision in Paul, *Vita* cap. 37, pp 555F–556A and added two further visions not found in the *Vita*. See also R. Schnitzer, *Die Vita B. Herlucae*, pp 105–6.   111 Paul, *Vita Gregorii VII* cap. 122, p. 544: Udalric was 'the ordainer of this humble author', who when he died at the age of 105 (in 1121) left behind 'no one like himself among all the prelates of Germany'.   112 Paul, *Vita Herlucae* cap. 30, p. 555A. On the date see J. Mois, *Das Stift Rottenbuch*, p. 111.   113 P. Classen, *Gerhoch von Reichersberg*, p. 25; R. Schnitzer, *Die Vita B. Herlucae*, p. 69; W. Wattenbach, R. Holtzmann & F.-J. Schmale, *Deutschlands Geschichtsquellen*, p. 247.   114 Bernold of Constance, *Chronicon* 1092, p. 496.   115 Paul, *Vita Gregorii VII* cap. 122–3, p. 545.   116 By Paul's first editior, J. Gretser, *Opera omnia* 6 (Regensburg, 1735), 162H (marginal note). Cf. M. Maier, 'Ein schwäbisch-bayerischer Freundeskreis' (as n. 17), p. 314. The

detailed accounts of visions that he specifically ascribed to 'the virgin Herluca of happy memory'.[117] Paul described the virgin of chapters 122–3 as the 'special pupil' of Bishop Udalric of Passau, while, as we have seen, in the *Vita Herlucae* he identified Herluca's 'most excellent advisers' as Abbot William of Hirsau and his pupil Theoger. The virgin of chapters 122–3 was educated by a holy mother (named here as Helisea) and by virgin aunts, while the only kindred of Herluca to be mentioned in the *Vita* were a deceased father and a niece.[118] We are evidently confronted in the appendix of Paul's *Life of Gregory VII* with two different virgin visionaries, the second being anonymous.[119] What is clear from Paul's account is that Udalric of Passau, like William of Hirsau, 'educated virgins, widows and women in cleanliness and chastity'[120] and was equally active in persuading lay women 'to renounce marriage and the world'.[121]

Herluca ended her life under the protection of the house of regular canons in Bernried; during her years in Epfach she and her circle had links with the house in Rottenbuch. A connection with a third congregation of regular canons is found in the *Vita Herlucae*, namely that of Beuerberg (in the diocese of Freising). The *Vita* indeed presents significant evidence about the origins of Beuerberg in the context of a vision of Herluca (the first of the many occasions that St Laurence appeared to her when she received communion). The occasion was the burial of Gepa, 'the sister of the hermit Conrad', in *Berga* near Eurasburg.[122] On her journey from Epfach to *Berga* Herluca met her friend Paul of Bernried and his pupil Gebhard, who were also attending the funeral. In *Berga* the companions met Henry, described here as 'provost of Beuerberg' (although that congregation was not founded until 1121, the year of Herluca's departure from Epfach). Henry was accompanied by 'the lady Bertha, the mother of Otto', whom Paul described as 'the defender of both houses', that is, the advocate both of the hermitage of *Berga* and the house of regular canons in Beuerberg. This Otto, son of Adalbert of Eurasburg, is identified as the founder of Beuerberg in Pope Calixtus II's privilege for the foundation.[123] The hermit Conrad, 'unwillingly absent' from his sister's burial, is described in the *Vita* as 'the originator of the house of Beuerberg'. That foundation, therefore, had originated as a settlement of hermits before it was converted into a com-

identification was rejected by the Bollandists, *Acta Sanctorum Maii* 6, 143F notes q, r. Cf. J. Greving, *Pauls von Bernried Vita Gregorii VII.*, p. 118; R. Schnitzer, *Die Vita B. Herlucae*, p. 117.   **117** Paul, *Vita Gregorii VII* cap. 114–15, pp 542–3.   **118** See above n. 24.   **119** M. Hansizius, *Germania Sacra* 1 (Augsburg, 1727), 296 identified this virgin visionary as Judith (daughter of Hadewig) on whom Udalric of Passau conferred the veil. One vision is indeed attributed to Judith in the *Vita Herlucae* cap. 28, p. 554F: a vision of heavenly voices singing *Alleluia*, which prompted her to accede to Herluca's exhortations to embrace a life of virginity.   **120** Haimo, *Vita Willihelmi* cap. 6, p. 213. See above p. 179.   **121** Bernold of Constance, *Chronicon* 1091, p. 491. See above p. 182.   **122** Paul, *Vita* cap. 36–7, pp 555F–556A. See R. Schnitzer, *Die Vita B. Herlucae*, p. 146 n. 100 on the place-name *Berga*.   **123** A. Brackmann (ed.), *Germania Pontificia* 1: *Provincia Salisburgensis* (Berlin, 1910), 381 (printed in *Monumenta Boica* 6, 403–4). See J. Mois, *Das Stift Rottenbuch*, p. 210.

munity of regular canons in 1121. Like Paulina's foundation of Paulinzella in
the Thuringian Forest, which developed from a hermitage into a monastery of
the Hirsau connection,[124] Beuerberg is a reminder of the fluidity of reforming
institutions in the early twelfth century.

The circle of Herluca also had contacts with a religious house in the
immediate neighbourhood of Epfach, the Benedictine monastery of
Wessobrunn (in the diocese of Augsburg). Because of the sparseness of the
documentation it is difficult to determine the affiliation of Wessobrunn and
its relations with the reformed monasteries of southern Germany.[125] The evidence of the Wessobrunn necrology, however, suggests many connections
with centres of reform.[126] The strongest evidence of a positive attitude
towards monastic reform is an incident of 1103, the year in which the leader
of the Gregorian party in Germany, Bishop Gebhard III of Constance was
expelled from his city by the imperialist anti-bishop Arnold. In consequence
the loyal Gregorian Abbot Theoderic of Petershausen, a monastery of the
Hirsau observance, fled with twelve of his monks to Wessobrunn, where he
was honourably received by Abbot Adalbero.[127] The *Vita Herlucae* refers to
the abbey on a single occasion, when recording that it was 'in the cemetery
of the monastery that is called Wessobrunn' that Herluca's pupil Judith was
buried.[128] A friendship that connected Herluca herself with Wessobrunn
seems to be recorded in Paul's *Life of Gregory VII* in an account of a vision
concerning an unchaste priest. The informant who reported the vision to Paul
was 'the monk Adelbero of blessed memory, beloved of God and men, who
himself suffered reproaches and threats from the enemies of our Gregory
[VII] because of his obedience to his decrees'. The vision concerned the priest
who served the 'church that is in the place called Rott' and Paul noted that
'that neighbourhood, that is, the frontier of the lands of the Bavarians and the
Swabians that are separated by the River Lech, was not far away from the
dwelling of both the venerable old man [Adelbero] and the blessed virgin
[Herluca], who deeply loved one another in Christ'.[129] As the only monastery

---

124 See above p. 181.   125 H. Jakobs, *Die Hirsauer* does not include a discussion of
Wessobrunn as a monastery of the Hirsau connection but see H. Jakobs, *Der Adel in der
Klosterreform von St. Blasien*, pp 112–13 (Wessobrunn 'during the Investiture Contest was
at least for a time close to the anti-imperial front of the monastic reformers'); J. Hemmerle
and I. Andrian-Werburg, *Das Bistum Augsburg 2: Die Benediktinerabtei Wessobrunn* (Germania
Sacra, new series 39: Berlin, 1991), 89 (contacts with Bernried and Rottenbuch); A.I. Beach,
Women as scribes: book production and monastic reform in twelfth-century Bavaria (Cambridge,
2004), pp 27, 69 (Wessobrunn and the Hirsau reform).   126 P. Lindner, *Profeßbuch der
Benediktiner-Abtei Wessobrunn* (Beiträge zu einem Monastico-benedictinum Germaniae 1:
Munich, 1909), pp 3–4.   127 Casus monasterii Petrishusensis III.32, *MGH Scriptores* 20,
657. See G. Meyer von Knonau, *Jahrbücher des Deutschen Reiches unter Heinrich IV. und
Heinrich V.* 5 (Leipzig, 1904), 181–2; H. Feierabend, *Die politische Stellung der deutschen
Reichs-abteien*, pp 89–90.   128 Paul, *Vita Herlucae* cap. 31, p. 555A.   129 Paul, *Vita
Gregorii VII* cap. 115, p. 542. The anecdote is repeated in *Vita Herlucae* cap. 24, p.
554DE, without the reference to Adelbero.

in the close neighbourhood of Epfach, Wessobrunn was the probable dwelling of Adelbero.[130] The monk Adelbero's communication to Paul suggests that Wessobrunn preserved a detailed tradition of Herluca's visions such as Gerhoch of Reichersberg found in Rottenbuch.

A direct connection between Herluca and Wessobrunn was made by the late fifteenth-century bibliographer Petrus Wagner, monk of SS Udalric and Afra (and later abbot of Thierhaupten), identifying a correspondence between Herluca and Diemut, the renowned anchoress of Wessobrunn. 'There still exist extremely pleasant letters in the monastery of *Beronica*, which is now commonly called Bernried, some sent to the holy virgin Herluca and others sent back by Herluca in reply.'[131] Diemut had lived as an *inclusa* in the monastery of Wessobrunn since *c.*1080 and was famous for her work as a scribe, producing a large number of biblical, patristic and liturgical manuscripts.[132] Petrus Wagner's evidence suggests a friendship between Diemut and Herluca in the period of the latter's residence in Epfach, which continued after her removal to Bernried in the form of this correspondence. The correspondence is no longer extant but scholars have accepted the accuracy of Wagner's evidence – despite Paul of Bernried's emphatic statement in the prologue of the *Vita* that Herluca was 'entirely unaware of literature'.[133] This phrase did not necessarily mean that Herluca was unable to read or write: it might mean only that she could not claim to be truly learned by early twelfth-century standards.[134] Certainly when Paul used the expression 'entirely unaware of literature' in his prologue, his purpose was to contrast Herluca with a distinguished prelate, 'trained in humane studies'.

Explaining in the prologue of the *Vita* why he saw fit to compose an account of the unlearned Herluca, Paul presented a surprising juxtaposition. He and his pupil Gebhard had come to the conclusion that they 'had never savoured God more sweetly from the mouth of a man than from the mouth of Archbishop Walter of Ravenna, and from the mouth of a woman than from the mouth of Herluca'.[135] Archbishop Walter of Ravenna, whom Paul

---

130 R. Schnitzer, *Die Vita B. Herlucae*, p. 70.   **131** Petrus Wagner, *Congestum monachorum illustrium aliarumque personarum sanctarum atque nobilium de Ordine s. Benedicti* (1493), quoted from Munich, Staatsbibliothek codex latinus 1211 by R. Bauerreiß, *Kirchengeschichte Bayerns* 3 (St Ottilien, 1951), 45 n. 79. Wagner included a catalogue of the codices written by Diemut and quoted some sentences from the *Vita Herlucae*. See H. Fuhrmann, 'Zur handschriftlichen Verbreitung' (as n. 29), p. 367 n. 2.   **132** R. Schnitzer, *Die Vita B. Herlucae* pp 48–50; A.I. Beach, *Women as scribes*, pp 32–64. See also K. Bodarwé, 'Verlorene Zeugnisse einer Frauenfreundschaft. Diemut von Wessobrunn und Herluca von Epfach' in G. Signori (ed.), *Meine in Gott geliebte Freundin. Freundschaftsdokumente aus klösterlichen und humanistischen Schreibstuben* (Bielefeld, 1995), pp 50–9.   **133** Paul, *Vita*, prologue, p. 552B: *prorsus litteraturam non cognoscente*.   **134** H. Grundmann, 'Litteratus-illitteratus: Der Wandel einer Bildungsnorm vom Altertum zum Mittelalter', *Archiv für Kulturgeschichte* 40 (1958), 52–65; R. Schnitzer, *Die Vita B. Herlucae*, p. 50 observes that 'neither in Epfach nor in Bernried would it have been difficult for [Herluca] to obtain the services of a clerk' to write her letters.   **135** Paul, *Vita*,

had known first as a clerk in Regensburg, was the illustrious prelate who had played a prominent part in the First Lateran Council (1123) and who, around the time of the composition of the *Vita Herlucae*, played a major diplomatic role in the papal schism of 1130, as the legate of Pope Innocent II in Germany.[136] It was not to be wondered at, wrote Paul, that a prelate, 'holy and adorned with miracles' and 'nevertheless trained in humane studies', should be such a source of edification to the faithful. When, however, spiritual instruction came from a woman, 'entirely unaware of literature, the miracle of divine inspiration was much more obvious'.

For the individuals converted or advised by Herluca, for the religious houses and the individual reformers who preserved her memory, Herluca's importance lay in 'the signs of holiness in her *conversatio*', such as were recorded by the hagiographer Paul in his *Vita*. Her renown consisted partly in her constant access to St Laurence and to Bishop Wikterp of Augsburg as her spiritual mentors,[137] partly in the visions affirming the transcendent importance of virginity and celibacy, which dictated her own *conversatio* and the spiritual advice that she gave to her *alumni*. In Paul's view, Herluca's visions demonstrated 'how much God's grace attended those who obeyed Gregorian teaching', notably Gregory VII's decrees against clerical marriage. Herluca was one of those Gregorian heroes 'who prevailed against unchaste priests and their adherents'.[138] A vision of the bleeding Christ, interpreted for her by Wikterp, revealed to Herluca that Richard, the parish priest of Epfach did 'not preserve the chastity appropriate to his high office'. 'Thereafter she opposed him by publicly avoiding him and by her example she encouraged the people to do the same'. Eventually Richard of Epfach 'was improved by the incessant chiding and reproaches of Herluca'.[139] The vision of Herluca reported to Paul by the monk Adelbero revealed the fate of a priest in the neighbourhood of Epfach, Adalbert of Rott, 'who through his enslavement to fleshly desires contaminated that church' and whose spirit was carried off to hell by evil spirits.[140] Such visions demonstrated how 'the wrath of God promoted the decrees of our Gregory ... in our land' of Germany.[141]

Herluca's visions seemed to the hagiographer of inestimable value in giving divine confirmation of the validity of Gregorian reforming decrees that remained controversial while Paul was writing his work. There is perhaps a topical and polemical dimension in Paul's account of the visions of Herluca. It is possible that between his stay in Bernried (in the early 1120s) and his

prologue, p. 552B. 136 F.-J. Schmale, 'Die Bemühungen Innozenz II. um seine Anerkennung in Deutschland', *Zeitschrift für Kirchengeschichte* 65 (1953/4), 240–70; I.S. Robinson, *The Papacy, 1073–1198*, p. 134. 137 Paul, *Vita* cap. 33, 41, 43, 45, pp 555B, 556BD (Laurence); cap. 12, 22, 41, 43, 46, 52, pp 553E, 554D, 556BD, 557B (Wikterp). 138 Paul, *Vita Gregorii VII* cap. 114, 118, pp 542, 543. 139 Ibid., cap. 114, p. 542; *Vita Herlucae* cap. 22–3, p. 554CD. 140 Paul, *Vita Gregorii VII* cap. 115, pp 542–3; *Vita Herlucae* cap. 24, p. 554DE. 141 Paul, *Vita Gregorii VII* cap. 113, p. 541.

final residence in St Mang from (1138 onwards) Paul returned to
Regensburg[142] and that it was here that both the *Life of Gregory VII* and the
Life of Herluca were written. For the situation in Regensburg was now radically different from that in 1121, the year of Paul's expulsion. The key event
had been the unexpected emergence of the reformer Cuno as bishop of
Regensburg in the disputed election of 1126. Cuno was formerly abbot of the
monastery of Siegburg (1105–26), which during his abbatiate had become an
important centre of reform. As bishop of Regensburg (1126–32) he proved
equally indefatigable in promoting both monastic and canonical reform in his
diocese.[143] In recruiting Gerhoch of Reichersberg to promote his reforming
initiatives, Cuno brought to Regensburg a scholar who, like Paul of Bernried,
was keenly aware of the Gregorian reform programme.[144]

Both as abbot of Siegburg and as bishop of Regensburg Cuno had actively
promoted scholarship. During his abbatiate he had encouraged and guided the
composition of the great theological works of Rupert of Deutz, who was for a
time a monk in Siegburg.[145] As bishop he encouraged Gerhoch of Reichersberg
to write his first theological treatise, having introduced him to the writings of
Rupert of Deutz.[146] Cuno probably also encouraged the work of Paul of
Bernried. It happened that in the autumn of 1130 – most likely the year in
which the *Life of Herluca* was composed – an accusation of heresy was made by
members of the clergy in Regensburg against Gerhoch of Reichersberg. His
offence was a declaration that the sacraments of 'evil priests' (those guilty of
simony and unchastity) were invalid. Gerhoch (who was later to use the visions
of Herluca in his *Expositio super canonem missae* as evidence to support his
eucharistic teachings) was accused of holding a view similar to that implied by
Herluca when she publicly avoided the priest Richard of Epfach 'and by her
example encouraged the people to do the same'. It was also a view implied in
the letters of Pope Gregory VII that Paul quoted in his *Life* of the pope.[147] The
judge who vindicated Gerhoch against his accusers was the papal legate,
Archbishop Walter of Ravenna,[148] the friend of Paul of Bernried, who in the
Vita Herlucae compared his beneficial influence to that of Herluca. Hence for
Paul, writing in 1130, there was an urgent topicality in Herluca's visions. For
her admirers those visions were a valuable reminder of pure Gregorian doctrine.

142 C. Märtl, 'Regensburg in den geistigen Auseinandersetzungen des Investiturstreits',
Deutsches Archiv 42 (1986), 158–60.   143 J. Semmler, *Die Klosterreform von Siegburg. Ihre
Ausbreitung und ihr Reformprogramm im 11. und 12. Jahrhundert* (Rheinisches Archiv 53:
Bonn, 1959), pp 46–8, 84–7, 96–102.   144 P. Classen, *Gerhoch von Reichersberg*, p. 55:
Gerhoch 'deliberately preserved the memory of Gregory [VII]'.   145 J. Semmler, *Die
Klosterreform von Siegburg*, pp 48, 372–83.   146 Gerhoch, *Opusculum de aedificio domus
Dei*, MGH *Libelli de lite*, 3, 137, 139. See P. Classen, *Gerhoch von Reichersberg*, p. 34.   147
Paul, *Vita Gregorii VII*, cap. 36, 37, 39, 40, pp 489–92, 493–5 = Gregory VII, *Epistolae
Vagantes* 8, 9, ed. H.E.J. Cowdrey (Oxford, 1972), pp 16–22; Gregory VII, *Registrum*,
II.45, II.11, MGH *Epistolae selectee*, 2, 182–5, 142–3.   148 P. Classen, *Gerhoch von
Reichersberg*, pp 48–51.

Eleanor of Aquitaine and the women of the
Second Crusade

CONOR KOSTICK

There is a very striking contrast between the sources of the First Crusade (1096–9) and those for the Second (1147–8). It is hard, although some narrative historians of an earlier era did so, to miss the references to women in all the sources for the First Crusade. In even the tersest accounts of the Crusade there can be found mention of women participants. So, for example, The Anglo-Saxon chronicler, writing in Peterborough, had only a few lines of comment about the Crusade, but he did think it noteworthy that countless people set out, with 'women and children'.[1] The near contemporary Annals of Augsburg stated that along with warriors, bishops, abbots, monks, clerics and men of diverse professions, 'serfs and women' joined the movement.[2] When the longer accounts of the expedition are examined it becomes clear that women participated in the First Crusade in their thousands and they even led popular contingents of departing crusaders.[3]

The sources for the events of 1147–8, however, very rarely mention women. The presence of women on the Second Crusade is only evident from a small number of references and even then in more fragmentary fashion than is the case with regard to the material concerning the First Crusade. This contrast provokes the question that is investigated here. Does the absence of women in the sources for the Second Crusade genuinely reflect the fact that fewer women participated in it? Or is it that those contemporaries who wrote about the Second Crusade paid less attention to the presence of women and therefore created a false impression that there were fewer women crusaders than in the expedition of 1096–9?

For the First Crusade historians have a relative abundance of source material. Fulcher of Chartres, Raymond of Aguilers and the anonymous author of the *Gesta Francorum* were all crusaders who wrote substantial accounts of the expedition.[4] Soon after its completion, a well-informed Lotharingian monk,

1 Michael Swanton (ed.), *The Anglo-Saxon chronicles* (London, 2000), p. 323: *wifan and cildan.* 2 *Annales Augustani*, MGH SS 3, 134: *coloni et mulieres.* 3 Baldric of Dol, *Historia Hierosolymitana*, RHC Oc. 4, 1–111, hereafter BD, here 17. For women and the First Crusade see C. Kostick, *The social structure of the First Crusade* (Leiden, 2008), pp 271–86. See also S.B. Edgington, '*Sont çou ore les fems que jo voi la venir?* Women in the *Chanson d'Antioche*', in S.B. Edgington and S. Lambert (eds), *Gendering the Crusades* (Cardiff, 2001), pp 154–62. 4 Fulcher of Chartres, *Historia Hierosolymitana (1095–1127)*, ed. H. Hagenmeyer (Heidelberg, 1913); Raymond of Aguilers, *Historia Francorum qui cepe-*

Albert of Aachen, also wrote a very rich and valuable history.[5] But for an account of what happened to the major armies of the Second Crusade there is only one history of comparable length written by a participant: Odo of Deuil's *De profectione Ludovici VII in Orientem*.[6] The other participant historian, Otto of Freising, was so disheartened by the experience that when he came to the year 1147 in his history of Frederick I, king of Germany, he stated that he would leave the subject to others, as he had not set out to write a tragedy.[7] So for eyewitnesses we are left with Odo, a monk from the monastery of St Denis, who accompanied King Louis VII on the Second Crusade as his chaplain. In 1152 Odo replaced the very important figure of Suger, regent of France and confidant of the king, as abbot of St Denis, a position he retained until his death in 1162.

The structure of Odo's work is that of an extended letter, as if he were explaining events for the benefit of Suger back in France. It covers the events from the large assembly on Easter Sunday in 1146 at Vézalay, where Louis launched the French contingent by distributing crosses, to the king's arrival at Antioch in March 1148 at which point Odo probably wrote his history. Frustratingly, it therefore says nothing of the subsequent political crisis at Antioch in which Louis' wife, Eleanor of Aquitaine, played an important part, nor the siege of Damascus in 1148.

There is only one clear reference to the presence of women on the Second Crusade in the *De profectione Ludovici VII in Orientem*. In writing of the negotiations between Louis and Manuel I Comnenus, the Byzantine Emperor, Odo reported that the emperor demanded two things: a kinswoman of the king's, who accompanied the queen, as wife for one of his nephews and the homage of the French barons. While the French crusading nobility were considering these demands, Robert, count of Perche, Louis' younger brother, took matters into his own hands. He 'secretly abducted his kinswoman from the queen's retinue, thereby releasing himself and certain barons from paying homage to the emperor and his relative from marrying the emperor's nephew'.[8]

It is not possible to identify the Capetian noblewoman at the centre of this dispute. But the example is crucial nonetheless as it shows the participation of the French queen, Eleanor of Aquitaine, was not an isolated example of a

runt Iherusalem, ed. John France (Ph.D. thesis, University of Nottingham, 1967); R. Hill (ed. & trans.), *Gesta Francorum et aliorum Hierosolimitanorum* (London, 1962). For the complex relationship between the *Gesta Francorum* and a very similar account by the eyewitness Peter Tudebode, see J. Rubenstein, 'What is the *Gesta Francorum*, and who was Peter Tudebode?' *Revue Mabillon* 16 (2005), 179–204.   **5** Albert of Aachen, *Historia Ierosolimitana*, ed. S.B. Edgington (Oxford, 2007), hereafter AA.   **6** Odo of Deuil's *De profectione Ludovici VII in Orientem*, ed. V.G. Berry (New York, 1968), hereafter OD.   **7** *Ottonis et Rahewini Gesta Frederici I. Imperatoris*, G. Waitz and B. Simson (eds), *MGH Scriptores rerum Germanicarum in usum scholarum*, vol. 46, 3rd ed. (Hanover, 1912), hereafter OF, p. 65.   **8** OD 57: *cognatam suam reginae clam subripit se cum quibusdam baronibus illius subducens hominio et cognatam suam nepotis eius matrimonio.*

noblewoman being present on the crusade: she had a female retinue with her. This information derived from the key source, although only momentarily drawing attention to the presence of women on the crusade, is sufficient to substantiate the later and more distant reports that have to be examined to flesh out the issue.

Henry of Huntington, the influential English historian, wrote, *c.*1154, a very brief summary of the events of the Second Crusade in his *Historia Anglorum*. He contrasted the success of the humble naval expedition that captured Lisbon in 1147 with the failure of the great armies led by kings and explained this by the fact the humility of the former earned God's favour, while the pride of the latter caused God to despise them. Moreover, their incontinence, open practice of fornication and adulteries rose up in the sight of God.[9] That this sinful activity involved women who had departed with the crusading armies was a major theme of another English historian, William of Newburgh.

William wrote a history of England at his priory in the final years of his life, around 1196–8, in other words, some 50 years after the events, although with an interest in Eastern affairs. In his youth, William had met a monk who had lived at Antioch for many years.[10] When William described the departure of the Second Crusade he wrote that following the example of Louis and Eleanor, 'many other nobles followed this example and brought their wives with them.'[11] Since the wives of princes could not be without ladies-in-waiting, he explained, the resulting multitude of women (*feminarum multitudo*) brought about licentiousness in the Christian camp: a lack of chastity that polluted the army and resulted in the withdrawal of God's favour.[12] William then continued with a more convincing historical and political explanation of the failure of the expedition, but his attempt to offer a reason for why the Christians lacked God's favour draws attention to a wider body of women participants in the crusade than is visible from the work of Odo of Deuil alone.

Rather closer to the events of 1147–8 was William of Tyre. William was Chancellor of the Kingdom of Jerusalem from 1174 and Archbishop of Tyre from 1175 to his death *c.*1185. Thus he was familiar with the traditions of the region and explicitly stated that he had heard accounts from those who had participated in the events of the Second Crusade.[13] William of Tyre's *Chronicon* was commissioned by King Amalric of Jerusalem in 1167 and took its final form after redrafting by William in 1184. The presence of women among the crusading army is quite explicit in the *Chronicon*. In describing the enormous numbers who came with Conrad III alone, William of Tyre wrote

9 Henry of Huntingdon, *Historia Anglorum* ed. D. Greenway (Oxford, 1996), p. 752. 10 William of Newburgh, *Historia Rerum Anglicarum*, ed. R.G. Walsh and M.J. Kennedy (Warminster, 1988), hereafter WN, p. 96. 11 WN 92: ... *multi alii nobiles uxores suas secum duxerunt.* 12 WN 92–4, 128. 13 William of Tyre, *Chronicon*, ed. R.B.C. Huygens, CC vols LXIII and LXIII A (Turnholt, 1986), hereafter WT, pp 742, 747.

that there were 'up to 70,000 with breastplates, not including the footsoldiers, infants and women and riders with light armour'.[14]

On 7 January 1148, the French contingent split. The vanguard, having ascended Mount Cadmus (about 25 miles south east of Laodicea in Phrygia), pushed on in search of a better camping place, leaving a considerable gap to the baggage train and the rearguard. A Turkish force that had been monitoring the Christian army seized the opportunity and attacked from the heights of the mountain, inflicting great losses on the French. That night, wrote William of Tyre, those in the camp waiting for news of the battle were oppressed by grief. 'This man sought his father, that his lord; that woman sought her husband, this her son and when they did not find what they sought, they spent the night kept awake by the burden of their cares.'[15] William therefore believed that considerable numbers of women, of unspecified social rank, were accompanying the French army.

In these sources then, the evidence for women on the Second Crusade indicates that noblewomen were present, along with their ladies-in-waiting, but – apart from the deduction that female servants of these noble ladies were likely to have been present – there is no indication of the presence on the crusade of a large body of women of the lower social orders, such as was the case on the First Crusade. Since we have only a limited number of near contemporary sources it cannot necessarily be concluded that such women were not present: it might be that the lack of information concerning lower class women reflects more on the interests and outlook of these particular medieval historians than the actual role of women on the crusade.

A survey of the annalistic sources offers some insight into this question. As noted above, two chroniclers specifically noted the presence of large numbers of women among the popular contingents of the First Crusade setting out in 1096, and their testimony is supported by the chronicle of Bernold of St Blaisen (Constance), as well as eyewitnesses to the departure of the crusade who subsequently wrote histories of the expedition.[16] Do we have similar information in the annals of 1147? Certainly we get a picture of a huge popular response to the appeal for a new crusade: German and Lotharingian annals in particular emphasized the great numbers of people of all social backgrounds who participated in the Second Crusade. The Annals of Aachen, the Annals of St Peter of Erfut, and those of the Premontre Continuator of

---

14 WT 742: *... exceptis peditibus, parvulis et mulieribus et equitibus levis armature.*   **15** WT 752–3: *Hic patrem, ille dominum; illa filium, hec maritum cuncta Iustrando perquirit; dumque non inveniunt quod querunt, noctem percurrunt pondere curarum pervigilem.*   **16** Bernold of St Blaisen (Constance), *Chronicon*, 1096, pp 527–9; *Historia peregrinorum euntium, RHC Oc.* 3, 167–229, here 174; AA i.25 (48); Ekkehard of Aura, 'Chronica', in F.-J. Schmale and I. Schmale-Ott (eds), *Frutolfs und Ekkehards Chroniken und die Anonyme Kaiserchronik* (Darmstadt, 1972), pp 140, 144; Guibert of Nogent, *Gesta Dei per Francos*, ed. R.B.C. Huygens, *CC* LXXVIIa (Turnhout, 1996), hereafter GN, p. 331; BD 17.

Sigebert of Gembloux all refer to an 'innumerable multitude' taking part in the journey.[17] The later works of Lambert of Ardres and the *Historia Welforum Weingartensis* state that those setting out included 'uncountable thousands of people'[18] and 'men of every condition'.[19] The near contemporary Annals of Klosterrad (just north of Aachen) talk of a tenth of the entire land participating.[20] This corresponds with an 1147 letter from Bernard of Clairvaux, the main preacher of the crusade, who rather proudly wrote to his fellow Cistercian, Pope Eugenius III that as a result of his agitation for the expedition 'towns and castles are emptied, one may scarcely find one man amongst seven women, so many women are widowed while their husbands are still alive.'[21] It is notable that Bernard reported men leaving women to participate and not entire families joining the movement.

More precise detail about the departing crusaders is available in the description provided by the eyewitness Gerhoch, provost of Reichersberg (in 1162) of the gathering of the crusading forces:

> There was not a city that did not send forth multitudes or a village or town that did not at least send a few. Bishops together with magnates were each setting out with his own squadrons, carrying shields, swords, armour and other instruments of war with abundant preparation of finances and of tents, which they convoyed with carts and innumerable horses. The highway and that of the neighbouring plains could scarcely contain the innumerable carts and horses; the breadth of the Danube could hardly hold the multitude of boats. For so infinite was the army that from the times when nations began to exist I should have thought that never had so great a multitude of knights and footsoldiers been concentrated together. No markets of goods were lacking for the sale of the necessities, nor were there any fields that lacked carts or horses for conveying food. No lack either of peasants and serfs, the ploughs and services due to their lords having been abandoned without the knowledge or against the will of their lords.[22]

17 *MGH SS* 16, 686; *MGH SS* 16, 20; *MGH SS* 6, 453: ... *multitudine innumerabili.* 18 *MGH SS* 24. 633: ... *innumeris populorum milibus.* 19 *MGH SS* 21, 468: ... *cuiuscumque conditionis hominibus.* 20 *MGH SS*, 16, 718. 21 Bernard of Clairvaux, *Epistola* 247.2 in J. Leclercq, H.M. Rochais & C.H. Talbot (eds), *Sancti Bernardi opera*, 9 (Rome: Cistercienses, 1957–77), pp 8, 141. 22 Gerhoch of Reisenberg, *De Investigatione Antichristi Liber I*, *MGH Historica Libelli de Lite Imperatorum et pontificum, Saeculis XI et XII conscripti* 3 (Hannoverae, 1897), p. 374: *Non fuit civitas, que multitudines, non villa seu vicus, que non saltim paucos emitteret, episcopi cum magnates singuli cum suis turmis incedebant, scuta, gladios et loricas aliaque belli vasa secum perferentes cum capiosa preperatione sumptuum ac tabernaculorum, que plaustris et equis innumeris subvehabant. Vix terrestris via simul et campi contigui per terram gradientes, vix Danubii decursus navium multitudines capiebat. Tam enim erat infinitus exercitus, quod, ex quo gentes esse ceperunt, numquam tantam hominum, equitum simul et peditum, multitudinem in unum congregatam estimarverim. Nulla earum necessitatibus*

It is clear from these sources, particularly Gerhoch, that in a similar manner to the First Crusade, the preaching of the Second inspired great crowds of all social condition to take up the cross. This seems especially true of the Rhineland, where a Cistercian monk Radulf responded to the idea of the crusade by preaching his own agitational message against the local Jewish population with considerable destructive effect until checked by Bernard of Clairvaux. But it is less obviously the case that women of the lower social orders participated in the same proportions as they did in 1096. In fact the impression, especially from Bernard's letter, is that the crowds who set out in 1147 were overwhelmingly male. In contrast to the First Crusade, where it was a much-commented on phenomenon, only a handful of annalists explicitly mentioned the presence of women among the departing crowds of the Second Crusade. The Annals of St Giles of Brunswick, although heavily dependent of the Annals of Pöhlde for its account of the Second Crusade, deviated from the latter in making the point that in 1147 'an infinite number of people of both sexes were inspired' to take the cross.[23] The Annals of Würzburg stated that 'both sexes of mankind therefore hurried unwisely [to join the crusade], men with women, poor with rich, princes and great magnates of the realm with the king himself, clergy, monks with abbots and bishops.'[24] The Chronicle of Hainaut by Giselbert of Mons is less valuable, being written more than a generation later, *c*.1193. Giselbert echoed the theme of Henry of Huntingdon in saying that 'but because very many had their wives and their company marched women of every condition, marching in rows neither sensible nor lawful, they accomplished nothing.'[25] Writing with a similar theme, but significantly closer to events was Vincent of Prague, chaplain to Bishop Daniel I (1148–67), whose annals noted that 'in as much as the aforementioned kings together with their wives and other barons did not reject the company of foolish women when they took hold of so great a journey, they generated much filthiness which was detestable to God. It is well known that nothing good comes of having military equipment and foolish women in the same tent.'[26]

The survey of the chronicle evidence then suggests that there were women among the popular crowds that took up the crusading message in 1146 and

venalium rerum fora, vix ulli campi cui plaustra et equi victualibus perferendis deerant, non rusticanorum ac servorum, dominorum suorum relictis aratris ac servitiis, ignorantibus quoque nonnulli vel invitis dominis. **23** *MGH SS* 30.1, 14: *... populus infinitus sexus promiscui animatur.* **24** *MGH SS* 16.3: *Currit ergo indiscrete uterque hominum sexus, viri cum mulieribus, pauperes cum divitibus, principes et optimates regnorum cum suis regibus, clerici, monchi cum episcopis et abbatibus.* **25** *MGH SS* 21.516: *... sed quia uxores suas quamplures secum habebant et in eorum comitatu cuiusque conditionis mulieres incedebant, ipse non sano vel iusto ordine incedentes, nihil profecerunt.* **26** *MGH SS* 17. 633: *... predicti namque reges cum uxoribus suis aliique barones consortia muliercularum non repudiantes, talem viam arripuerunt, ubi plurime Deo abhominabiles oriebantur spurcicie; non autem bene conveniunt nec in unu sede morantur arma bellica et muliercularum contubernia* [Ov. Met. II.846].

1147, but they represented – probably – a smaller proportion of the crusade than in 1096.

Why was this? In part the explanation might lie in the message of the crusading preachers. Although the official papal message with regard to the First Crusade, as evidenced from Pope Urban II's letter to the clergy and people of Bologna,[27] was to dampen down the unexpected enthusiasm of non-combatants, the itinerant popular preacher, Peter the Hermit, consciously sought a following among women.[28] Bernard of Clairvaux, however, checked the activities of Radulf, the most notable popular preacher of 1146, and so the main recruiting message for the Second Crusade was more definitely the official voice of the papacy. Ideologically, therefore, it might have been more difficult for women in 1146 to claim that they too were to be included than those women who in 1096 claimed to found a cross fallen from heaven as a signal they should set off for Jerusalem.[29]

Bernard's boast that he had left towns abandoned by their men indicates he was not attempting to give the mobilization the emmigratory character it had for thousands of peasants in 1096. The Second Crusade was a more strictly military undertaking and one from which on the whole the Christian forces seem to have intended to return. In 1096 there were many who brought their plough teams and sold their land before departing, providing evidence that they intended to settle in the Near East.[30] A far larger proportion of such crusaders would be accompanied by women than those who planned to return once the military pilgrimage was concluded.

Does the difference in the numbers of women noted among the popular crowds also reflect a tightening of social roles in the 50 years since 1096? Had the lives of women become more regulated in the first half of the twelfth century? Was there less opportunity for women to act in the independent manner, such as was reflected in reports of women dressing in manly attire in order to participate in the First Crusade? There is a considerable literature on the evolution of marriage in the twelfth century.[31] The wider issues cannot be entered into here, but insofar as an comparison of the role of women on the First Crusade and the Second offers any material for the discussion, it suggests that there was less freedom for independent action by women of the lower social orders in 1147 than in 1096.

---

27 Urban II, letter to the clergy and people of Bologna: Hagenmeyer, *Epistulae et Chartae*, pp 137–8. 28 GN 121. 29 BD 17. 30 GN 120. 31 See especially Georges Duby, *Medieval marriage: two models from twelfth-century France* (Baltimore, 1978); Georges Duby, *The knight, the lady and the priest: the making of marriage in medieval France* (New York, 1983); James A. Brundage, *Law, sex and christian society in medieval Europe* (Chicago, 1987); J. Goody, *The development of the family and marriage in Europe* (Cambridge, 1983); D. Herlihy, *Medieval Households* (Cambridge, MA, 1985); C.N.L. Brooke, *The medieval idea of marriage* (Oxford, 1989); R.F. Berkhofer III, 'Marriage, lordship and the "greater unfree" in twelfth-century France', *Past and Present* 173 (2001), 3–27.

In regard to one particular woman, however, the Second Crusade shows a marked contrast with the First. From 1096–9 no Christian woman played a significant role in directing the course of events of the expedition. Only one incident – and that suspiciously like an episode from a *chanson* – showed a woman crusader affecting the strategic considerations of the expedition. Albert of Aachen reported that a certain Emeline, wife of Fulcher a knight of Bouillon, was captured by the illustrious Turkish knight, a general of Omar, lord of Azaz. At the suggestion of Emeline, this Turkish general contacted Duke Godfrey of Lotharingia with a view to leading a revolt against Ridwan of Aleppo.[32] For the Second Crusade, however, there is the very interesting issue of the role played by Eleanor of Aquitaine, the queen of France. Eleanor's long and colourful career has attracted a great deal of attention both from scholars interested in the role of noble women in the medieval period and from a wider public interest.[33]

One problem with establishing Eleanor's role on crusade with any clarity is that our main source, Odo of Deuil did not care to comment on the queen's activities and he never named her. This may well reflect the fact that Odo had a rather idiosyncratic notion of the *libra vita*, the 'book of life' mentioned in a letter of Paul to the Phillipians and in Apocalypse.[34] Odo seems to have treated his history as a part of the *libra vita* and was very anxious that only worthy persons be named in it. Several pious individuals were described as being 'worthy of mention', while other, less reputable figures were not named since they 'did not deserve to be in the book of life'.[35] Eleanor of Aquitaine seems to have belonged in the latter category and if this was a conscious censorship by Odo, it was almost certainly because he was writing in the aftermath of the events in Antioch described below: events that were very damaging to Louis, the subject of Odo's devotion.

On 31 March 1146 at Vézelay in the presence of Bernard of Clairvaux, King Louis VII took the cross and when he departed on the expedition he took his wife Eleanor with him, because, wrote William of Newburgh much later, he could not bear to leave her at home. There is a version of this event which has been repeated for some 70 years now and remains the dominant one in the public domain, which is that Queen Eleanor, along with many companions among the women of the French aristocracy formed a distinct female company, compared to the classical Amazons, with Eleanor their Penthesilia, riding around handing out spindles and distaffs to those reluctant to commit themselves.[36] Even recent academic writing that avoids such fanciful speculations has nevertheless repeated that several noblewomen came on

---

32 AA v.7 (346). See also S. Geldsetzer, *Frauen Auf Kreuzzügen* (Darmstadt, 2003), p. 185.   33 For Eleanor of Aquitaine see Jean Flori, *Aliénor d'Aquitaine: La Reine insoumise* (Paris, 2004).   34 Phil 4:3, Rev 13:8.   35 OD 10, 12, 20.   36 For example, A. Weir, *Eleanor of Aquitaine* (London, 2000), p. 51.

the expedition with Eleanor, those most frequently named being Sybilla, countess of Flanders, Mamille, or Maybel of Roucy, Faydide of Uzés, countess of Toulouse, Florina of Bourgogne, the countess Torqueri of Bouillon and the countess of Blois.

The problem here is that there is no evidence for any of these individuals having been present on the crusade and quite strong evidence that the whole idea of a contingent of noblewomen has arisen through a mistaken assembly of certain associations between some of these women and crusading. Mamille was a crusader, but she came to the Kingdom of Jerusalem in 1107, not 1146.[37] A Florina of Burgundy appears in Albert of Aachen's history, dying in Anatolia in the winter of 1097, ambushed while travelling with a company of Danes who were attempting to catch up with the main army of the First Crusade.[38] Sybilla did travel with her husband, Thierry I of Flanders to the Kingdom of Jerusalem, but not until 1157. In 1147 she was acting as regent of Flanders and Lambert of Waterlos describes her as defending the territory from incursions by rivals.[39] Faydide was married to Alphonse-Jordan of Toulouse, who was a participant in the Second Crusade and might have travelled with him but there is no record of this, such as might be expected to appear in William of Tyre's history. Nor is there any contemporary record of the presence of Torqueri, but Sabine Geldsetzer notes that she might be connected to the Emeline of Bouillon, the participant in the First Crusade mentioned above.[40]

Curiously, while admirers of Eleanor of Aquitaine have tended to exaggerate her enthusiasm for the crusade and attribute to her much more initiative than the sources allow for they have tended to slide over the one clear period in which she appears on the crusade as a political leader in her own right, that of the sojourn of the French forces in Antioch, in the spring of 1148. On Louis' arrival at the port of Saint Symeon on 19 March 1148, Raymond, the prince of Antioch rode to meet the French army with his household to give them an enthusiastic welcome. Hopes were high in the Latin principality that the united French – Antiochene army could reverse the gains of Nur ad-Din, the emir of Aleppo, who had been successfully capturing Christian towns and castles on the Christian frontier east of the Orontes. As the uncle of Eleanor of Aquitaine, Raymond had every reason to anticipate close collaboration with the newly arrived knights. But Raymond's fellow Christian magnates based around Jerusalem also desired the assistance of the French army for their own goals. They considered it would be a waste if Louis campaigned in the region of Antioch and sent envoys to him urging that he come to the Holy City. The greatest concern of the Jersualem magnates was that Louis would be detained in Antioch especially because of the 'intervention of the queen.'[41]

---

37 WT 14.15.   **38** AA 224.   **39** *MGH SS* 16, 516–17.   **40** S. Geldsetzer, *Frauen Auf Kreuzzügen*, p. 185.   **41** WT 16.29, p. 757: ... *interventu regine.*

As it became clear that Louis favoured taking his forces to Jerusalem and did not intend to fight in the region of Antioch, Raymond made plans to salvage something from the situation. According to William of Tyre:

> Frustrated in his hope, [Raymond], changing his efforts, began to hate the ways of the king and to openly construct ambushes and to arm himself to harm the king. For he planned, either violently or with secret machinations, to seize from the king his wife [Eleanor] who consented in this same plan as she was a foolish woman. For as we deduce, she was an imprudent woman, as she demonstrated both before and afterwards with clear evidence: contrary to the dignity of royalty, the law of marriage was neglected and the fidelity of the conjugal bed forgotten. After the king learned of this, forestalling the efforts of the prince, taking measures for his life and safety, on the advice of his magnates, hastening his journey he secretly left the town of Antioch with his followers.[42]

John of Salisbury, the celebrated English philosopher, spent the years 1149–53 at the papal court in Rome, and wrote an account of his experience there, the *Historia Pontificalis*, *c.*1163–7. From the perspective of a papal insider, John gave some attention to the Second Crusade and provided a version of the events at Antioch that matches that of William of Tyre. According to the *Historia Pontificalis* the constant conversations between Raymond and Eleanor made the king of France suspicious. When Raymond asked Louis for consent to keep the queen at Antioch, Louis prepared to bring her away, only to be confronted by Eleanor raising the question of consanguinity. At this the king, though he loved the queen, was shaken and would have been willing to consent to divorce if his advisors hand not pointed out that if, in addition to the military disasters, it was reported that Louis had also been deserted by his wife, it would bring everlasting shame to France. Moreover, argued one particular hostile knight, the queen might be party to incest, for, 'guilt under kinship's guise could lie concealed' (as Ovid put it in the *Heroides*, IV. 138). As a result of the policy of the king's French counsellors, Eleanor was forced to leave Antioch when the king departed.[43]

Georges Duby, in an important essay on Eleanor of Aquitaine, held to a theme that historians have tended to exaggerate her independence of action

---

42 WT 16.27, p. 755: *Spe frustratus mutato studio regis vias abhominari et ei prestruere patenter insidias et in eius lesionem armari cepit: uxorem enim eius in idipsum consentientem, que una erat de fatuis mulieribus, aut violenter aut occultis machinationibus ab eo rapere proposuit. Erat, ut premisimus, sicut et prius et postmodum manifestis edocuit indiciis, mulier imprudens, et contra regiam dignitatem legem negligens maritalem, thori coniugalis fide oblita. Quod postquam regi compertum est, principis preveniens molimina, vite quoque et saluti consulens, de consilio magnatum suorum iter accelerans urbe Antiochena cum suis clam egressus est.*

in a vain search for an example of a strong twelfth-century woman. In the main his argument is convincing, but for this particular incident Duby probably went too far in describing the conflict as entirely between Raymond and Louis.[44] William of Tyre explicitly stated that Eleanor colluded with Raymond and that it was her intervention with the French army that the nobles of Jerusalem feared, while John of Salisbury attributed the raising of the issue of divorce to Eleanor herself.

It probably is the case here that, for the first time, a woman of the nobility was an important figure in the strategic direction of a crusade. Eleanor found herself in a situation where she could threaten to break away from Louis and take her vassals into alliance with her uncle, Raymond of Antioch, and, indeed, she came close to implementing this threat. But it has to be recognized that a very particular set of circumstances gave rise to the opportunity for Eleanor to raise her own political and military agenda: the hegemony of the king over the French army had been undermined by the great losses it had experienced and the shameful abandonment of many of the foot soldiers; Eleanor as an heiress had the vassalage of many crusading knights in her own right, a minority faction of the army but an important one; and two powerful male figures, the king of France and prince of Antioch, were in conflict, creating space into which she could assert her own goals. The moment was short-lived. With what was effectively a kidnapping – the forcible removal of Eleanor from Antioch by Louis' advisors – this combination of circumstances collapsed and she once more became an invisible appendage of the king's. There are no other references to the queen on the crusade.

One final piece of evidence worth noting with regard to women on the Second Crusade comes from the naval expedition that in 1147 captured Lisbon for an alliance of Christian forces. An Anglo–Flemish fleet had sailed to the city from Dartmouth, arriving on 28 June and, with the assistance of the Christian king of Portugal, had captured the city on 24 October. To ensure discipline across the disparate force the various regional factions agreed to a common set of laws by which to regulate their conduct. Among these statutes was a decree that women should not go out in public.[45] This decree provides a useful summary of the contrast between the First Crusade and the Second. Without doubt women were present on the Second Crusade, but in much fewer numbers and – but for a moment of political crisis in which Eleanor of Aquitaine briefly strove to implement her own goals – very much more under the direction of men than had been the experience of women on the First Crusade.

43 John of Salisbury, *Historia Pontificalis* ed. M. Chibnall (London, 1956), pp 51–3.   44 Georges Duby, *Women of the twelfth century* (Cambridge, 1997), pp 9–11, 16.   45 Raol, *De Expugnatione Lyxbonensi*, ed. C.W. David (New York, 2001 [1936]), p. 56.

Consolation and desperation: a study of the letters of Peter of Blois in the name of Queen Eleanor of Aquitaine

STEPHEN HANAPHY

The name Peter of Blois is known today chiefly because of his skill as a writer of fine Latin. One of his poems, indeed, has recently been recorded in order to demonstrate 'the medieval love-lyric at the height of its sophistica-tion'.[1] It was as a writer of letters, however, that Peter came into employment at the courts of kings and archbishops. Through these letters he communi-cated with popes, advised and admonished friends and colleagues, and com-mented on events of such significance as the rebellion of King Henry II's children against their father, the murder of Thomas Becket, and the circum-stances that gave rise to the Third Crusade.[2] It is intended in this essay to throw light on certain key literary qualities displayed in the letters of Peter of Blois by focusing on an aspect of his writing which characterizes the pieces written on behalf of Queen Eleanor of Aquitaine, and which also distinguishes a number of other letters in his once-famous collection. This aspect, the *locus consolationis* or 'topic of consolation', had, as we shall see, its own vocabulary and mode of expression. It belonged to the rhetoric of letter-writing, other-wise known as the *ars dictaminis*, which art allowed Peter to succeed in what was once called 'his bid for literary fame'.[3]

It is with the circumstances under which Peter became a member of the household of Eleanor that we should begin. After the death of his employer,

---

1 Clive Brooks, *Reading Latin poetry aloud* (Cambridge, 2007), p. 181. The poem, known by its opening words *Vacillantis trutine*, is recited by the author on Disk 2 of the two accompanying CDs. All of Peter of Blois' poems have been edited recently in Carsten Wollin (ed.), *Petri Blesensis Carmina* 128 (Turnhout, 1998). Further discussion of Peter's poetical works is contained in Peter Dronke, 'Peter of Blois and poetry at the court of Henry II', *Mediaeval Studies* 38 (1976), 185–235. 2 The most recent edition of Peter of Blois' letters is still that of J.A. Giles, reprinted with notes by Pierre de Goussainville in *PL* 207, cols. 1A–560C. Professor Rolf Köhn (Universität Duisberg-Essen) is reported, however, to be preparing a new critical edition for *CCCM*. An edition of *Epp* 1, 14, 26, 30 and 150 is found in Lena Wahlgren, *The letter collections of Peter of Blois: studies in the manuscript tradition*, Studia Graeca et Latina Gothoburgensia 58 (Gothenburg, 1993). The letters written by Peter in the latter period of his life have also been edited in Elizabeth Revell (ed.), *The later letters of Peter of Blois*, Auctores Britannici Medii Aevi 13 (Oxford, 1993). References in this paper to Peter's letters will be to those printed in *PL* 207, unless otherwise stated. 3 R.W. Southern, 'Peter of Blois: a twelfth-century humanist', *Medieval humanism and other studies* (Oxford, 1970), pp 105–32, here 112.

the archbishop of Canterbury Baldwin of Forde, during the siege at Acre in November 1190, Peter's participation in the Third Crusade came to an end. This involvement had been marked by his composition of a number of letters and treatises, in which he had urged King Henry II in particular to take up the cross and deliver Jerusalem from the forces of Saladin.[4] Moreover, a revised version of one of these treatises indicates that Peter was present at Acre in the months leading up to Archbishop Baldwin's death.[5] Bereft of his employer, Peter left Palestine and made his way back to England. It is possible that he found himself in Sicily at the same time as Queen Eleanor in the spring of 1191.[6] It is clear however, as we shall see below, that he was a member of the queen's retinue by 1192.

It is important to note at this point, and it will become especially relevant when we examine those letters in which Peter applies his knowledge of the language of consolation, that the period at issue here was one of some difficulty for the letter-writer. On 6 July 1189 King Henry II, to whom Peter had dedicated the first version of his letters as well as a now-lost *gesta* entitled *De praestigiis fortunae*,[7] died. Peter had worked at the court of the king as chief letter-writer to the archbishop of Canterbury since 1177, and in spite of derogatory remarks made in relation to courtly life under Henry II in what is his most famous letter, *Ep.* 14, Peter owed much of the development of his career to his proximity to the king. Indeed, one of the earliest letters of Peter's collection, written probably in 1165, was addressed to King Henry II and treated of so important an issue as the education of his son, the future rebel Young King Henry.[8] It has been suggested that it was on the strength of this letter that Peter was rewarded by his then-employer, Archbishop Rotrou of Rouen, with a mission to the royal court of Sicily in 1167, where

---

4 *Epp* 98 and 211; R.B.C. Huygens (ed.), *Dialogus inter regem Henricum et abbatem Bonevallis*, CCCM 171 (Turnhout, 2000), pp 375–408; R.B.C. Huygens (ed.), *Petri Blesensis Tractatus Duo: Passio Raginaldi Principis Antiochie; Conquestio de dilatione vie Ierosolimitane*, CCCM 194 (Turnhout, 2002). For extensive discussion of Peter's crusade-writings see R.W. Southern, 'Peter of Blois and the Third Crusade', in Henry Mayr-Harting & R.I. Moore (eds), *Studies in medieval history presented to R.H.C. Davis* (London, 1985), pp 207–18; Michael Markowski, 'Peter of Blois and the conception of the Third Crusade', in B.Z. Kedar (ed.), *The horns of Hattin* (London, 1992), pp 261–9. For Peter's role in the Third Crusade generally see Joseph Armitage Robinson, 'Peter of Blois', in idem, *Somerset Historical Essays* (London, 1921), pp 100–40: especially pp 115–16, 120–1; Southern, *Scholastic humanism and the unification of Europe 2 – the heroic age* (Oxford, 2001), pp 196–203; Egbert Türk, *Pierre de Blois: ambitions et remords sous les Plantagenêts* (Turnhout, 2006), pp 210–13. 5 Southern, 'Peter of Blois and the Third Crusade', p. 216. 6 For details of Eleanor's movements at this time see Roger of Howden, *Chronica*, ed. William Stubbs, 4 Rolls Series (London, 1868–1871), III, pp 100, 179; cf. J.T. Appleby, *England without Richard, 1189–1199* (London, 1965), pp 57–9. The possibility that Peter encountered the queen's household in Sicily is raised in Southern, 'Peter of Blois and the Third Crusade', p. 215, and in Türk, *Pierre de Blois*, p. 388. 7 For references to this work see *Ep.* 4, col. 12B; *Ep.* 19, col. 71B; *Ep.* 77, col. 239C. 8 *Ep.* 67.

he became tutor to King William II and keeper of the royal seals.[9] Later, while Peter was secretary to Archbishop Baldwin's predecessor, Richard of Dover, he composed treatises on the transfiguration of Christ and the conversion of St Paul.[10] These works seem to have impressed King Henry II, for Peter says in the preamble to his *Compendium in Job*, written probably by the beginning of 1183,[11] that the king had ordered him to compose this work along the same lines as the two earlier treatises.[12] Peter's proximity to the king, therefore, allowed him to indulge in the activity in which he was most skilled, and for which he was most famous, namely, the composition of what one scholar has described as his 'finely wrought Latin'.[13]

Upon his return to England in July 1191,[14] Peter found his position *vis-à-vis* the royal court altered for the worse. His two most important employers of the previous decade, King Henry II and Archbishop Baldwin, were deceased. Also, his friendship with the bishop of Bath and archbishop-elect of Canterbury Reginald fitzJocelin, through which Peter had acquired the archdeaconry of Bath, had turned cold.[15] Peter's state of mind at this time does not appear to have been much healthier than his professional prospects. In a self-pitying letter to the new archbishop of Canterbury Hubert Walter, he attributes his delay in reaching the archbishop's household to 'a fear of sickness, or rather of death'.[16] This fear was aroused by Peter's stated anticipation of the return of the malaria which had affected him initially after his ill-fated adventure to Sicily at the end of the 1160s.[17] We might note that

9 On Peter's references to this ill-fated mission see *Epp* 10, 46, 90, 93 and 131; cf. Robinson, *Somerset historical essays*, p. 103; Southern, *Scholastic humanism*, p. 189. On the connection between *Ep.* 67 and Rotrou's reward for Peter, see *idem*, p. 188.   10 *De Transfiguratione Domini*, *PL* 207, cols. 777A–792A; *De Conversione S. Pauli*, *PL* 207, cols. 791A–796B.   11 Rolf Köhn, *Magister Peter von Blois* (c.1130), 'Eine Studie zur Bildungsgeschichte der Geistlichkeit in der höfischen Gesellschaft' (D.Phil., U. Konstanz, 1973), p. 66, n. 96.   12 Joseph Gildea (ed.), *Compendium in Job*, in idem, *L'Hystore Job: an old French verse adaptation of 'Compendium in Job' by Peter of Blois* (Liege, 1974), p. xx (=*PL* 207, col. 795C–D): *Praecepistis mihi ut ad similitudinem illorum tractatuum, quos feceram de transfiguratione Domini et de conversione beati Pauli, vitam sancti Job summatim, et sub quodam compendio delibarem, ea duntaxat interserens, quae ad patientiam et caeteras virtutes vos plenius informarent.* Discussion of a general nature concerning this work is found in Gildea, 'Extant manuscripts of *Compendium in Job* by Peter of Blois', *Scriptorium* 30 (1976), 285–7.   13 Ian Short, 'Language and literature', in Christopher Harper-Bill & Elisabeth van Houts (eds), *A companion to the Anglo-Norman world* (Woodbridge, 2003), p. 201.   14 For the determination of this date see Southern, 'Peter of Blois and the Third Crusade', p. 215, n. 25; *idem*, *Scholastic humanism*, p. 203.   15 A full discussion of the relationship between the two men is contained in Lena Wahlgren, 'Peter of Blois and the later career of Reginald fitzJocelin', *English Historical Review* 111 (1996), 1202–15: on the deterioration of this relationship see especially 1211–12.   16 *Ep.* 199, col. 333A: *Moram itaque meam excuset apud gratiam vestram, non timor aegritudinis, quam patior, sed potius mortis.*   17 Col. 332C–332D: *Verumtamen quartanae insidiantis et imminentis praeambulos aestus iam praesensi; et quia nunc biennio continuato expertus sum eius malitiam, vereor ne in me ipsius malitia recidivet.* For the description of Peter labouring under the effects of malaria in Sicily see *Ep.* 90, col. 282A.

fears such as these have led a number of scholars to detect 'hypochondriac tendencies' in Peter of Blois.[18] Whether or not his fear of suffering a second bout of malaria was justified, it should be noted that Peter, more than many of his contemporaries, would have recognized the symptoms of quartan fever should they have arisen, since in *Ep.* 43 he demonstrates an acute understanding of the condition.[19]

Peter's letter to Hubert, which might at first glance be dismissed simply as a sick-note, is sombre and fatalistic in tone, and is indicative of the change in outlook which he seems to have undergone during his experience of the Third Crusade. His writings on the crusade, to which reference was made above, have been studied in the context of the spirituality and concern for religious reform to which they attest.[20] They were the result, in the words of one scholar, of the 'profound impression' made upon Peter by the news of the fall of Jerusalem.[21] We note the piety and selflessness ascribed to Reynold of Châtillon in the *Passio Raginaldi*; the contrition of King Henry II in the *Dialogus*; and the emphasis on penitence and humility in the *Conquestio*. Peter's articulation of these attributes is key to our understanding of what Ethel Higonnet described as his 'spiritual and intellectual growth'.[22] Another sign of this growth is evinced in Peter's composition of a *Tractatus de fide*, which dates probably to the months after Archbishop Baldwin's death at Acre.[23] The contents of this unprinted treatise 'seem to reflect Peter's growing interest in doctrine and devotion in the 1190s'.[24] This interest is evident also throughout the letters written by Peter in the final stages of his life. In the words of the editor of these later letters, we see Peter of Blois' 'concern shifting from engagement with diplomacy and law, and courtly and secular affairs, to a deeper interest in the spiritual and contemplative life, partly under the influence of Cistercian ideals'.[25] The clearest sign of all of Peter's intensified spirituality in the years following his experience of the Third Crusade is his decision to enter the priesthood. In *Ep.* 123 he had explained his reluctance to be ordained by insisting that 'no-one is suitable for ministry until he be cleansed by the fire of the Holy Spirit'.[26] At some point in the 1190s, however, Peter looked back at the days he had wasted, regretted that he had spent all his life 'soldiering' (*militavi*) in schools and at court, and considered himself ready to seek ordination.[27]

18 Wahlgren, *The letter collections of Peter of Blois*, p. 15; cf. Southern, *Scholastic humanism*, p. 212.   19 Peter's knowledge of medicine is examined in U.T. Holmes & F.R. Weedon, 'Peter of Blois as a physician', *Speculum* 37 (1962), 252–6; see also the remarks on this subject in Türk, *Pierre de Blois*, pp 18–20.   20 Michael Markowski, 'Peter of Blois and the conception of the Third Crusade', pp 261–9.   21 Southern, 'Peter of Blois and the Third Crusade', p. 208.   22 'Spiritual ideas in the letters of Peter of Blois', *Speculum* 50 (1975), 218–44: 243.   23 For this dating see Revell (ed.), *The later letters of Peter of Blois*, p. 323, n. 1.   24 Ibid.   25 Ibid., p. xxvii.   26 Col. 363A: *Nemo enim aptus est ministeriis spiritualibus, donec sancti Spiritus ardore purgetur.*   27 *Ep.* 139, col. 414B: *Volens itaque redimere dies meos, quos perdidi, quia perniciose et perdite vixi; ibid.*, col. 415B: *Noveritis*

It is against this backdrop of professional insecurity and intensified religiosity that Peter's employment at the household of Queen Eleanor must be placed. Between 1192 and 1193 he seems to have been occupied at her court,[28] yet the precise nature of that occupation is not altogether certain. Three letters written by Peter in the queen's name, in which he appeals to Pope Celestine III to deliver her son, King Richard I, from captivity at the hands of Duke Leopold of Austria, are the most famous source for Peter's employment at this stage of his career.[29] In what remains the fullest discussion of these letters, Beatrice Lees makes a strong case for doubting that they were sent, or even intended to be sent, by Peter to the pope.[30] First, no evidence exists in the contemporary sources to suggest that Eleanor brought any influence to bear upon the pope in the matter of Richard's captivity.[31] Second, Peter's description of Richard languishing in chains does not stand up to scrutiny, to the extent, Lees notes, that it is hardly conceivable that they [the three letters] were ever intended seriously to influence a pope who was familiar with the true facts of the case'.[32] Indeed, the depiction of Richard bound in a 'furnace of tribulation'[33] does not square with Ralph of Coggeshall's account of Richard keeping 'his spirits up by making his guards drunk and playing practical jokes on them'.[34]

Lees also challenges the assumption that Peter wrote the letters at Eleanor's instigation, treating them merely as 'rhetorical exercises masquerading in the guise' of historical letters.[35] Though it is convincing in its categorization of the three letters as works of rhetoric rather than of diplomacy, Lees' article is less persuasive in its distancing of Peter of Blois from the company of the queen. She assumes that a rejection of the overt purpose of the letters must 'carry Peter's secretaryship with them'.[36] This assumption is based on Lees' belief that Peter did not witness any of the queen's extant charters.[37] Two charters issued by the queen in 1193, however, were witnessed by Peter of Blois and therefore show this belief to be mistaken.[38] Also,

---

autem, quod ab ineunte aetate semper in scholis aut curiis militavi; ibid., col. 416A: *Rogate Dominum unctionis, ut ungat me oleo misericordiae suae; unctio enim docet de omnibus; ipsa me doceat facere voluntatem Dei, captivare totum intellectum meum in obsequium Christi, fungi sacerdotio, et offerre illi incensum dignum in odorem suavitatis.* On Peter's use of the metaphor of 'soldiering' in the schools and at court see Rolf Köhn, 'Militia Curialis – Kritik am geistlichen Hofdienst', *Soziale Ordnungen im Selbstverständnis des Mittelalters* 12 (1979), 227–57, here 256.   **28** H.G. Richardson, 'The letters and charters of Eleanor of Aquitaine', *English Historical Review* 74 (1959), 193–213, here 202.   **29** *PL* 207, *Epp* 144–6. The text itself of the letters is printed in *PL* 206, cols. 1262C – 1272D, and also in Thomas Rymer (ed.), *Foedera, Conventiones, Litterae*, 20 (London, 1704–35; reprinted 1967), I, 23–5.   **30** B.A. Lees, 'The letters of Queen Eleanor of Aquitaine to Pope Celestine III', *English Historical Review* 21 (1906), 78–98.   **31** Ibid., 79.   **32** Ibid., 89.   **33** *Ep.* 144, *PL* 206, col. 1265B: *in fornace tribulationis.*   **34** John Gillingham, *Richard I* (London, 1999), p. 257.   **35** Lees, 'The letters of Queen Eleanor of Aquitaine to Pope Celestine III', 78.   **36** Ibid., 81.   **37** Ibid.   **38** Richardson, 'The letters and charters of Eleanor of Aquitaine', 202. The charters in question are numbered 26 and 155 in Nicholas

Lees' scepticism of the formality of Peter's office under Eleanor, based on the fact that Peter nowhere calls himself the queen's chancellor, must be questioned in light of H.G. Richardson's finding that 'however her household was organized, it is certain that it included nothing like a scriptorium, no officer like a chancellor'.[39]

Notwithstanding the likelihood that Peter's three letters on behalf of Eleanor were never sent to the pope, and were simply rhetorical exercises composed 'at a time when the captivity of the king of England was interesting him keenly',[40] they nevertheless offer an important insight into the mindset of Peter of Blois at this particular period of his life. These three letters, written ostensibly at the behest of Queen Eleanor, may be viewed as personalized expressions of the same religious renewal that we find in Peter's later letters and crusade-writings. It may be shown, in other words, that the captivity of Richard I provided Peter with yet another subject through which he could communicate to his readers what has been called his 'new spirituality'.[41] Peter's composition of the three letters was motivated, therefore, by the concept of *aedificatio ad salutem*, which has been identified as a central theme of his letter-collection.[42] The three letters also throw light on the question of his writing style, by which we may understand 'the structuring and ordering of language',[43] which brings us back to the main theme of this essay. That Peter was, in the words of King Richard I's biographer, 'a famous stylist' is well known;[44] and yet the precise nature of that style has attracted little attention. This lack of attention was referenced by G.R. Evans in her review of Elizabeth Revell's edition of Peter's later letters when she noted that there remained 'a rich mine for research' into questions of the letter-writer's style.[45]

There have, however, been some general statements made concerning the style in which Peter of Blois' letters were written, which should be reflected upon at this point. R.W. Southern once described Peter as 'a master of language', and one of the earliest and most successful practitioners of an ancient style of eloquence, of which St Bernard of Clairvaux was the father, and which

Vincent (ed.), *The acta of Eleanor of Aquitaine and of Richard Duke of Aquitaine and count of Poitou* (Oxford, forthcoming). For this reference I am indebted to J.D. Cotts, whose new book, *The clerical dilemma: Peter of Blois and literate culture in the twelfth century* (Washington DC, 2009), of which he kindly sent me proofs, contains a summary of the controversy relating to the precise nature of Peter's employment under Eleanor: see *The clerical dilemma*, pp 40–2. **39** Richardson, *The letters and charters of Eleanor of Aquitaine*, p. 209. **40** Lees, 'The letters of Queen Eleanor of Aquitaine to Pope Celestine III', 81. **41** Rolf Köhn, 'Autobiographie und Selbststilisierung in Briefsammlungen des lateinischen Mittelalters: Peter von Blois und Francesco Petrarca', in J.A. Aertsen & Andreas Speer (eds), *Individuum und Individualität in Mittelalter*, Miscellanea Mediaevalia 24 (Berlin, 1996), p. 697. **42** Michael Markowski, 'Peter of Blois, writer and reformer' (PhD, Syracuse University, 1988). **43** Janet Martin, 'Classicism and style in Latin literature', in Robert L. Benson & Giles Constable (eds), *Renaissance and renewal in the twelfth century* (Oxford, 1982), pp 537–68: p. 537. **44** Gillingham, *Richard I*, p. 43. **45** 'Review of *The later letters of Peter of Blois*, ed. Elizabeth Revell (Oxford, 1993)', *Speculum* 69 (1994), 1248–50, here 1248.

had at its core 'burning words' (*ignita verba*).[46] Success in this endeavour was achieved, according to Southern, because of Peter's thorough acquaintance with Biblical imagery and his ability to give 'to small matters the flavour of the wide world of scholarship'.[47] A more specific description of Peter's language is found in the aforementioned article by Beatrice Lees, where she identifies Peter's 'elaborate, antithetic constructions, his twisted and affected turns of expression, his excessive fondness for Scriptural and classical quotations, and for puns and verbal conceits, and his outbursts of rhetorical enthusiasm'.[48] Peter's letters, Lees notes, are full of 'his own peculiar phrases and of his pet texts and plays on words, which recur constantly in his writings'.[49] This account gives the impression that Peter of Blois' language is contrived, artificial and bombastic. And yet his letters were extremely popular, to the extent that they are contained in approximately 250 extant manuscripts.[50] An indication of the enduring popularity of these letters is found in one scholar's observation that 'they were used as models for epistolary composition into the sixteenth century'.[51] More specifically, it has been demonstrated that the *De curialium miseriis* of the fifteenth-century humanist Aeneas Silvius Piccolomini contains 'an elegant variation of Peter's themes and language'.[52] By focusing on certain critical works of Peter of Blois we shall now elaborate on the subject of this style, and in particular on his use of the language of consolation. In the process we shall throw light on that period of his career in which he took up his pen in the name of Queen Eleanor.

When addressing Peter of Blois' epistolary style it is important to have regard to his *Libellus de arte dictandi*, which appeared around the same time as the publication of his first collection of letters in 1184.[53] Though the attribution to Peter of this theory-based handbook, of which only one copy is extant in the form of a fourteenth-century manuscript,[54] was once called into question by Tore Janson,[55] the prevailing opinion is that the *Libellus* was

---

46 *The making of the Middle Ages* (London, 1967), pp 205–6.   **47** Ibid., p. 204.   **48** Lees, 'The letters of Queen Eleanor of Aquitaine to Pope Celestine III', 80.   **49** Ibid.   **50** Wahlgren, *The letter collections of Peter of Blois*, p. 17.   **51** A.G. Rigg, *A history of Anglo-Latin literature, 1066–1422* (Cambridge, 1992), p. 85. On the popularity of Peter of Blois' letters throughout the late Middle Ages see also Southern, *Medieval humanism*, p. 105; Higonnet, 'Spiritual ideas in the letters of Peter of Blois', 218–219, n. 5; Martin Camargo, *Medieval rhetorics of prose composition: five English artes dictandi and their tradition*, Medieval and Renaissance texts and studies 115 (New York, 1995), p. 3, n. 6.   **52** Keith Sidwell, 'Aeneas Silvius Piccolomini's *De curialium miseriis* and Peter of Blois', in Zweder von Martels & Arjo Vanderjagt (eds), *Pius II 'el più expeditivo pontifice'. Selected studies on Aeneas Silvius Piccolomini (1405–1464)* (Leiden, 2003), pp 87–106, here p. 104.   **53** Edited in Martin Camargo, *Medieval rhetorics of prose composition: five english artes dictandi and their tradition*, Medieval and Renaissance Texts and Studies 115 (New York, 1995). On the dating of the *Libellus* see F.J. Worstbrock, Monika Klaes & Jutta Lütten, *Repertorium der Artes Dictandi des Mittelalters. Teil 1: Von den Anfängen bis um 1200*, Münstersche Mittelalter-Schriften 66 (Munich, 1992), p. 92.   **54** Cambridge University Library MS Dd. 9. 38.   **55** *Prose rhythm in medieval Latin from the ninth to the thirteenth century*, Studia

indeed the work of the letter-writer.[56] The handbook contains instructions as to how letters should be divided, and as to the content of those sections in terms of modes of address, syntax, punctuation and the use of metaphor. It also provides would-be writers with useful expressions germane to particular themes, such as the description of places, physiognomy, and of personal attributes such as prudence, fortitude and modesty. Most importantly from our point of view, Peter's treatise presents seven different ways in which a letter-writer might assuage a person's grief arising out of bereavement or general misfortune. These are introduced as variations on the same theme, which is that 'consolation is the mitigation of grief based on the benefit of reason'.[57]

Consolation might be offered first, according to the *Libellus*, by reminding the afflicted that the misfortune endured has been experienced by others in the past.[58] Second, the writer could ascribe the death of a friend or serious infirmity to the necessity of nature, rather than to fortune.[59] Third, the hardship may be shown to be trivial and destined to last only a short time.[60] Fourth, the adversity may be imputed to divine providence, and designed to challenge, rather than destroy us.[61] Fifth, all worldly things may be shown to be empty and transitory.[62] Sixth, the evils one suffers may be shown to bring glory rather than ignominy.[63] Lastly the student is advised that consolation may be offered by demonstrating the fickleness and mutability of fortune.[64] Peter then concludes this section on consolation by explaining briefly that the same seven approaches need only be applied negatively, in order for the letter-writer to instill desperation.[65] The first of these, which is designed

---

Latina Stockholmensia 20 (Stockholm, 1975), pp 88–92, 97–8.   **56** See for instance Southern, *Medieval humanism*, pp 115–16; *idem*, 'Towards an edition of Peter of Blois' letter-collection', *English Historical Review* 110 (1995), 925–37: 929, n. 1; James J. Murphy, *Rhetoric in the Middle Ages: a history of rhetorical theory from Saint Augustine to the Renaissance* (Berkeley, 1974), pp 229–30; *idem*, 'Caxton's two choices: "modern" and "medieval" rhetoric in Traversagni's *Nova Rhetorica* and the anonymous *Court of Sapience*', in idem (ed.), *Latin rhetoric and education in the Middle Ages and Renaissance* (Aldershot, 2005), p. 245; Camargo, *Medieval rhetorics of prose composition*, pp 39–40.   **57** *Libellus*, ed. Camargo, p. 69: *Est autem consolacio doloris mitigacio racionis innixa beneficio.* **58** Ibid., pp 69–70: *Primus locus est cum ostendimus incommodum quod aliquis sustinet <non> nouum et inusitatum, set frequenter eciam summis uiris accidisse.*   **59** Ibid., p. 70: *Secundus locus consolacionis cum ostendimus eam calamitatem que nos ducit in merorem non fortune temeritati, set nature necessitati pocius imputandum, sicut de amicorum morte vel graui infirmitate.* **60** Ibid.: *Tercius locus consolacionis est cum erumpna que toleratur aut in se leuis aut parum duratura esse ostenditur.*   **61** Ibid.: *Quartus locus consolacionis est cum aduersitas que nos deprimit diuine prouidencie imputatur, ut sit nobis ad exercicium, non ad excicium.*   **62** Ibid.: *Quintus locus consolacionis est cum omnia mundana uana et caduca esse monstrantur, nec efficere quod pollicentur.*   **63** Ibid.: *Sextus locus consolacionis est cum exemplis probamus mala que aliquis patitur non ignominiam set gloriam paritura.*   **64** Ibid.: *Septimus locus consolacionis imperfectis conuenit, cum fortunam mobilem mutabilemque et facilem in partem alternam et conuertibilem demonstramus.*   **65** Ibid.: *Eisdem locis possumus aliquem desolari et, utendo contrariis, cogere desperare.*

cogere desperare, translates thus: 'Nobody has experienced such misfortune'. The second *locus* reads: 'Your luck is doing you harm', and so on.[66]

Let us now consider the practical application of these devices in the letter-collection of Peter of Blois. Addressing King Henry II after the death of the Young King Henry on 11 June 1183, Peter rebukes the king in *Ep.* 2 for allowing his grief to exceed the bounds of reason. The tone of the letter is in stark contrast to that of *Ep.* 1, in which Peter dedicates his collection to the king and alludes to his *magnificentia*.[67] We read in the following letter that the reverence of the king's majesty has been cast off, his magnanimity is being worn away by effeminate softness, and he is indulging childishly in sobs and tears.[68] Peter employs the first *locus consolationis* contained in his *Libellus* by reminding the king that his grief has been endured before, for example by Job upon the death of his sons, Abraham upon the death of his wife Sarah, and by Jacob upon the presumed death of his son Joseph.[69] Peter takes no issue with the fact that the king grieves, but rather with what he perceives as an excess of grief.[70] He appeals to Henry to restrain himself, and not to allow his sorrow to consume him *ultra modum*.[71] These censures contrast with the subsequent description of the king's deceased son, whom Peter calls *Christi miles*, and who has shown his father the way of the penitent man.[72] He goes on to write of Henry the Young King: 'nobody was more humble in confession, more contrite in self-blame, more devoted to better living, more cruel in the affliction of his own flesh, more fervent in thorough exculpation'.[73] By calling Henry the Young King a soldier of Christ, and by listing his pious struggles for the purpose of edifying his father, Peter applies the sixth *locus consolationis* prescribed in the *Libellus*, the full translation of which reads:

> Where we prove by examples that the misfortunes one suffers will bring forth not ignominy but glory; thus it was for Hercules, Aeneas and Ulysses, and others for whom continual labour and courage, which was exercised in adversity and never to be overwhelmed by the flood-

---

66 Ibid.: *Primus locus est: 'Numquam alii tale accidit infortunium'. Secundus est: 'Temeritas tua tibi nocet'.* Note that *temeritas*, which normally translates as 'rashness', can also mean 'chance' or 'accident': see C.T. Lewis and Charles Short, *A Latin dictionary* (Oxford, 1879; reprinted 1969), p. 1848.   **67** Col. 2B.   **68** *Ep.* 2, col. 4A: *vestra magnanimitas ... in morte filii vestri mortificata est, et quadam mollitie muliebri degenerans, gemitibus indulget ac lacrymis, atque reverentia maiestatis abiecta, supervacuis doloribus pueriliter intabescit.*   **69** Cols 4A–5A: *Nam et Job, audita filiorum suorum morte, vestimentorum scissione et aspersione pulveris vim doloris expressit. Abraham, mortua Sara, venit ut fleret eam et plangeret. Jacob existimans filium suum Joseph devoratum a bestia, multos dies continuavit in planctu.*   **70** Col. 4A: *Doloris affectum in vobis non arguo, sed dolendi excessum.*   **71** Col. 5B: *Sed sit, quaeso, hic dolendi modus, ne vos dolor rapiat ultra.*   **72** Ibid., col. 7A: *in abiectione temporalium et humilitate poenitentiae factus et defunctus est Christi miles. Exemplum dedit vobis, ut et vos sequamini vestigia poenitentis.*   **73** Ibid., col. 7A: *Nemo enim fuit in confessione humilior, in sui accusatione contritior, in emendatione devotior, in propriae carnis afflictione crudelior, in omni satisfactione ferventior.*

waters, brought honour, rather than shame, for whom exile was happier than life at home, as is shown well in Ovid's letters from Pontus.[74]

Henry the Young King is therefore characterized as the hero who has been rewarded for his worldly struggles with eternal glory. His father, Peter reasons, should follow his pious son's example and be consoled by the fact that by turning his lamentations into 'weapons of penitence' he too might achieve everlasting rewards.[75] It should be said that by urging the king to see in his son's life and death an example to follow and challenge to meet, Peter employs the fourth *locus consolationis* contained in the *Libellus*. We find also the fifth *locus* being employed when the letter-writer reminds the king that this world is deceptive, that life is short, and the end unpredictable.[76]

If Peter's letter to King Henry II represents a model of twelfth-century *consolatio*, his writings on behalf of Queen Eleanor during the captivity of Richard the Lionheart seem to represent an exercise in the art of *desperatio*. Nowhere is this better demonstrated than in the last of this set of three letters, in which he addresses the pope thus: 'You alone force me to despair; after God, you have been my hope, the trust of our people'.[77] In using the words *desperare me cogitis* Peter clearly has in mind the principles set out in his own *Libellus* regarding the inversion of consolation. By not acting to liberate Richard I, Pope Celestine III is causing Eleanor despair. Consider also the following extracts from *Ep.* 146:

> I cannot take one breath free from the persecution of my troubles and the grief caused by my afflictions, which beyond measure have found me out. I have completely wasted away with torment and with my flesh devoured, my bones have clung to my skin. My years have passed away full of groans and I wish they could pass away altogether.[78]

---

74 Peter of Blois, *Libellus*, p. 70: *Sextus locus consolacionis est cum exemplis probamus mala que aliquis patitur non ignominiam set gloriam paritura; sicut Erculi, Enee et Ulixi et aliis quibus labor continuus et virtus aduersitatibus excercitata et nunquam mersabilis undis honori fuit non dedecori, quibus exilium fuit patria felicius, sicut in Ouidio de Ponto satis ostenditur.* For Peter's reading of the *Epistulae ex Ponto* of Ovid, see Stephen Hanaphy, 'Ovidian exile in the letters of Peter of Blois (*c.*1135–1212)', *Viator* 40 (2009), 93–106. 75 Col. 7A–B: *Exemplum dedit vobis, ut et vos sequamini vestigia poenitentis ... Planctus itaque, quos impenditis mortuo, in arma poenitentiae convertatis; ut sicut turbato fatalitatis ordine filius vos praecessit ad mortem, sic ordinato huius mortalitatis excursu caeteros praecedatis ad vitam.* 76 Col. 7B: *fallax enim est hic mundus, vita brevis, finis dubius.* 77 *Ep.* 145, *PL* 206, col. 1271C: *Solus desperare me cogitis, qui solus post Deum spes mea, populique nostri fiducia fueratis.* Translated in Anne Crawford (ed.), *Letters of the Queens of England* (Bath, 1994), p. 42. 78 *PL* 206, col. 1269A: *nec ad momentum mihi respirare liberum est a tribulatione malorum et dolore a tribulationibus, quae invenerunt nos nimis. Tota dolore contabui, pellique meae consumptis carnibus adhaesit os meum. Defecerunt anni mei in gemitibus, et utinam omnino deficiant.* Translated in Crawford (ed.), *Letters of the Queens of England*, p. 9.

I am pitiable, yet pitied by no-one; why have I, the Lady of two king-
doms, the mother of two kings, reached the disgrace of this abominable
old age? I am the mother of two kings. My insides have been torn out
of me, my family has been carried off, it has rolled away from me; the
young king and the count of Brittany[79] sleep in the dust, and their
most unhappy mother is compelled to live, so that without cure she is
tortured with the memory of the dead.[80]

Here Eleanor is depicted as being just as inconsolable as King Henry II after
the death of the Young King Henry. While in *Ep.* 2 Peter sought to appeal
to the king's sense of reason in order to mitigate his grief, he characterizes the
queen in *Ep.* 144 as having lost self-control entirely. Peter puts in her mouth
the following words:

Certainly grief is no different from insanity while it is inflamed with
its own force. It does not recognise a master, is afraid of no ally, it has
no regard for anyone, and it does not spare them – not even you.[81]

Though it is implied at the end of *Ep.* 144 that some solace may be found in
the idea that Richard will be rewarded for his sufferings in prison with eternal glory, the predominant theme of these letters is one of desolation.[82] This
is encapsulated in the opening section of *Ep.* 145, in which Peter laments that
his, or rather the queen's, 'expectation of greater cruelty has cut off all hope
of consolation'.[83] Whatever rational advice Peter could offer King Henry II by
way of consolation after the death of the Young King Henry, it is clear in
these three letters that the Queen-mother is impervious to such reasoning.

And yet it is essential to remember that the words and sentiments of *Epp*
144–6 are those of Peter, not of Eleanor. Moreover, they are words of per-
suasion. This point has been observed by Peter von Moos in his study of the
genre of consolation in medieval literature.[84] He notes that the guidelines con-

79 Note that Eleanor's son Geoffrey, duke of Brittany, is described by Peter elsewhere
more accurately as *dux Britanniae: Ep.* 113, col. 340D.   **80** *PL* 206, col. 1269C: *Ego misera,
et nulli miserabilis, cur in huius detestandae senectutis ignominiam veni, duorum regnorum
domina, duorumque regum mater exstiteram: avulsa sunt a me viscera mea; generatio mea
ablata est, et revoluta est a me. Rex iunior et comes Britanniae in pulvere dormiunt, et eorum
mater infelicissima vivere cogitur, ut irremediabiliter de mortuorum memoria torqueatur.*
Translated in Crawford (ed.), *Letters of the Queens of England*, p. 40.   **81** *PL* 206, col.
1262C–D: *Sane non multum ab insania differt dolor, dum in impetu suae accensionis est, domi-
nos non agnoscit, socium non veretur, nec defert, nec parcit alicui, sed nec sibi.* Translated in
Crawford (ed.), *Letters of the Queens of England*, p. 36.   **82** For the idea of Richard being
'cleansed in the furnace of affliction' see *Ep.* 144, *PL* 206, col. 1265B: *Nam si nunc in fornace tribulationis purgatur a Deo, qui circa eum adversa et prospera saluberrima moderatione
disponit, vexatio transibit in gloriam, atque pro confusione duplici et rubore, in terra sua dupli-
cia possidebit.*   **83** *PL* 206, col. 1265D: *exspectatio durioris eventus omnem gratiam consolationis abscidit.*   **84** *Consolatio. Studien zur Mittellateinischen Trostliteratur über den Tod und*

tained in Peter of Blois' *Libellus* show that the function of consolation is deliberative, rather than simply epideictic. In other words, the technical language of consolation belongs to the art of rhetoric in that it can be used to persuade or dissuade.[85] In his consolation of King Henry II in *Ep.* 2, Peter gives a practical demonstration of the theories contained in his *Libellus de arte dictandi* by persuading a father that the death of his son should not cause him excessive grief. The inverse of these theories, that is the language of *desperatio*, is applied by Peter in *Epp* 144–6 in order to evoke sympathy in Queen Eleanor's plight.

    Given the unlikelihood, as argued convincingly by Beatrice Lees, that Peter sent these letters to Pope Celestine III, the question remains as to why he wrote the letters in the first place. The answer lies in Peter's circumstances as he entered the company of Eleanor of Aquitaine. We saw earlier how Peter's proximity to the court of King Henry II had provided him with many opportunities to demonstrate his skill as a writer, and how the king's death, along with that of Baldwin, had left a vacuum in the writer's career upon his return from the Holy Land. He now found employment under Eleanor, and just as the fall of Jerusalem had fired him into composing his propaganda pieces for the Third Crusade, so the imprisonment of the king of England provided inspiration. The same impulse that had moved him to write passionately about the need to liberate Jerusalem now drove him to write of a mother's grief. The expressions of anger, sorrow, fear and frustration encountered in *Epp* 144–6 are all too familiar: they are found on every page of Peter's crusade-writings. The tearful yearning for consolation that permeates the letters written under Eleanor's name is a recurrent theme in the *Conquestio de dilatione vie Ierosolimitane*. Note the following textual and conceptual comparison:

Ep. 146, *PL* 206, col. 1269A-B	*Conquestio*, ed. Huygens, p. 76
Utinam totus sanguis corporis mei iam emortui, cerebrum capitis, ossiumque medulae ita dissolvantur in lacrymas, ut in fletus tota pereffluam.	Utinam in fletum totus effluam et pascatur lacrimarum solatio dolor meus, deducant oculi mei lacrimas, deficiat in dolore vita mea et anni mei in gemitibus.

Just as Peter's hope of a most longed-for consolation (*spes desiderantissime consolationis*)[86] rested upon the Western princes and magnates making good on their pledge to come to the aid of Jerusalem, so the consolation of Eleanor is said to depend solely upon Pope Celestine III's intervention. The same sense

zum Problem der Christlichen Trauer 4 (Munich, 1971–2), I, p. 44.   **85** Ibid.   **86** Huygens (ed.), *Conquestio*, p. 80.

of urgency that pervades Peter's call to arms in the *Conquestio* is evident in
the second letter addressed to the pope:

Ep. 145, *PL* 206, col. 1270C-D	*Conquestio*, ed. Huygens, p. 84
Redde igitur mihi filium meum, vir Dei, si tamen vir Dei es, et non potius vir sanguinum ... Heu, heu, si summus pastor in mercenarium pervertatur, si a facie lupi fugiat, si commissam sibi oviculam imo arietem electum, ducem Dominici gregis, in faucibus cruentae bestiae derelinquat!	Quanta, queso, insania est, in tam anxie necessitatis articulo dilationes innectere, suam protelare salutem, Christi dissimulare iniurias, permittere ut lupus in ovile deseviat et tunc primo parare subsidium, cum oves devoraverit universas?

Here we find Peter recycling the language employed by him in his earlier
writing on the crusade. First Saladin was the wolf threatening the sheepfold
of Jerusalem; now Duke Leopold of Austria is portrayed as the public enemy.

Peter's thought-process is revealed to us in his references to Richard's
captor as a tyrant and son of perdition: *tyrannus* and *filius perditionis* are Peter's
favourite names for Saladin.[87] The same language of lament and desolation
employed by Peter in his crusade-writings thus reappears in his letters in the
name of Eleanor. We are introduced to a desolate figure in the opening lines
of the *Passio Raginaldi*, in which Peter laments the death of the prince and the
fall of Jerusalem: 'I sigh before I eat, and my roarings pour out like the waves,
because that which I have feared has occurred'.[88] Such sorrow and helplessness are expressed by Peter at the end of his last letter in Eleanor's name: 'my
writing is interrupted by my sobbing, my sadness saps the strength of my soul
and it chokes my vocal chords with anxiety'.[89] Likewise, Peter has Eleanor
lament in *Ep.* 145 that the very thing she feared has occurred.[90] Note also how
Peter's frustration at the failure of the western princes to fulfill their crusading vows is reworked in the context of Richard the Lionheart's imprisonment.
Like the sons of Ephraim, who bend and shoot with the bow, and are turned
on the day of battle (Psalm 77:9), so the cowardly crusaders of the *Passio
Raginaldi* and the papal legates of *Ep.* 146 are said to fail to come to the assistance of Jerusalem and Eleanor of Aquitaine respectively.[91]

---

87 Leopold is referred to as a tyrant in *Ep.* 144, *PL* 206, col. 1263B, 1263C; *Ep.* 145, *PL*
206, cols. 1266C, 1267C, 1268A, 1268B (twice); *Ep.* 146, *PL* 206, col. 1270B. He is called
perditionis filius in *Ep.* 146, *PL* 206, col. 1272C. Peter calls Saladin a *tyrannus* in Huygens
(ed.),, *Passio Raginaldi*, pp 58, 59 (twice), 61. He calls him a '*filius perditionis*' in ibid., pp
40, 46 and in Huygens (ed.), *Conquestio*, p. 84.   88 Huygens (ed.), *Passio Raginaldi*, p. 31:
*Antequam comedam suspiro et quasi inundantes aque sic rugitus meus, quia timor quem timebam
evenit michi et quodcumque verebar accidit.*   89 *PL* 206, col. 1272D: *Spiritum enim singultus
intercipit, et animae vires moeror absorbens vocales meatus anxietate praecludit.* Translated in
Crawford (ed.), *Letters of the queens of England*, p. 43.   90 *PL* 206, *Ep.* 145, col. 1265D:
Quidquid enim verebar, accidit.   91 Huygens (ed.), *Passio Raginaldi*, p. 32: *Iactati autem*

The letters written by Peter of Blois in the name of Eleanor of Aquitaine highlight the danger involved in using his collection as an historical source. They exemplify Giles Constable's assertion that 'no clear line can be drawn between the "historical" and "literary" aspects of medieval letters ... their worth as historical sources must always be evaluated in the light of their literary character.'[92] On the other hand, it is possible, and it has been the objective of this study to show, that the letters written by Peter of Blois in the Queen-mother's name contribute to our knowledge of the life and *modus operandi* of one of the most important and influential letter-writers of the Middle Ages. A good indication of this influence, indeed, is discernible in MS Trinity College Dublin 603. Compiled in England in the first half of the thirteenth century, this manuscript contains excerpts not only from the letters of Peter of Blois, but also from the moral letters of Seneca the Younger, the *Historia Anglorum* of Henry of Huntingdon and the *Versus de nominibus aequivocis* of the poet Serlo of Wilton.[93] It also contains sections of general discussion on philosophy and the liberal arts, as well as a list of medical maxims and verses concerning medical practice.[94] In the margin of one of the letters of Peter of Blois, namely the consolatory *Ep. 2* addressed to King Henry II on the death of his son, we find written the words *de fletu et planctu*.[95] This explanatory note, together with the inclusion of *Ep. 2* in a compilation such as that represented by MS TCD 603, shows that Peter of Blois' language of consolation was considered a model of the genre for the purpose of instructing students in the generation after the writer's death.

By examining the language of consolation and desolation in the letters of Peter of Blois, and by seeing in it an application of particular rhetorical techniques, we gain a valuable insight into the art of a twelfth-century letter-writer. What appear at first to be the desperate appeals of Queen Eleanor for assistance from Pope Celestine III, emerge as the careful application of the rhetoric of consolation by a skilled practitioner of the *modus epistolaris*. Considered in the context of his experience of the Third Crusade, and of the intensified spirituality that marked the later years of his life, the language of Peter's letters in the name of Eleanor also helps us to mark an important stage in the writer's life and in the development of his outlook.

---

vento iactancie, quasi filii Effren intendentes et mittentes arcum conversi sunt in die belli; *Ep.* 146, *PL* 206, col. 1271A–B: *Nunc autem filii Ephrem intendentes et mittentes arcum in die belli conversi sunt.*   **92** G. Constable, *Letters and letter-collections* (Turnhout, 1976), p. 11. **93** The *Historia Anglorum* has been edited as part of the Oxford Medieval Texts series: Henry, Archdeacon of Huntingdon, *Historia Anglorum*, ed. & trans. Diana Greenway (Oxford, 1996). See also Jan Öberg's edition of the poetical works of Serlo of Wilton: *Serlon de Wilton: Poèmes latins* (Stockholm, 1965), pp 79–88.   **94** For a description of this MS see Marvin Colker, *Trinity College Library Dublin: descriptive catalogue of the medieval and Renaissance Latin manuscripts* 2 (Aldershot, 1991), II, pp 1055–7.   **95** Fol. 48ra.

Bardic poems of consolation to bereaved Irish ladies

KATHARINE SIMMS

The following paper originated as a contribution to one of the all-day conferences on medieval and Renaissance women's history annually hosted at Trinity by our honorand in her capacity as a member of the Irish National Committee for the International Federation for Research in Women's History (Council of the Irish Association for Research in Women's History). It was a distinctive theme running through this series of conferences that women in the medieval and early modern period should not be studied simply in terms of marriage and child-rearing, but also for their wealth, intellectual attainments or social and political influence. I offer the present more fully referenced version of that talk in acknowledgement not only of Christine's contribution to women's history as one aspect of her many converging academic interests, but to recall in particular her encouragement of Irish women's history through these conferences and the resulting publications.

Irish bardic poems were composed between the thirteenth and the seventeenth centuries by hereditary families of professional poets. They were publicly performed by trained reciters to a musical accompaniment during banquets held by the Irish and even the Anglo-Irish nobility.[1] The poets themselves were a privileged, highly-educated and highly-paid class within Irish society. While compiling a descriptive catalogue of the surviving corpus of these poems, including both the published and unpublished texts,[2] I came across a distinct group of poems of condolence and consolation for the death of a spouse or close relative. There are, of course, plenty of elegies or memorial poems honouring the dead themselves, to be recited at funeral feasts following either the burial itself or a commemorative mass,[3] but these consolation poems are quite different in theme and emphasis, since their focus is on the emotions and plight of the survivor. It is a small category: out of 1,968 poems surveyed, I have only identified about a dozen which fit this description, the numerical uncertainty reflecting the existence of some borderline examples. The most interesting feature is that all twelve or so are addressed to women. This would be less remarkable if they were all addressed to widows, the presumed hostesses at the funeral feast, but some are to griev-

---

1 K. Simms, 'Literacy and the Irish bards' in H. Pryce (ed.), *Literacy in medieval Celtic societies* (Cambridge, 1998), pp 238–58 at pp 244–8.   2 Now published on the web at http://bardic.celt.dias.ie.   3 See P.A. Breatnach, 'The poet's graveside vigil: a theme of Irish bardic elegy in the fifteenth century' in *Zeitschrift für Celtische Philologie* 49/50 (1997–8), 50–63.

ing mothers or sisters – why then are there no poems of consolation to griev-ing fathers and brothers? It is not because the Irish had a convention that 'men don't cry', since the formal elegies abound in references to warrior bands in floods of tears at the death of their leader.[4]

When I first set myself to explore the reasoning behind the consolation poems, I went back to an earlier study of mine on a common motif found in formal elegies whereby the bardic poet himself takes on the persona of a bereaved widow.[5] Recalling scenes from the sagas, where the grief-stricken wife or lover hurls herself onto her loved one's corpse, or into his grave, and dies of a broken heart, the poet apologises for living on after his beloved patron has died, with exclamations like 'My God! How can these [tears] be thought genuine while (I) his poet remain alive?' ... 'I must not shrink back from my burial-day; is it not a miracle that I have lived (in spite of my grief)?' ... 'Alas O God that he and I are not buried together'.[6] Similarly in a poem of condolence addressed by the early seventeenth-century Fearghal Óg Mac an Bhaird to Mary and Margaret, the daughters of Ó Domhnaill (O'Donnell), lord of Tír Conaill, two sisters who had lost four brothers one after another in the course of the Nine Years War and its aftermath, the poet muses:

> 'Tis strange that Mary should live, while the rivers no longer bear ships, and the withered forests of the fold of Uisneach are ever weep-ing for those four.
>
> Throughout fair Banbha the apple-trees bend not with apples, nor the woods of hazelboughs with nuts – strange that Margaret should live.[7]

Bardic poetry is about increasing and defending a patron's honour and repu-tation. I wondered if there was an old tradition whereby the mourning wife felt an element of shame at surviving her husband, and these poems were intended to eliminate such feelings and restore her dignity. However the sur-viving body of such compositions does not encourage this idea. Most date from the seventeenth century. Certainly they are conscious heirs to a tradi-tion that goes back at least as far as the late tenth or early eleventh century, but the message changes with time.

4 E.g. J. O'Donovan, 'Donnchadh Ó Futhail's poem on the death of Sir Finghin Ó hEidirsceoil and his son Conchobhar, about the year 1619' in J. O'Donovan (ed.), *Miscellany of the Celtic society* (Dublin, 1849), pp 370–83; T. Ó Donnchadha (ed.), *Leabhar Cloinne Aodha Buidhe* (Dublin, 1931), pp 75, 261; D. McManus, 'An elegy on the death of Aodh Ó Conchobhair (d. 1309)', *Ériu* 51 (2000), 69–91; C. Mhág Craith, *Dán na mBráthar Mionúr* 1 (text, Dublin, 1967), pp 16–22; 2 (trans. Dublin, 1980), pp 6–10; E. Knott, 'Mac an Bhaird's elegy on the Ulster lords', *Celtica* 5 (1960), 169.   5 K. Simms, 'The poet as chieftain's widow: bardic elegies' in Liam Breathnach, Kim McCone and Donnchadh Ó Corráin (eds), *Sages, saints and storytellers: Celtic studies in honour of Professor James Carney* (Maynooth, 1989), pp 400–11.   6 Ibid., pp 404–5.   7 O. Bergin, *Irish bardic poetry*, ed. D. Greene & F. Kelly (Dublin, 1970), p. 231.

A poem ascribed to Mac Coise, a tenth-century court poet to the kings of Tara, addresses Derbáil, daughter of the king of Connacht and widow of Domnall Ó Néill (d. 980), high-king of Ireland, consoling her for the death of her son Áed Ó Néill.[8] The message to her is resignation to God's will, it is God who gave her son and He has now taken him back. Her grief for Áed is no greater than that of Échtach for her son, the legendary high-king Cormac mac Airt, or Sadb's sorrow for the death of her son, Eógan and her brother, Art, killed in the Battle of Mag Mucraime, or Bébinn's sorrow for her son Fráech, killed by the champion Cúchulainn. Not less did Caintigern mourn for Mongán, when he died pierced by Arthur, or the queen who lamented Láegaire the high-king, slain by the wind and the sun. Not less did Hecuba mourn Hector when slain by the spear of Achilles. Let the queen take up the cross of Christ, follow the Heavenly King to the home of the apostles and avoid frightful Hell.[9] Thus the poet manages in quite a short space to demonstrate his knowledge of both native Irish and classical legends and his orthodox grasp of Christian teaching. His tone is typical of the pre-Norman period, when such poems as were written down often bear strong signs of clerical influence, but strangely from the very same period, and perhaps from the same author, comes a gentle parody of this theme, an address to the wife of the high-king Máel Shechlainn II (d. 1022), exhorting her not to grieve for the death of her goose:

O Mór of Moyne ... loss of a bird is no great occasion for grief. If you consider that you yourself must die, is it not an offence against your reason to lament a goose?

Daughter of ... Donnchad ... are you unacquainted with the tale of Solomon of old,[10] when your lovely goose so inflames your heart?

Have you not heard that Conn of the Hundred Battles ... is dead, and Cormac too, and Art?

Have you not heard that the good warrior Mongán fell ... that he

8 This queen died in 1010, and her dead son is either Aodh Ó Néill the king of Aileach who died in battle in 1004 'in the 29th year of his age and in the tenth of his reign', or, if the poet's own death date of 990 is to be relied upon (*Annals of Ulster (to 1131 AD)* eds S. MacAirt & G. MacNiocaill (Dublin, 1983), pp 422, 432–4, 440), the poem possibly refers to an earlier son of the royal couple who bore the same name, as was quite often the case in medieval society, and particularly in Irish noble families, a solution suggested by Prof. M. Ní Dhonnchadha at a paper read to the 'Tionól', or symposium of the School of Celtic Studies, Dublin Institute for Advanced Studies, November 2000. It is also possible that the poem is a pastiche dating between the twelfth and fourteenth centuries, composed to illustrate one of the many tales and legends that grew up about the kings and queens reigning at the period of the great Battle of Clontarf, the last and most decisive victory of the Irish over Viking forces. See J. Carney, 'Notes on early Irish verse', *Éigse* 13 (1970), 305–11. 9 K. Meyer (ed.), 'Mac Coissi cecinit', *Zeitschrift für Celtische Philologie* 6 (1908), 269–70. 10 Murphy's translation of this clause is emended in accordance with Carney's reading, Carney, 'Notes', p. 311.

of the nimble hand has perished, Cú Chulainn who was a delightful champion?[11]

Both these Middle Irish examples sternly reprove the woman for feeling grief, whereas later poems in this class show more fellow-feeling, perhaps reflecting the change from a clerical to a secular environment. A mid-thirteenth century elegy for an infant princess of the Ó Domhnaill (O'Donnell) dynasty of Donegal, who died of disease at the early age of five, has passages which anticipate this more human approach. In this case we know that the poet himself, Giolla Brighde Mac Con Midhe had lost all his own children in early infancy, and felt their loss very deeply,[12] so we find that his sympathy extends from the noble foster-mother and the mother to the bereaved father also, though the poem is formally an elegy for the child herself:

> Her foster-mother spends a while weeping, a while telling stories of her; what recollection would be more sorrowful to her foster-mother than the remembrance of her gaiety ...
>
> She (Gormlaith) never struck another child, she never earned the sighs for a daughter; I see everyone's despair because of her ...
>
> She has not brought forth a mere sigh from the heart of the daughter of Cathal (her mother); there is nothing that does not leave a person except physical grief.
>
> The daughter of the daughter of Cathal is missing to her noble father; soft, lovely, bright, wavy, fresh hair, the pet calf, the first care of Cruachan.[13]

The first explicit poem of condolence, directly addressed to the feelings of the bereaved woman to be preserved since the Middle Irish texts mentioned earlier, is an unusual fourteenth-century example. It is strongly reminiscent of a celebrated elegy from the mid-fourteenth century 'Repair ye the prince's tunic' in which the poet addresses the palace ladies who received the torn and blood-stained clothes of the murdered king Aodh Ó Conchobhair, slain in 1356 in revenge for his abduction of his vassal's wife. This laments each separate mark left by the stab-wounds, as Mark Anthony is represented lamenting the bloodstained robes of Julius Caesar.[14] But the poem of condolence which echoes it is a short amateur piece, 'O tunic of Dermot's son' and it is composed by the third earl of Desmond, Earl Gerald the Rymer, for the bereaved Mór, daughter of Mac Donnchaidh, widow of his Irish ally Cormac son of Diarmaid Mac Carthaigh of Muskerry.[15] Though she asked to have the

11 G. Murphy (ed.), *Early Irish lyrics: eighth to twelfth century* (Oxford, 1956), no. 37. 12 N.J.A. Williams (ed.), *The poems of Giolla Brighde Mac Con Midhe* (Dublin, 1980), poem no. 19. 13 Ibid., poem no. 2, verses 15, 19–21. 14 L. McKenna (ed.), *Aithdioghluim Dána*, 2 vols, text in vol. 1, transl. in vol. 2 (Dublin, 1939, 1940), poem no. 3. 15 This

bloodstained tunic of the dead man sent back to her, he says, it would only increase her sorrow. The Earl sorrows too, as he thinks of Cormac's wounds. A similar bloodstained tunic, was sent home to the widow of Diarmaid, Cormac's father, and the legendary Gráinne, daughter of the highking Cormac mac Airt also received a bloodstained garment after the death of her lover Diarmaid Ó Duibhne.[16]

It is not until the fifteenth century that we have once more a fully professional, classical poem of condolence addressed by a court poet to a bereaved Irish queen. The date is 1424, when the annals tell us that Gráinne, daughter of Ó Ceallaigh (O'Kelly), and wife of Tadhg Ó Briain (O'Brien), king of Thomond or north Munster, made or perhaps caused to be made a coffin for her son by an earlier marriage, the prince Ruaidhri Ó Conchobhair (O'Conor), who died in that year and was buried in Roscommon.[17] For this event to gain entry to the annals may imply either that the queen really did make the casket with her own hands, or that she commissioned an exceptionally ornate and beautiful one, in either case suggesting she was deeply affected by her son's death. The poet, Tadhg Óg Ó hUiginn was the supreme practitioner of bardic verse in his own day, patronized by both the chief governor of Ireland, the 4th earl of Ormond and by the Great O'Neill. He had a long-lasting attachment to Gráinne's own family, the Uí Cheallaigh of Uí Mhaine (east county Galway), and he sent this poem of condolence by messenger, presumably to the court of Ó Briain in Ennis (county Clare), where Gráinne now lived. The words explicitly refer to the tenth-century Mac Coise's poem to the queen Derbáil and repeat the message of that earlier text:

> Gráinne I hear is in chains of woe, and 'twill be hard to free her; the prison of the lady of Í Maine oppresses me (too).
>
> The grief of the queen ... will be felt no longer by her if only she will hearken to my first words.
>
> Though to the queen of Ros Comáin her son's death is heavy affliction, yet she would find the anger of the Lord who created Ruaidhri to be worse still.
>
> If it be her separation from Ruaidhri that casts her down ... let her find any two folk who are never separated!

Cormac's regnal dates are normally given as 1387–1410 e.g. T.W. Moody, F.X. Martin, F.J. Byrne (eds), *A new history of Ireland, ix, Maps, genealogies, lists: a companion to Irish history part II* (Oxford, 1976) p. 156, or S.T. MacCarthy, *The MacCarthy's of Munster* reprint with commentary by The MacCarthy Mór (Arkansas, 1997), p. 497, but on the evidence here Cormac would appear to have died on or before 1398, the year the earl himself died. Mac Niocaill, see note 16 below, suggests 1388 as the date of Cormac's death. **16** G. Mac Niocaill, 'Duanaire Ghearóid Iarla' in *Studia Hibernica* 3 (1963), 46–7. **17** *A. Conn.*, pp 468–9.

Let her reflect that the (loss of) the world's glory is no cause for unhappiness; let this thought take hold of her; the world is a shadow or a dream.

Ruaidhri was given to her, ... He who took that gift away was he who gave it ...

Long ago, MacCoise, chief poet, sent as I am now sending to Gráinne southward, a messenger to the daughter of Tadhg in the North

Bitter at first Dearbháil found the wise man's words, but they caused her grief to ebb ...

Remove from thy heart, O princess the mist of sorrow for him, even though thou art loth not to yield to dejection after his loss.

Of two others I shall speak who gave poetry its due honour; do thou imitate them in giving such honour to me, if thou feelest inclined to reject my advice.

... Eochaidh's eye was given to a poet,

for a whole year Maoileachlainn entrusted rule over all Ireland to a poet like me ... thy rescue from grief shall be the third honour done to the profession of poetry

Canst thou, I ask thee now, bear to consider what I have said? If my words meet not with thy good will – well, at all events I have said enough.'[18]

The repeated statements that Gráinne may not want to listen to the poet are unusually emphatic. Since the poem is sent as a message, it was possibly commissioned by Gráinne's own family, the Uí Cheallaigh, in the hope of alleviating a real case of depression that was giving them cause for concern. Bardic poets were often commissioned to convey a blessing or good luck, for example when a new house was built, a new boat was launched, or when their patrons were seriously ill. It was taboo to the nobility of Ireland to refuse a poet's request, and they reasoned that if God was addressed with a poem which specifically asked for the patron's recovery as the reward of the eulogy, God himself would be honour-bound to grant this request.[19] In this case the poet is reinforcing the Christian message of resignation to God's will with the secular taboo against refusing a poet's request, to pressurize Gráinne into making an effort to resign herself.

Since the occasion of this poem's composition was so unusual and noteworthy, and the poet was so famous, many of his compositions being used as

18 McKenna, *Aithdioghluim Dána*, poem no. 13, verses 2–9, 16, 19–24.   19 Examples of healing poems are L. McKenna (ed.), *The book of O'Hara* (Dublin, 1951), poem no. 1; J. Carney (ed.), *Poems on the O'Reillys* (Dublin, 1950), nos. 9, 21; S. Mac Airt (ed.), *Leabhar Branach* (Dublin, 1944), nos. 10, 11, 33, 54; P. Ó Riain, 'Dán ar Shéafraidh Ó Donnchadha an Ghleanna', *Éigse* 12, pt ii (1967), 123–32.

a model for student poets to imitate in later generations,[20] and since he himself refers so explicitly to the consolation of Dearbháil as his model, it seems to me possible that it was this much-admired poem by the fifteenth-century Tadhg Óg Ó hUiginn that inspired the later poems of condolence, and that the growing practice of addressing poems directly to bereaved mothers or widows, rather than simply composing elegies in memory of the deceased, reflects the increased social and economic status of the female members of the Irish and Anglo-Irish noble families in the early modern period.

All the remaining poems in this class appear to belong to the seventeenth century. The earliest may be that addressed by Brian Ó Domhnalláin to Síle, daughter of Éamonn and widow of MacWilliam Bourke of Mayo,[21] who had earlier been scolded by the eminent poet Tadhg mac Dáire for daring to question the accuracy of the genealogy he had traced for her.[22] She may have been a comparatively young widow, for as well as being told that earthly sorrow is transient, and God wills that she should be resigned, she is also adjured not to let mourning spoil her looks: the poet deplores that through sorrow she should deliberately darken those red lips and sky-blue eyes, that curling yellow hair, snow-white side and tender knee and foot. She can hardly be reproached for the degree of sorrow she feels if one considers all that she has lost: tribute came to the house from Athlone to Limerick and from the western Owles of Mayo, poets came from Leinster and Munster, scholars from Donegal flocked to the house. She heard tales recited from every part of Ireland, musicians performed lays at the banquets. However she should put this out of her mind. Nature itself reflects the gloom she feels, but if she turned her back on sadness, the sun would shine again, and the earth yield its fruits once more. She will never again find a husband worthy of her among either the Irish or the Anglo-Irish after the death of Mac Uilliam, the best king to plunder nobles and maintain hospitality, supporter of the O'Donnells of Tír Conaill and pillar of the Bourkes.[23] These closing details seem to identify her husband as Theobald son of Walter *Ciotach*, the rebel 'marquis of Mayo' who died in 1606.

20 D. McManus, 'The Irish grammatical and syntactical tracts: a concordance of duplicated and identified citations', *Ériu* 48 (1997), 83–101 at pp 91–8, entries 7–8, 10, 16, 18, 22–3, 26, 28–9, 31, 35, 39–40, 48, 50–1, 59, 61, 70–1, 73, 75, 78, 82, 88, 93–4, 103, 108, 110–11, 113, 118, 121, 125.   21 Moody, Martin & Byrne, *A new history of Ireland*, ix, p. 121, cites three possible MacWilliam Bourkes of Mayo who flourished around AD 1600 – Theobald son of Walter *Ciotach*, deposed 1600, d. 1606; Theobald 'of the Ships', created Viscount Mayo in 1627, died 1629, and Richard son of 'the Devil's Reaping Hook' made MacWilliam in 1600, date of death unknown. The internal reference to MacUilliam as 'supporter of Uí Chonaill' makes the first of the three the most likely, as he was created by Red Hugh O'Donnell, and died before the flight of the earls took Rughraidhe O'Donnell, earl of Tirconnell, out of the country.   22 McKenna (ed.), *Aithdhioghluim Dána* no. 41.   23 'Léig thart do thuirse a Shíle' unpublished poem in Royal Irish Academy MSS 2 (23/F/16), p. 170 and 743 (A/iv/3), p. 796.

The theme of a young woman's good looks being spoiled by grief also occurs in a poem addressed by the seventeenth-century Munster poet Cúchonnacht Ó Dálaigh to a certain Úna, whose surname is not given. In this case she is mourning the death of her father. The poet counsels her to control her mind, to abandon her wild distress, the limbs the Creator made should not be wasted through any one person's death, her sunny face should not be wintered over – what could be more damaging than the change to her shining form – though she has great cause for grief, there is no point in wilfully reawakening it, she should not be a party to the death of her own soul. She should take the Virgin's Son in place of any other father, and spend her time in heartfelt grief over the wounds of His crucifixion.[24]

A series of poems written by Ulster poets during the period of the plantation of Ulster in the early seventeenth century mingle personal and political themes. Fear Flatha Ó Gnímh addresses Sorcha the wife of Captain Toirdhealbhach (mac Airt) O'Neill of Castletown, on the death of her young son, Art Óg. The whole province of Ulster, he claims, is troubled by the weeping of this one woman for her son. They were gloomy enough already after the departure of the earls of Tyrone and Tyrconnell to the east, and the confiscation of their patrimony. The death of Art Óg is another major blow. Sorcha's torment is as great as that of the tenth-century queen Gormlaith, wife of the high-king Niall Glúndubh, to whom is ascribed a poem lamenting the drowning of her son Domhnall.[25] This sombre poem would have to be described as one of condolence rather than consolation. There are no suggestions that the bereaved mother should cheer up, rather her personal grief is magnified to symbolize the political grievances of the Ulster Irish during the confiscation and plantation of their lands. A similar political message runs through the poems to the O'Donnell sisters, both Fearghal Óg Mac an Bhaird's address to Mary and Margaret, cited above, and Eoghan Ruadh Mac an Bhaird's address in 1609 to a third sister, Nuala, who was living in exile in Rome where her brother, the Earl of Tirconnell was buried. In Eoghan Ruadh's poem, the silent deserted site of the grave in Italy, which would have been crowded with noisy mourners had it been located in Donegal, symbolizes the indifference of their continental allies to the political disasters suffered by the O'Donnell family:

> Dismiss from thee for the sake of God that weighing sorrow, O daughter of O'Donnell; shortly shalt thou go on the same path, behold the steps before thee!

---

24 'Lámh ar h'aigneadh a Úna' ed. T.F. O'Rahilly, *Measgra Dánta: Miscellaneous Irish poems*, 2 (Cork 1927) 2, poem no. 60. 25 'Buaidhreadh cóigidh caoi én-mhná', unpublished poem in Trinity College Dublin Library MSS 1378 (H.5.6), p. 211 (frag.); 1291 (H.1.17), fo. 93; National Library of Ireland MS G 24, p. 27.

In hand of clay set not thy hope ... we thought, as didst thou, that
the Children of Mil had a prospect of help through those three in the
tomb when they set forth from the cold peaks of Ireland.[26]

Like the earl of Tirconnell and his brother, Hugh O'Neill, the earl of Tyrone
and his son Aodh Ruadh or Hugh the Red died in exile in Italy, and the
young Hugh's tutor, the Franciscan poet Aodh MacAingil addressed a poem
of spiritual consolation to the youth's sister Bridget O'Neill, according to the
colophon. But the poem itself is in the form of a sermon preached by the
young man's skull:

> O man who looks on this skull ... I am the head of Aodh O Neill, I
> will teach you a swift lesson, never to love this world, much that it
> promises is false: this treachery was played on me – grandson of
> O'Donnell, heir to O'Neill I was promised a territory as great as any
> in the British Isles, but all that Aodh obtained was six feet of earth in
> exile far from his homeland. Of the noblest blood in the three king-
> doms, I was about to have any wife I chose, but I lie beside a cold
> flagstone forever. I was promised hall, castle court and beautiful bower,
> I dwell till judgement day in a narrow earthen grave.[27]

As with the poem to O'Donnell's sister, lamentation over the deceitfulness of
this world of sin mingles with lamentation over the disappointment of the
political exiles at their failure to win much support for their cause from the
king of Spain or the pope.

A much more personal and less political tone is struck by the letter of
Father Bonaventura Ó hEoghasa to Janet Marward, wife of William Nugent
the poet, son of the baron of Delvin, condoling with her on the death of her
son, Richard Nugent. He reverses a cynical proverb of the Irish, "'Tis easy
sleeping on a friend's wound' meaning the sorrows of others never affect us
as much as our own. He begins his poem.

> 'Tis hard to sleep on a friend's wound ... Comrades of tested affec-
> tion, their grief is the same, their sorrow is the same, and their glad-
> ness is the same.
>
> So is it with me ... concerning thy grief, O daughter of Walter: the
> venom of the wound that has grieved thee is another wound upon my
> mind.
>
> Thy sigh, caused by suffering, is wont to overcome my sense of
> hearing: thy tear, heart's beloved, sucks the blood from my heart.

26 E. Knott, 'Mac an Bhaird's elegy on the Ulster lords', *Celtica* 5 (1960), 169–71.   27 C.
Mhág Craith (ed.), *Dán na mBráthar Mionúr*, 2 vols, 1 text, 2 trans. (Dublin, 1967, 1980),
poem no. 35.

> There has been taken from thee – how sad – thy son, the heir to thy heritage; thy sorrow's cure, thy only fosterling is dead – thy glory in this life, Janet
>
> … And yet, however painful it be to thee, if thou art vexed with Him who bestowed [him]…it is right to rebuke thee for it.
>
> God the Father – what artist is nobler – made Richard for himself: not from thee has He taken that bright hand, and not to thee did He give it in the beginning.
>
> The man's death is the door of life; his fate is no ground for anxiety … Clear now thy mournful face; dry thy sunny cheek. The pang that has entered thy heart shall depart from thee at my prayer.[28]

Once again we find a reference at the end of this poem to the almost supernatural efficacy of a poet's prayer.

The theme of the poet being wounded by his patron's grief also appears in an exceptional poem to Martha Stafford, the wealthy English wife of Sir Henry O'Neill of Clannaboy, who is being comforted, not for the death of her husband, but for an accident suffered to her arm as a result of a fall from a horse, which led to the arm itself being amputated. The Ulster bard, Domhnall Ó hEachaidhéin, told her:

> I fell from a horse in Ulster early on that Sunday morning, though I was not riding him, my heart was tortured that day while I was in Connacht beside the Sligo river. We (poets) all fell in a single day, through the maiming of one woman.[29]

The latest poem in this class dates between 1635 and 1640 and is addressed to a Scottish lady, Janet Mackenzie, wife of Domhnall Gorm MacDonald of Sleat, condoling with her on the death of her daughter Catherine. It is probably the work of the foremost Scottish bard of his day, Cathal Mac Mhuirich. It has the same elements of rebuking despair and resistance to God's will, and urging the lady to reward and honour the poet by granting his petition that she should cheer up, that are found in the tenth century poem to queen Derbáil or the fifteenth-century poem of Tadhg Óg Ó hUiginn to the Ó Ceallaigh princess:

> O Janet, comfort your heart, understand now, my dear, that you must do the Lord's will and avoid giving Him offence …
>
> For God's sake cease from your mourning: offer your daughter to the High King; give joys precedence over sorrow that you may abandon your career of grief.

---

28 Bergin, *Irish bardic poetry*, poem no. 36, verses 1, 3–5, 8, 14–17.   29 T. Ó Donnchadha (ed.), *Leabhar Cloinne Aodha Buidhe* (Dublin 1931), poem no. 32, verses 6–8.

Abandon your grief for high spirits, for mirth, for dalliance with warriors; exchange your dejection for merriment, ... understand that God only gave mankind a temporary lease on this world.

It is fitting for you of the languid eye, if you listen to my words, to receive a lay to check grief and be silent in honour of my art.

Although we are loth that she should go to heaven, it is joyful for Catherine ... She is among angels and virgins ... we should not mourn because she is gone.

If sadness of heart because of her death were of any profit to her or to us, I would have something whereby to help grief with a ready pledge of poems.[30]

There are certainly archaic aspects to this class of poems, the theme of rebuking grief for the death of a loved one, because it implies rebellion against God's will is constant throughout, as is the theme of the respect due to a poet's admonition, and the almost magical efficacy of his verse. But I think it is no accident that the overwhelming majority of the surviving examples are addressed to ladies in the first half of the seventeenth century. This was a period of transition into the modern world when the feelings of women as individuals, and their intellectual capacity were receiving greater attention in the context of the humanist ideals of the North European Renaissance. More importantly, from the second half of the sixteenth century onwards the Gaelic system of 'bride-price' marriages was giving way to English-style arrangements with jointures and widow's dower giving a new financial standing to the wives and especially the widows of Gaelic lords.[31] Many wives or sisters of exiled Gaelic chiefs were in receipt of quite generous pensions from the Spanish, or in some cases the English government.[32] In the first half of the seventeenth century women, to a greater extent than ever before, had the economic power to act as patrons in Gaelic Ireland, and the poets responded to this practical consideration.

30 A. Matheson (ed.), 'Poems from a manuscript of Cathal Mac Muireadhaigh', *Éigse* 11 (1964), 7–10.   **31** K.W. Nicholls, 'Irishwomen and property in the sixteenth century' in M. MacCurtain & M. O'Dowd (eds), *Women in early modern Ireland* (Edinburgh 1991), pp 17–31; M. Mac Neill, *Máire Rua: Lady of Leamaneh*, ed. M. Murphy (Whitegate, Co. Clare 1990), pp 13–15, 20–1, 40–1, 67, 79; P. Breatnach (Paul Walsh), 'Dánta Bhriain Uí Chorcráin' in *Irisleabhar Muighe Nuadhad* (1929), 47–8.   **32** P. Walsh, 'Red Hugh O'Donnell's youngest sister, Mary' in idem, N. Ó Muraíle (ed.), *Irish leaders and learning through the ages* (Dublin, 2003), pp 331–2; ed. N. Ó Muraíle, *From Ráth Maoláin to Rome* (Rome, 2007), pp 423–5, 427, 442; *Calendar of state papers Ireland, 1608–10*, pp 183, 216, 429, 540, 543–4.

Lover of widows: St Jerome and female piety

CATHERINE LAWLESS

In a vision of the Swedish mystic St Birgitta (1302–20) the Blessed Virgin recommended St Jerome (c. 362–420) to her as a 'lover of widows'.[1] The soul of the Roman mystic Francesca Romana (1384–1440) was led by St Jerome to witness the heavenly court presided over by Christ.[2] Catherine of Siena (c. 1347–80) wrote of St Jerome as one of those ministers who had shed great light 'on this bride, as lamps set on a lampstand, dispelling errors with their true and perfect humility'.[3] Aged seven, Colomba of Rieti (1467–1501) had a vision of Christ with Saints Peter, Paul, Dominic and Jerome, the latter accompanied by his lion. After deciding to consecrate her life to virginity the saints and Christ disappeared, but the lion of St Jerome remained with her throughout the night, disappearing only at dawn and leaving behind a sweet perfume. She took this to mean that the lion would protect her consecrated virginity.[4]

To modern sensibility, St Jerome is an unlikely spokesman for female emancipation. His often quoted text: 'as long as woman is for birth and children, she is different from man as body is from soul. But if she wishes to serve Christ more than the world, then she will cease to be a woman and will be called man' does little to endear him to contemporary female students although it does provoke interesting discussions on gender, the body and soul, and history.[5] Yet, as I shall show, St Jerome had a distinct cult among medieval women. His cult has been examined by Eugene Rice who argued that devotion to the saint was particularly appropriate in the Renaissance, because as the translator of the bible from Greek to Latin he could be seen as a proto-humanist.[6] Millard Meiss examined his treatment in medieval Italian art and argued that his penitential, ascetic life spent in the deserts of North Africa made him a saint dear to the penitential movement of the late Middle Ages.[7] Bernard Ridderbos examined the cult and its iconography in

1 Birgitta of Sweden, *The Liber Celestis of Saint Bridget of Sweden*, ed. Roger Ellis, Early English Text Society (Oxford, 1987), p. 448.   2 Santa Francesca Romana, *Fioretti Spirituali (Visioni e Divine Consolazioni)*, ed. D. Modesto Scarpini (Florence, 1923), pp 48–9.   3 Catherine of Siena, *The Dialogue*, ed. Susanne Noffke (New York, 1980), p. 222. See also pp 155–6.   4 Alfredo Cattabiani, *Santi d'Italia*, 2 (Milan, 2004), I, 273.   5 *Commentariorum in Epistolam ad Ephesios libri III*, in *Mariae* in *PL* 27, col. 533: *Sin autem Christo magis voluerit servire quam saeculo, mulier esse cessabit, et dicetur vir, quia omnes in perfectum virum cupimus occurrere*. Translation taken from Bonnie S. Anderson & Judith P. Zinsser, *A history of their own: women in Europe from pehistory to the pesent* (London, 1981), p. 83.   6 E.F. Rice Jr, *Saint Jerome in the Renaissance*, Johns Hopkins Symposia in Comparative History, 13 (Baltimore, 1985).   7 Millard Meiss, 'Scholarship and penitence

greater detail, with reference to medieval penitence and humanistic learning.[8] Katherine Gill, one of the few authors to examine the role of St Jerome in the female piety of the later Middle Ages, has demonstrated the dissemination not only of his own texts but also that vast corpus of writings which claimed to be by him and showed its importance for medieval women in the production and reception of vernacular literature in Italy.[9]

The late Middle Ages saw a massive growth in lay involvement in religious activity. Influenced by Cistercian spirituality, the mendicant orders and increased interest in Eucharistic and Marian cults, a spirituality emerged that has often been described as affective, involving deep emotional involvement with the life and sufferings of Christ. In practice this was seen in the growth of lay confraternities, flagellant movements and anchoritic and penitential lives often led within the orbit of the mendicant orders. This 'devotional revolution', to borrow the phrase coined by Emmet Larkin in his study of religious revival in nineteenth-century Ireland, has been seen by scholars to be of particular importance to women.[10] The penitential movement of the Middle Ages also allowed a meaningful role for the laity, and lay women in particular. As noted by Anna Benvenuti Papi, women began to outnumber men in the ranks of lay saints 'even if these laywomen were increasingly monasticized, cloaked in religious habits, and assimilated (often in retrospect) as members of some regular community'.[11]

Penitential movements offered a way in which the laity, which was barred from traditional monastic life, could live a life of piety, charity and devotion. Some of these were affiliated to the mendicant orders, but nearly all were operating within the same framework of piety.[12] Female piety could partake of these more flexible penitential arrangements, and indeed, the penitential movement of the twelfth and thirteenth centuries has been identified as almost synonymous with the women's religious movement during the same

in the early Renaissance: the image of St Jerome', *Pantheon*, 32:2 (1974), 134–40. Also see John Henderson, 'Penitence and the laity in fifteenth-century Florence', in Timothy Verdon & John Henderson (eds), *Christianity and the Renaissance: image and religious imagination in the Quattrocento* (Syracuse, NY, 1990), pp 229–49 (especially at 237).   8 Bernard Ridderbos, *Saint and symbol: images of St Jerome in early Italian art* (Gronigen, 1984).   9 Katherine Gill, 'Women and the production of religious literature in the vernacular, 1300–1500', in E.A. Matter & John Coakley (eds), *Creative women in medieval and early modern Italy: a religious and artistic Renaissance* (Philadelphia, 1994), pp 64–104. On the 'Pseudo-Jerome' Corpus, see also E.F. Rice, *St Jerome*, passim, but especially at pp 39, 152.   10 Emmet Larkin, 'The Devotional Revolution in Ireland, 1850–75', *American Historical Review*, 72 (1972), 625–52.   11 Anna Benvenuti Papi, 'Mendicant friars and female pinzochere in Tuscany: from social marginality to models of sanctity,' in Daniel Bornstein & Roberto Rusconi (eds), *Women and religion in medieval and Renaissance Italy*, trans. M.J. Schneider (Chicago, 1996) pp 84–103 (at p. 84).   12 The difficulties of defining various groups of penitential men and women and of separating them from the more traditional monastic groups have been outlined by Duane Osheim, 'Conversion, conversi, and the Christian life in late medieval Tuscany,' *Speculum* 58 (1983), 368–90.

period.[13] Women sometimes lived in small communities without the sanction of a male-authored monastic rule. In Northern Europe these women were called beguines, in Italy they were known as *pinzochere*, or *bizzoche* and the church made many attempts to bring them within the confines of clerical control, usually by making them members of the more flexible third order rather than the supposedly cloistered second order of nuns.

St Jerome was a useful model for female penitence; he was himself a penitent, and he had given advice and inspiration to women living penitential lives. Thus, it could be said that he endorsed female penitence whether *in domis propriis* or in small communities. Not only were there the extant letters that he wrote to the Roman widow Paula (d. 404) and her daughter Eustochium (d. 418) in their monastery, but his admission that he had lost count of his daily letters to the latter facilitated the growth of a large body of literature attributed to him, including a late thirteenth or early fourteenth century rule for nuns.[14]

Another reason why Jerome was popular with women was that his piety could be imitated. The Christian ideal of martyrdom was difficult to achieve for the urban lay woman in the late Middle Ages, but the ascetic lives of the early desert fathers and mothers could be imitated, either in one's own home, or in religious communities, or within an anchoritic cell. Jerome's own writings linked asceticism, sanctity and martyrdom, for example, in his letter to Eustochium on the death of Paula: '... your mother is crowned by her long martyrdom. It is not only the shedding of blood that is computed in confession, but the service of a devoted mind is also a daily martyrdom.'[15] Jerome was the perfect role model for penitence for both sexes. His desperation, recounted in his famous letter on virginity to Eustochium, evoked the penitence of Mary Magdalen: 'When all else failed, I lay down at Jesus' feet, watered them with my tears, and wiped them with my hair'.[16] His sanctity had more in common with those saints of the later Middle Ages, described by Vauchez as 'new' saints than with early Christian saints in that his holiness was achieved through prayer, penitence, fasting and teaching rather than through blood martyrdom.[17] This was a sanctity that could be imitated, and Jerome had given gender specific information on how to achieve it.

> Have a set of letters made for her, of boxwood or of ivory, and tell her their names. Let her play with them, making play a road to learning,

13 Katherine Gill, 'Open monasteries for women in late medieval and early modern Italy: two Roman examples', in C.A. Monson (ed.), *The crannied wall: women, religion and the arts in early modern Europe* (Ann Arbor, MN, 1992), pp 15–47 (at p. 18).   14 Regula Monachorum, *PL*, 30, 391–426. E.F. Rice, 'St Jerome's "Vision of the Trinity": an iconographical note', *Burlington Magazine* 125:960 (1983), 151–3, 155 (at p. 152).   15 Jerome to Eustochium, Epistle 108, 31 in *PL*, 22, 878–906 (905); also in *Sancti Eusebii Hieronymi Epistulae*, ed. Isidorus Hilberg, 3 (New York, 1970).   16 Jerome, Epistle 22. *PL*, 395–425 (at 398).   17 See E.F. Rice, *Saint Jerome*, p. 30.

and let her not only grasp the right order of the letters and remember
their names in a simple song, but also frequently upset their order and
mix the last letters with the middle ones, the middle with the first.
(Letter 107, to Laeta, 403)[18]

The authority to practice penitential lives at home or in a religious community could be found in the writings of St Jerome, and those writings attributed to him. Jerome encouraged his female friends to read and to bring up
their daughters to read, as can be seen in the letter, written in 403, advising
on the education of Paula, the young granddaughter of St Paula. Medieval
female literacy is hard to measure, and literacy itself is a question complicated
by whether one means by the word the ability to read and write in Latin, or
just in the vernacular, or the ability to read but not write, or that of reading
certain types of texts but not others.[19] Although there was certainly a discourse which did not encourage women reading, the number of devotional
anthologies owned by, and in some cases, copied by, women is numerous.
Gill has demonstrated how devotional texts were disseminated from convents
such as the Dominican S. Caterina in Pisa, encouraged by the charismatic
Dominican friar Fra Domenico de Cavalca (*c.*1260–1342), who translated St
Jerome's Lives of the Desert Fathers into the vernacular, and the Florentine
female Dominican convent of S. Jacopo de' Ripoli, which later in the fifteenth
century also became an important centre for printed book production.

Jerome's writings, legends about St Jerome and texts attributed to him are
ubiquitous in the vernacular anthologies in Florentine libraries, often owned
by the laity and loaned to friends for copying and then passed down through
generations. Biblioteca Nazionale Centrale di Firenze (henceforth BNCF) MS
Palatino 93, a fourteenth century manuscript, added to in the sixteenth century, contained the legend of St Jerome 'The blessed Jerome, according to
what he himself says at the end of one of his books'.[20] The fourteenth century BNCF MS Palatino 5 contained Jerome's Letter to Demetrias, his consolatory letter to a sick friend, his letter to a monk on monastic life, his letter
to Heliodorus on contempt of the world and the solitary life, and his letter
to Eustochium on 'on the love of virginity'.[21] The same material is found in a
manuscript owned at one stage by the Adimari family in Florence, this time

18 Letter 107 to Laeta, in *Select letters of St Jerome*, pp 344–5. *PL*, 22, Epistle 107, col.
867–73 (at 871).   19 On female literacy, see Christiane Klapisch-Zuber, *Women, family
and ritual in Renaissance Italy*, trans. Lydia Cochrane (London, 1985), and Judith Bryce,
'Les livres des Florentines: reconsidering women's literacy in quattrocento Florence', in
Stephen J. Milner (ed.), *At the margins: minority groups in premodern Italy* (Minneapolis,
2005), pp 133–62.   20 BNCF MS Palatino 93, ff.1r–24v. See Luigi Gentile, *I Codici
Palatini*, 2 (Rome, 1885–9), I, 86–8. The best discussion of these anthologies is in Dale
Kent, *Cosimo de' Medici and the Florentine Renaissance* (London, 2000), ch. 6.   21 BNCF
MS Palatino 5, f.1r–28v; 29r–43r; 64r–73r, 79v–115r. L. Gentile, *I Codici Palatini*, I, 5–6.

translated, according to the inscription, by a friar of the religious order dedicated to St Jerome, the Gesuati.[22] Laywomen, such as Costanza, widow of Benedetto Cicciaporci, commissioned copies of Cavalca's Lives of the Desert Fathers for her own instruction and that of her daughters.[23] Another manuscript copy of the lives of the Desert Fathers was, according to an inscription, copied in 1463 in the house of Maria della Rossa of Siena.[24] Through texts such as the Lives of the Desert Fathers, women could emulate the piety of the old hermits of both sexes. Despite its name, the text contained the lives of many female saints such as Mary Magdalen, Mary of Egypt, Thais, Pelagia, and Melania the Elder and showed that women could even aspire to sanctity through penitence, rather than martyrdom.

Part of the attraction of St Jerome was that his authority could be used to legitimize various forms of female religious life that could otherwise be condemned as unorthodox and possibly even heretical. Female monasticism had always posed a problem in terms of legitimacy and authority. As sacramental authority was vested in a male priesthood, no female religious community could be entirely enclosed without any male contact. Various religious rules were drawn up which in different measures allowed or restricted male access to female religious houses. *Cura monialium*, or care of (or responsibility for) nuns was a continuous source of tension between female convents and their male counterparts, or between monastic orders and local bishops. Some of these tensions can even be seen in the times of Jerome himself, but they were to be become ever more frequent in the later Middle Ages with the development of new religious orders, notably the second and third orders of the mendicant movement.

For instance, although the early Clarissan nuns worked for their own needs and were provided for by the nearby Franciscan friars, their struggles reveal much about the problems facing female communities in the Middle Ages. A community of undefended women living together without any clear male authority or rule was highly subversive and soon attempts were made to force the women to submit to older forms of Benedictine monasticism.[25] Such

---

22 BNCF MS Palatino 19, f.1r–5r (Life of St Jerome); 5v–20r, and 75r–105r (letter to Demetrias); 20r–30v (letter to a monk on monastic life); 36v–75r (letters to Eustochium). This codex also contains texts by Jerome and the pseudo-Jerome on the Assumption of the Virgin. L. Gentile, *I Codici Palatini*, I, 19–21. See also BNCF MSS Palatino 35; 13; 41 (where the translation is explicitly given to Cavalca); 73; *Palatino* 39 (also including a life of St Paula); 42 (letter to Susanna, 'fallen into fornication'); 68 (also including Cavalca's text *Medicina dell'cuore*); 69 (owned by Vespasiano da Bisticci, the bookseller); 104; 30; 35. 23 BNCF MS II, III, 89. See Carlo Delcorno, 'Cavalca, Domenico', *Dizionario Biografico Italiano* (Rome, 1979), XXII, 577–86. 24 BNCF MS Palatino 130, f.185r. For details see L. Gentile, *I Codici Palatini*, I, 117–18. *Biblioteca Riccardiana* MS 1273 contained Cavalca's Meditations on the Life of Christ and the Mirror of Sins and was owned, according to the inscription on the flyleaf, by Antonia, wife of Cristofano di Leonardo Rondinelli. D. Kent, *Cosimo de' Medici and the Florentine Renaissance*, p. 429 n. 25 For

attempts were highly distressing to St Claire, as the Benedictine rule allowed for the holding of property, an idea which denied the Franciscan ideal of apostolic poverty. In 1216 Claire was granted the Privilege of Poverty by Pope Innocent IV (d. 1254), although the women were forced to follow the Benedictine rule in other respects. Claire redacted her own rule, based on the rule of St Francis and on his last testament, which was accepted only two days before her death in 1253, and which soon became binding not on the Clarissan order itself, but only on her own convent of S. Damiano and one or two others.[26] The 'problem' of female monasticism was not only one of uncontrolled female piety, but resentment from the male mendicant houses who were charged with their spiritual and material governance, a duty made explicit by Gregory IX in 1227.[27] The figure of St Jerome could thus be seen as useful model for male authority within the world of female piety.

Clarissan devotion to St Jerome can be shown by several images. A painting of *c.*1360–5 in Altenburg by Giovanni del Biondo (fl. 1356–92) shows St Jerome with three Clarissan donor figures. St Jerome is accompanied by an inscription*: Ornate o filie lampades vestras occurrite sponso quia jam ad hostium pulsat.*[28] A panel in the Vatican attributed to the Master of the Straus Madonna (fl.1390–1420) shows St Eustochium dressed in a Clarissan habit, accompanied by her mother, St Paula. The Clarissan nun Suor Battista, daughter of Benedetto de' Nobili commissioned Sano di Pietro (1405–81) to paint an altarpiece for the Sienese Clarissan convent of S. Petronilla in 1479.[29] The painting depicted the Assumption of the Virgin with Sts Catherine of Alexandria (a popular conventual choice due to her mystic marriage with Christ, a model of the sister's own nuptial vows), Michael the Archangel, Jerome and the titular of the convent, Petronilla. The scene was flanked by SS. John the Baptist (Battista's name-saint) and John the Evangelist. In 1508 the Clarissan nuns of the Florentine convent of Monte Domini commissioned Andrea del Sarto to paint an altarpiece for a church in Monte Albano depicting the Virgin and Child with Sts Justus, Francis, Jerome and Claire.[30]

Unregulated piety was feared as it had the potential to lead to heresy. A Sienese, Giovanni Colombini (1304–67) converted when his wife, angry at

disquiet on groups of religious women living without any particular rule, see V.M. Talò, *Il monachesimo femminile: La vita delle donne religiose nell'Occidente medievale* (Milan, 2006) p. 286, citing canon 26 of Lateran II, and p. 289 on Lateran IV, cos.XII, *De nimia*.   **26** André Vauchez, *Ordini Mendicanti e società italiana (XIII–XIV secolo)* (Milan, 1990), p. 52.   **27** Chiara Frugoni, *Una solitudine abitata: Chiara d'Assisi* (Bari, 2006), p.12.   **28** Epistle 9, in *PL*, 30, col. 142. George Kaftal, *Saints in Italian art: iconography of the saints in Tuscan painting* (Florence, 1952), cols. 521–34, no.158 (k); C.B. Strehlke, *Italian paintings 1250–1450 in the John G. Johnson collection and the Philadelphia Museum of Art* (Philadelphia, 2004), p.79, n. 24, for attribution and dating; C. Frugoni, *Una solitudine*, p. 82 for the nuns. **29** Now in Siena, Pinacoteca no. 259–60. Diana Norman, 'Sano di Pietro's Assunta Polyptych for the convent of Santa Petronilla in Siena', *Renaissance Studies*, 19:4 (2005), 433–57 (at 437).   **30** Andrea Natali, *Andrea del Sarto* (New York, 1999), pp 14–15.

him for his impatience for his dinner, threw him a copy of the legend of St Mary of Egypt, a penitent prostitute who had lived and died in the desert.[31] His conversion involved founding a movement which received its name of Gesuati due to the frequency with which its members praised the name of Jesus. His wife wryly complained that she had asked for rain, not a flood.[32] Gesuati devotion to St Jerome as a penitent and as a learned authority was profound, and was found even more in the female branch of the order, founded by Colombini's cousin, Caterina.[33] She promoted the movement among women and was influential in setting up a Gesuati house for women in Florence under the dedication of St Jerome: S. Girolamo delle Poverine.[34] The Franciscan female tertiary house of S. Girolamo sulla Costa was in existence by 1417, having its foundation in a looser group of penitent women from 1377 onwards.[35] A number of female tertiary houses in Tuscany were dedicated to St Jerome.[36]

> A widow who is freed from the marital bond has but one duty laid upon her, and that is to continue as a widow. It may be that some people are offended by her sombre garb: they would be offended also by John the Baptist, and yet among those born of women there has not been a greater than he. (Jerome, Letter to Marcella, 384.)[37]

The reasons why Birgitta of Sweden was drawn to St Jerome are not hard to find: she was a widow herself for forty years, led a life of religious penitence and, like Paula, travelled to the Holy Land.[38] She had founded her own order and given it the Rule dictated to her by an angel and could thus be consid-

---

31 D. Weinstein & R. Bell, *Saints and society: the two worlds of western Christendom, 1000–1700* (Chicago, 1982), p. 116.   32 E.F. Rice, *Saint Jerome*, p. 69.   33 Gesuati houses were often dedicated to St Jerome, for instance, S. Girolamo in Siena, which housed an elaborate altarpiece by Sano di Pietro in 1444 (Diana Norman, *Painting in late medieval and Renaissance Siena* (London, 2003), p. 184); S. Girolamo in Pistoia and S. Girolamo in Pisa (Isabella Gagliardi, *I trofei della croce: L'esperienza gesuata e la soccietà lucchese tra Medioevo ed Età Moderna* (Rome, 2005), p. 16n).   34 Giuseppe Richa, *Notizie istoriche delle chiese fiorentine*, 10 (Florence, 1754–62), X, 234; Anna Benvenuti Papi, *'In castro poenitentiae.' Figure e modelli femminili nella rappresentazione della santità (sec. XII–XIV): Santità e società femminile nell'Italia medievale*. Italia Sacra. Studi e Documenti di Storia Ecclesiastica 45 (Rome, 1990), pp 520, 524–5, 528.   35 Walter Paatz & Elizabeth Paatz, *Die Kirchen von Florenz*, 6 (Frankfurt-am-Main, 1940–54) II, 344–9; G. Richa, *Notizie*, X, 233; V, 274. There was a convent of Gesuate nuns in Lucca, also dedicated to St Jerome (Alessandro Da Morrona, *Pisa illustrata nelle arti del disegno* (Livorno, 1812), p. 214).   36 For example, one in Arezzo, founded by a widow in 1439, Castiglion Fiorentino founded between 1429 and 1450, Colle Valdelsa, founded before 1568, Montepulciano and S. Girolamo di Campansi in Siena (Benvenuti Papi, *'In castro poenitentiae'*, pp 547–8; 550–2, 568).   37 Letter 38 to Marcella, in *Select letters of St Jerome*, ed. F.A. Wright (Cambridge, MA, 1933). *PL*, 22: 463–5 (at 464).   38 *Vita Brigittae*, in J. Bolland & G. Hensen (eds), *Acta Sanctorum* (Antwerp, 1643–), *Octobris* 4 (1780), 368–560.

ered, like Jerome, as a founder of a monastic order. The Virgin, in one of her frequent appearances to St Birgitta, advised her that those who followed the teachings of St Jerome were blessed, and that he was a lover of widows.[39] However, the association between virtuous widowhood and St Jerome was not confined to the visions of St Birgitta. The fiery Franciscan friar Bernardino of Siena (1380–1444) cited St Jerome as his authority when telling Italian women how they could be widows of God: they were to always be active, to read their hours of the Virgin and other devotional texts, and to do needle-work and other useful things. If clothes were not needed for themselves and their families, they could make them for the poor.[40] Bernardino quotes Jerome's letter to Eustochium in telling mothers to bring their daughters to sermons so that she will learn what is of God and the saints, adding helpfully that 'you know nothing of God, don't teach her, she will not learn'.[41] He reit-erated Jerome's advice on keeping virginity, 'guard, guard well, guard! Guard her from her brother: guard her from her brother-in-law or from her cousin; guard her from however many relatives you have: even from her father she should be guarded.'[42] Like Jerome, Bernardino stressed the importance of not remarrying and time and again used as an example of a widow of God the prophetess Anna, so often cited in Jerome's letters to the Roman matron Marcella.[43] The Dominican Giovanni Dominici (1355–1419) in his advice to Bartolomea Obizzi reminded her of how, if she were widowed, to behave in her widowhood, 'Staying in your choice to live as a common widow among your family, you will avail of the holy rules of Paul teaching on Timothy; and more broadly in many letters the doctor St Jerome will teach you'.[44] Catherine of Siena, in a letter to an elderly widow, Colomba, also cited Jerome's advice to widows on how to lead a humble and penitent life.[45]

Jerome's letters were also in sympathy with medieval conceptions of the incompatibility of sanctity with family life, or at least the difficulty in recon-ciling sanctity and family life. Jerome's distaste for remarriage and his advice

---

39 *Liber Celestis*, p. 278.   **40** Bernardino da Siena, *Le Prediche Volgari Inedite, Firenze 1424–1425–Siena 1425*, ed. P. Dionisio Pacetti (Siena, 1935), pp 243–4.   **41** Ibid.: *Tu non sai niente di Dio, non gli insegni, et essa non impara.*   **42** Ibid.: *… guarda, ben guarda, guarda! Guardala dal fratello: guardala dal cognato e dal cugino: guardala da quanti parenti che tu hai: insino dal padre si vogliono guardare.*   **43** San Bernardino da Siena, *Le Prediche*, pp 249–50. Anna the Prophetess is repeatedly cited as an example of a virtuous widow, see Domenico Cavalca, *I Frutti Della Lingua, Volgarizzamento del Dialogo di San Gregorio e dell'Epistola di S. Girolamo ad Eustochio*, ed. G. Bottari (Milan, 1837), p. 13; Giovanni Dominici, *La Regola del Governo di Cura Familiare*, ed. D. Salvi (Florence, 1860), pp 104–5. For her use by Savonarola in the late fifteenth century, see Girolamo Savonarola, *A guide to righteous living and other works*, ed. Konrad Eisenbichler (Toronto, 2003), pp 192, 196.   **44** Giovanni Dominici, *Regola*, p. 101: *Stando tua elezione di viver come vedova comune infra' tuoi, serverai le sante regole di Pagolo insegnando sopra ciò Timoteo; e più dif-fusamente in molte pistole t'insegnerà san Ieronimo dottore.* See p. 104.   **45** Caterina da Siena, *Le Lettere di Santa Caterina da Siena*, ed. P. Giuseppe di Caccia, 3 (Bologna, 1996–9), 1, letter 166 (at p.96).

to widows can be seen enacted in the lives of many religious women; an example is seen in the Pisan Tora Gambacorta (1362–1419), forced into marriage at thirteen and widowed by fifteen, who fled home and took refuge in a Franciscan convent, taking the name of Chiara (Claire), in order to avoid another marriage. Under the influence of Alfonso Pecha, himself a brother of the Girolamite Fray Pedro Fernandez de Pecha, Chiara's parents allowed her to profess as a religious.[46] The replacement of earthly family with spiritual families is recounted in a heartbreaking fashion by the Dominican Jacobus De Voragine (d. 1298) in the *Legenda Aurea*, when he recounts St Paula leaving her little son Toxocius as she departed for Jerusalem: 'While the sails were hoisted and the ship, propelled by the rowers, was heading toward the deep, little Toxocius stood on the shore with outstretched, pleading hands. Yet Paula, dry-eyed, looked toward heaven, putting her love of God above her love for her children. She knew not herself as a mother in order to prove herself Christ's handmaid. As she fought her grief, her entrails were twisted in pain as if being torn from her body. Her full faith made her able to bear this suffering: more than that, her heart clung to it joyfully, and for love of God she put aside love of her sons and daughters.'[47]

The renunciation of children is a recurring *topos* in the *Vitae* of many female saints. The life of the thirteenth-century widow, the blessed Chiara Ubaldini recounted how she had left her twin sons after having spent a night in between them crying. She yearned for peace to meditate upon God in the quiet of the Clarissan house of Monticelli.[48] Voragine stressed how Elizabeth of Hungary (1207–31) married out of respect for her parents' wishes rather than carnal desire, and that upon her husband's death she refused to remarry, donning the habit of the Franciscan tertiary instead. He then told of how Elizabeth prayed to be rid of maternal love in order to free herself to serve God:

> Then, in order that her spirit might move more totally to God and her devotion be unhampered by distraction or impediment, she prayed the Lord to fill her with contempt for all temporal goods, to take from her

46 A.M. Roberts, 'Chiara Gambacorta of Pisa as patroness of the arts', in E.A. Matter & John Coakley (eds), *Creative women in medieval and early modern Italy: a religious and artistic Renaissance* (Philadelphia, 1994), pp 120–54 (at p. 122). On the Hieronymites or Girolamites, see Ignazio de Madrid, 'Gerolamini', in Giancarlo Rocca (ed.), *La sostanza dell'effimero. Gli abiti degli ordini religiosi in Occidente* (Rome, 2000), pp 431–2. **47** Jacopo de Voragine, *The Golden Legend*, ed. W.G. Ryan, 2 (Princeton, 1993), II, 122; his source was Jerome's letter to Eustochium, *Sancti Eusebii Hieronymi Epistulae*, ed. Isidorus Hilberg, 3 (New York, 1970), ep. 108. *PL*, 22, 6 (891): *Jam carbasa tendebantur, et remorum ductu navis in altum protrahebatur. Parvus Toxotius supplices manus tendebat in littore.* Translation and text available at http://epistolae.ccnmtl.columbia.edu/letter/445.html, accessed 31 July 2009: Already with the sails hoisted and the oars bringing the ship out to sea, little Toxotius held out his hands a supplicant on the shore ...' **48** G. Richa, *Notizie*, IV, 190.

heart her love for her children, and to grant her indifference and constancy in the face if every insult.[49]

Her prayer was answered and she told her women that she cared for her children no more than for others around her. Her earthly family was thus replaced by a more general spiritual kinship. However, the female kinship groups, found so much in the letters of St Jerome, can be found replicated in late medieval devotional networks. Claire of Assisi's sisters, Beatrice and Agnese, followed her into a life of penitence.[50] Chiara of Montefalco's younger sister Giovanna had set up a community of penitent women under the dedication of S. Leonardo, and was the first abbess of S. Croce in 1290.[51] Catherine of Siena's aunt, Agnese, was a Dominican tertiary,[52] as was her sister-in-law, Lisa Colombini,[53] and her mother, Lapa Piagenti.[54] Vanna, the widowed mother of Colomba of Rieti, became a Dominican tertiary and joined her daughter in Perugia.[55] The sister of Filippa Mareri (1200–36) renounced her impending marriage to join Filippa in a nascent Clarissian community near Rieti, and her niece was the recipient of one of her early miracles when, after having fled to the convent, her brothers tried to take her back but she became too heavy to lift.[56]

The link between Birgitta of Sweden, Catherine of Siena and the Girolamite congregations of Italy is provided in the person of the Spanish bishop, Alfonso Pecha, who edited the Revelations of Birgitta and presented them to the pope in Avignon in 1373.[57] Alfonso's brother, Fra Pedro Fernandez, was a follower of the Girolamites in Italy led by Fra Tommasuccio da Foligno and founded a house in Spain, near Toledo.[58] In March 1374 Catherine of Siena wrote of Alfonso's visit to her in a letter sent to Bartolomeo Dominici and Tommaso Caffarini.[59] Alfonso accompanied the Pisan Girolamite, Piero Gambacorta, on his pilgrimage to the Holy Land.[60] He ended his days as a hermit near Genoa, inspired by the penitent seclusion of St Jerome.[61]

Before I became acquainted with the household of the saintly Paula, all Rome was enthusiastic about me. Almost everyone concurred in judg-

49 De Voragine, *Golden Legend*, 2, 307. **50** J.A.K. McNamara, *Sisters in arms: Catholic nuns through two millennia* (Cambridge MA, 1996), p. 306; V.M. Talò, *Il Monachesimo Femminile*, p. 306. **51** Ernesto Menestò, 'The Apostolic canonization proceedings of Clare of Montefalco, 1318–19', in Daniel Bornstein & Roberto Rusconi (eds), *Women and religion in medieval and Renaissance Italy* (Chicago, 1996), pp 104–29 (at p. 118); V.M. Talò, *Il Monachesimo Femminile*, p. 317. **52** Girolamo Gigli, *Diario Sanese. Parte prima, seconda edizione* (Siena, 1854), p. 196. **53** Caterina da Siena, *Lettere*, III, 615n. **54** Caterina da Siena, *Lettere*, II, 603n. **55** A. Cattabiani, *Santi*, I, 277. **56** A. Cattabiani, *Santi*, II, 995–6. **57** C.B. Strehlke, *Italian paintings 1250–1450 in the John G. Johnson collection and the Philadelphia Museum of Art* (Philadelphia, 2004), p. 345. **58** E.F. Rice, *Saint Jerome*, p. 69. **59** F.T. Luongo, *The saintly politics of Catherine of Siena* (New York, 2006), p. 56. **60** A.M. Roberts, 'Chiara Gambacorta', p. 144. **61** E.F. Rice, *Saint Jerome*, p. 69.

ing me worthy of the highest office in the Church. My words were always on the lips of Damasus of blessed memory. Men called me saintly. (Letter 45, to Asella.)[62]

Jerome provided instruction and support for women despite contemporary disapproval. Accusations of improper behaviour with Paula led to his departure from Rome in 385.[63] This guidance to pious women was echoed in the leadership of men who encouraged female piety, such as the Dominican, Giovanni da Salerno (d. 1242) who translated works for the *convertite* or repentant prostitutes of the Florentine convent of S. Elisabetta. He was criticized by contemporaries for doing so, 'especially at the request of women' but justified himself by referring to St Jerome.[64] Cavalca, the translator of St Jerome in Pisa, was able to intervene on behalf of the nuns of S. Anna al Renaio so that they could be released from some of the harsher effects of enclosure, and was spiritual leader of the women of S. Marta.[65] The authority of St Jerome, along with that of St Paula and St Augustine was cited by Giovanni Dominici in his *Regola*, as it was some decades later by St Antoninus, the Dominican Archbishop of Florence, in his *Opere a ben vivere* dedicated to another woman in search of spiritual consolation, Dianora Tornabuoni.[66]

I would like to conclude by looking at the convent of Annalena in Florence and the Adoration of the Child altarpiece by Fra Filippo Lippi (*c.*1406–69) as a number of the themes isolated so far – female piety and male authority, pious widowhood and devotion to St Jerome – can be seen in the ethos and daily life which influenced the commission of this artwork for this fifteenth-century Florentine convent.[67] The Adoration of the Child was painted between 1450 and 1455 and shows the Virgin and Child with Sts Joseph, Hilarion, Jerome and Mary Magdalen. The painting is unusual on a number of levels: the strange perspectival tricks played with differing levels and plains – common with Fra Filippo Lippi but otherwise little seen in Florentine art. The landscape filling the picture surface suggesting an enclosed, perhaps claustrophobic green space, is typical of the heavily forested area south of Florence which was home to spiritual retreats such as Vallombrosa and Camaldoli – the latter a hermitage patronized by the Medici and site of a similar Adoration by Lippi.[68] The cropped figure of the saint is again, unusual in Florentine painting but not in the oeuvre of Lippi. Magdalen is a figure who often appears with St Jerome and symbolizes penitence. The presence of the early desert hermit St Hilarion is more unusual, and indeed, his identity would be hard to guess without documentation surrounding the painting.

---

62 Letter 45 to Asella, in *Select letters of St Jerome*, ed. F.A. Wright, p. 183. *PL*, 22, 3 (480–4) (at 481). 63 E.F. Rice, *St Jerome*, p. 14. 64 K. Gill, 'Women and the production of literature', p. 79. 65 Ibid., p. 75. 66 Antonino Pierozzi (St Antoninus), *Opere a ben vivere*, ed. Francesco Palermo (Florence, 1858). 67 Florence, Uffizi, 8350. 68 Florence, Uffizi, 8353, *c.*1463.

The painting was, in fact commissioned by Filippo Malatesta, a relative of Annalena Malatesta (1426–90) for the female Dominican convent of San Vincenzo Ferrer founded by her.[69] Annalena was the widow of a famous soldier of fortune, Baldaccio d'Anghiari (*c.*1400–41) who had been recently murdered.[70] The murder was followed in 1450 by the death of their son, Guido Antonio.[71] Annalena, already known for her piety, wished to live a penitential life surrounded by her kinswomen and female friends. Her brother, Roberto, a Knight of Jerusalem, offered to help her remarry; Annalena refused but needed her brother's help to secure the return of her dowry and to act as her legal procurator regarding the Florentine authorities. With the help of Roberto, her dowry was returned and permission was sought from the pope and granted to found a Dominican house.[72] The choice of saints in the painting can be closely related to Annalena's personal life and choices: the Adoration of the Child itself, a theme that was popular in female piety and was also Eucharistic in nature, with the combined motif of childhood and the Eucharist embodied in the figure of the Child; the figure of Mary Magdalen, a woman who had, in popular legend, achieved sanctity despite lack of virginity through penitence and asceticism; Hilarion, clothed in the robes of the Jerusalemite knights, anachronistically, was one of the desert fathers, a disciple of St Anthony Abbot, who had lived an ascetic life in the Holy Land – the spiritual home of the Jerusalemite Order, the order of her brother; and finally, Jerome, who embodied the penitential life style to which she and her nuns aspired, whose writings gave them the power to claim patristic authority for their choice of life, and whose own spirituality seemed so close to their own.

69 A.V. Coonin, 'New documents concerning Desiderio da Settignano and Annalena Malatesta', *Burlington Magazine* 37 (1995), 792–9 (794).   70 Giovanni Cavalcanti, *Istorie fiorentine*, ed. Guido di Pino (Milan, n.d. [1943]), pp 250–1.   71 G. Richa, *Notizie*, X, 131.   72 G. Richa, *Notizie*, X, 133.

Women's experiences of war in later medieval Ireland

GILLIAN KENNY

The one thing that can be said with a degree of certainty about medieval Ireland is that throughout the period some kind of warfare was going on somewhere on the island. This activity may have consisted of raiding parties, sieges or even pitched battles and these happenings were, of course, not without consequences especially for those among the most vulnerable in society: women. There are therefore many examples of women as victims of war. Such women people the pages of the various sources as victims of rape, kidnap and murder. While such horrible episodes tell the pitiful stories of some women's experiences of warfare in their localities, they do not speak for the many and varied experiences of the whole. The fact that warfare may be said to have been endemic in medieval Ireland led to the development of women's roles not only as long-standing victims but also as inciters, facilitators, peacemakers and perhaps sometimes even warriors within the martial societies of Ireland. The term 'societies' is chosen on purpose for to all intents and purposes medieval Ireland supported two very different, yet at times overlapping, worlds. There was that of Gaelic Ireland, a society in which skirmishing and cattle raiding were vital warrior pursuits; and alongside that society existed Anglo-Ireland: a world which looked to the common law and feudalism for its inspiration and which was primarily concerned militarily with actions against the Gaelic Irish. Within these two worlds women's sufferings and triumphs make for illuminating study because of their engagement with the processes of warfare.

Despite that fact that Gaelic Ireland and Anglo-Ireland were often at odds with each other, their expectations concerning the role of women and their behaviour were similar. As in the rest of medieval Europe so in Ireland women were expected to marry, bear children and perform all the tasks related to these events. Marriage in both of these cultures was the normal state of existence for most adult women; however, there were profound differences in how women from Gaelic Ireland and Anglo-Ireland conducted their lives as married women and these differences are manifest when we examine their activities during periods of conflict in particular. The rights of the wife at marriage and her behaviour and freedoms within marriage varied enormously between the Gaelic and Anglo-Irish worlds. These differences could sometimes lead to Gaelic married women, in particular, taking sustained and active parts in the prosecution or resolution of conflict in a variety of roles that were quite unavailable to their Anglo-Irish contemporaries. Anglo-Irish women were freer to act as widows but the relatively settled areas they occupied as well as the strength of cultural expectations and taboos surrounding their behaviour meant that very few of them took advantage of their legal freedoms as widows to engage in warlike behaviour.

The key to understanding how Gaelic married women could have active roles to play in times of war lies within the Gaelic legal system. Gaelic marriage was a secular affair and within Gaelic society married women of equal status to their husbands wielded extensive legal powers regarding their own property as well as their joint property. A Gaelic Irish wife had the freedom to administer the goods she brought with her to the marriage as well as any marriage-portion settled on her by her husband. She was to be consulted in every case involving their joint land and property and had veto rights over them just as her husband had those same rights to any contract she made on her own. If her husband made a bad decision concerning joint property then his wife had the right to rescind it.[1] With respect to property that the wife may have held separately, she was allowed to sell or let it independently.[2] The married woman was regarded under Gaelic law, as having wide powers of independent contract, almost as wide as her husband.

The Gaelic woman's continuing control over her own property after her marriage could have interesting repercussions especially if, as could sometimes be the case, that property consisted of soldiers. The Annals of Loch Cé, for example, refer to the marriage of Aedh O Connor and Ailin, the daughter of Dubhgall MacSomhairle, upon which the young wife brought as her dowry 160 galloglass.[3] Dowries in Gaelic Ireland are not very well documented before the sixteenth century but, in general, they probably consisted of movables, including soldiers. In the early fourteenth century Angus Óg, lord of the Isles, married Agnes, the daughter of Cú Mhuighe O Cathain of Ulster, and he is said to have received a dowry (or a tocher, as it was known in Scotland) of 140 men of every surname in O Cathain's territory with his new wife.[4] This ability to manage such property led to certain women becoming able to wield an amount of power in their localities. By the sixteenth century, for example, there is evidence that Gaelic Irishwomen were freely accepted as witnesses and some noblewomen acted as arbitrators in disputes over property.[5] It is reasonable to assume that this was not an entirely new practice but one that had its roots in the medieval era. This ability to control her own property after marriage was the crucial difference between the lives of Gaelic

---

1 R. Thurneysen, N. Power, M. Dillon, K. Mulchrone, D.A. Binchy, A. Knoch & J. Ryan, *Studies in early Irish law* (Dublin, 1936), p. 228. 2 Ibid., p. 227. 3 *ALC* 1259. 4 Rosalind K. Marshall, *Virgins and viragos: a history of women in Scotland from 1080–1920* (London, 1983), p. 29. 5 K.W. Nicholls, 'Irishwomen and property' in Margaret MacCurtain & Mary O'Dowd (eds), *Women in early modern Ireland* (Edinburgh, 1991), pp 17–31, here p. 18.

and Anglo-Irish wives and influenced their ability to participate in martial plots and activities. For, according to the common law as it was enacted in later medieval Ireland, wives were not entitled to hold property by themselves.[6] Thus their economic independence and their power of independent action was curtailed. The married women of Anglo-Irish society were legally subject to their husbands who upon marriage effectively assumed control of all their wives' property as well as their persons.[7]

The two societies therefore differed in how they facilitated freedom of action for their women. As we shall see some of this freedom took on an actively martial aspect, not always approved of or supported by their men. The idea of a woman actively engaging in warlike activity was both feared and admired within both societies. The Gaelic Irish especially loved stories of warrior women, war goddesses and witches involved in sexual conflict and political plotting with the added bonus of magical events thrown in. The early Irish in particular were obsessed with arms-bearing women in contest with men. These may be said to represent a literary subversion of formal social roles. For in the Irish sources the war between hostile armed females and their male enemies illustrated the worst threat to social order imaginable. And so the warrior women who appear in the sagas and stories always represented trouble as they turned the world upside down through their very existence. Women like these who overstepped the bounds of social convention were – precisely because of the perversity of their behaviour – nevertheless attractive figures and a residual fascination with such rebels is found in saga, myth and poem.[8] Conversely in real life women who exhibited such behaviours were bound to have alarmed and upset their male and female contemporaries and so when they do appear in the record their impact is dramatic and unforgettable.

In a remarkable entry in the Annals of Connacht dated 1315 it is written that:

> Aed O Domnaill, king of Tir Conaill, came into Carbury and ravaged the whole district, being advised thereto by his wife, the daughter of Magnus O Conchobair. She herself, with all the gallowglasses and men of the Clan Murtagh that she could obtain, marched against the churches of Drumcliff and plundered many of its clergy.[9]

The following year Rory O Connor made peace with O'Donnell and yielded the lordship of Carbury to him. However, Dervorgilla (for that was her name) refused to acknowledge the peace her husband had made and hired another

---

6 Ibid., p. 17.   7 Peter Fleming, *Family and household in medieval England* (Basingstoke, 2001), p. 38.   8 Lisa M. Bitel, *Land of women: tales of sex and gender from early Ireland* (Ithaca, NY, 1996), pp 212–16.   9 *A. Conn.*, 1315.20, 1316.2.

band of galloglass to which she offered a reward for killing Rory. The galloglass did their job and Rory was killed in direct contravention of the wishes
of her husband and also of oaths sworn on the relics of Tirconnell.
Dervorgilla's actions indicate a woman with enormous freedom of action but
also very importantly apparently without any fear of her husband's reaction.
This lack of fear can, in part, perhaps be explained by that fact that when a
Gaelic Irish woman married guardianship of her was transferred to her husband but he was not her sole guardian. Marriage did not sever the tie
between a woman and her original family and so her own kin never relinquished all their rights and interest over her.[10] A woman like Dervorgilla, the
wife of an important Gaelic chieftain, was independently wealthy and was
also, by virtue of her marriage, entitled to some share of her husband's
authority over his territories.[11] These factors undoubtedly contributed to some
wives effectively wielding a large amount of martial and political power within
Gaelic Ireland.

To her Anglo-Irish contemporaries the military antics of Dervorgilla if
they were aware of them at all would have probably seemed both unbeliev-
able and unrealistic. Anglo-Irish wives surrendered control of themselves and
their property to their husbands when they married. That was what law and
custom expected of them. It was as widows, however, that they could begin
to approach the same sort of freedom of action (and in many cases even surpass) demonstrated by their Gaelic contemporaries. Take for example the
(somewhat fantastical) tale of Roesia de Verdun. 'Daughter', 'heiress', 'wife',
'widow', 'soldier', 'nun' and 'murderer' are just some of the titles accorded to
her over the course of her life. Her grandfather, Bertram de Verdon, was the
man who started that family's connection with Ireland. The de Verduns
quickly became an influential family in Ireland and thanks to astute marriages
they became very well connected in the Anglo-Norman community. After
Bertram's death he was succeeded by Nicholas, who was eventually succeeded
by Roesia, who was heiress to all her father's lands in Ireland and England.
Roesia married Theobald Walter in 1225 when she would have been in her
early twenties: a fairly late age for a first marriage. It is worth noting that
after her marriage to Theobald (his second marriage) she retained her maiden
name, as did her children by him (none of whom were heirs to Ormond).
Roesia bore a child every year during her short marriage. Theobald died at
Poitou in 1230 for which mercy she must have heaved a sigh of relief.

10 R. Thurneysen et al., *Studies*, pp 180–1; this included a right to a proportion of her
goods at death and also of the wergild if a stranger had killed her and they were also partly
liable for any wrongdoing she may commit. The mother-kin also had certain limited rights
in regard to her children.   11 James Hardiman, *Ancient Irish deeds and writing, chiefly
relating to landed property, from the twelfth to the seventeenth century* (Dublin, 1828), pp 93–
5 as cited in Katharine Simms, 'The legal position of Irishwomen in the later Middle
Ages', *Irish Jurist*, n.s., 10 (1975), 96–111, here p. 108.

Widowhood was no doubt welcome if only to end the exhausting cycle of endless childbearing that was the unenviable lot of upper-class women.

The year of her husband's death in 1230 marks a turning point in Roesia's activities, for a series of events followed which she very quickly capitalized on both to bolster her own power and to boost her family's power base in Louth. Shortly after she was widowed, her father died in 1231 and she was awarded his lands in 1233. Roesia was now owner of her family lands as well as administrator of her dower lands from Theobald, she was a wealthy prize whose future husband would have to be carefully considered by the king. It appears that she was in no hurry to remarry, as her first act was to pay the fine of 700 marks both for her inheritance and to ensure that she would not have to marry again. Roesia came into her own as a landholder and proved to be a very capable woman at maintaining not only her lands from her husband but also her own inheritance.

Roesia was as careful as any of her male predecessors in defending an inheritance that had vulnerable borders and she was substantially more successful than they in fortifying those lands. In 1236 she successfully erected a castle, Castleroche, to defend her lands against Irish raiders, which none of her ancestors had been able to do. The castle is still very striking today sitting as it does on a large outcrop of natural rock. While this was undoubtedly done to supplement its defensiveness, the placement was also designed to impress and strike awe into the native population. This castle would have been viewed by the local population as a blatant display of power and one of female power at that.

Roesia also built a motte at Mountbagnall and had a manor near Castletown, both outside Dundalk. Castleroche, however, is of interest as it is the focus of various local legends concerning Roesia and her martial pursuits. One is that there was in Roche Castle a window, subsequently called the 'murder window' as it was from there, on her orders, that a workman (or, in other versions, the architect of the castle) had been thrown. Another story is that she rode at the head of her men against her Gaelic enemies the O'Hanlons. According to the story she was a ferocious fighter and wore body armour. She is thus portrayed as a powerful and malicious figure, acting in a very male fashion even to the extent of wearing armour and displaying a strong ruthless streak. The reputed riding out of Roesia at the head of her troops is a striking and unusual image and akin to that of Dervorgilla and her gallowglass.

Whether events happened in Dervorgilla and Roesia's lives as they have been portrayed in both the annals and within folklore is uncertain. They may have been remembered so well precisely because they were truly anomalous in their alleged eagerness to engage in battle. No matter how wealthy or independent, for any Gaelic Irishwoman was to take up arms and lead soldiers was a remarkable event, even in the often-disturbed condition of the later medieval period. The same applies to independent-minded Anglo-Irish widows who one is more likely to find waging battles through the courts than on a field of conflict. But the possibility does also arise that at times in the violent and disturbed later medieval period in Ireland, some women emerged from the shadows and brought the fight to their enemies. Both societies provided a solid legal base (depending on whether a woman was a wife or widow) for women to do so. There is also the fact that unsettled times could also facilitate extraordinary actions. Whether either of the women described above actually wielded a sword is unknown and probably unlikely but their stories and their status as leaders of war-bands may hint at the possibilities of action that manifested themselves for women during times of extreme dislocation and stress associated with ongoing warfare. These possibilities perhaps coupled with unusually forthright and strong personalities on the part of certain women may have allowed some whose names are now lost to have played an active military part in the ongoing squabbles and vicious in-fighting of later medieval Ireland.

The lack of evidence, however, for the activities of such women leads to the conclusion that for a woman to appear on a battlefield as a prosecutor of war was a rare, if not impossible event. Both societies, however, Gaelic and Anglo-Irish, provided opportunities for differing levels of independent action depending on one's marital status. So the opportunities were there for women to behave just as violently as their male contemporaries considered it their right to. The liminal nature of societies at war allied with the economic independence of upper-class women may have enabled some women, in both societies, to ape their fathers' and brothers' military exploits (and, in Roesia's case, better them by building Castleroche) in their defence of their family lands. There can be no doubt, though, that in both societies, the role of the warrior woman was a very unusual one indeed. So unusual, in fact, that women who pursued aggressive martial policies, such as Roesia, have survived in folk memory as archetypes rather than as the flesh-and-blood creatures that they once were.

Of course not all women led soldiers on raids or were even reputed to have done so. More commonly a woman's participation in war was as an inciter of action perhaps or maybe paymaster for a band of fighters. As part of a prolonged period of particularly vicious fighting during the mid-thirteenth century for example two women appear to have issued orders resulting in various deaths. In the first instance in 1232 Donal MacCarthy, supposedly on the orders of Magnus O Coffey and his wife murdered the three sons of a neighbouring king and plundered his lands. Twenty years later Donal himself was (unsurprisingly) killed in battle against the Anglo-Irish. Popular rumour stated that this was done on the orders of Sadb, the daughter of O Brien and wife of O Donnchadha. Two years later Sadb, her husband, their three sons and her brother-in-law as well as numerous others were burned to death by Donal MacCarthy, prince of Carbury, the son of the man she had ordered killed. They were supposedly betrayed by family members.[12] Thus women entered fully into the cycle of violence and feud within Gaelic Irish society by inciting and commissioning the extreme violence that so often characterized Irish society in this period. Similarly amongst the Anglo-Irish certain women were blamed for entering into feuds and inciting men to violence. In 1333 the de Mandevilles murdered William de Burgh, the Brown Earl of Ulster, near Carrickfergus. Gyle de Burgh was blamed for inciting her husband Richard de Mandeville to take revenge on William for the death of her brother Walter de Burgh, whom William starved to death in 1332.[13] Gyle thus had a very personal reason for aiding her husband in murdering the earl of Ulster but she was not the only woman implicated in this act. It is possible that the widow of Walter de Burgh may also have had a part in pushing the Mandevilles to kill the Brown Earl.

Power politics amongst the Gaelic and Anglo-Irish elite sometimes called for women to use subtle means of survival in order to stay in favour with husbands and families. Therefore threatened women were characterized as treacherous enemies, untrustworthy and cunning and quick to use betrayal as a tactic of war. Consider the following, terse entry in McCarthy's Annals: 'The castle of Athlone was taken from the English, having been betrayed by a woman who was in it'.[14]

The reasons for the betrayal by this anonymous woman were not listed but this incident indicates just how much damage well placed women could inflict by using treachery, one of the more powerful and insidious weapons in a woman's arsenal of survival. Women were, however, by no means the only practitioners of treason: they could just as easily be the victims of it. In 1367, according to the Annals of Ulster:

> a hurtful attack was made by the sons of Aedh Mac Cathmail and the royal chief of Cenel-Feradhaigh, namely, Gilla-Patraig Mac Cathmail and his good son, Cu-Uladh junior and his wife, the daughter of Maghnus Mag Mathgamna, were killed by them in treachery. Murchadh, his brother, [succeeded] in his place after him.[15]

Perhaps the most reprehensible act of betrayal recounted in the annals, certainly one that deeply shocked Gaelic Ireland, was that involving a woman, namely the wife of Piers de Bermingham. When Piers murdered nearly 30 members of the O Connor Faly family in 1305 his wife quietly but crucially helped him. Bermingham had invited a group of the O Connors to his castle and when they arrived he murdered over 20 of them, including children he

---

12 John Lodge, *The peerage of Ireland: or a genealogical history of the present nobility of that kingdom*, 8 (Dublin, 1789), II, 12. 13 Katherine O Neill, 'Women and warfare in the Middle Ages' (unpublished M. Phil.: University of Dublin, 1998), pp 26–7. 14 *AFM*, 1455, 10. 15 *AU*, 1367, 5.

had acted as godfather to: an act that was viewed as being particularly bar-
baric by the Gaelic Irish. The annals reported that his actions against them
were so successful because his wife watched and warned him when any of the
O Connors tried to hide. Thus she was blamed for the deaths of many of the
victims.[16]

The truly horrible nature of warfare in later medieval Ireland is revealed
when a man expects his wife to call out to him the hiding places of small
children so he can throw them from his castle battlements. It is impossible to
know whether Pier's wife joined in enthusiastically or whether it was an
action that she was ashamed of and hated doing. Was she a victim or a murderer just as culpable as her husband? Her reasons for her actions and her
story has been lost but this small but affecting episode does show how women
either used or were allocated the more pernicious background roles in a society nourished by war. They may have pointed out the victims but they rarely
gave the fatal push or plunged the sword in.

When they did kill by their own hand, the medium they used could be a
subtle one: that of poison. In the Annals of the Four Masters there is the following entry under the year 1417:

> Art the son of Art, son of Murtough, son of Maurice, Lord of Leinster
> a man who had defended his own province against the English and
> Irish from his sixteenth to his sixtieth year; a man full of prosperity
> and royalty; the enricher of churches and monasteries, by his alms and
> offerings died (after having been forty-two years in the lordship of
> Leinster) a week after Christmas. Some assert that it was of a poison-
> ous drink which a woman gave to him and to O'Doran, Chief Brehon
> of Leinster at Ros-Mic-Triuin, that both died. Donough his son
> assumed his place after him.[17]

Art MacMurrough Kavanagh is generally regarded as the most formidable of
the later kings of Leinster. One might tremble at the thought of attacking Art
with a body of soldiers but he could not defend himself against poison and so
a mere woman allegedly killed the redoubtable warrior using the delicate tools
that were available to her. As to why she did it we will never know but a man
with Art's colourful biography must have made very many enemies including
women over the years only too willing to try and kill him.

Other women, particularly Gaelic Irish wives, seem to have pursued more
diplomatic courses in dealing with their enemies. In 1392–3 a safe conduct
pass was issued to Una, the wife of Niall Óg O Neill, who was going to and
from Drogheda accompanied by 12 men and women to meet with the Lord
Justice and Council.[18] A wife such as Una acting as an intermediary is not,

16 *AI*, p. 397.   17 *AFM*, 1417.   18 James Graves (ed.), *A roll of the proceedings of the*

perhaps, very unusual in wartime but a wife concluding a formal peace with her husband's enemies can be judged as more remarkable. This appears to have been the case in 1433 when Fionnuala, the wife of O Donnell and daughter of O Connor Faly, along with Nachtan O Donnell made peace with the O Neills who had been attacking them. This agreement was made without the consent or involvement of her husband as he was absent, fighting elsewhere.[19] In these instances it can be seen that high-ranking Gaelic wives were involved in political and military affairs at the highest levels and often exercised remarkable independence of action. A clear example of this arose in 1210 when a woman contributed to strategic wartime decision-making concerning the fate of her family. In that year, when King John told Cathal Crobhdearg O Connor to bring his son Aedh to meet him to receive a charter for the third part of Connacht, Cathal with 'his wife and his people' decided not to take his son to the king. The king it was reported subsequently 'took some hostages with him to England'.[20] The O Connors (including the boy's mother) had declined to approve the sending of their son as a hostage.

These women's power bases that emboldened them to participate in war councils and offer advice also enabled them to control and unify their husband's family if he was taken captive. Certainly, at the higher levels of Gaelic society, the independent action of wives was accepted in wartime and their continuing control over their own property could also come to their family's aid in times of trouble. For example, in 1422 Owen O'Neill was ransomed by his wife and family who gave his captor cattle, horses and '*other gifts*'. This type of ongoing participation in their families' wartime and political affairs was not mirrored in the Anglo-Irish world, not by wives, widows or singe women. This was a Gaelic phenomenon facilitated by the mix of social, legal and cultural traditions that enabled Gaelic wives to take active roles in the ongoing pursuit of advantage through warfare within that society.

A large part of that warfare consisted of the taking of hostages. It appears to have been a common enough practice for a man's wife to be used as a hostage in order to place a check on his behaviour. This was a tactic used both by Gaelic and Anglo-Irish lords. In 1316 the Justiciar Edmund Butler was ordered to ascertain:

> ... whether the release of More, wife of O Hanlon from prison in the town of Drogheda where she was placed by Nicholas de Verdun by whose men she was captured in war, would be injurious to the king or to the disturbance of the peace and if he finds that she can be released safely to deliver her to Nicholas to make his profit of her and if not to make *gratium* with Nicholas for what pertains to him for her capture.[21]

King's Council in Ireland for a portion of the 16th year of the reign of Richard II AD 1392–3 (London, 1877), no. 161. **19** *AFM*, 1433. **20** *ALC*, 1210. **21** Brendan Smith, 'The

The opportunities for abduction appear to have been plentiful. The sources are full of references to women being taken by opposing armies. Like in 1227 when:

> Aed mac Cathail Chrobdeirg went to Ó Domnaill in Tir Conaill. He returned south and brought away his wife. The sons of Toirrdelbach [Ó Conchobair] came upon him in the Curlew Hills and he left his wife and horses behind. The wife was afterwards delivered up to the Galls.[22]

Thus this nameless victim lost her home, her husband, probably her children too and was handed over to her enemies probably as a hostage to try and control the actions of her husband and his family: a terrible predicament but simply another story to add to a very long litany of women's travails in lawless times. Consider the case of Etain MacCarthy. In 1243 her and her husband were taken prisoner by her son (not her husband's son). She was then given away by her own son Tadhg to Cu-Connacht O Reilly (as his new wife) who had just released Tadhg from captivity. This capture of his mother appears to have been the price agreed to by her son with Cu-Connacht for his release. Her bridegroom very soon after proceeded to 'blind and emasculate' her son, as the annals claimed, 'on the orders of the Gall'.[23]

The Gall were not slow to utilize the hostage-taking traditions of the Gael. In 1227 the annals claim that:

> a depredation was committed in Sligo by the Justiciary and by Brian son of Toirdelbach when they took many women prisoners.[24]

Later on the annals record that in January 1315 Achy MacMahon left his wife and three of his sons as hostages in Dublin castle to ensure his payment of 30 cows to the king and also as an incentive to capture a notorious robber in the area, Philip O Scathal.[25]

Whether or not these women's captivity proved a restraining hold on their male relatives' actions is, in most cases, unknown. Yet, for the policy to have survived within both societies it must have achieved at least a demonstrable level of success. The threat of violence against loved ones held as hostages was used as a bargaining chip by both sides in efforts to stem or halt ongoing violence, much of which left many female victims dead or injured. The available records list many instances of attacks endured by women and their even more vulnerable children. The annals record such instances in broad and pitiless terms. In 1310 states one, on:

medieval border' in Raymond Gillespie & Harold O'Sullivan (eds), *The borderlands: essays on the history of the Ulster-Leinster border* (Belfast, 1989), pp 41–53, here p. 50. **22** *A. Conn.*, 1227, 10. **23** *AU*, 1243.1, 2; *ALC*, 1244 (p. 363). **24** *ALC*, 1227,13. **25** B. Smith, 'The medieval border', p. 46.

The first of January [- - - -]. A great foray, called Creach an Tóiteáin [The Foray of the Burning], was made by Aodh Bréifneach [Ó Conchobhair] on Maol Ruanaidh Mac Diarmada in Clochar Ó Muirghile, and Donnchadh son of Donnchadh Mac Diarmada was captured, and his wife, the daughter of Ó Flannagáin, was killed there. Many women and children were burned there.[26]

The last sentence, a factual aside, does not and cannot convey the horror, distress and fear of such an event. It is no wonder that for those outside the military elite in both societies, war was an event to be dreaded and guarded against. Perhaps women who went as hostages hoped that their captivity might buy some time for their children to grow up in, for crops to be harvested, and for peace to develop – rather that than the year-on-year devastation wrought by the raiding and harrying that were the pursuits of the male warrior classes. A description of the aftermath of one such raid describes the scene afterwards as follows: 'women and boys and [whole] families included; whereby that murderous far-secluded area became a mere heap of carnage thickly stacked'.[27] Perhaps the following example further serves to illustrate the hardships experienced by women in both societies due to such actions. A court sitting in Carlow in 1311 heard the Jurors state that certain Irish and English men burned the house of Betoun widow of John de Valle, knight, at Arbrystyn and killed Thomas de Valle and Philip de Valle and stole cows and sheep and other goods. This was done, it was claimed, in revenge for an attack upon the O'Tooles.[28] The apparently unstoppable cycle of war at all levels of society was one that must have plunged many into despair. The actions attributed to the widow of Richard de Clare after his death encapsulates those feelings of utter helplessness that must have attended such events.

> After her husband Richard de Clare and his son were killed at the battle of Dysert O Dea it is said that de Clare's wife at Bunratty abandoned the castle, set fire to the place and said farewell to the country and none of her descendants ever came back to claim it.[29]

PEACE-MAKING

Most women's experiences of war were then suffused with sadness and suffering and they knew that this was a situation that was, if at all possible, best

26 MacCarthaigh's Book 1310, 1 (http://www.ucc.ie/celt/published/T100014/index.html – accessed 24/09/2009).   27 John Mac Rory Magrath, *Caithréim Thoirdhealbhaigh*, II, trans. S.H. O'Grady (London, 1929), p. 71.   28 Margaret C. Griffith (ed.), *Calendar of justiciary rolls of Ireland, 1308–14* (Dublin, 1956), pp 173–4.   29 Mervyn Archdall, *Monasticon Hibernicum* (Dublin, 1873), p. 92, n. 25.

avoided. One way to try and ensure this was through reconciliation, most notably through marriage alliances. For that reason over the course of several centuries the Papal offices sometimes found themselves inundated with requests from the Irish for dispensation for marriages specifically designed to end war and conflict. This excuse was used as a form of blackmail, that is to dispense a marriage, which would bring peace to the unstable locality in question. In such an instance it was argued that providing a dispensation was performing a public service, in that it kept the peace. This could be a persuasive argument in a war-torn country such as Ireland. In 1406 the bishop of Kilmore dispensed the marriage of Richard Orayly (O Reilly) and Lasrina Macgamrugan. They had already had children and were related but they wanted to marry with the stated desire of the 'quelling of wars between their followers, kinsmen and friends'.[30] In 1426 it was advised that the Pope remove the impediments delaying the marriage of the 'noble and puissant' Roger Mccmahuna of Clogher diocese and Alice White of the Armagh diocese. These impediments were that they were closely related on several levels but the marriage was advised for several reasons. These included the legitimization of the children who had already been born as well as the peace that their union brought to the warring English and Irish.[31]

Similarly, Thomas, the son of the earl of Desmond, and Elis, the daughter of William lord Barry, were granted dispensation to marry in 1455 despite being related, 'in order to assuage and prevent the continuation of enmities, discords, homicides, burnings, depredations and plunderings and breakings of towns and castles on the part of their parents, friends and kinsmen'.[32] The description of the types of violence and unrest that these marriages hoped to end, are, in themselves, an implied threat. For example, the grant of a dispensation in 1447 to Thomas FitzMaurice, the son of the earl of Desmond, and Annora de Geraldinis, the daughter of the baron of Ardfert, was made because of continued trouble between their respective families. To whit:

> great wars have arisen, whence slaughter, burnings of towns and castles, depopulation etc. have been perpetrated and are perpetrated daily so that there seems to be no hope of peace, wherefore they desire to find a remedy by means of marriage.[33]

An appeal by Henry O Neill in 1469 to marry Joan MacMahon was made with the explicit hope that the marriage would put an end to violence.[34] To

---

30 *CPL, 1404–15*, p. 106.   **31** D.A. Chart (ed.), *The register of John Swayne, archbishop of Armagh and primate of Ireland, 1418–39* (Belfast, 1935), pp 45–6.   **32** *CPL, 1455–64*, p. 232   **33** *CPL 1447–55*, p. 359.   **34** The MacMahons as a powerful Ulster family could aid O Neill as effective allies, see C.T. Cairney, *Clans and families* (London, 1989), p. 89; A. Lynch, 'The administration of John Bole, archbishop of Armagh, 1457–71', *Seanchas Ardmhacha* 15:1 (1991), 113–83, here p. 167.

back up this exalted reason O Neill gave the archbishop of Armagh a quantity of gold on condition that the archbishop would write to Rome recommending the dispensation. The archbishop's (purchased) sympathies were clear when he stated that he noted how difficult it was for the Gaelic chiefs to find suitable marriage partners and especially ones who would bring longed-for peace in their wake. Perhaps the dispensing of marriages for the sake of peace indicates just how little the input of the prospective brides mattered when it came to their own marriages. Here, very obviously, women were used as pawns for military and political ends, whether their marriages were actually being used as a means to obtain peace or not. It may be that in a country exhausted by feuds and warfare this excuse was found to be a powerful and effective way for the families involved to gain a political or military advantage, by dint of an honourable reason for marriage. Whether the brides (or grooms) were happy about it was of no consequence whatsoever.

For these marriages were bargains made to keep the peace and to ensure good relations in troubled localities. Women's experiences of war in these instances was one of subjection to the martial plans of their families and those of the bridegroom's. No active part could be played by such women until after they married and even then, depending on factors such as the cultural traditions of their society and their own status and economic power, their influence could either be powerfully and outwardly expressed or it may have had to take a more hidden and less public course. The majority of women must have dreaded and feared conflict but there were some who saw it as an opportunity to exert power and wield influence and as a means to become actively and publicly involved in the worldly affairs of their families. This particularly applies to upper-class Gaelic Irish wives. In times of crisis and uncertainty women could and did exercise an independence of both thought and action that at other times was almost unheard of. For some women then while war was on the one hand disruptive, debilitating and dangerous it could also be advantageous, empowering and freeing. During periods of prolonged conflict normal social rules could be subverted and some women were able to use such situations in order to gain advantages both for their families and also for themselves as well as redress grievances. They did so efficiently, sometimes ruthlessly and although the sources are silent on feelings it is hard to believe that they weren't sometimes not only afraid but also exhilarated, emboldened and possibly appalled by their own actions.

Bonae litterae and female erudition in early sixteenth-century Nuremberg

HELGA ROBINSON-HAMMERSTEIN

This paper will draw attention to manuscripts and printed works available to nuns of St Clare's convent in Nuremberg, especially loans and gifts of books and dedications prefacing Latin translations of newly available Greek texts. Willibald Pirckheimer (1470–1530), renowned humanist, imperial diplomat and Nuremberg Councillor, had uncovered many of these treasures. He was very excited about his finds and considered his sister Caritas (1467–1532, since 1503 abbess of the Nuremberg Convent of the Poor Clares), an ideal recipient. The loans and gifts started with a confident attempt to win her over to the humanist love of 'good literature' (*bonae litterae*) and to encourage her to become an erudite female – the muse of contemporary humanist studies in the classical tradition. The siblings' views of what made a truly erudite female did not coincide for long. Distinguishing herself from her brother, Caritas cautiously created her own model of erudition. Their correspondence is evidence of an arduous, often acrimonious, learning process for both. Willibald eventually became aware of the futility of attempting to pursue what looked to Caritas like 'secularist' – even pagan – studies. The intervention of Willibald's close friend Conrad Celtis seems to have marked the turning point which directed the Abbess' search more energetically away from 'philosophy' towards a thoroughly Christian version of humanism. The foundation of her intellectual development in the convent was an understanding of crucial elements of medieval learning. This paper will therefore include a brief examination of the nature of some medieval and late fifteenth century manuscripts and books in the library of St Clare in Nuremberg. Since 1483 Caritas had been responsible for looking after and extending the collection. She had enthusiastically engaged in this task, and seamlessly linked the exploration of Christian humanist books – loans and gifts to which Willibald eventually restricted himself – to the study of works written in the Franciscan and mystical traditions.

There is no doubt that Willibald provided a strong stimulus to learning in the convent and that his dedications and donations played a seminal role in the cultural life of the community, which has still not been fully appreciated. He encouraged his sister Caritas to make humanist learning her main concern, arguing that God had given her special gifts of understanding which should be devoted to 'true studies'. The reformed regulations of the Observant Franciscans that had been adopted in the fifteenth century were not averse to learning, but there was a built-in stumbling block when defining the aims of the Franciscan commitment to learning compared with the humanist fervour to recover ancient literature and be guided by its ethos.

Before assessing the literary works in question it will be useful to say more about the relationship of the two Pirckheimer siblings and the influence they could exercise on each other. The appearance[1] and the activities of Willibald Pirckheimer are familiar to early modern historians. His fame as the first humanist to translate several classical works from Greek into Latin has never faded since it was first spread by his humanist friendship network that included Erasmus of Rotterdam and Conrad Celtis. The current work of the German Pirckheimer society stimulates critical appreciation of Willibald Pirckheimer in its *yearbook* and the edition of his correspondence is reaching completion.[2] It is not known what Caritas Pirckheimer looked like, but scholarly interest in her career has recently grown. It has greatly benefited from Josef Pfanner's edition of the *Denkwürdigkeiten* and her correspondence.[3]

Caritas was the eldest of nine daughters and one son of Dr Johannes Pirckheimer and his wife Barbara, née Löffelholz. Although both members of extremely influential families in Nuremberg, the couple had moved to Eichstätt, where the husband had taken the position of counsellor to the bishop. After the death of his wife Johannes Pirckheimer returned to Nuremberg and entered the service of the Council. With the exception of their daughter Juliane who married the Nuremberg patrician Martin Geuder, all other sisters joined cloistered communities, two of them, Barbara – who

---

1 For his image see the portrait by Albrecht Dürer in Giulia Bartrum, *Albrecht Dürer and his legacy* (London, 2002), p. 217, description no. 165 with references to several other contemporary portraits. 2 The *Pirckheimer Jahrbuch* has been published since 1986. The edition of his correspondence, started by Emil Reicke (vol. 1, 1940), is now in the hands of Helga Scheible (vol. 7 is scheduled for publication in 2009). The extensive publications of the Pirckheimer *Gesellschaft* are summarized in the Willibald Pirckheimer entry on their website:< www.pirckheimer-gesellschaft.de.>. This also offers brief biographies of Willibald and Caritas by Dieter Wuttke. 3 Josef Pfanner (ed.), *Die 'Denkwürdigkeiten' der Caritas Pirckheimer (aus den Jahren 1524–1528)* (Landshut, 1962); Josef Pfanner (ed.), *Briefe von, an und über Caritas Pirckheimer (aus den Jahren 1498–1530)* (Landshut 1966). The most important works: Lotte Kurras & Franz Machilek (eds), *Caritas Pirckheimer (1467–1532)* ([Exhibition Catalogue] Nuremberg, 1982); Lotte Kurras, 'Pirckheimer, Caritas OSCl' in *Die deutsche Literatur des Mittelalters. Verfasserlexikon*, 7, 1989, cols. 697–702; Ursula Hess, '*Oratrix humilis*. Die Frau als Briefpartnerin von Humanisten, am Beispiel der Caritas Pirckheimer', in Joseph Worstbrock (ed.), *Der Brief im Zeit alter der Renaissance (Acta Humaniora)* (Weinheim, 1983), pp 173–203; Eva Lippe–Weissenfeld Hamer, '*Virgo docta, virgo sacra* – Untersuchungen zum Briefwechsel Caritas Pirckheimers' in *Pirckheimer Jahrbuch* (1999), 121–55; idem, Caritas Pirckheimer, das Klara–Kloster und die Einführung der Reformation' in *Pirckheimer Jahrbuch* (2000), 238–75; Eva Cescutti, '*Quia non convenit ea lingua foeminis* – und warum Charitas Pirckheimer dennoch lateinisch geschrieben hat', in Michaela Hohkamp & Gabriele Jancke (eds), *Nonne, Königin und Kurtisane. Wissen, Bildung und Gelehrsamkeit von Frauen in der Frühen Neuzeit* (Königstein im Taunus, 2004), pp 202–24.

took the name Caritas – and Clara, remained in Nuremberg and became prominent among the Poor Clares. Unusually for a young girl, Caritas had received a thorough Latin education in the house of her grandfather in Nuremberg. Her great-aunt Catherine, well known as a learned female of great distinction, had been her instructress until the age of 12 when Barbara/Caritas was sent to the convent. At St Clare she was able to continue her education until she was professed in 1483, when she became the teacher of young girls as well as librarian of the convent. The Vicar General of the Observant Franciscans had admired her knowledge of Latin already when he visited the convent in 1481.[4]

At that time Willibald was devoting himself, like his friend Conrad Celtis, to the intellectual *translatio imperii et studii* to bring about the transfer and continuation of the Roman Empire from Italy to Germany by studying and cultivating the ancient languages and their literatures. These friends were united in the conviction that no empire could survive unless it promoted learning and studies. Celtis, who was for some months a guest in Willibald Pirckheimer's house in Nuremberg, elaborated the conditions of such a transfer of empire through studies *inter alia* in his ode to Caritas, of which more below.[5]

Although Willibald corresponded with all his sisters (often dealing with merely practical questions), Caritas was closest to him in the shared pursuit of learning. He sought to cultivate in her the *virgo docta* whose accomplishments he praised to many members of his humanist friendship circle. Some of her admirers compared Caritas with Paula and Julia Eustochium, the learned ladies with whom St Jerome had conducted an influential correspondence.[6] Caritas began to familiarize herself more thoroughly with the meaning of such a comparison. It was to become the question that preoccupied her throughout her career. A crucial difference in attitude of brother and sister to classical learning soon revealed itself. He was the active explorer, who considered himself privileged to stand at the threshold of a new age, she remained the receptive and often highly critical correspondent, accommodat-

4 The conversation with the Vicar General of the Observant Franciscans Wilhelm Bertho is reported in a letter by the Abbess Margarete Grundherr, 1481, in Kurras & Machilek, exhibit no. 104. See also Eva Schlotheuber, 'Humanistisches Wissen und geistliches Leben. Caritas Pirckheimer und die Geschichtsschreibung im Nürnberger Klarissenkonvent', in *Pirckheimer Jahrbuch* (2006), 89–118, here 94–5.   5 Josef Pfanner (ed.), *Briefe*, No. 46. See also Susanna Knackmuß, '"Meine Schwestern sind im Kloster…": Geschwisterbeziehungen des Nürnberger Patriziergeschlechtes Pirckheimer zwischen Klausur und Welt, Humanismus und Reformation', in *Historical Social Research* 30 (2005), 80–106.   6 See examples in Josef Pfanner, *Briefe*, pp 37, 139, 142. On the early sixteenth-century enthusiasm for St Jerome see article by Berndt Hamm, 'Hieronymus-Begeisterung und Augustinismus vor der Reformation. Beobachtungen zur Beziehung zwischen Humanismus und Frömmigkeitstheologie (am Beispiel Nürnbergs)', in Kenneth Hagen (ed.), *Augustine, the harvest, and theology (1300–1650)* (Leiden, 1990), pp 127–235, here pp 196–202. For St Jerome and female piety, see above, chapter 16.

ing classical literature to her deeply anchored Christian convictions. Venturing too far into the 'pagan' classical humanist intellectual realm did not suit her and she never stayed silent when she sensed that her core Christian values were being undermined.

It is important to discover what had been the determining influences on her in the convent. Caritas was expected to possess a basic knowledge of Latin when she took the veil. This had been the key – at least in theory – to the reform of the Franciscan Order in the fifteenth century. It laid stress on understanding the liturgy, with the emphasis on comprehending what was being sung rather than mindlessly reciting incomprehensible words. In the reformed rules a crucial distinction existed between reading (and comprehending) and writing Latin. The former was the aim, the latter was frowned upon, especially in female communities. It is illuminating not to neglect Thomas Lentes' insight that the reform relied on a change of attitude to the text. No longer was it merely a sacred object and therefore part of the Church's treasures; instead it could become the subject of intellectual enquiry and analysis. That suited the humanists very well because it provided the preconditions for an initiation to *bonae litterae* and true erudition. On the other hand one must bear in mind that with this ruling the Franciscans had, inadvertently, departed from the traditional conviction of the Church which believed that female knowledge of Latin led to immorality because it gave access to so much pagan literature with which the female brain could not cope.[7] The differentiation between female reading and writing of Latin was an attempt to recover some of the original thinking. It is easy to imagine that such a categorical rejection of nuns writing in Latin, a ruling that was eventually extended to the prohibition of reading 'pagan books', led to conflict with the humanist scholars who corresponded with these ladies. Willibald's letter of December 1503 to Caritas on the occasion of her election as Abbess throws light on the significance of such a restriction.[8] He said that he was not sure whether to congratulate her or console her, since he was quite sure that this new position would absorb too much time and energy. To Erasmus he wrote that she had been raised to the rank of abbess but the Franciscans had forbidden her to write in Latin.[9]

The convent of the Poor Clares had been sedulous and successful in implementing the reformed rules, especially those relating to the moral con-

---

7 Erasmus lampooned this 'absurdity of the Church's attitude' in his Colloquium *Abbatis et Eruditae* (1524). Celtis in the Third Book of his *Amores* expressed his strong conviction that priests feared for their controlling influence on contemporary society if women were not kept ignorant. Thomas Lentes, '"Andacht" und "Gebärde": Das religiöse Ausdrucksverhalten', in Bernhard Jussen & Craig Koslovsky (eds), *Kulturelle Reformation. Sinnformationen im Umbruch, 1400–1660* (Göttingen, 1999), pp 29–67, here p. 33.   8 Josef Pfanner, *Briefe*, no. 36, 20 December 1503.   9 Willibald to Erasmus, 14 March 1504, cited by Eva Cescutti, '*Quia no convenit ea lingua foeminis*', p. 211.

duct of the nuns.[10] The Library collection played a crucial part in the endeavour to make education the sheet-anchor of the reform of the order. It shows, however, that the reform resulted not in a radical rejection of the past but in the co-existence of old and new and, where necessary, the transformation and revision of what had been the focus of attention before. The best Franciscan tradition was reflected in the accumulation of manuscripts copied at the convent: collections of sermons, prayer books, Latin and German histories of the convent compiled by a priest with the assistance of nuns. These works belonging to the genre of 'consolation literature' were of especial significance to Caritas herself, as her correspondence with Sixtus Tucher, Provost at St Laurence, shows.[11]

Abbess Caritas' high esteem for these works shows not only that the manuscripts of the fourteenth century were not removed from the Library as a result of the reforms but instead they fed into the reform endeavours. A few observations on the collections that shaped the reform period will be necessary before dealing with the intellectual challenge of humanist studies that faced Abbess Caritas and her convent. Among the liturgical works marking one of the aims of reform was the *Liber Ordinarius*, a directory combining individual books used in the Mass and the Hours throughout the year. It listed suitable antiphons, psalms, responses, prayers and hymns as well as chants and readings from epistles and the gospels.[12] A *Missale Plenum* also belongs to this category. It is a German translation of the full text of the gospels and epistles read during Mass in the course of a year.[13]

The following items, presented by Heinrich Meichsner, a close friend of the sisters, were welcome donations that revealed three special preoccupations of the convent in the process of reform. The first was a two-volume Bible in

---

10 The Nuremberg convent of the Poor Clares accepted the Statutes of the Reformed Observance on the occasion of Giovanni di Capistrano's visitation in 1452, and was soon recognized in Southern Germany and Austria as the model institution that could help with the reform of other convents. See Eva Schlotheuber, 'Humanistisches Wissen und geistliches Leben', pp 93–9, cites many instances of this as well as presenting excerpts from various Reform Statutes inspired by St Clare of Nuremberg.   11 Lotte Kurras has given a reliable brief assessment of the manuscripts copied and the holdings of the library in the exhibition catalogue of 1982. The article is entitled: 'Klostergeschichte im Spiegel der Bibliothek', pp 90–103, relating to exhibits nos. 72–95. Josef Pfanner's edition of *Briefe* also contains many references to loans of books to be copied in the convent, e.g. Letters 31–66. The absence of any inventory renders firm conclusions impossible. See Franz Machilek, 'Klosterhumanismus in Nürnberg um 1500', in *MVGN* 64 (1977), 10–45, here p. 43. The location of the scriptorium is unknown, although it is likely to have been near the chapel. See description of the layout of the convent (in Kurras & Machilek), Exhibit No. 42 and *passim*. Irene Stahl, 'Alltagsleben im Kloster' in Kurras & Machilek, pp 103–108 also reminds the reader that Sister Felicitas Grundherr asked her father in July 1527, as on several previous occasions, to have a manuscript bound for her.   12 Lotte Kurras (in Kurras & Machilek) commenting on exhibit no. 51.   13 Lotte Kurras (in Kurras & Machilek) commenting on exhibit no. 91.

German, copied in Nuremberg in 1455, a version of the famous *Kuttenberg Bible*.[14] The Aesop manuscript is the oldest German prose translation of 63 of Aesop's fables.[15] Another interest of the reform is indicated by the manuscript of a work by Johannes Nider entitled (in a printed edition of 1493) *The Four-and-Twenty Golden Harps, the nearest way to Heaven*.[16] The printed version was copied by Abbess Helena Meichsner from the incunable. It is more than likely that the Poor Clares quite often made copies of printed works donated to them so that these could be lent to other convents. There is ample evidence of the mutual bond of spiritual friendship between convents that intensified with the reform period gathering momentum.

Typical of the manuscripts produced in response to the reform are the mystical works by various authors. *Eighty Sermons* were mostly copied by Sister Catherine Ockers in 1470.[17] These sermons, fervently studied by the nuns, are by Johannes Tauler (*c.*1300–61), the most prolific and influential mystic after Heinrich Seuse, following in the footsteps of Master Eckart.[18] Mystics exercised considerable influence on the course of reform which was consciously promoted as an intensely spiritual movement. Thomas à Kempis' *De Imitatione Christi* was the main representative of the *Devotio Moderna*.[19]

The influence of mysticism – surprisingly – was intensified in the new century precisely at the time when humanist studies were beginning to make their impact. A typical example is Ulrich Pinder's *Mirror of the Passion of Christ* printed in Nuremberg in 1507. It combined all the features that made mysticism so useful to the reform. Its texts–inspired by Bonaventure and Bernard of Clairvaux – marked the stages of the perfect accomplishment of the true Christian spiritual life: *contemplatio, compassio, imitatio, administration, exultatio, resolutio, quies*. Its aim was to update the message in text and image. There are 76 woodcuts by the most renowned masters of the age, Hans Baldung Grien, Hans Schäufelein and Heinrich von Kulmbach. Karl Schlemmer, commenting on the significance of this work, points out that it prompted new endowments dedicated to St Sebald and St Laurence, the main churches in Nuremberg, of chants to commemorate the Last Supper at the beginning of Lent 1499. There was also the *Patris Sapientia* endowment to sing the Seven Hours of the suffering of Christ at St Sebald every Friday in 1514.[20] The latter exercised a special influence on Abbess Caritas. Of equal

14 Lotte Kurras (in Kurras & Machilek), commenting on exhibit no. 80.   15 Lotte Kurras (in Kurras & Machilek), commenting on exhibit no. 81. The manuscript of 70 fols. originated around 1412 in Southern Bavaria. It is known as the *Nuremberg Aesop*. It is now among the holdings of the *Herzog August Bibliothek in Wolfenbüttel*, acquired by Duke Augustus when he started his library.   16 Lotte Kurras (in Kurras & Machilek), commenting on exhibit no. 80.   17 She was a nun of the Nuremberg convent from 1454 until her death in 1486.   18 Irene Stahl (in Kurras & Machilek) commenting on exhibit no. 97. This version of the *Eighty sermons* is almost identical with the text printed at Augsburg in 1486.   19 Franz Machilek (in Kurras & Machilek), commenting on exhibit 132 a.   20 Karl Schlemmer (in Kurras & Machilek), commenting on exhibit 132 b.

significance for Abbess Caritas was the *Miserere* by the Dominican revivalist preacher Girolamo Savonarola. It is a meditation on Psalm 50 with prayers Savonarola had written in his Florentine prison, awaiting execution. Caritas lent it to her two younger sisters at the Convent of Bergen.[21] These books were not mere prestige possessions of the convent library of St Clare. They had been collected for the purpose of private reading and use in services or at table.

Caritas Pirckheimer's appreciation of the works of mysticism that had been accumulated in the convent library before her time becomes obvious in her comments on these works, especially in her correspondence with Sixtus Tucher. Here she demonstrated that they did not restrict her intellectual religiosity but had an influence on her contemplative exercises.[22] Caritas Pirckheimer responded to mysticism by seeking to combine emotion with close, rational reading of the texts. She was able to integrate remarkably seamlessly mysticism with Christian humanism as the following considerations will show. Adapting Jean Gerson, the Parisian theologian, she explicitly stated in her second letter to Conrad Celtis: 'the theology of mysticism is the art of love or Caritas [she alluded to his use of her name in the dedication] to love God in *scientia*'.[23] In her position of responsibility for the library collection and later as abbess she furthered the acquisition of works that made possible a smooth transition to a thorough reception of Christian humanism without overturning what might be considered the canon of the existing holdings. Caritas acquired the reputation of an avid and discerning book collector.[24]

Stephan Fridolin (*c*.1430–98) was no doubt the crucial mediator who affected the convergence of the Franciscan tradition with humanism. As a member of the Observant Franciscans he was preacher as well as confessor to the nuns of St Clare. He had impressed the patrician elite with his carefully researched historical work *Kaiseransichten* – the physiognomies of German emperors – dedicated to the Council. Fridolin reached out most effectively to all inhabitants with his famous *Schatzbehalter*, a meditation on the suffering and death of Christ, published by Anton Koberger in 1491.[25]

---

21 Lotte Kurras commenting on exhibit 89 (in Kurras & Machilek) the German translation of the work, a Nuremberg imprint of around 1499 points out that Eufemia and Sabina Pirckheimer at Bergen asked their brother Willibald, after 1504, to obtain the German imprint for them since they had to return the copy they had borrowed from St Clare. This is one of the few instances where the ready availability of – admittedly less extensive – works in print is likely to have discouraged the copying of a printed book in the convent's scriptorium.   22 Josef Pfanner, *Briefe*, nos. 1–32.   23 Josef Pfanner, *Briefe*, no. 47, p. 106, lines 31–2: '... *mystica theologia nihil alius est nisi ars amoris vel charitatis ut scientia deum amandi ...*'   24 Franz Machilek, 'Der Klosterhumanismus in Nürnberg um 1500', in *MVGN* 64 (1977), 10–45, especially pp 13 ff.   25 It is recognized as one of the two most significant works produced in Nuremberg. The other is the so-called Nuremberg Chronicle initiated by Hartmann Schedel, also published by Koberger. See Berndt Hamm, 'Humanistische Ethik und reichsstädtische Ehrbarkeit in Nürnberg', in *MVGN* 76 (1989),

Peter Strieder has discussed it as the outstanding expression of the new flowering of Franciscan religiosity.[26] Fridolin's influence on Caritas' own spiritual and intellectual development can best be seen in her record of his sermons, preached in the last years of his life at St Clare. They deal with the breviary and various observances, closely interpreted from passages of the Bible. It is more than likely that she discussed her notes with Fridolin, extending them and filling in gaps before she had them copied again by other nuns. Caritas was anxious to have the authentic text read out at the communal meals of the nuns.

Heinrich Vigilis was another preacher, also confessor at the convent from 1487–99, and writer who, like Fridolin, placed great emphasis on the compassionate suffering with Christ. Neither of them encouraged fasting and other deprivations as a means of identification with Christ.[27] From her general reaction one may hazard a guess that this coincided with Caritas' general disposition. Evidence of this may be seen in an illuminated manuscript of his sermons, completed in 1494, on the gospels of each Sunday from Easter to the 23rd Sunday after Trinity. She is said to have noted them down word for word for discussion with the author and to be read out at meals.[28]

The third Franciscan who exercised a similar influence on the nuns of St Clare was Nicholas Glassberger from Moravia, living in the cloister of the Discalced between 1483 and 1508 and acting as occasional confessor to the nuns. He encouraged them to write a chronicle of their Order in Latin and German. It is evident that the composition of this chronicle relied very much on original sources in the convent library.[29] This enterprise was motivated by one of the key humanist convictions that a community could only be sustained now and in future through accurate knowledge of its past from original sources.[30] The second chronicle, *A short general history of the Order of St Clare* combined with the *History of the Nuremberg community* is in Latin. The manuscript shows that the sisters made excerpts from documents held at St Clare. The manuscript itself was corrected by Caritas. There is also a

65–147, here p. 128; Petra Seegets, *Passionstheologie und Passionsfrömmigkeit im ausgehenden Mittelalter. Der Nürnberger Franziskaner Stephan Fridolin (gest. 1498) zwischen Kloster und Stadt* (Tübingen, 1998). **26** Peter Strieder, 'Frömmigkeit und Spiritualität im Umkreis von Caritas Pirckheimer' (in Kurras und Machilek), p. 119 as an introduction to exhibits, pp 120–7. **27** Klaus Guth, 'Wege der Nachfolge – Klosterleben am Vorabend der Reformation' (in Kurras & Machilek), 13–25; Eva Schlotheuber, 'Humanistisches Wissen und geistliches Leben', pp 105–18. **28** Exhibit no. 85 (in Kurras & Machilek). See also Johannes Kist, 'Heinrich Vigilis, ein Franziskanerprediger am Vorabend der Reformation', in *Zeitschrift für bayerische Kirchengeschichte* 13 (1938), 144–50. **29** Paula Datsko Barker, 'Caritas Pirckheimer: a female humanist confronts the Reformation', in *Sixteenth Century Journal* 26:2 (1995), 259–72, here p. 261. **30** See Berndt Hamm, 'Humanistische Ethik', p. 86. Hamm points out that a work with original sources does not preclude the occasional flights of fancy, for instance citing the Romans as the founders of Nuremberg. Such assertions, however, facilitated the *translatio imperii* desire in its literary strategy, which dominated Conrad Celtis' and Willibald Pirckheimer's thinking.

German version, possibly translated and copied by Apollonia Tucher, with corrections by Caritas.[31]

Caritas was fortunate to find herself in charge of an institution that had practised a moderate version of late medieval piety in its manuscript and book collection policy. The works of mysticism encouraged her to the kind of sympathetic suffering with Christ that provided ample room for the exercise of her intellect. No hatred and castigation of her body or excessive fasting were demanded. She firmly rejected the *Heilsautomatismus* that some nuns might find advocated in contemporary works in the Library.[32] For the period after 1500 more extensive contacts 'with the world outside the cloister' – not forbidden by the tradition of her Order – enriched Caritas' spirituality also by more manuscript or book donations. Eminent humanists, in their dedications of recently-recovered ancient knowledge, opened up enticing prospects by inviting her to join a new kind of intellectual friendship network.

Initially Willibald Pirckheimer lent Caritas well-known works not available in her library. A typical example of her appreciation of this service is her letter to him of 1502.[33] She wrote that she and their sister (Clara) found daily 'consolation' – a key word in her vocabulary – in the 'holy books' which he had placed at their disposal. The community derived great satisfaction from this 'treasure of life and divine salvation'. Although they were no theologians, they tried to absorb as much as they could of 'everything that is written for our salvation'. Caritas was referring to two books.

The first, which she returned with expressions of overflowing gratitude, contains poems by the fourth-century Christian poet Clemens Aurelius Prudentius. Caritas praised the verses, 'which please me greatly'. She stressed that, although she had been unaware of the name of the author, she recognized many of the hymns as those which the nuns sang in choir at different times of the day and various seasons of the church year.[34]

The author of the second work is St Jerome. From Caritas' comments one must assume that she was referring to his correspondence with Julia Eustochium and Paula, whom she described as 'the saintly women he especially befriended and who persuaded him to translate a large part of Holy Scripture from the Hebrew tongue into Latin'. This was the book she begged to be allowed to retain longer because she had 'found in it such a very precious treasure that she must love Jerome before all other saints'.[35]

---

31 Lotte Kurras (in Kurras & Machilek), commenting on exhibits 87 and 88, both around 1500.   32 Klaus Guth (in Kurras & Machilek), p. 23; Josef Pfanner, *Briefe*, No. 33.   33 Josef Pfanner, *Briefe*, no. 33, pp 78–80.   34 On Prudentius see article by Eckhard Reichert in *BBKL* vol. VII (1994), cols. 1010–1013. The work is likely to have been the *Liber Cathemerinon*, containing an extended introduction with biographical information and 12 hymns. It was circulating in manuscripts and used in the monastic liturgy throughout the Middle Ages. The hymns by Prudentius – there is a larger collection of which the *Cathemerinon* forms part – were frequently printed and reprinted around 1500.   35 Josef

The two books are 'proof-texts' of the late medieval reform interest in learning. From the humanist perspective they could, however, also serve to prepare the nuns' minds to a reception of *bonae litterae* and true erudition. This is not to imply that Willibald made the loans as part of a precisely calculated educational strategy. In this instance it is much more likely that Caritas had actually asked for them and Willibald readily complied because he could appreciate their 'bridging' function.

Caritas' relationship with her brother as the provider of learning through books was untroubled as long as he sent her what she valued as 'consolation literature'. He, however, wished her erudition to extend further. Willibald's own approach to humanist studies was to explore what he might find. There was no self-imposed restriction, certainly not as far as the secular, 'pagan' writings were concerned. He was anxious to plumb the depth of ancient 'philosophy'. An extreme form of secular humanism, which he seems to have greatly enjoyed was shared only with close male friends like Albrecht Dürer. Their correspondence encodes promiscuous and even pornographic allusions, which he understandably never revealed to his sister. Willibald could not pursue a precisely calibrated target in the humanist instruction of Caritas. There is no doubt, however, that he wished to further an open-minded interest in exploring the Greek and Roman classics which could coexist with Christian teaching. The substance of his teaching could be adjusted in accordance with new discoveries he might make. He was aware that Caritas would never become an author; she would always remain a corresponding member of a friendship circle. Willibald enlisted the help of famous humanists to encourage his sister to use her God-given talents.[36] He sang her praises to Conrad Celtis, the *poeta laureatus*, Albrecht Dürer, Johannes Reuchlin, Johannes Cochlaeus, Philip Melanchthon and Hieronymus Emser, all of whom responded favourably.

After 1503 Willibald became much more decided in his pursuit – possibly under the influence of Conrad Celtis, who was staying at his house – to turn Caritas into a truly learned *virgo*. As already mentioned above, he was disappointed when Caritas was elected abbess. Although he expressed his misgivings fairly cautiously, there is no doubt that he saw the position as a hindrance to the pursuit of 'true learning'. The burdens of office in caring for the cloistered community would make it impossible to devote herself to what her gifts had really equipped her for: the joy of humanist studies.[37] Caritas, on the other hand, was not only anxious to derive as much benefit as she possibly could from Christian humanism to integrate it with her life's work, but also to persuade the great men, especially her brother and Conrad Celtis, to

Pfanner (ed.), *Briefe*, no. 33, pp 78–80.   **36** See Ursula Hess, *'Oratrix humilis'*, p. 173. See also Franz Machilek, 'Klosterhumanismus in Nürnberg um 1500', *MVGN* 64 (1977), 10–45.   **37** Josef Pfanner, *Briefe*, no. 36, pp 83–4.

devote themselves exclusively to Christian humanism. She looked for an opportunity to apply and elaborate what she had learned from her correspondence with Sixtus Tucher.[38] Conrad Celtis, whose offer of Platonic love savoured too much of eroticism for her liking, became the first target of her offensive.[39]

What had Celtis done to incur Caritas' severe censure? In his dedication to her of the works of Hrotsvit of Gandersheim he had praised her as the true successor to this eminently learned tenth-century Benedictine abbess, the greatest medieval female scholar.[40] He also wrote a Sapphic Ode to her and sent her a copy of his *Amores*. While accepting Hrotsvit as an example of an erudite female, she made her disgust with what she considered Celtis' 'advances' absolutely clear in her second letter to him. In her view he had misread her offer of a literary partnership. She was looking for spiritual friendship. She also pointed out that while apparently confirming the Christian tradition by putting her in a line with the great Hrotsvit, he was so fascinated with 'pagan' literature that it controlled all his intellectual and moral values.[41] Not only could she not approve of his representation but she also wished to relocate him in a line with St Paul, St James and Bernard of Clairvaux, the twelfth-century reformer of religious orders.[42]

Willibald tried a different method to win Caritas over to his view of erudition and his belief in *virtus* with the dedication of his translation of Plutarch's *Of the Godhead's delayed revenge*.[43] Significantly, he separated her life's calling from her devotion to *bonae litterae*. Realising that it was a tricky enterprise to persuade Caritas of the value of stoic *virtues*, he adopted a shrewd, inoffensive ploy to render the subject more palatable. He sketched a picture of the historic devotion of the Pirckheimer family to erudition. They had always been especially endowed with divine grace and blessed with a long line not only of learned men but also women. Departing from the medieval notion of the inferiority of women, he considered them the intellectual equal of men if they really devoted themselves to erudition. Willibald cited the example of their great-aunt as the most impressive adornment of their family.[44] He expected that the reference to the family's impressive tradition of learning

38 Josef Pfanner, *Briefe*, nos. 1–31, from 1498?–1506. Paula S. Datsko Barker, 'Caritas Pirckheimer: a female humanist confronts the Reformation', in *Sixteenth Century Journal* 26:2 (1995), 259–72 briefly sketches the influence of Tucher on Caritas.   39 Josef Pfanner, *Briefe*, nos. 45, 46 & 47, pp 100–8.   40 Dieter Wuttke (in Kurras & Machilek), commenting on exhibit 136. For a brief biography of Hrotsvit see *TRE* 15 (1986), 610–11.   41 I cannot fully agree with Ursula Hess' observation that Celtis saw linguistic skills as a variant of erotic play, Ursula Hess, '*Oratrix humilis*', p. 175.   42 Josef Pfanner, *Briefe*, no. 47, p. 100, line 33; p. 101, line 2.   43 Josef Pfanner, *Briefe*, no. 39, 1 June 1513.   44 This is Catherine, sister of Willibald's and Caritas' grandfather Hans, who was the first tutor of Caritas. A learned man like Christoph Scheurl, not a member of the family, spoke in the same sense of the seminal influence of the great-aunt on Caritas in his letter of 1 September 1506 when he sent his *Utilitates Missae*, see Josef Pfanner, *Briefe*, no. 66.

and – arising from this – their unassailable reputation in Nuremberg for service to the common good would have a positive effect on Caritas. He had found a solid foundation from which to project the work he was dedicating to Caritas as something that would have pleased their great-aunt. Caritas' frequent references to herself in her letters as 'humble' seemed to imply a rejection of that intellectual equality. Too much has been made of this reference as an inhibiting self-imposed restriction. *Humilis* is not an adjective chosen by her to deny her obvious abilities: instead it is a biblical injunction that relates to moral, not intellectual life: 'God opposes the proud, but gives grace to the humble'.[45] The reference to *humilitas* can also be treated as a conventional *captatio benevolentiae* in humanist correspondence. Willibald certainly did not regard it as a flaw in Caritas' intellectual disposition.

The Stoic philosopher Plutarch's tract dealt with the *Question why the wicked often seem to escape the divine punishment of their evil deeds*.[46] Willibald started with a fundamental premise that may have worried Caritas. He stated that it was 'the gift of God that we live, the gift of philosophy, however, that we live well'. Philosophy was the wisdom humans acquired through their erudition. Willibald then narrowed down the application of the general premise, observing that this philosophy healed the soul and allowed humans to suffer the insults of the unscrupulous. There seems to have been a topical occasion for saying this because he added: 'you know what I mean'. The general purpose of the donation of this translation from the Greek into Latin was also mentioned in the dedication. It related to the quality of Caritas' erudition. The famous humanist brother wished her to recognize that some pagan authors believed in the inevitability of divine justice even if it was slow in coming. He wished to make Caritas understand that the ancient philosophers were not far from the truth. Here it becomes clear that he was concerned to make his sister realize that 'true erudition' must fit the reception of Christianity into the context of classical learning which conditioned it. He called for a reversal in his favourite sister's thinking, attempting to turn her away from making received medieval teaching the vessel into which to pour classical precepts that conformed with it: to switch the container for the content.

Caritas was not ready for this, as her reply makes clear, she preferred to see St Jerome as the crucial conduit of 'true erudition' and her brother as the contemporary successor of the learned saint, the translator of the Vulgate. In that frame of mind she thanked him profusely for his gift. She gave him her

Ursula Hess '*Oratrix humilis*' describes Willibald's adoption of this device as 'the creation of a family myth'.   **45** 1 Pet 5:5 & Jas 4:6. Compare this with Ursula Hesse's treatment in '*Oratrix humilis*'.   **46** Dieter Wuttke (in Kurras & Machilek), commenting on exhibit no. 145. The Letter of Dedication is dated Nuremberg 1 June 1513. The tract is addressed to famous men *De His Qui Tarde A Numine Corripiuntur Libellus*. Nuremberg, Friedrich Peypus. Date of release 30 June 1513. According to Wuttke, Willibald must have had a copy before the official publication date.

own reading of virtue from which she completely excluded his appeals to 'philosophia'.[47] The virtue she recognized was that of charity/*caritas*. She thus utilized the reference in the dedication to make her own point about the Christian meaning of her chosen name. She conceded that he had done well 'to associate such a splendid work with the name of Caritas, for Caritas is the virtue that shares out all goods'. Caritas was essential in earthly life and heavenly bliss, 'where there will be beautiful fruit of all good deeds'.

The salient point of her letter is that she must not be called a *docta virgo*. She loved the learning of humanists and benefited from it.[48] She refers to the recent find of the manuscript translated by Willibald as 'a precious pearl which God has happily allowed you to unearth from Greek literature'. Significantly, she treats Greek literature as a heap of rubble from which some treasures can be rescued. She pointed out that Plutarch in 'advocating patience did not write like any of the other pagan authors'. From the remainder of her letter it becomes even more obvious that very few Greek writers offer the kind of 'good literature' she was looking for. Adopting the language of mysticism she likened Plutarch to the 'best theologians and imitators of the perfection of the gospel'.[49]

There was much the abbess found inspiring in classical literature but she assembled her erudition from selections of that literature which fitted into her Christian humanist *philosophia*. The liturgy of the convent, the tradition of reading at table, of study and contemplation allowed her to create her own model of the learned female. To re-emphasize what was said above, Caritas explicitly rejected the image of the *virgo docta* – that of the classical muse – first sketched out for her by Conrad Celtis.[50]

For several years Willibald used Christmas or New Year gifts of translations of the works of Early Church Fathers – they were within the compass of humanist search for sources – to retain some influence on the formation of Caritas' learning. In the accompanying letters of dedication he liked discussing the obstacles to research and editing of ancient manuscripts. This is not so evident in his gift for the year 1515 – the *Praecepta* of Father Nilus, one of the Desert Fathers (*c*.400) – because the letter itself has not survived.[51] Willibald had rediscovered the *Praecepta* together with the *Apophtegmata*.[52] In 1516 he dedicated to the sisters two speeches by St Gregory of Nazianze, a manuscript of which he had discovered and translated from Greek into Latin.[53] In his dedication he pointed out that he had almost completed the work when he found out that these letters and some other speeches had

47 Josef Pfanner, *Briefe*, no. 40, June 1513.   **48** Josef Pfanner, *Briefe*, no. 40, lines 25–37.
49 Josef Pfanner, *Briefe*, no. 40, lines 5–10.   **50** Josef Pfanner, *Briefe*, no. 46, April 1502 contains Celtis' Ode to Caritas as the classical muse admired in Germany, making her part of his *translatio imperii* design.   **51** Josef Pfanner, *Briefe*, no. 41, the letter relating to the gift for 1516 briefly mentions the booklet.   **52** Emil Reicke, *Willibald Pirckheimers Briefwechsel*, vol. II, no. 377, pp 596–8.   **53** Josef Pfanner, *Briefe*, no. 41.

already been published under the name of Rufinus. On closer inspection, however, he discovered that he had not wasted his time because there were so many omissions and interpolations in Rufinus' text that his treatment did not do justice to St Gregory. He therefore decided to publish his own edition.

The distinctive feature of humanist scholarship (that includes the study of the Early Church Fathers) was its meticulous research and editorial technique, which is also evident in Willibald's other works. He wished the Poor Clares to benefit from this research by giving them an insight not only into the intellectual excitement of pursuing such research but also into the editorial techniques he applied. One thing he learned as time went on, however, he must be careful not to shock the sisters with Ciceronian Neoplatonism that offered only an inferior place to God.

In the course of the year 1516 he was able to present the sisters with the fruits of Erasmus' quest for 'good literature'. He sent them the newly published dual language edition of the New Testament based on what Erasmus considered the authentic Greek manuscripts of the writers of the New Testament and a new Latin translation that by implication challenged the authority of the Vulgate. As is clear from contemporary correspondence, the nuns read the works of Erasmus avidly and seem to have had no problem with the potentially controversial New Testament.[54] Other works of Christian humanism were dedicated by Willibald's friends to the famous abbess in her widely renowned convent.[55]

Then there came a quarrel, followed by silence, between Willibald and Caritas for over a year. Somewhat surprisingly, the point at issue did not concern the interpretation of what constituted 'good literature'. The bone of contention was Willibald's propensity to flout long-established Nuremberg conventions. He upset Caritas' sense of communal order and how it was maintained by allowing his daughter Barbara to marry a commoner (in February 1518). He defended his decision in a letter to his sister in the convent in which he announced that he preferred a decent commoner to a pretentious patrician. Caritas warned him not to offend public sentiments. Willibald took great exception to this unsolicited advice.[56] The reconciliation

---

54 Karl Schlemmer (in Kurras & Machilek), commenting on exhibit 125. Josef Pfanner, *Briefe*, no. 165, 20 May 1516, Willibald to Erasmus.   55 The letters edited by Josef Pfanner furnish ample proof of this.   56 This is the interpretation of relevant sources studied by Helga Scheible, the editor of Willibald Pirckheimer's correspondence, in her article: 'Willibald Pirckheimers Persönlichkeit im Spiegel seines Briefwechsels am Beispiel seines Verhältnisses zum Klosterwesen', in *Pirckheimer Jahrbuch* (2006), 73–88, here p. 76. She argues on the basis of her thorough knowledge of the sources. *Willibald Pirckheimers Briefwechsel*, III, 572, p. 445, lines 4–12; IV, 613, p. 67, lines 42–4; 617, p. 85, lines 57–8. I am grateful to Helga Scheible for allowing me to consult an earlier version of this article. Looking ahead, it seems poetic justice that Barbara Straub was to become the main lifeline between the city, her father and the convent, as is evident in the correspondence between Clara Pirckheimer and Willibald in the name of the abbess. See Josef Pfanner,

was only brought about – after their sister Clara had made several futile attempts – at the end of 1519, when on 23 December Willibald submitted his most dramatic dedication to his sisters Caritas and Clara. It reveals the 'headaches' of a dedicated researcher. The rediscovered works in question are by Fulgentius Afer (467–533) and Johannes Maxentius (sixth century).[57] Fulgentius, bishop of Ruspe in North Africa, opposed Arianism and upheld Augustinian teaching on divine grace, a subject that was very much discussed among theologians at the time and that came to dominate the theological discourse in the early 1520s. Willibald announced that his aim was to 'improve all Christian theology and to perfect the intellectual, philological and moral education of Christians'. He presented a typical humanist project.

In his letter of dedication to the sisters he gave a gripping account of the tantalizing circumstances that surrounded the recovery of the text. Even after nearly five centuries the reader can still sense a swing between excitement and frustration of the devoted scholar. On a diplomatic mission on behalf of Emperor Maximilian Willibald stopped at Würzburg where he discussed the progress of scholarship with the learned Abbot Johannes Trithemius,[58] who was at the centre of a comprehensive humanist friendship network. From him Willibald learned of the existence of important ancient manuscripts in his keeping, which Trithemius promised to prepare for publication. On his return from the Low Countries Willibald heard about Trithemius' sudden death, which prevented this venture from coming to fruition. Willibald decided to take the matter in hand himself in Trithemius' memory only to find that the collection had somehow disappeared. Just one manuscript was eventually found, but it proved illegible. Willibald did not give up. He taught himself to

Briefe relating to 1525. I have written at some length about this in my edition of the translation of *Denkwürdigkeiten*, which I have called *Defen*ce (forthcoming).   57 See Helga Scheible, 'Willibald Pirckheimers', p. 77; *Willibald Pirckheimers Briefwechsel*, VI, 652, pp 157–61; Josef Pfanner, *Briefe*, no. 43 also dates the letter to 23 December 1519. December 1519 makes perfect sense in view of the fact that their sister Clara tried to mediate between Willibald and Caritas in August 1519; see *Willibald Pirckheimers Briefwechsel*, IV, 613 and 617. Dieter Wuttke (in Kurras & Machilek), commenting on exhibit no. 146, the first edition of the book, argues that the letter and the gift were sent in 1518. The title of the publication is descriptive and ignores the device of eye-catching brevity of popular early modern book titles: *Opera B. Fulgentii Aphri, Episcopi Ruspensis, Theologie Antiqui. Nuper in vetustissimo codice apud Germanos inuenta, obsoletis et Langobardicis literis conscripta. Antea numquam impressa. Nunc primum ad rectiorem veteris Theologie institutionem, qua vt eruditione intellectus, sic lingua eloquio et uita moribus cultior fiat, Deo auspice, pro desyderiis votisque multorum in lucem emissa. Item opera Maxentii Johannis, Servi Dei, pulchra vetustatis Monumenta, in eodem codice reperta.* Dieter Wuttker adjusts the dating on the basis of the Koberger edition of the Fulgentius/Maxentius copy (held in Staats-und Stadtbibliothek Augsburg). His researches have suggested that the corpus of the text was printed in Hagenau by Thomas Anselm for Johannes Koberger in January 1517, the date of publication was after 9 February 1520.   58 Trithemius, highly regarded by his fellow humanists, coordinated a great deal of contemporary research. This is also evident in the letter of dedication to Caritas.

read this text and established its authorship. To keep his spirits up, he secured the support of the printer Johannes Koberger who agreed to publish the important work. Koberger remained committed to this project through thick and thin. There were indeed still many obstacles to overcome. The friends had not anticipated the next problem that presented itself. The owner of the manuscript – it must have been sold after Trithemius' death – refused to sell it or give permission to use it. Willibald and Koberger did not succeed with their offer to have it merely copied: only a considerable bribe could secure access to the manuscript for a limited period. Copying, however, presented an almost impossible task, since those recruited to undertake it, refused to assume responsibility for the accuracy of their work. At that critical moment the tide began to turn with the arrival of Johannes Cochlaeus on Willibald's doorstep. This distinguished scholar had just been appointed to a distinguished position at Frankfurt (Oder). When the plague broke out he returned to Nuremberg and was able to assist Willibald. The transcript and translation were completed in 1517.[59]

Willibald denied having enumerated all these headaches in the course of his researches simply to demonstrate the trouble to which he had gone in the service of humanist studies. In the final section of his letter he explained that his design had been to give the sisters an impression of his toils in order to show how crucial Fulgentius was to Christian scholars of the reform period of the early sixteenth century. He ended his account by detailing the bishop's own story of persecution and suffering. The explicitly stated reason for dedicating the works of Fulgentius and Maxentius to the sisters was an acknowledgement of Caritas' understanding of Christian scholarship. The dedication expressed Willibald's confidence that Caritas would appreciate the writings since she was renowned for her learning, true knowledge of 'good literature' and moral conduct. It is evident that Willibald adopted his sister's definition of 'good literature' when corresponding with her. Cochlaeus also sent a letter of dedication to Caritas. In it he drew attention to a crucial issue.[60] Far from trying to fashion her into a passive, receptive Ciceronian Neoplatonic muse – as Celtis and Willibald had first attempted to do – he expressed the hope that her fame as a saintly and learned lady would in association with that of Fulgentius be the best advertisement for his writings.

Already in 1515 Friedrich Peypus had acknowledged Caritas' celebrity when he published a set of her letters written in Latin. In his preface he explained that these letters had come into his hands and although they had originally been intended exclusively for the eyes of the recipient, he was convinced that their publication would serve an important purpose. Caritas was after all an outstanding example of female erudition and a model of wisdom

---

59 See note 57 above.   60 Josef Pfanner, *Briefe*, No. 57, 11th Calend of January 1519 = 22 December 1519.

that should be emulated by all. He was also convinced that her name would make the little book more saleable.[61] Her fame and her virtues would become more deeply engrained in the consciousness of society. This is the role of the erudite female committed to *bonae litterae* which Caritas felt she could accept without injuring her conscience. Peypus (with an eye to his sales), but more pertinently, Cochlaeus recognized the model she had elaborated for herself taking her inspiration from St Jerome's esteem for his female correspondents Paula and Julia Eustochium. The erudite female enshrined a *virgo sacra*.

APPENDIX

[English translation of the letter of dedication to Abbess Caritas by her brother Willibald Pirckheimer reprinted and translated into German. Josef Pfanner, *Briefe*, No. 43, 23 December 1519.]

Preface to the books of the blessed Fulgentius, discovered and edited [by Willibald Pirckheimer]. Willibald Pirckheimer sends his greetings to the Reverend Mother Caritas Pirckheimer, Abbess of St Clare at Nuremberg, his beloved sister.[1]

A few years ago I travelled as the emissary of our free republic[2] to Lower Germany on behalf of the invincible Emperor Maximilian whose fame will never die.[3] On my way I stopped at Würzburg and visited among others Johannes Trithemius, the former Abbot of Sponheim, my old friend.[4] He received me very cordially. And after we had, as so often happens, talked about our studies, he mentioned the old manuscripts of which this city could be justly proud. They had been assembled from bequests to monasteries, even in Upper Germany.[5] I encouraged him to publish these for the benefit of all

---

61 Josef Pfanner, *Briefe*, No. 53: *Cum autem ea matrona foeminei sexus et nostrae civitatis praecipuum sit ornamentum, in quam unam Salvator noster plus eruditionis contulit quam in multas alias huius temporis mulieres, putavi eas publicandas fore, quatenus libellus ipse, vendibilior fieret et in argumentum a foemina caperes bonis litteris incumbere et Deo servire frugalissimum esse.*

1 On the dating see note 56 above. 'Fulgentius von Ruspe' in *TRE* 11 (1983), 723–7.   2 He is referring to the free imperial city of Nuremberg in the manner of a scholar of humanist studies.   3 Emperor Maximilian had died 12 January 1519.   4 Trithemius was a key figure in the revival of *bonae litterae*. For further information see 'Johannes Trithemius' in *BBKL*, vol. XIX (2001), cols. 1449–54. Harald Müller, 'Graecus et fabulator. Johann Trithemius, Leitfigure und Zerrbild des spätmittelalterlichen "Klosterhumanisten"', in Horst Kranz & Ludwig Falkenstein (eds), *Inquirens subtilia diversa* (Aachen, 2002), pp 210–23.   5 This was not the result of any dissolution of monasteries but possibly of reforms within the monastic system in the late fifteenth century, which concentrated on practical, moral reformation and by implication downgraded ancient learning. Humanist scholars on the other hand were very anxious to collect such learning and build church reform on the revival of precisely such ancient learning. The

those devoted to [scholarly] studies. I was especially interested in the manuscripts which were considered lost but [thought] to be [hidden] intact somewhere.

He graciously assured me that he would undertake this task, but it was not very long before jealous death swept him away. His passing brought matters to a standstill and prevented the publication of some very valuable Greek and also Latin books, not without causing considerable damage to the whole learned world. It was my endeavour, however, after such a great man had been so cruelly removed [from us] to use all my powers to ensure that what he had not been able to accomplish during his life, should at least be taken care of after his death [to commemorate his life]. For a long time I tried to bring it about, but without success, for everything he had left behind had disappeared.[6] No trace of it could be found anywhere.

Finally, after I had almost given up hope, I came across one book. It was of rare age and written in almost illegible letters. At first inspecting it I was so moved by the venerable age [of this manuscript] that I believed I had found a most precious treasure. But soon I was overcome by great embarrassment since I was unable to read even a single word of it. The letters were so obsolete and belonged to a time long gone. This forced me to learn the first elements [of linguistic competence]. I assessed the script more closely in order to be able to distinguish the letters more carefully, put the words together again and then separate them once more into individual letters [that could be used for comparison].[7] In the end I discovered that this book contained the writings of St Fulgentius, a man distinguished by the saintliness of his life as well as the scholarship of his works.[8] [When I was certain of this] I considered it highly worthwhile not to leave such a brightly shining light of Christian faith under a bushel but to make sure that it reached the hands of men, especially of those who are sedulously devoted to the study of Holy Scripture. As soon as I was free I asked our dear Koberger[9] to come and see me. I encouraged him to publish this book. As a man committed to serving the public good, he promised to do it without considering the cost.

At this stage a new problem arose which prevented the expeditious accomplishment of my dearest wish by placing seemingly insuperable obstacles in

sifting of these manuscripts by humanist scholars raised great expectations among the learned that some valuable works, which were known about but whose texts could never be closely studied, might be rediscovered. **6** His whole literary legacy had been lost, either through carelessness or by giving away or selling parts of his collection. **7** This was quite a tedious but successful method to use which palaeographers still resort to when first acquainting themselves with an antiquated script. They concentrate on identifying familiar words, list the individual letters and look for these letters in other words. **8** 'Fulgentius von Ruspe', in *BBKL* 2, 1990, cols. 153–5, with extensive bibliography. **9** Johannes Koberger was the heir of Anton Koberger, the most famous entrepreneur publisher in Nuremberg. He expanded the family tradition of editing, printing and publishing.

my way. The new owner of the book refused to sell it to us. We were, however, not particularly interested in purchasing it and begged him to allow us to make at least a copy of it but it was all in vain.

We therefore tried a different approach. The man had become suspicious. [The bidders were too keen. He suspected that he had quite a valuable manuscript and that there was more money to be extracted]. Step by step we moved the matter forward by offering him money. We furthered our wish not by begging him but by making a substantial offer. The sum was so great that another [bidder] would hardly have offered it or he might have bought several books with it.[10] He further complicated matters by adding the condition that after use [after copying the text] the codex had to be returned [immediately] and to this end a document and a sealed receipt had to be drawn up. We had only just received the codex when a new problem arose. We had recruited several copyists but not a single one of them was willing to sign responsible for their work.[11] They considered the task not merely too difficult but hopeless, and it was of no use that I promised to assume overall responsibility of overseeing it. Whenever necessary I would throw light into the deep darkness. We did not find a way out.

At that stage a fortunate chance brought our [friend] Johannes Cochlaeus [to us], a man distinguished by his intellect and scholarship.[12] He had just returned from Italy where he had in the sweat of his brow and with extraordinarily hard work acquired the so-called dignity of a doctor of theology. At first he had travelled to Frankfurt where he had been appointed to the deanship of the *Liebfrauenstift*. He had hardly arrived when a rampant plague forced him to flee. We appealed to him to undertake the task and persuaded him in the end so that he completed it in the most rigorous fashion.

I have probably spun out the fate of the book, dear sister, more than was strictly necessary. I did it deliberately so that you might know with what difficulties and at what cost the writings of this saintly man were rescued from the darkness of oblivion and dusty imprisonment.

To give you a clearer impression of the man [I add the following]. Fulgentius was African by birth, living at Carthage. There he was elected bishop, not so much on account of his noble birth, although he was the offspring of a very eminent family, as on account of his learning and saintliness.

10 They came to the conclusion that a bribe was the best persuader.   11 This suggests that when the copyists saw the script they realized that they were not up to the task. It is interesting to find here that copyists did not necessarily know the script they copied, let alone understand the content of the text. It was a mechanical job, but Willibald Pirckheimer was also very demanding. He was known not to pay a copyist, if he considered his work shoddy.   12 Johannes Cochlaeus (1479–1552) had been rector of the school attached to St Laurence in 1510. He acted as mentor of three of Willibald's nephews on their study tour in Italy. In 1517 he was ordained in Rome and appointed dean of the *Liebfrauenstift* in Frankfurt (Oder). A little later he became one of Luther's most implacable opponents. 'Johannes Cochläus', in *TRE* 8 (1981), 140–6.

When the Vandals – to please the Arians[13] – persecuted the Catholics, murdering and expelling them and closing their temples, Fulgentius and the rest of the [Catholic] bishops were deported to the island of Sardinia. He never stopped instructing them, admonishing them [to adhere to the Catholic faith] and consoling them in their great distress. At last he was summoned back from his exile, and the citizens of Carthage received him with great honours as their most eminent inhabitant. Finally he relinquished all his ecclesiastical offices and decided to conclude his days on the island of Circinna,[14] reading and writing, he contended in the service of God.

I dedicate the works of the blessed Fulgentius to you, dearest Caritas and to our sister Clara. [I also dedicate to you] all the other writings of Johannes Maxentius,[15] which we had found together with Fulgentius and did not wish to separate from them. I know very well that such a spiritual gift will be much more acceptable to you. It will mean more to you than if I had sent you the most precious but transient works [dealing with worldly rather than spiritual matters]. The books of this great man are redolent not with worldly concerns that might originate in human tradition but encompass purely divine and heavenly things. You will become all the more convinced of the truth of my judgment the more closely you read the texts. There is no need to admonish you to do this, I know.

Farewell, my excellent sister with your entire convent, you who are no less renowned for your erudition and your appreciation of good literature as for the purity of your morals and conduct of life.

Nuremberg, at my house, on the 10th Calend of January, in the year of our human salvation 1519.[16] [*decimo calendas Januarii, anno salutis humanae 1519*]

---

13 A heretical Christian sect that did not believe in the Trinity, see *TRE* 3 (1978), 692–719. R.P.C. Hanson, *The search for the Christian doctrine of God: the Arian controversy* (Edinburgh, 1988).   14 Small island on the coast of North Africa.   15 Sixth-century monk, also in the tradition of St Augustine.   16 See note 56 above.

Important ladies and important families: Lucrezia Borgia and Caterina Cibo Varano

M. GRAZIA NICO OTTAVIANI

The two ladies who appear in the title never actually met, even though they shared experiences 'of government' that were similar but, at the same time, contained differences. Lucrezia and Caterina have recently been the subject of discussions, during the cycle of Borgia conferences (Lucrezia)[1] and during a conference held at Camerino (Caterina),[2] the city over which Caterina ruled. The meetings gave the opportunity to shed some light on the figures of both ladies: Lucrezia as a victim of the political projects of her father and brother[3] and Caterina as an 'unconventional' *ducissa* with a strong character in a small court modelled on the court of Urbino.[4]

My own studies on the two ladies have been conducted through archival documents kept in the cities over which they ruled (Foligno-Spoleto near Perugia and Camerino), and through the correspondence which they exchanged with the town priors or magistrates, or with characters of equal 'rank'. From this research a very colourful picture emerges, in which government duties, directives and orders intertwine along with anxious concerns about dynastic, economic and family problems.

To begin with the *pontificis maximi naturalis filia*,[5] we know that Lucrezia was appointed governess of Spoleto and Foligno in Umbria in the summer of 1499.[6] Her presence in that position was brief – about 50 days – but significant. A marriage with Giovanni Sforza, lord of Pesaro, resulting from the papal policy of favouring the ducato of Milano did not last long. Lucrezia had no better luck with her second husband, Alfonso, duke of Bisceglie, the natural son of Alfonso II of Naples, whom she married in July 1498. A further change of papal policy rendered Bisceglie *persona non grata;* he was therefore brutally murdered.[7]

1 C. Frova & M.G. Nico Ottaviani (eds), *Alessandro VI e lo Stato della Chiesa* (Roma, 2003). 2 P. Moriconi (ed.), *Caterina Cybo, duchessa di Camerino (1501–1557)* (Camerino, 2005). See also A. De Marchi & P.L. Falaschi (eds), *I volti di una dinastia. I da Varano di Camerino* (Milano, 2001) and *I da Varano e le arti* (Camerino, 2003).   3 See M.G. Nico Ottaviani, 'Cesare e Lucrezia Borgia nei loro rapporti con le città e i castelli dell'Umbria', in Frova & Ottaviani (eds), *Alessandro VI e lo Stato della Chiesa*, pp 265–79 and, for a bibliographical view on Lucrezia, P. Corsi, 'I Borgia nella storiografia letteraria moderna e contemporanea', in O. Capitani, M. Chiabò, M.C. De Matteis, A.M. Oliva (eds), *La fortuna dei Borgia* (Roma, 2005), pp 25–31.   4 M.T. Guerra Medici, 'La "civil conversazione" alla corte di Caterina Cibo', in *Caterina Cybo*, pp 89–92: *una piccola corte marchigiana.*   5 See A. Esposito, 'Il notaio Benimbene e la famiglia Borgia', in Capitani et al. (eds), *La fortuna dei Borgia*, p. 174. 6 Nico Ottaviani, 'Cesare e Lucrezia Borgia', pp 270–7.   7 N. Rubinstein, *Lucrezia Borgia* (Roma, 1971), pp 4–15; F. Gilbert, 'Borgia, Cesare', *Dizionario Biografico degli Italiani*, 12

Lucretia moved to Spoleto, accompanied by a large entourage and took her seat in the fortress on the 14 August 1499. The following day she received the homage of the town priors.[8] There are two important documents concerning Lucrezia: the first is Alexander VI's very well-known letter in which it is recalled that *mictamus dilectam in Christo filiam nostram mulierem Lucretiam de Borgia ad gubernium Ducatus spoletani et Fulginei*. The second letter is addressed to the *dilecta in Christo filia*, to whom the pope acknowledges 'all authority, honour, onus and wages relating to the office of government'; including, we might add, the rich income obtained by the territory of Spoleto.[9]

A large body of literature has generated various reflections on the reasons for the pope's appointment of Lucrezia,[10] reasons which go beyond the desire to distract his daughter's attention from other, more unpleasant events, or to prevent her reunion with her husband, Bisceglie. These reasons are better understood when Lucrezia is viewed as one of many actors in the Borgia story, with her own role and capabilities, yet always at the centre of projects constructed in a masculine frame of mind. In that context, we might perceive a desire to 'prepare' the daughter for her next and final marriage, to Alfonso d'Este.[11]

This, however, could only have been a secondary consideration for the pope in the appointment of his daughter as governess of a rather vast territory such as the Ducato of Spoleto so dangerously close to Perugia. More than one historian has suggested that the appointment represents in part an instrument of the pope's government in a region which the Holy See controlled 'only with difficulty'.[12] Recently also Gabriella Zarri examined the orders of Lucrezia's government, maintaining that it is 'una indubbia novità sul piano della giurisdizione femminile'.[13] Achille Sansi, a Spoleto historian, wrote that 'nelle scritture pubbliche s'incontrano alcune orme del governo di Lucrezia' (in the public documents we can find Lucrezia's marks).[14] In fact Lucrezia tried to resolve a dispute caused by a raid involving some of the citizens of Spoleto against some citizens of Terni. Lucrezia's auditor, *Antonius de Humiolis de Gualdo* famous for his *verborum elegantia et facundia*, convinced the citizens of Spoleto to agree to a temporary truce of about three months, followed by the governess looking to a definitive truce.[15]

(Roma, 1970), p. 700.   8 A. Sansi, *Storia del Comune di Spoleto dal sec. XII al XVII*, 2 (Spoleto, 1972), pp 103–6.   9 Spoleto, Sezione di Archivio di Stato, *Riformanze*, 75, c. 89rv.   10 For which see Nico Ottaviani, 'Cesare e Lucrezia Borgia', p. 270.   11 Op. cit., pp 274–6.   12 Quoting Mario Caravale and cited by myself, op. cit., p. 275. About Baglioni family, see C. Regni, 'Le istituzioni comunali a Perugia al tempo di Alessandro VI', in *Alessandro VI e lo Stato della Chiesa*, pp 229–54. About other areas of government, such as Nepi and Sermoneta, see the papers in G. Pesiri (ed.), *Il Lazio e Alessandro VI. Civita Castellana, Cori, Nepi, Sermoneta* (Roma, 2003).   13 G. Zarri, *La religione di Lucrezia Borgia. Le lettere inedite del confessore* (Roma, 2006), p. 23.   14 Sansi, 'Storia di Spoleto', p. 135.   15 Spoleto, Sezione di Archivio di Stato, *Riformanze*, 60, cc. 97r–98r and 109r, 22, 25 August and 11 September. See also L. Silvestri, *Collezione di memorie storiche tratte dai protocolli delle antiche riformanze della città di Terni dal 1387 al 1816 rel-*

In the Spoleto Riformanze (such as communal records) so full of news about Borgia family, is copied the appointment letter of *Antonius de Gualdo* in charge to go *ad civitatem nostram Spoletanam ... facturus que tibi dicta ducissa iniunxerit et offitio auditoratus incumbent* (he will do what the Duchess and his role require).[16] If then we add some letters, saved in Todi, dated between 1499 August and October *ex arce spoletina*,[17] and written by the Secretary[18] (except the third letter) where Lucrezia signed herself as *Lucretia Borgia de Aragonia ducissa et Spoleti Fulgineique gubernatrix*, the sum of her presence grows, involving Todi as well.

The governess undertook with the Priori to get back everything stolen and to punish the criminal (letter I); promised help against Altobello da Canale (letter III); in the end ordered them to bring to justice sons of Thomasso de Vallo (Spoleto's district) who murdered and robbed near porta Romana in Todi, warning that *se procederà contra li vostri homini* (we have to proceed against commune of Todi), a fact that happened, of course (letters II, IV, V).[19]

The second issue seems certainly more significant and with regards to the help promised to defeat Altobello da Canale who, with his brother Vittorio, fought against the guelfi and Degli Atti families; she compelled him to escape in 1496 and to go to the castles of Todi's district, then destroyed by himself.

The duchess showed considerable skill in dealing with the situation: providing a gift (probably sent with the letter) and stating her *displicentia et amaricazione* (regret) about of *ad quel tanto che ce scrivete delli insulti et crudele occissione et altre enormità proxime perpetrate da Altobello* (crimes committed by Altobello who must be punished). She guaranteed the pope's help; in fact Alexander VI sent his soldiers, while the governess sent her troops from Spoleto and Altobello was defeated and made prisoner in Acquasparta.[20] All of Lucrezia's letters seem strong, sure, and written with sense of justice, kindness and firmness; their contents were suggested perhaps by the astute Secretary, whose name appears in two letters.[21]

After Lucrezia's departure, other Borgias took over power in the Ducato, beginning with Ludovico, one of the pope's nephews.[22] It seems to me that,

ative al suo stato politico morale civile industriale ed ai suoi rapporti colle altre città e luoghi convicini non che alla storia contemporanea* (Terni, 1977), p. 182. **16** Spoleto, Sezione di Archivio di Stato, *Riformanze*, 60, c. 113r, 6 August 1499. **17** Todi, Archivio Storico Comunale, sala VI, fascicoli I e I bis; F. Mancini (ed.), 'Lucrezia Borgia governatrice di Spoleto', in *Archivio Storico Italiano* 115 (1957), 182–7; see also G. Comez, 'Lucrezia Borgia e i Priori di Todi', in *Volontà Nuova* 5 (1979), 25–7. **18** Appointed by the Pope *cancellarius comunis, procurator et notarius Camere apostolice* of Spoleto for three years. **19** Comez, 'Lucrezia Borgia e i Priori di Todi', p. 27. **20** F. Mancini (ed.), 'La cronaca todina di Joan Fabrizio degli Atti', in G. Italiani, C. Leonardi, F. Mancini, E. Menestò, C. Santini, G. Scentoni (eds), *Le cronache di Todi (secoli XIII–XVI)* (Spoleto, 1991), pp 540–7; A. Fabretti (ed.), 'Cronaca della città di Perugia dal 1492 al 1503 di Francesco Matarazzo detto Maturanzio', in *Archivio Storico Italiano* 16:2 (1981), 148–51; P. Pellini, *Della historia di Perugia* (Venezia, 1664), pp 136–7. **21** Mancini, *Lucrezia Borgia*, p. 184. **22** Todi, Archivio storico comunale, *Lettere ai Priori di Todi*, busta 2 n.n., *Ludovicus Borgia*

starting with Lucrezia's, the sequence of appointments represents nothing more than the adherence to a principle (the *pietas erga parentes*, which is to say privileges or favour for his family) which guided the pope's policy throughout Borgia's papacy.[23]

Caterina Cibo is another prominent figure, and has therefore attracted the attention of many scholars for a variety of reasons: the family to which she belonged; the ties with important families (Cibo of Genova and Medici of Firenze), and even with popes (Leo X and Clement VII); her renown as a lady of culture; her relationships – which were not always well looked-upon – and the rather liberal exercise of her patronage (towards the so-called *spirituali*); the strong opposition to her marriage with Giovanni Maria da Varano; her life as a widow and her regency of a much sought-after state; and finally her quiet departure from the political stage, which itself raises a number of questions.[24]

Quite a character, then.[25] Caterina's parents were, for their part, also characters of some interest: her father was Franceschetto Cibo, the son of Giovanni Battista, who was to become pope under the name of Innocent VIII, and her mother was Maddalena de' Medici, one of the daughters of Lorenzo the Magnificent.[26] Francesco Serdonati, the author of an 'addition' to Boccaccio's *De mulieribus claris*, provides a great deal of descriptive information about 'Lady Caterina Cybo Duchess of Camerino': from him we learn that she was beautiful and pious, intelligent and kind; that she knew four languages – Hebrew, Greek, Latin and 'Tuscan'; and that she studied 'humanities', theology and philosophy.[27] One presumes that she was the recipient of a careful upbringing, of which, however, little else is known.[28]

At the age of 12, she was promised in marriage to Giovanni Maria da Varano from Camerino: a union which was at first well looked-upon but then

nepos signs a letter *ex arce Spoleti*, 25 agosto 1500. Other documents in Spoleto, Sezione di Archivio di Stato, *Riformanze*, 78, cc. 286v–287r and 288v–289r (a. 1503). **23** M. Miglio, Le ragioni di una revisione storica, *Roma di fronte all'Europa*, pp 15–18. **24** M.G. Nico Ottaviani, '*Me son missa a scriver questa letera …*'. *Lettere e altre scritture femminili tra Umbria, Toscana e Marche nei secoli XV–XVI* (Napoli, 2006), pp 89–91. **25** For the many aspects of her strong character see the important paper from G. Zarri, 'La spiritualità di Caterina Cybo: indizi e testimonianze', in Moriconi (ed.), *Caterina Cybo duchessa di Camerino*, pp 313–31, particularly for the spiritual aspects, the relationship with 'riformati' as Bernardino Ochino, and the patronage towards Cappuccini of Marche. About this last point see also S. da Campagnola, 'Caterina Cybo e un Ordine di successo: i Cappuccini di Renacavata', in A. De Marchi & P.L. Falaschi (eds), *I volti di una dinastia*, pp 138–9. **26** G. Pieraccini, *La stirpe de' Medici di Cafaggiolo: saggio di ricerche sulla trasmissione ereditaria dei caratteri biologici* (Firenze, 1924), I, 145–6. **27** *Libro di m. Giovanni Boccaccio delle donne illustri. Tradotto di latino in volgare per m. Giuseppe Betussi, con una giunta fatta dal medesimo, d'Altre Donne Famose. E un'altra nuova giunta fatta per m. Francesco Serdonati d'altre Donne Illustri Antiche e Moderne. Con due Tavole una dei nomi, e l'altra delle cose più notabili*, in Fiorenza per Filippo Giunti, 1596, p. 613. **28** F. Petrucci, Cibo, Caterina, *Dizionario Biografico degli Italiani*, 25 (Roma, 1981), pp 237–41.

strongly opposed by the bride's mother, Maddalena, who was more disposed to give her daughter's hand to Giovanni Maria's nephew Sigismondo.[29] In 1520, after her mother's death, Caterina did marry the da Varano, the heir to a state which had suffered the violence of the Borgia 'tempest', in that Camerino had been occupied in 1502 by Borgia's troops.

The sudden fall of Valentino brought Giovanni Maria back to his own city. The situation had changed, and, for Giovanni Maria, was to change again, in a very palpable way: having once again assumed the reigns of power, he was confirmed in his power by the new pope, Juilius II, and then Leo X (de' Medici) granted him the title of Duca.[30] When Giovanni Maria died of the plague in 1527, the succession seemed to be clear: the duke recognized his daughter Giulia as heir, and his wife Caterina as governess for the period of her life (*tutrix* and *Gubernatrix generalis Ducatus*),[31] thereby placing both under the protection of the pope and the emperor, and Clement VII recognized the title with a famous letter.[32]

In his will, Giovanni Maria instructed his daughter to marry one of Ercole Varano's sons (Varano of Ferrara),[33] as soon as she should reach the age of 14, in order to strengthen the position of his dynasty. Caterina, however, had other goals in her mind. She had forged an alliance with the duke of Urbino, Franceso Maria I Della Rovere, promising to Guidobaldo II, the duke's heir, what she should not and could not promise, namely the hand of her daughter Giulia. Caterina was absolutely determined to achieve her projects for her daughter's marriage, regardless of the groom's resistance to the idea.[34]

In October 1534, the marriage contract between Giulia, barely twelve, and the much older Guidubaldo, was signed in the utmost secret. The marriage met with universal disapproval, first from the College of Cardinals, and then from the newly elected pope, Paul III, who was hostile to Della Rovere family.[35] These last events were very complicated for Caterina: besides the

---

29 Son of Venanzo, Giovanni Maria's brother; M.G. Nico Ottaviani, '*Me son missa a scriver questa letera …*', p. 92; M.T. Guerra Medici, *Famiglia e potere in una signoria dell'Italia centrale. I Varano di Camerino* (Camerino, 2002), pp 43–4.   **30** J.E. Law, 'City, court and countryside in Camerino', in T. Dean & C. Wickham (eds), *City, court and countryside in late medieval and Renaissance Italy: essays presented to Philip Jones* (London, 1990), pp 171–81; *idem*, 'Relazioni dinastiche tra i Della Rovere e i Varano', in B. Cleri, S. Eiche, J.E. Law, F. Paoli (eds), *Storia del Ducato*, 4 (Urbania, 2002), I, 21–34.   **31** Caterina, as *ducissa*, sent many letters to the priors of some towns of the Duchy of Camerino; see I. Biondi, 'Documenti relativi a Caterina Cybo nei comuni del ducato di Camerino', in *Caterina Cybo, duchessa di Camerino*, pp 195–232. See also M.G. Nico Ottaviani, '*Me son missa a scriver questa letera …*', pp 107–8.   **32** M.G. Nico Ottaviani, '*Me son missa a scriver questa letera …*', pp 98–9.   **33** 'Signori senza terra' (lords without land): P.L. Falaschi, 'Splendori di una Signoria inedita', in A. De Marchi & P.L. Falaschi (eds), *I volti di una dinastia*, p. 18. For Varano of Ferrara see L. Chiappini, 'I rapporti tra i Varano e gli Estensi', in A. De Marchi & P.L. Falaschi (eds), *I da Varano e le arti*, pp 171–3, and D. Ferrigoni, 'La quadreria dei Varano da Ferrara a Camerino. I ritratti degli avi', in A. De Marchi & P.L. Falaschi (eds), *I volti di una dinastia*, pp 26–35.   **34** Guidobaldo was in love with Clarice Orsini; op. cit., p. 100.   **35** Petrucci, *Cibo Caterina*, p.

pope's hostility, she had to deal with Guidubaldo's dissent, arising from what J.E. Law describes as 'the ungainly two-headed government'[36] created by the marriage, with Caterina holding the fortress and presumably the state income, while Guidubaldo considered himself the duke. This conflict was resolved by means of several agreements which granted Caterina the right to hold the office of governess for the period of her natural life, if she so decided, and the young couple half the state's income.

In 1535 the regent elegantly departed the scene, leaving the little court of Camerino; she left because she couldn't stand to see any diminution of her own authority at Camerino where disputes between herself and her son-in-law and daughter had become very frequent.[37] The consequences of this disagreement are evident in several letters exchanged between Caterina and Guidubaldo. In a letter from Florence (December 18, 1536) Caterina begged His Excellency, Guidubaldo, for some help as 'I am broke', she wrote, until 'my dowry is given back to me as promised'. While she complained at her greedy son in law 'with one thousand scudi ... you would offend me very deeply', she reminded him of her affection 'I have no other happiness than you both'.[38]

In two later letters (13 August 1537 and 29 February 1538) she asked again to have her 'dowry and cottage' back, this time with higher hopes as, 'thanks God, Your Excellency has become the nephew of His Beatitudine' the pope Paul III Farnese, the uncle of Vittoria, whom Guidubaldo had married soon after his first wife's death. According to Feliciangeli, there is some irony in Caterina's phrasing,[39] but it seems to me that these letters are more respectful than the previous ones, with some loving words for 'la nostra piccinina' (our little girl), that is, her granddaughter Virginia, who had been left motherless.

In a letter to Guidubaldo dated 1530, probably written by a secretary, as was customary for these noble women, the duchess of Camerino informed him that she had sent 'un paro di capriuoli' (a couple of roe deers) and asked him for 'buone novelle del meglioramento della Illustrissima signora Duchessa sua Madre' (good news about the health of the very Illustrious Duchess Your Mother). This was Eleonora Gonzaga, who had contracted 'il mal francese' (the French disease) from her husband.[40]

Caterina wrote two respectful letters to Eleonora Gonzaga: the first one, in July 1541, contains some information (gossip?) about the Medici's court,

238.   **36** J.E. Law, *Relazioni dinastiche tra i Della Rovere e i Varano*, p. 30.   **37** B. Feliciangeli, *Notizie e documenti sulla vita di Caterina Cibo Varano duchessa di Camerino* (Camerino, 1891), pp 216–17; J.E. Law, *Relazioni dinastiche tra i Della Rovere e i Varano*, p. 31; M.T. Guerra Medici, *Famiglia e potere in una signoria dell'Italia centrale*, p. 54.   **38** Firenze, Archivio di Stato, *Ducato di Urbino*, classe I, filza 236, cc. 1105rv–1106r; B. Feliciangeli, *Notizie e documenti sulla vita di Caterina Cibo*, letters 10–11, pp 278–9 and pp 218–19, but the letters are not kept.   **40** ASF, *Ducato di Urbino*, classe I, filza 14, c. 553r, 1530 agosto 11. B. Feliciangeli, *Notizie e documenti sulla vita di Caterina Cibo*, p. 265; S. Pellizzer, 'Eleonora Gonzaga, duchessa di Urbino', in *Dizionario Biografico degli Italiani* (Roma 1993), 42, 425.

particularly with regard to Duke Cosimo I, the son of Giovanni delle Bande Nere and of Maria Salviati, who had married the beautiful Eleonora of Toledo, the daughter of the viceroy of Naples, who provided him with many children.[41] At the court of Florence Caterina could gather useful information for 'la Signora Madama di Urbino' (the Lady of Urbino) as she was related to the Medici family through her mother.

About one year later Catherine wrote to Eleonora Gonzaga again,[42] this time about some affinity between the Della Rovere and the court of France, the link being Giovanni, brother of Giuliano (Giulio II) and father of Francesco Maria I, who had been at the service of the king.[43] The two letters are polite and grateful to Eleonora, who had helped Caterina against the awkward attempt of Mattia, a man from the Ferrara branch of the family, to invade the duchy. Caterina wrote the letters in praise of the *Madama* (her own pleasure is to be generous), who was respected in all the courts for her intellectual and moral qualities, as we know from a sonnet by Pietro Aretino on the famous portrait by Titian. Aretino wrote that the portrait 'shows the harmony that in Leonora holds honesty ... shyness ... modesty and beauty ... prudence'.[44]

If we attempt, by way of conclusion, a comparison of the two ladies, it becomes evident that, regardless of the shared legal title, there was a great deal of difference between them: Caterina Cibo seems energetic, determined, influential and, above all, autonomous in her decision-making as she confronted, often alone, both the internal and external problems of her little state.

It must be said of Lucrezia Borgia that, notwithstanding the brevity of her period of rule (a few days against the seven or eight years during which Caterina, widow, ruled the duchy), she was always subject to her father's wishes, controlled by secretaries, to the effect that her space for manoeuvre was very restricted.

This is not to belittle Lucrezia's virtues, the expression of which was always limited by paternal wishes, while Caterina used the period of her widowhood to enjoy her *ducissa*'s powers, or, as Serdonati says, 'this woman understood well the government of states and discoursed very prudently on world affairs, and showed great constancy and strength of spirit, both in times of good and of adverse fortune always displaying a well balanced countenance'.[45]

---

41 Maria Salviati was the daugther of Iacopo Salviati and Lucrezia di Lorenzo il Magnifico: see G. Pieraccini, *La stirpe de' Medici di Cafaggiolo*, I, 240–6 and 465–85, and II, 5–49 about Cosimo I and Eleonora.   42 The two letters are in ASF, *Ducato di Urbino*, classe I, filza 266, cc. 659rv and r. B. Feliciangeli, *Notizie e documenti sulla vita di Caterina Cibo*, letters 8–9, pp 276–8.   43 M. Bonvini Mazzanti, 'Aspetti della politica interna ed estera di Francesco Maria II Della Rovere', in *I Della Rovere nell'Italia delle Corti* (2002) I, 77–91.   44 The sonnet is quoted in the short profile written by G. Pezzini Bernini in *I Della Rovere*, 2, 307.   45 *Libro di m. Giovanni Boccaccio delle donne illustri*, pp 615–16: *Fu questa donna molto intendente de governi di stati, e discorreva con grande prudenza sopra gli affari del mondo e mostrò gran costanza, e fortezza d'animo in diversi tempi di buona, e di ria fortuna mostrando sempre una medesima faccia.*

Contributors

BRENDA BOLTON taught medieval and ecclesiastical history in the University of London for many years. In retirement, she continues to write and has edited a series for Ashgate since 2000. A joint editorial venture with Christine Meek resulted in *Aspects of power and authority: international medieval research 14*, a volume of selected papers from the Leeds' International Colloquium published by Brepols in 2007.

M.E. BRATCHEL teaches medieval and Renaissance history at the University of the Witwatersrand, Johannesburg. His publications include *Lucca, 1430–1494: the reconstruction of an Italian city-republic* (Oxford, 1995).

WILLIAM CAFERRO teaches history at Vanderbilt University. He is the author of several monographs, including *John Hawkwood: English mercenary in fourteenth-century Italy* (Baltimore, 2006), which won the Otto Grundler Prize from the Medieval Academy.

EDWARD COLEMAN teaches medieval history at University College Dublin. His publications include 'Lombard city annals and the social and cultural history of northern Italy' in S. Dale, D.J. Osheim, A. Williams (eds), *Chronicling history: chronicles and historians in medieval and Renaissance Italy* (Philadelphia, 2007) and a translation of the Annals of Cremona in the same volume.

GEORGE DAMERON teaches medieval history and humanities at Saint Michael's College, Vermont. He is the author of *Florence and its church in the ages of Dante* (Philadelphia, 2005) and *Episcopal power and Florentine society, 1000–1320* (Cambridge, MA, 1991).

WILLIAM R. DAY JR is a former Research Associate of the Fitzwilliam Museum, Cambridge University. His publications include 'The population of Florence before the Black Death: survey and synthesis', *Journal of Medieval History*, 28:2 (June 2002), 93–129.

STEPHEN HANAPHY recently completed a Ph.D. on Peter of Blois' use of classical Latin texts. He is currently completing a degree in law in the Honorable Society of King's Inns.

GILLIAN KENNY is a former graduate student of Christine Meek's. She teaches medieval history in the Dept of Adult Education in University College Dublin. She is the author of *Anglo-Irish and Gaelic women in medieval Ireland, c.1170–1540* (Dublin, 2007).

CONOR KOSTICK is the author of *The siege of Jerusalem* (Continuum, 2009) and *The social structure of the First Crusade* (Brill, 2008), and teaches the subject of the Crusades at Trinity College Dublin.

CATHERINE LAWLESS lectures in the history of art at the University of Limerick. Along with Christine Meek she edited two of the volumes in the Four Courts Press series Women in Late Medieval and Early Modern Europe.

ANDREAS MEYER teaches medieval history at the University of Marburg, Germany.

M. GRAZIA NICO OTTAVIANI teaches medieval history at the University of Perugia. Her publications include '*Me son missa a scriver questa letera....*' *lettere e altre scritture femminili tra Umbria, Toscana e Marche nei secoli XV–XVI* (Liguori, 2006).

DUANE OSHEIM is Professor of History at the University of Virginia. His works include *An Italian lordship: the bishopric of Lucca in the late Middle Ages* (Berkeley, 1977).

JENNIFER PETRIE taught Italian at University College Dublin. Her main research interests are the works of Dante and Petrarch. She was joint editor (with John C. Barnes) of the volume *Dante and the human body* (Dublin, 2007).

IGNAZIO DEL PUNTA teaches history at the University of Pisa. His publications include *Mercanti e banchieri lucchesi nel Duecento* (Pisa, 2004).

I.S. ROBINSON is Lecky Professor of History in Trinity College, Dublin and specializes in eleventh- and twelfth-century European history.

HELGA ROBINSON-HAMMERSTEIN is Fellow Emerita of Trinity College, Dublin and specialises in early modern European history. She was co-founder of the first M.Phil. degree (in Reformation and Enlightenment Studies) in TCD.

KATHARINE SIMMS teaches the history of Gaelic Ireland at Trinity College, Dublin. Her most recent book is *Medieval Gaelic sources* (Dublin, 2009).

Index

285